The One-Block Feast

THE
ONE-BLOCK FEAST

An Adventure in Food
from Yard to Table

MARGO TRUE & the staff of *Sunset* MAGAZINE

TEN SPEED PRESS
Berkeley

Contents

FALL

WINTER

Introduction

It's the start of the day at Sunset magazine. On the way to the coffee machine, I pass Kimberley and Margaret. Kimberley is an imaging specialist; she color-corrects the cascade of photographs that streams into our office every month. Margaret is our production coordinator, adjusting every detail of the layouts until the pages are ready for publication. But right now, Kimberley and Margaret are beekeepers. They're both in bulky white jumpsuits, with veiled helmets tucked under their arms, heading out to inspect our hives.

As for me, I'm carrying a white bucket filled with leftover spinach, fennel trimmings, and chile seeds. With my coffee in the other hand, I go out to see the girls—the squawking hens in Sunset's test garden who dive-bomb the bucket as soon as I set it down. I collect a couple of still-warm eggs from the nest box and go back inside, past the egg sign-up sheet with its list of colleagues waiting their turn for eggs, past the big crocks of vinegar with their bracingly tangy smell, and into the kitchen to put away the eggs. It makes me happy to know that our under-the-counter fridge holds wheels of Gouda that we made a few weeks ago from the milk of our own cow, that the latest batch of beer is percolating in a corner, and that the shelves in the pantry are lined with bottles of our own olive oil and jars of honey from the hives.

Although it may sound like we're running a farm here, we aren't. Our main business is putting out a monthly lifestyle magazine about the West. But the Sunset office is a little different from other magazine offices.

It was designed by its longtime former owners, Bill and Mel Lane, to be what Bill liked to call "a laboratory of Western living." On its five acres, landscape architect Thomas Church planted extensive gardens that start with the cacti of the Southwest and arc over to the ferns and firs of Washington and Oregon, with California redwoods in between. The Lanes installed a test garden, too, for trialing the newest flowers, fruits, and vegetables, so

we could tell our readers which varieties to count on. The building itself, constructed in the early 1950s by architect Cliff May, embodied the then-new idea of outdoor living, with sliding glass doors to bring in the view, tile floors that flowed from inner rooms to outer patios, and courtyards with shady overhangs and comfortable seating. Many of the home stories in the magazine over the years have focused on bringing the outdoors in and vice versa. We've built patios in our parking lots, put together an adobe oven, and made all kinds of garden structures— from tool sheds to benches to raised beds—and published the plans. In the sand volleyball court we used to have, we once pit-roasted a pig, Hawaiian style. It ended in a visit from the fire department, but in a laboratory, not all experiments go smoothly.

In the kitchen, we made a point of celebrating Western foods like Meyer lemons and abalone, starting when some of them were barely known outside the West. (One of my favorite bits of display type, from a 1970 article: "It's endlessly versatile. It's a dip, a sauce, a dressing, a spread. It's *guacamole*.") We've been fans of local eating for a long time. So we were thrilled when, several years ago, it became a bona fide movement: People everywhere were seeking out ingredients close to home, grown by farmers they could meet or at least learn about. It was civilized and humane, healthy in the largest sense of the word, and it produced great-tasting food.

The gardens at Sunset

Although there's a lot of advice and information in this book, we designed it to be used by all kinds of readers and meet different kinds of needs.

Make a Fast Recipe

Say it's a Monday night after work, and you want a quick recipe for that nice farmers' market produce you just bought. You'll find dozens of choices here—actually, more than half of the recipes in the book take less than an hour.

Plant a Vegetable or Two

Or, try growing some of that produce yourself. We've provided planting and harvesting advice for every fruit or vegetable in the book, in the sections titled "Garden." We also have a short section on gardening basics.

Grow a Whole Feast—or All Four

If you want to grow and cook an entire seasonal feast, like we did, you can decide which menu sounds appealing (every chapter begins with one) and then follow that menu's planting plan, which is included in the garden section. The recipes we cooked for our feasts—plus more dishes we developed using that season's ingredients—are at the end of the chapter. Or if you're an expert gardener who enjoys a challenge, check out the warm-season and cool-season planting plans (pages 4 to 7) that will take you through a whole year of one-block feasts—and some really interesting plants, too.

Make Food from Scratch

Maybe you love the idea of from-scratch cooking and want to make as much of your own food as possible. Our project guides can help you make cheese, olive oil, vinegar, beer (from wheat, barley, and hops), and wine; and even salt from seawater. These are true adventures, and will change the way you look at food. You'll be surprised by how easy some of them are.

Raise Food-Producing Animals

Once, "A Chicken in Every Pot" was a countrywide dream; now it seems to be a chicken (or flock) in every backyard. If you're curious about getting laying hens, read our guide on page 59. We've also included guides to raising honeybees (page 39) and a dairy cow (page 213).

Or Just Read

And, if you just want to plop on the sofa and read a story, we wrote one for you. The chapter introductions describe our successes and failures as we gardened, cooked, and otherwise worked our way toward making the book you have in your hands.

Lastly, if you see something you especially like in these pages (or omissions or errors), or want to share your stories about raising your own food, let us know! Come comment on our facebook page for this book, www.facebook.com/SunsetMagazine, or stop by our blog about this project, http://oneblockdiet.sunset.com, whose readers have helped shape and improve everything we've done.

As we saw people (even restaurants) setting food-gathering boundaries for themselves, experimenting with 150-mile, 100-mile, and even 50-mile diets, we looked around at our living laboratory—which occupies a full city block—and thought, why don't we try a one-block diet? It would take local eating to its logical conclusion, since you can't get much more local than your own back yard. Starting in May, we'd grow everything we needed in our organic garden for an end-of-summer feast in August. (Our planting plans and timelines are included on pages 4 to 7.)

To make it interesting, we'd raise more than just plants. We would figure out how to make absolutely everything we needed for a well-rounded meal, from protein to cooking fat to seasonings to sweetener to even wine—the kinds of ingredients you would typically buy at the store, even if you're a dedicated locavore.

Almost before we knew it, we had formed Team Chicken, Team Olive Oil, and Team Bee to explore exactly how to produce the eggs, oil, and honey that we wanted. Several other teams materialized—you'll read about them in the first chapter—and we became like an old-fashioned neighborhood of do-it-yourselfers heading for the best block party ever.

After a little more thought, we decided that the block should be reduced to a medium- to large-size backyard, so that it would be easier for our readers to replicate all that we were planning. We began describing our adventures on a blog, called One-Block Diet (http://oneblockdiet .sunset.com), where we recorded what worked and what didn't, the practical tips we learned from experts, and the fun we had.

By the time we sat down to our summer feast in August, the project had assumed a larger life. Various strands of it were still evolving: for instance, the Syrah

we'd made was nowhere near ready to drink (it was still aging); our cheeses were tasty, but we wanted to explore making different and more ambitious kinds; and we thought it would be fascinating to turn our honey into mead. We found ourselves not only continuing the projects we'd started, but coming up with new ones and planning menus for the seasons ahead. And pretty soon it all added up to this book, with extra recipes developed along the way.

However, we ended up doing our research in fits and starts, skipping to winter and then to fall and back to spring. For the sake of seasonal continuity and flow, and so that our plan is helpful to anyone following it, I've condensed some of our experiences and adjusted dates where it made sense.

When we started the project, we knew nothing about the time-honored skills we were trying to explore, apart from gardening and cooking. We had no idea how to make wine, or keep bees, or milk a cow. We are people with full-time office jobs and home lives, and yet we found that all of these things are completely possible and extremely rewarding.

Although this book is as comprehensive as we could possibly make it, with recipes that use only what we grew or raised ourselves, we designed it to be a resource that anyone—backyard garden or no—could dip into and still really enjoy. All the recipes work with store-bought or farmers' market ingredients, for instance. And even if you choose just one project, like homemade vinegar, you will feel the undeniable pride that is part of what makes food from scratch so rewarding.

But if you want to dive in deeper, say, and collaborate with your neighbors so that one of you raises chickens and another bees, and maybe the woman on the corner grows tomatoes and corn, and your buddy across the street makes the beer—then just imagine how great your block parties could be.

THE ONE BLOCK GARDEN:
Warm-Season Planting Plan

The illustrations and timelines on this page and immediately following show every plant we raised for our one-block feasts, with dimensions indicating how much space we allotted for each. Some plants from the warm-season garden (like the citrus trees, most of the herbs, the fennel, and the butternut squash) remain in the cool-season garden plan (see next page), either because we used them during the cool season or because we relied on them year-round.

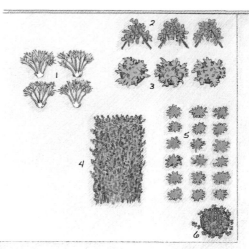

Planting and Harvesting Timeline for Northern California

The timeline below shows when we planted and harvested all the crops for our four seasonal one-block feasts in Menlo Park, California; the information on specific crops in the garden section of each chapter reflects the general guidelines for each plant. If you live outside Northern California, turn to page 250 for other region-specific planting and harvesting timelines. To learn how to produce your own transplants (seedlings) from seed, see Starting Plants from Seed, page 11.

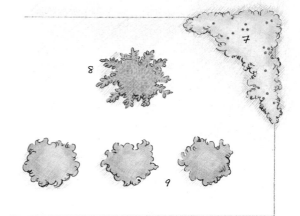

MARCH

PLANT

25 Chives ● ▼
21 Lemon tree (any time in mild climates, but best in spring after last frost) ■
19 Marjoram (and year-round) ● ▼
7 Nasturtiums ●
18 Oregano (and year-round) ▼
20 Parsley (and for fall and spring feasts; succession sow; replant in cool season) ● ▼
10 Peppermint ▼
3 **11** Potatoes (from seed potatoes; plant in towers or trenches)
14 Rosemary (and year-round) ▼
15 Tangerine tree ■
16 Tarragon, French ▼
17 Thyme (and year-round) ▼

PROJECTS
    BEER (for spring feast)
    BEES (through April)

APRIL

PLANT

26 Basil (in batches, every 2 weeks through August) ▼
2 Beans (through August) ●
5 Chiles (and for fall feast; through May) ● ▼

30 Corn (in batches, every 2 weeks through August) ●
22 Cucumbers ●
24 Edamame (in batches, every 2 weeks through May) ●
13 Hops (through May) ✳
23 Lemongrass ▼
12 Pattypan squash, 'Bennings Green Tint' (in May) ● ▼
12 Pattypan squash, 'Sunburst' (in May)
5 Peppers (through August) ▼
8 Pineapple guava ■
6 Purslane ●
4 Quinoa ●
28 Tomatoes (through May) ● ▼
32 Zucchini

PROJECTS
9 TEA ■
    COW ❖

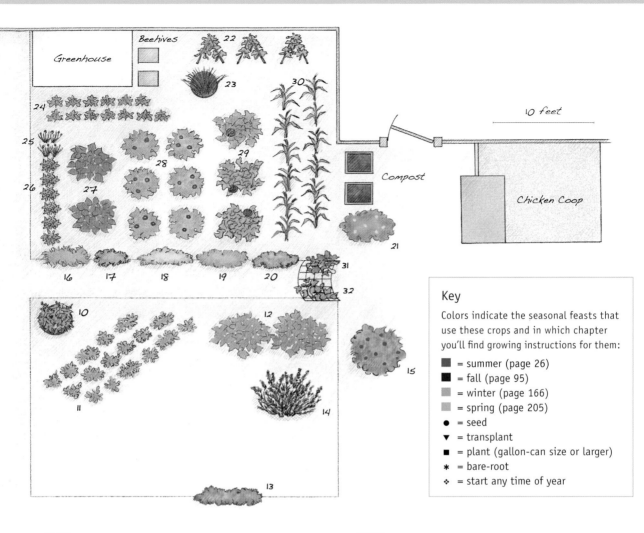

Key

Colors indicate the seasonal feasts that use these crops and in which chapter you'll find growing instructions for them:

■ = summer (page 26)
■ = fall (page 95)
■ = winter (page 166)
■ = spring (page 205)
● = seed
▼ = transplant
■ = plant (gallon-can size or larger)
✳ = bare-root
❖ = start any time of year

MAY

PLANT
31 Butternut squash (through June) ▼
29 Melons (through June) ●
1 Florence fennel (through August) ●

HARVEST
All crops for spring feast (see page 205)

JUNE

HARVEST
Barley (planted in November)
Onions, 'Spanish White' (planted in October) and let cure
Potatoes
Wheat (planted in January)

PROJECTS
BEER (for summer feast)
CHEESE ❖

JULY

HARVEST
Garlic (planted in October) and let cure
Onions, cippolini (planted in February) and let cure

AUGUST

HARVEST
All other crops for summer feast (see page 26)

PROJECTS
CHICKENS (buy chicks; raise indoors until fully feathered, 8 to 10 weeks) ❖

THE ONE BLOCK GARDEN:
Cool-Season Planting Plan

Planting and Harvesting Timeline
for Northern California

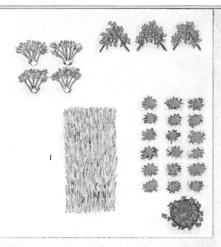

> ### Key
>
> Crops not numbered or mentioned are carryovers from the warm-season planting plan on the preveious page. Colors indicate the seasonal feasts that use these crops:
>
> ■ = summer (page 26)
> ■ = fall (page 95)
> ■ = winter (page 166)
> ■ = spring (page 205)
> ● = seed
> ▼ = transplant
> ■ = plant (gallon-can size or larger)
> ✳ = bare-root
> ❖ = start any time of year

SEPTEMBER

PLANT

(If using seeds for crops below, start them in August)

18 Arugula (also for spring feast; succession sow through March) ●
9 Broccoli rabe ● ▼
10 Broccoli romanesco ▼
16 Cabbage, Savoy (through October) ▼
11 Cauliflower ▼
14 Kale, Tuscan ● ▼
15 Kale, Curly-Leafed ● ▼
17 Lettuce, Red Butterhead ● ▼
12 Mustard (every few weeks through December) ●
20 Radicchio ▼
13 Swiss chard (and for winter feast; through January) ● ▼
19 Thyme

HARVEST
26 Hop flowers and let dry

LATE SEPTEMBER–EARLY OCTOBER

PLANT
23 Parsley (also for spring and summer feasts; succession sow February through March) ● ▼
22 Sage ▼

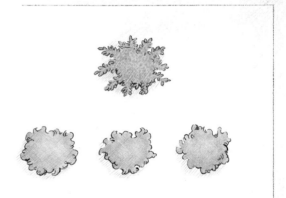

HARVEST
1 Quinoa

PROJECTS
WINE (harvest and crush grapes)

OCTOBER

PLANT
2 Fava beans ●
27 Garlic (late October to early November, from cloves)
25 Onions, 'Spanish white' ● or sets

HARVEST
■ All crops for fall feast (see page 95)

PROJECTS
MUSHROOMS (order logs ❖; plant morels)

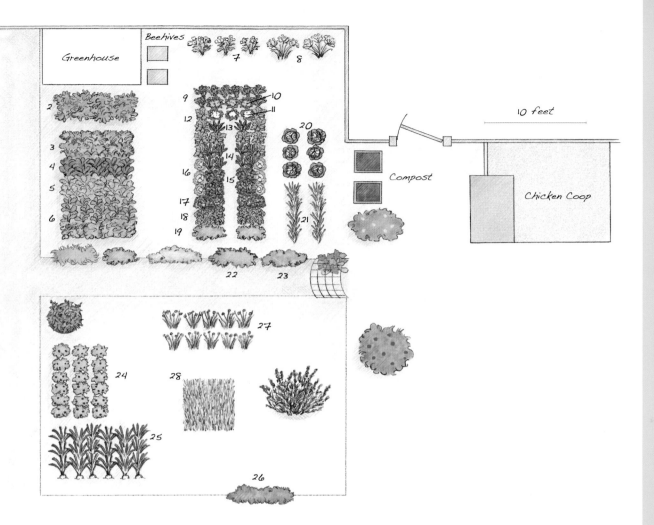

NOVEMBER

PLANT
1 Barley (after harvesting quinoa; through February) ●

PROJECTS
    OLIVE OIL
    VINEGAR ❖

JANUARY

PLANT
24 Strawberries (into February) ✱
28 Wheat ●

PROJECTS
    SALT ❖
    ESCARGOTS ❖
    MEAD ❖

FEBRUARY

PLANT
4 Beets (through August) ●
3 Carrots ●
7 Chervil (through March) ●
8 Dill ●
21 Green onions ● ▼
6 Mesclun (through mid-March for late spring harvest) ●
5 Radishes (through June) ●
26 Onions, cippolini (very end of February) ● ▼ or sets

HARVEST
    ■ All crops for winter feast (page 166)

Essential Gardening Guidelines

The following information is bare-bones basic for organic gardening. If you would like to learn about mulching (to keep soil moist and squelch weed growth), ways to protect young plants (with row covers, netting, or fencing), training and staking plants, and other details about organic fruit and vegetable gardening, see our *Western Garden Book of Edibles* (Sunset Publishing Corporation, 2010). For specifics on how to grow each plant we raised for our feasts, see the garden guides at the beginnings of the first four chapters in this book. Because growing conditions vary by region (and even within neighborhoods), the best source for local planting information is your county's agricultural cooperative extension office; find yours at www.csrees.usda.gov/Extension/index.html.

BEFORE YOU PLANT

It is extremely tempting to put your seeds and seedlings in the ground right away. But if you want them to flourish and feed you well, you must create a hospitable environment for them first. The two most important elements are sun and soil.

Sun: More Is Better

Most vegetables, herbs, and fruits need 6 to 8 hours of full sun daily. Plant them in a spot that is not shaded by buildings, trees, or shrubs. Shadows lengthen in fall and winter to the north of tall structures, so use a compass to figure out where north lies, and make sure any tall plants or structures to the south won't cast shadows over your growing bounty.

Soil: The First Ingredient

Rich, well-drained soil gives your plants the edge they need to produce abundant, flavorful harvests with minimal attention. If your garden is organic, as ours is, keeping the soil healthy is key to plant health, too.

ASSESSING YOUR SOIL

How do you know whether your soil is good, just okay, or a plant-killing disaster? Most soils fall more or less into one of these three categories.

Loam This is the good stuff, dark, rich, crumbly, and wonderful-smelling, especially when slightly damp. It drains well but doesn't dry out too fast, can hold nutrients longer than other soil types, and contains enough air for healthy root growth. Give it the squeeze test: Thoroughly wet a patch of soil and let it dry out for a day. Then, pick up a handful and squeeze it firmly in your fist. If it is slightly crumbly but still holds a loose ball, it's loam.

Clay (heavy) soils These are made up of very small particles that pack together tightly, producing a compact mass with microscopic pore spaces (the areas between soil particles). Because water and nutrients percolate slowly through the tiny spaces, drainage usually takes a while. It's not easy for roots to penetrate clay soil, and during long rainy spells (or if overwatered), the soil stays wet, sometimes to the point of causing root rot. When subjected to the squeeze test, heavy soil forms a tight, slippery ball.

Sandy (light) soils At the other end of the spectrum are soils with large, irregularly rounded particles and

In the Sunset test garden, we have two side-by-side wooden-slat bins that look like big open crates. We also like the three-bin system often used for composting, which can handle a greater amount of material, but our garden doesn't have room. One of our two bins holds a "hot" pile and the other a "cold" pile. The "hot" pile you build all at once, and you get finished compost in about 3 months. The "cold" pile, which you build gradually, breaks down more slowly. Having the two piles gives us a way to deal with both a whole load of raw materials at once and a smaller, steadier stream from the garden and kitchen.

Build a Two-Bin Compost System

1. **Set up bins** You can use pretty much any kind of bin—wooden, plastic, or chicken wire shaped around rebar—set directly on the soil. That way, beneficial fungi, bacteria, and worms have a better chance of finding their way into the compost, and the bins keep the piles from getting messy. Ours are 3 feet square (the minimum size for efficient "hot" composting), about 3 feet tall, and/or open on the top and one end for easy pile turning.

2. **Add materials** Any compost pile has four main ingredients: **browns** (carbon), including dried grass, dried leaves, woody stems, straw, and eggshells, with the biggest pieces no larger than 6 inches; **greens** (nitrogen), including animal manure (not dog or cat), fresh grass, fresh leaves and other fresh plant parts (stalks, roots),

coffee grounds and kitchen scraps (no fat or meat), and coffee grounds (with the biggest pieces no larger than 6 inches); **water,** usually with rainfall and condensation providing all that is needed to keep the pile as moist as a wrung-out sponge; and **air,** which reaches the compost through the open top and front of the bin. **To keep out of your compost:** Weeds with seedheads, cat and dog feces, disease- or insect-infested plants, meat scraps, and copious amounts of other food scraps (keep the food scraps to less than 50 percent of the greens; otherwise, they will rot and attract flies and rodents). Feed both piles a good range of greens and browns. Treat your compost like your diet—diversity is best.

3. **Build and tend the hot pile** Alternate 6-inch-thick layers of browns and greens, watering each layer thoroughly and ending with a brown layer. This is a great place to toss the still-green summer crops you ripped out at the end of the season.

    The pile will heat up from the inside over the next week or so. Then use a spading fork to "turn" (that is, mix) the pile, and keep turning it once a week. We drag all of it out onto a tarp to turn it and then pile it back in the bin.

    You'll have finished compost in about 3 months. It's ready when the majority of the contents smell and look like lush, earthy, dark brown soil. It might need to be sifted if harder-to-break-down additions (like branches) haven't decomposed.

4. **Build the cold pile** You worry less about the ratio of browns to greens in a cold pile. Just toss in whatever might be coming from the garden or kitchen. It decomposes from the bottom up and no turning or any other maintenance is necessary: If it starts to smell, add more browns. It's ready when it turns a rich, dark brown; smells earthy; and has the look and feel of coffee grounds, which can take from 6 to 12 months.

Our two-bin setup is not a perfect system. The space isn't big enough to hold all of the garden scraps, and can't produce enough compost to feed all of our new plantings, so we end up buying bagged compost from the garden store.

But it's a start, and we have one thing working strongly in our favor: readily available chicken excrement from our coop to add to both piles. This amendment, high in nitrogen, jump-starts any pile's breakdown. You need to let it age in the compost pile for at least a month, however, before you can use the compost on plants. Otherwise, it will burn them.

We get immense satisfaction out of shoveling the chicken poop into the compost bin, and a satisfaction just as great from putting finished compost back out into the planting beds. We feel like we're helping along one of nature's most miraculous systems: using "waste" to become food once again. Not everyone would get such pleasure out of shoveling crap. But we like seeing the loop close, so we wouldn't have it any other way.
—**Johanna Silver**

large spaces between them that allow water and nutrients to drain away freely. Plants growing in sand are unlikely to suffer root rot, but you need to water them more often to keep their roots moist. The frequent watering leaches nutrients away, so you'll have to fertilize more often, too. Try the squeeze test: If the soil feels gritty, doesn't hold its shape, and crumbles in your hand, it's sandy.

FIXING YOUR SOIL

Compost This "gardener's gold" is an easy, natural way to create good soil. Plenty of compost loosens clay soils and improves drainage. Added to sandy soils, it increases moisture retention by wedging into the large pore spaces between the soil particles. To learn how to make it yourself, see Cultivating Compost, opposite. You can also buy bagged compost at nurseries.

A few days before planting, dampen the soil slightly to make it easier to dig. With a spading fork (also known as a digging or garden fork), dig to a depth of about 10 inches, breaking up clods of earth and removing any stones, weeds, and debris as you go.

Spread a hefty layer of compost (3 to 6 inches) over the soil and fork it in, along with granular controlled-release fertilizer (see How to Fertilize, page 15). Then level the bed with a rake, breaking up any remaining clods. Water well and let the improved soil settle.

Each time you replant a bed with new crops, you'll first need to rejuvenate the soil by repeating these steps, but adding only 1 to 2 inches of compost instead of 3 to 6 inches. Your soil will get progressively fluffier and richer.

HOW TO PLANT

Once you have prepared your soil and let it settle for a few days, your garden is ready to be planted. You can buy seeds and start your own plants, sow seeds directly in the ground, or buy transplants (seedlings) from a nursery. With seeds, you can order exactly what you want from a mail-order company if your local nursery doesn't carry it. Seek out All America Selections (AAS) seeds whenever possible. They have been judged as winners for their stellar performance in trials across the country by the AAS, a nonprofit organization whose mission is to promote new garden-seed varieties. Nursery transplants are more expensive, and the choice is more limited, but they can be planted immediately.

Starting Plants from Seed

When you start your plants from seed, you can experiment with more varieties than you ever knew existed. (Many of our one-block crops are only available as seeds.) It's also a fascinating science project and an exercise in patience and care.

Seeds are dormant until placed in a moist medium (such as potting mix) that encourages germination. We start ours in cell packs left over from buying seedlings, and either keep them in our garden's greenhouse until the seedlings are up before planting them outdoors, or sow them directly into the ground. Seed starting flats or peat pots, available at nurseries and home-supply stores, work too, and you don't need a greenhouse—a bright indoor windowsill will work fine.

The "hot" pile

When do you start seeds? For most warm-season vegetables, seeds should be sown in early spring (except in hot desert climates), so the plants are ready to set out in the garden when the weather has warmed up. For cool-season crops, you want the seedlings ready to plant in early spring or in fall. Each packet will give you exact guidelines for when to start that particular seed. The label will specify any special care the seedlings might need, too, like a heating mat set underneath the cell pack to speed germination. The packet will also tell you whether the plant does best sown directly in the ground (certain crops, like carrots, prefer not to be transplanted). For tips on direct sowing, see opposite.

FOUR SEED-STARTING SECRETS

1. Use a light, fluffy soil mix Make sure you use potting mix instead of planting soil or compost. Potting mixes or soils contain all the necessary ingredients (perlite, vermiculite, peat moss) to stay light and fluffy and drain properly. Dampen the soil before you sow your seeds.

2. Plant more seeds than you need Whether sown directly in the ground or into cell packs, it's a good idea to plant double the amount of seeds you think you need. In the ground, this means to drop two seeds, instead of one seed, into each hole. In cell packs, sow eight tomato seeds if you want four tomato plants. That way, you'll have backups in case any of the seeds fail to germinate. You can always carefully separate the starts, pot up the extras, and pass them along to friends or coworkers.

3. Plant shallow Sow seeds twice as deep as the seed is wide. This means barely under the surface for tiny seeds like lettuce or carrots and about $1/4$ inch deep for crops such as squash. And you don't need to pat the seeds into the soil. You can just sprinkle soil on top of them; it really is okay.

4. Water thoroughly Once you have sown your seeds, sprinkle them gently but thoroughly with water. Be extremely diligent about keeping the seeds moist until they germinate (sprout).

PLANTING SEEDLINGS (TRANSPLANTS)

1. Move the seedlings to a halfway house Once the seedlings have developed their first true leaves, transplant each one to its own pot (a 4-inch-deep pot is ideal) before hardening it off (see at right) and putting it into the ground. Or, you can keep the seedlings in their cell packs

Shallow-furrow sowing

until the second set of true leaves appear, then harden them off and transplant directly into the ground. If you opt to transplant the seedlings to pots, here is how to do it:

- Fill the pots with potting mix, moisten the mix, and let it drain.
- Remove each seedling from its cell pack by gently squeezing the sides of the pack with one hand, turning the pack on its side, and then cradling the soil ball between two fingers of your other hand as you tip the seedling out.
- Poke a hole in the moistened potting mix. Carefully lift a seedling and its root-ball, keeping your fingers under it for support, and ease it into the hole in the potting mix. Firm the mix around the base of the seedling.
- Once all the seedlings are transplanted, water them immediately, then set the pots in bright light in the greenhouse or indoors near a window (but keep them out of direct sunlight for a few days).
- Feed the seedlings weekly with an all-purpose fertilizer sold for starting seeds or with a liquid fertilizer diluted to half-strength. When they sprout a couple more leaves, they are ready to be hardened off.

2. "Harden off" the seedlings The seedlings will need to be gradually acclimated to the outdoors before they are planted permanently outside. This process, called hardening off, prevents transplant shock and will help your seedlings thrive once they are in the ground. The seed packets will tell you when to begin the process.

Over the course of a week or so, take the 4-inch pots of seedlings (or the seedlings in cell packs if you have decided against the halfway house) outdoors for several hours each day, steadily increasing the amount of time until you are leaving them outdoors all night. Bring your babies indoors, though, should the temperature suddenly spike or drop. If you buy your transplants at a nursery, they are already hardened off and can be planted directly in the garden (see next step).

3. Transplant the plants into the garden Dig a hole the same depth as the 4-inch pot and an inch or two wider. Ease the plant out of the pot. Try not to disturb the roots, unless the root-ball is very tight. If that's the case, tease apart the roots a little to encourage them to grow out, rather than around and around in a coil. Place each plant in its hole so that the top of the root-ball is even with the soil surface. (Tomatoes are an exception; they are planted more deeply.) Firm the soil around the roots, then water with a gentle flow that won't disturb the soil or the roots.

SOWING SEEDS DIRECTLY IN THE GARDEN

Many vegetables grow best if you plant the seeds in the garden from the start. These include root crops (carrots, beets, radishes, turnips, and parsnips), as well as corn, peas, and beans.

Sow the seeds after the soil has warmed up to at least 60°F. You can check the temperature with an instant-read kitchen thermometer or a soil thermometer, available at garden shops. Read the seed packet (or the plant entries in this book) for more information on when to sow each crop. Make sure that the soil is loose and finely crumbled, so the tiny seedlings can push through. Refer to the plant entries or to the seed packet for the proper planting depth; seeds planted too deep won't sprout. As with seeds you start indoors, plant them twice as deep as the seed is wide.

To be sure you get enough plants, sow a lot of seeds close together. Then, when the seedlings are 1 to 2 inches tall, thin the seedlings to their proper spacing (specified in the plant entries and on seed packets).

You can sow three different ways:

Shallow furrows This is the most common way to sow. Use a trowel or the corner of a hoe to make a furrow the correct depth for the seeds you are planting. Sow the seeds evenly, then pat the soil gently over them. To make straight rows, stretch a string between two stakes and plant beneath it. Or, lay a board on the soil and plant along its edge.

Clusters This is a traditional way to grow sprawling plants like squash and melons, because it gives them more room. Sow five or six seeds in a circle and pat soil over them. Check the plant entries or the seed packet for how far apart to space the circles.

Broadcast Scattering seeds in wide bands instead of planting in rows is more space efficient for smaller crops, such as lettuces, carrots, or radishes. Scatter the seeds evenly over the soil. Cover by scattering soil over the seeds or by raking gently, first in one direction and then perpendicular to it.

After sowing, water the planted area with a fine mist, being careful not to dislodge the seeds. You want to keep the soil moist but not soggy, and also prevent it from forming a crust (so that the germinating seed won't bang its head against a ceiling). In hot weather, covering the soil with damp burlap helps retain moisture. Be sure to remove the burlap as soon as the seeds begin to sprout. If you plan to water with basins or furrows, dig them before you sow your seeds (see page 14).

HOW TO STORE LEFTOVER SEEDS

Usually a packet gives you more seeds than you can use. If the leftover seeds are stored airtight in a cool, dark place, they will last for at least another year, especially if they were fresh when you bought them. (Check the date on the packet before buying.)

To store the seeds, put them (in their packets for easy identification) in mason jars, resealable heavy plastic bags, or sturdy plastic containers, and stick them in the freezer. If you're not certain whether your seeds are viable, wrap them in a moistened paper towel, pop them in a resealable plastic bag, and put the bag in the sun. If they sprout in the time specified on the packet, they're good for planting.

HOW TO WATER

Every garden has different needs depending on the weather, the soil, the age and variety of the plant(s), and a host of other factors, so figuring out the best way to water is an ongoing learning process. What follows are general guidelines. For more specific information on the watering requirements of a particular crop, see the plant entries in each season.

Frequency

Water new transplants at least once a day in 60° to 70°F weather and up to two or three times a day when it's hot and windy. Your goal is to keep the soil moist but not soggy. As the plants grow and their roots reach deeper, you can water less frequently. In general, vegetables that are flowering or beginning to set fruit, form heads, or develop edible roots need to be watered more often than older plants.

Your soil texture also influences how often you need to water. Clay soils need less frequent watering than loam soils, and loam soils can be watered less frequently than sandy soils. (For more on soil types, see page 9.)

Amount

Once the plants are established, water them deeply enough to moisten the entire root zone. This encourages roots to grow down farther. Deeper roots have access to more moisture, which allows the plants to go longer between waterings. Frequent shallow sprinklings are inefficient because they encourage shallow root growth, which leaves plants subject to stress from heat and drying winds. To check water penetration in your soil, dig a hole with a trowel after watering.

Ways to Water

We used the following methods in our one-block garden:

By hand with a sprinkler hose or watering can Using a sprinkler nozzle on the end of a hose or a watering can with a sprinkler snout is useful for newly seeded beds, new transplants, and container plants because you can apply the water gently and put it exactly where it's needed. This method also rinses away dust and discourages certain pests (especially spider mites). Sprinkling has some disadvantages, as well. It wastes water through evaporation, particularly in windy weather. It may also encourage leaf diseases on some crops, especially in humid climates. The best time to water by hand is in the

Drip irrigation

morning (leaves will dry off during the day) when the air is still.

By hand, flooding a basin or furrow Basins, which are used to water large fruiting plants such as our lemon tree, tea bushes, and pineapple guava tree, are doughnut-shaped depressions in the soil surrounding the plants. As the plants grow, you need to expand the basins. Furrows, or shallow ditches, dug near smaller plants that are growing in rows work well on level ground. Broad, shallow furrows are generally better than deep, narrow ones: The wider the furrow, the wider the root area you can soak, since water moves primarily downward rather than sideways. To avoid damaging the roots, dig basins and furrows before you set out plants or sow seeds. Furrows are great because they are a fast, efficient way to reach the plants' roots.

Soaker hoses These are long tubes made of perforated or porous plastic or rubber with hose fittings at one end. When you attach a soaker to a hose and turn on the water supply, water seeps or sprinkles from the soaker along its entire length. Soakers are ideal for irrigating rows of vegetables. To water beds, snake the soaker back and forth around the plants. To water trees, coil a soaker around the outer edges of the root zone. Soakers water efficiently and evenly, but you have to be there to turn on the hose.

Drip irrigation Drip systems deliver water slowly by drip emitters that you attach to plastic tubing yourself, or by emitter lines, tubes with factory-installed emitters spaced at regular intervals. Emitters can be adjusted so that the water is applied directly over plant roots, reducing your water use. Because most of the surface is not moistened, drip systems also cut down on weed growth. Drip-irrigation kits and supplies are sold by agricultural-supply stores, retail nurseries, garden centers, and mail-order suppliers.

HOW TO FERTILIZE

First, you'll need to figure out the label. All fertilizer labels list the percentage by weight of three primary nutrients, in this order: nitrogen (N), phosphorus (P), and potassium (K). Fertilizers labeled "general purpose" or "all-purpose" are complete fertilizers, meaning they contain all three nutrients. For example, a fertilizer labeled 10-10-10 contains 10 percent nitrogen, 10 percent phosphorus, and 10 percent potassium. A fertilizer labeled 20-10-5 contains more nitrogen (N) than the other nutrients, so it's sometimes called a high-nitrogen fertilizer. Complete fertilizers can be liquid, granular, or pellets.

Choosing Fertilizers

Light feeders such as lettuce, radishes, and tomatoes that have been planted in rich soil well amended with compost rarely, if ever, need supplemental fertilizer. But many other crops, including melons and onions, need extra food to thrive. Where fertilizer is called for in this book, we most often use the types listed below.

Fish emulsion This creamy, brown, sometimes fishy-smelling liquid fertilizer is made from whole fish, or oils and by-products of processed fish. Dilute it with water according to label directions and apply it with a watering can. (We also use it as a foliar spray for an added boost.) It is fast acting, slightly acidic, and relatively mild.

Granular organic blend Dr. Earth granular fertilizer for tomatoes, vegetables, and herbs is a 5-7-3 formulation that combines fish bonemeal, kelp meal, alfalfa meal, soft rock phosphate, seaweed extract, potassium sulfate, and more. It is usually added during the growing season.

Controlled-release fertilizer This is our one exception to organic gardening. We sometimes use it for containerized fruit trees, which tend to be heavy feeders. The beadlike granules release nutrients gradually—the rate depends on temperature, weather, and moisture—over several months. Scatter and dig the granules into freshly prepared soil at the rate of about 3 tablespoons for every 4 square feet.

—*Kathleen N. Brenzel and Johanna Silver*

The Summer Garden

SUMMER

I t all started with the menu. In the Sunset kitchen in mid-May, we cooks dreamed about the end-of-summer dishes we wanted to make: Peppery arugula salads with a rainbow of ripe tomatoes in oranges and yellows, greens and purples, reds and pinks. A platter of avocados and oranges with paper-thin red onions. Sweet corn on the cob, definitely. Ripe figs, because we had spotted a vine growing out back.

With a tentative menu drawn up, we sat down with the garden department and got a reality check. Arugula, a cool-season crop, would wilt in our summer heat. Our fig vine had been pruned so severely the year before that it probably wouldn't bear much fruit—not enough to plan on, anyway. We had no avocado trees, and even if we bought some young ones, they would take several years to produce.

There were consolations, however. We could grow good tomatoes, though they would be on the small side in our cool climate. Corn would not have the savory depth that it does in the Midwest, but it would be sweet and juicy. 'Yukon Gold' potatoes would be no problem. "How about zucchini?" suggested Lauren Swezey, our garden projects editor. "Zucchini does really well here." Privately, I was crushed—zucchini is just about the most boring summer vegetable I can think of. But then Lauren described a wondrous variety called 'Trombetta di Albenga'. She took out a seed packet with a picture on it. "It curves like a trombone," she said. "And it's sweet and a little crunchy. Completely delicious." We were sold.

Over the next few days, we settled on a cooking fat (not peanut oil, because peanuts need a southern climate, or corn oil, because three cups would require about sixty pounds of corn, and we wanted to eat our corn). What Sunset did have were twenty-one olive trees, planted all around the property as landscaping back in the 1950s. They were loaded with fruit, and surely it wouldn't be too hard to figure out how to press it.

For seasoning, we would plant chiles, lemons, and potent summer herbs. And, because we lived close to the Pacific, it seemed worth trying to make some salt from seawater.

What would we do for protein? Our menu sounded good, but gossamery. We asked ourselves what we were collectively capable of, and it did not include raising meat animals. Eggs and cheese seemed more doable. We could keep chickens right in the garden, and as for the milk for cheese, the closest dairy would do. We didn't dream (then) that we might someday have a cow.

For dessert, we'd need a sweetener, and honey seemed like the natural solution. Why not try keeping some bees? Plus, all those pollinators would help our crops produce.

Within a couple of weeks, we'd finalized our menu. I wandered out into the garden to imagine how it might all look. A pair of grapevines caught my eye. What if we made wine? Our little vines wouldn't supply enough grapes, but maybe we could find a vineyard nearby. Wine editor Sara Schneider loved the idea and agreed to launch Team Wine. In the meantime, Rick LaFrentz, our head gardener, volunteered to lead Team Beer. He had brewed

The One-Block Summer Feast

Skillet-Roasted Edamame (page 67)
Deviled Cucumber Cups (page 67)

✧

Corn Soup with Roasted Poblanos and Zucchini Blossoms (page 70)

✧

Tomato and Herb Salad with Fresh Chive Cheese (page 69)
Rosemary Potatoes Anna (page 74)
Pattypan Squash with Eggs (page 75)

✧

Watermelon, Cantaloupe, or Honeydew Sorbets (page 80)
Peppermint-Lemongrass Tisane (page 80)

✧

Chardonnay (page 110) and Summer Wheat Beer (page 49)

---

at home using kits, and wanted to try planting barley, wheat, and hops to make beer from the ground up. It was intriguingly medieval of him.

Our made-from-scratch project had not even started, and here we were, "importing" wine grapes and milk and ocean water. But we would transform the imports into foods that would be wholly our own: grapes into wine, milk into cheese, water into salt.

Italians have a lovely word for the locally grown produce in their farmers' markets: *nostrani*—"ours." It usually sells out first because it's often the best. That's exactly what this summer dinner would be, from start to finish. Ours.

✧

I walked around the office to see if any of my other colleagues wanted to join the project. Erika Ehmsen, our stately, calm copy chief, knew where we might get the hundreds of pounds of grapes we needed: Thomas Fogarty Winery, in the nearby Santa Cruz Mountains. Her dad and Dr. Fogarty, a cardiologist, had worked together, and she'd visited as a child and had always wanted to go back. She signed up for Team Wine. Researcher Elizabeth

Jardina and art director Jim McCann liked the idea of chickens. Garden associate editor Julie Chai, whose heritage is Korean and German, wanted to join Team Vinegar (formed in the wake of Team Wine). "I have kimchi on one side and sauerkraut on the other," she told me. "I love all things fermented." Margaret Sloan, production coordinator, and Kimberley Burch, imaging specialist, were drawn to Team Bee. Margaret had always thought bees were mysterious and fascinating, and Kimberley, concerned about colony collapse disorder, mainly wanted to help increase the bee population.

By early June, we had started researching our various projects and were ready to roll. The fact that we had no experience with any of them, except cooking and gardening and a bit of beer making, did not dim our enthusiasm a bit.

That was a good thing, because it would take us about a year and a half to create everything we needed for our summer feast. The wine grapes wouldn't be ready until October; then they'd need months to ferment and mature. The olives ripened in November. And we could not harvest the wheat and barley until the following summer.

At least we could get the chickens going. I personally yearned for fabulous-looking breeds like Silkies, whose feathers are as soft as kitten fur, or Polish, whose feather crests make them look like Tina Turner. Fancy chickens are not always the best layers, though. In the end, we just got what Half Moon Bay Feed & Fuel happened to have on the day we visited, which were tiny chicks from breeds known to lay well: Ameraucanas (exciting, since they would lay blue- and green-shelled eggs), Rhode Island Reds, and Buff Orpingtons.

We bought two of each, and fussed over them like crazy, hanging a heat lamp over their wire cage—which we put in a storage shed behind our main office building—and visiting them every couple of hours. The runt, a Rhode Island Red we called Ruby, immediately developed a condition that the feed store had warned us about: pasty butt. Untreated, it can block a chick's digestion and be lethal. This we handled as instructed by the feed store, gingerly applying cotton balls soaked in warm water to the tiniest butt imaginable. Ruby survived.

As our chickens grew that fall, we plunged into wine making. Fogarty Winery agreed to sell us both Syrah grapes (a relatively forgiving variety, so we would have a chance of making drinkable wine) and Chardonnay juice (since pressing white grapes is much trickier than pressing the red). On a golden October morning, we drove out to the winery and picked five hundred pounds of small, luscious Syrah grapes from Fat Buck Ridge, a vineyard with sweeping views to the west. It was surprisingly fast—a couple of hours of snipping and we had all the grapes we could handle. We had a quick picnic in the vineyard, with a bottle of Fogarty Syrah from that very ridge—"the prototype, the goal . . . the competition," Sara joked later.

We had to crush the grapes as soon as possible. Waiting for us back at Sunset, with a giant pile of equipment, was Dan Brenzel, husband of our garden editor, Kathy Brenzel, and a serious home winemaker himself. His crusher-destemmer was entirely capable of handling our harvest. But a couple of us had seen the grape-stomping episode of *I Love Lucy* at an impressionable age, so we did some foot crushing, too, there in the Sunset parking lot. We laughed so hard we practically fell out of the garbage cans we were using for crushing. As Erika pointed out, it was sort of like a StairMaster. Set in quicksand.

The next several days were tense for Team Wine. Sara woke up at 3:00 a.m. worried that our grape pulp (called

must), which was soaking under the eaves in a big vat to give the juice as much flavor and color as possible, might be spoiling. So we added yeast to kick off the fermentation and crowd out any unwelcome microorganisms. (We'd already added yeast to our Chardonnay juice.)

And at first everything went like it should. The yeast attacked the sugars and belched carbon dioxide gas, which made the pulp gurgle and foam as though it were alive. A warm, thick, seething cap of skins and seeds formed on the surface, and we punched it down a few times a day so it could deliver its goodness to the juice. But the sugar level wasn't dropping fast enough. This meant we risked a "stuck fermentation" that could lead to spoiled wine. We decided to move our vats into the warm building, hoping to prod the yeast into gobbling more sugar. It worked, and the sugar eventually hit zero. We had gotten through the hardest part.

Now we eased the Syrah into a slower, secondary fermentation by sprinkling in powdery, freeze-dried malolactic bacteria. It was as easy as adding salt to a stew. A few days later—once the bacteria had a chance to settle in—we pressed our wine off its skins and seeds. This involved using Dan's homestyle basket press, which looked not unlike a toy rocket. We poured the inky slurry into the press and set up a tag team running buckets from the press's spigot over to several waiting carboys (big

glass jugs). Then, once we'd popped airlocks into the tops of the carboys, we left our beast alone to be tamed by beneficial bacteria and the gentling hand of time.

Meanwhile, our chicks had become fully feathered young hens and were ready for their coop in the test garden. The henhouse itself, which opened right into a fully enclosed yard—to keep out raccoons and other chicken hunters—was a grand sloping-roofed structure given to us by Wine Country Coops, in Napa. The hens took to it as though to the manor born, hopping up to its comfortable perches and exploring the nest boxes. Pretty soon, their personalities—yes, they do have them, it turns out—began to show: Rhode Island Red Carmelita was the boss lady, the most aggressive and the shiniest feathered. (Elizabeth worried that she might be a rooster.) Ruby was a talker, croaking insistently whenever we came to visit, as though cussing us out for something. Alana, slightly shy, was named for our managing editor, Alan Phinney, because her lustrous head feathers resembled his hair (he is a good sport about this). Her fellow Ameraucana, Ophelia, was much more outgoing and instead of clucking produced a sort of low foghorn tootle. The two Buff Orpingtons, Honey and Charlotte—both big, fluffy, and blonde—were the most inclined to jump on your lap for a pat. They weighed as much as house cats and liked to be stroked under their wings, where the down was softest. It made them burble happily, as did an ear of corn or a bulb of fennel thrown down for them to peck. And the burbling of a happy chicken is a very sweet sound.

❖

Everything was going well. Then, in late October, disaster struck. Olives began pelting the ground weeks before we had expected to harvest them. Not only that, the fruit looked shrunken and deformed. We sent some off to The Olive Press, up in Sonoma, for advice, and were told that we had the worst infestation of olive fruit fly maggots that the store's owner had ever seen.

Apparently, you can press olives with a small percentage of maggots—although you might end up with a flavor flaw known in the olive oil trade as "grubby" (seriously). Our fruit, though, was riddled with them. We could try treating the trees in the future, but this year the grubs had won.

We badly wanted olive oil, and we really wanted to learn how to pick and press olives. Fortunately, Valencia Creek Farms, in the Santa Cruz foothills, agreed to sell us eight hundred pounds of olives, which we could pick

Ascolano olives at Valencia Creek Farms

ourselves. So we rented a U-Haul and drove off to the foothills again.

At the orchard, we picked big, fat green Ascolanos. The rest of our order had been harvested for us earlier that day, and although we felt a little sheepish about this, we were also very grateful when we realized that it would have taken our five Team Olive members about eleven hours to pick what we needed.

As with grapes, speed is of the essence when pressing olives. The second they are off the trees, they start to degrade. We loaded up our twenty-two crates and drove south, to Pietra Santa Winery, near Hollister, and its olive press. The olives were destemmed and washed, and then ground by three massive stones into a pinkish, brownish paste that looked exactly like chopped liver.

We tasted the olive oil right from the spigot. It was grass green, flecked with bits of olive, and extremely fresh and bright. The mild climate of Santa Cruz had tamed the olives, so the oil was not nearly as peppery as a typical "three-cough" Tuscan oil. We were absurdly and instantly proud of it. Our hens were not laying yet and our wine was still aging, but we had our olive oil and it felt great.

❖

Our first egg (behind the decoy)

'Trombetta' zucchini shooting out tendrils

We were now in January, and with every passing day of the new year, we expected eggs. Chickens usually start laying when they are between four and six months old, and ours were past the five-month mark. Team Chicken was beside itself with anticipation, especially when the hens started showing the classic signs of being on the verge: fat pink combs and a tendency to suddenly crouch in front of you, tail up high. This is called the egg squat, and the chicken hopes you are a rooster bent on mating. We stroked the squatters from head to tail, which is supposed to relax them and help the egg form—but still, no eggs! Elizabeth caught herself actually commanding the chickens to lay. Team leader Jim put a marble egg paperweight in the nest box to encourage them. We checked the nest boxes four or five times a day. And then, finally, in late January, on a quiet Sunday, our Ameraucana Ophelia laid a small and exquisite blue egg.

Over the next several days, Ophelia gave us two more eggs—enough for a group taste. The yolks were deep orange-yellow and the whites so firm they actually were hard to break up with a fork. I scrambled them very slowly, and we all stood around and had small bites. They were velvety and voluptuous, with a rich, round flavor that made ordinary eggs taste like imitations.

One by one, the other chickens stepped into the nest box. Alana laid a light green egg the shape of a kiwifruit, with splotches of darker green. Carmelita, after half an hour of squawking and cackling and thrashing, produced a brown egg with a dent in the bottom (we figured out later that she was standing up when she laid it). Ruby's egg was brown too, but tiny and freckled. The Buff Orpingtons brought up the rear with creamy beige eggs. Pretty soon we were getting five or six eggs a day, and no two were ever the same.

Our next project took us up into the hills again, but this time north, to Sonoma, and the home of cookbook author Paula Wolfert. Paula is famous for her meticulous research and had just finished a major investigation of vinegar. She gave Team Vinegar a start-to-finish lesson, complete with emphatic advice: "If it smells like furniture polish, throw it out!" We left with jars of her precious vinegar "mother," the live starter culture for vinegar, which she had gotten from a friend who had brought it over from France. It was probably at least forty years old. The slippery, gelatinous bits of this venerable mother would convert part of our stash of Syrah into the best wine vinegar ever. Or, so we hoped.

We fed the mothers with cautious dribbles and then healthy pours of Syrah, and in a matter of weeks, we had some incredible vinegar. It was exhilaratingly strong, fruity, and complex, and left deep purple stains on whatever it touched. "It knocked my socks off," said Kathy Brenzel, Sunset's garden editor and the team leader. "I could've sipped it from a wineglass and been happy." This was nothing like grocery-store red-wine vinegar. We actually had to add water to it, just to tame its jets.

By now we were well into spring, a good time to get started on some cheese. We knew mozzarella would be tremendous with the big tomato and herb salad we had planned, but we also knew that making it was kind of difficult and also possibly painful (you have to stretch the cheese while it's boiling hot). Instead, Team Cheese bought a copy of Ricki Carroll's *Home Cheese Making* and started experimenting with recipes.

We had only a handful of ingredients: organic milk, "imported" from the excellent Straus Family Creamery, just north of San Francisco; lemons and herbs from our garden; and sea salt, which recipe editor Amy Machnak had figured out how to make from pure Pacific Ocean water. (Her fiancé, Andrew, a diver, had hauled in forty gallons of it for her.) So it's not surprising that the recipes did not turn out exactly as Carroll described. Plus, we lost control of our heat, overwhisked the curds, and used too much lemon juice. But in the end we produced two simple cheeses (and have since fine-tuned the recipes): a crumbly, salty, oregano-flecked white cheese we could sprinkle into soup, and a firm, sliceable log flavored with chives, which we planned to use in the salad. We felt pleased with ourselves. "I never thought you could really *make* cheese," said features editor Christine Ciarmello, who had moved west the month before, from Florida. "I've just come from the land of fast food, and here I've been responsible for the birth of this little cheese."

Soon after, in May, when the weather grew soft and warm, we planted just about everything else we hoped to eat. Test-garden coordinator Ryan Casey, who was starting his own small farm in Half Moon Bay, turned the soil in our backyard-size plot with a digging fork until it was as loose and light as bread crumbs and then raked in a rich, dark layer of compost. He planted the little seedlings lightning fast, scooping out each hole with one tanned, bare hand and plopping the plant in with the other, then sliding soil around the stem. For seeds, he

Among the Syrah vines at Fat Buck Ridge, in the Santa Cruz Mountains

dropped them into furrows with an upswing of his hand and then pinched the furrows closed on the downswing. His grace and economy of motion were mesmerizing.

The warmth meant flowers, too, and nectar flow, the food supply for bees. It was time to set up our hives. We decided to get what are called nucs—brand-new little colonies, each with a queen, bees, and brood (bee larvae)—rather than packaged bees, which would take longer to get established. But we were nervous. Already all the equipment seemed overwhelming, and we were a little scared of the bees themselves.

Master beekeeper Randy Oliver had nucs to sell, and he offered to give us a crash course in beekeeping, too. Over the phone, he told me, "You guys give me two hours and I'll shift your paradigm." In his lush, pine-scented bee yard, in the Sierra foothills, that is exactly what happened. He showed us that if we moved calmly among the bees, as though practicing tai chi, they would ignore us completely. He taught us how to hold the frames to catch the sunlight, so we could see the tiny eggs—each smaller than a grain of rice—to make sure the queen was laying. Bare hands, he said, are better for working with bees, because gloves can crush them. Then he carefully shook dozens of bees into our bare cupped hands. Holding them was electrifying. It felt like holding a mass of warm, vibrating air. No stings. By the end of the afternoon, we were completely smitten, and drove home with two hives of gentle, golden bees—two living bee worlds—in the back of our rented truck.

❋

In the meantime, a minor crisis had erupted in the chicken coop. Honey, our sweetest chicken, was being terrorized by the other hens. They would peck her little pink comb till it bled, and she'd hide in the nest box all day, not eating, not drinking. We tried all kinds of things to disrupt the pecking order, such as squirting the attackers with water guns, painting Honey's poor chewed comb with nasty-tasting liquid baby soap, and yelling "No!" repeatedly. Nothing worked. Honey was wasting away, her keel bone poking out like the prow of a ghost ship.

Finally, we built her a separate enclosure within the coop, with her own little nest box. Elizabeth called it the Honeydome. Unfortunately, the minute we put her in it she flew out to join her oppressors. Elizabeth claimed Honey had "a crazy form of chicken Stockholm syndrome." To block another escape, we extended the chicken-wire fence to the ceiling of the coop. But Honey just pressed herself against the mesh, and the other hens pecked away at her. We were at wit's end. And then, miraculously, the others started to leave her alone, and we put her back in the yard.

That was handy, because we suddenly had a new resident for the Honeydome: a half-grown chick we named Nugget, because it had been found (implausibly) in a McDonalds parking lot. The family that found the chick had taken her to their vet's office, where one of our cooks, there with her cat, heard the story and asked us to please adopt the little thing. It was too good a story to resist, so Nugget joined the flock, settling down in the Honeydome. Eventually the chickens would accept her (we sure hoped it was a her), and we would integrate them.

All was now calm on the chicken front, but our bees having a bumpy ride. Betty and Veronica—the names we had given the hives—had been attacked by ants right after they arrived. Scrub jays ate the bees in midair. Then varroa mites, horrible ticklike parasites that suck bees' blood and spread disease, invaded the hives. We did everything we could to help, throwing rocks at the jays, setting out ant bait, putting the hive legs in water to deter the ants, and dusting the bees with powdered sugar (which makes the mites lose their grip and fall off, and prompts the bees to clean themselves, knocking off more mites). We doused the hives with Apiguard, a foul-smelling mite-fighting gel, taking the risk that it might make any honey-in-progress taste like Listerine. Although it didn't get rid of the mites, it put a nice dent in the population.

As we tried to protect our poor bees, we explored the hives, too, learning to spot the queens, with their elongated abdomens, and the big-eyed, square-bottomed drones, whose main purpose in life was to mate with a virgin queen. All the rest were worker bees, and they each progress through a series of jobs, which we started to recognize. Guard bees stood sentry at the edge of the landing board and on the tops of the frames. House bees stayed in the hive, taking care of the queen and feeding the larvae. Mortuary bees carried the bodies of their dead sisters out of the hive. Foragers brought back food—pollen and nectar—and as they landed, we could see bright balls of pollen packed into pouches on their fuzzy back legs. On hot days, the house bees would stand on the landing board (and inside, too) and fan with their tiny wings, ventilating the hive. It was hypnotic and comforting to watch this orderly, intelligent, collective universe go about its business. Kimberley and Margaret became so fascinated that they started stashing their beekeeping outfits next to their desks, so they could get to the bees faster.

❊

Ryan had put in drip irrigation in June, and the garden took off like something in a fairytale. The melon vines darted sideways, carpeting their beds. The pattypan squash plants sprouted leaves as big as baby elephant ears, with bright yellow flowers underneath and nubbins of baby squashes. One day in early July, Ryan dipped a hand under the potato bed and pulled out a marble-size 'Yukon Gold'; they were coming along nicely. The much-anticipated 'Trombetta di Albenga' zucchini twirled up their arched trellis. The corn was already past my knees. Everywhere, bees zipped and buzzed and buried their shiny golden bodies in the blossoms.

We were not having superb luck with our wheat and barley, however, which we'd planted back in the winter. Squirrels pillaged the wheat, and we worried the barley would be next. As insurance, Team Beer started up a batch of wheat beer using a kit, and the funky-malty smell of wort—the sweet liquid that would ferment into beer—hung in the kitchen as thick as fog. We poured it into the primary fermenter and slapped on an airlock to let carbon dioxide escape, and the yeast turned the wort into a bubbling mass that made the airlock dance for days.

Our chickens had been healthy and strong, popping out eggs like Pez dispensers. Then champion layer Ophelia developed a strange, puffy chest. It was a hard lump about the size of a tennis ball. Elizabeth did some quick research and figured out that Ophelia's crop—a little sac where a chicken's food sits and moistens before traveling down toward its two stomachs—was stuffed with some kind of indigestible mass. Impacted crop, it was called, and it was serious. A chicken could die from it.

We turned Ophelia upside down and massaged her. This was ineffective and stressful. Our next option: carefully slice her open with a sterilized X-acto knife and remove the mass (apparently many chicken owners do this successfully), or take her to the vet. Worried we would botch the backyard surgery, we went to the vet, who extracted a giant wad of soggy straw from Ophelia's chest. She had, it seemed, been munching on the flooring of the coop. Before she returned, we removed every scrap of straw from the coop, and replaced the straw with largish hunks of pine bark. No chicken could possibly eat those.

❊

It was August, and our first feast was now just a few weeks away. We did not have honey yet, but we had plenty of

First beekeeping lesson   'Honey Select' corn   Our summer feast

eggs, good olive oil, and our first beer (from the kit; we'd save our homegrown grain for round two). We had not yet bottled the Chardonnay, but we could pour some of it into bottles just for the occasion. (The Syrah wouldn't be ready for at least another six months.) Our own crops were finally ripe enough for us to see how they worked in the recipes we'd developed. It was the moment we cooks had been waiting for.

We brought in armloads of vegetables, so fresh they still seemed to be growing. The ears of corn were plump and firm, with tassels as fragrant as grass, and not sticky and brown the way they often are at the store and even the farmers' market. When we sliced kernels off the ears, sweet, milky juices ran down the knife—they hadn't had time to thicken into starch. The cucumbers, picked small, were crisp and mild, without a hint of bitterness. We had grown edamame (soybeans) to see how they would do, and the pods were unexpectedly fat and fuzzy, with creamy beans inside. The sun-warmed tomatoes tasted like candy. Everything we had planned for the menu would work just fine.

Days before the dinner, we got our final ingredient. Margaret and Kimberley rushed into the kitchen with four dripping frames of golden honey laid out on sheet pans. With pastry scrapers, we cut the combs from the frames, sending thick, shiny, voluptuous rivers of honey streaming into the bowls beneath. Margaret said she wanted to lick her fingers and sing like Pooh Bear. Kimberley was so happy she was practically quivering. I couldn't stop eating the honeycomb: It was soft and supple, and gushed honey with every chew.

❋

On a hot late-summer evening, we set our table in the garden, a few feet from the plants that we had so carefully tended. We started with smoky, skillet-roasted edamame—just soybeans and salt—and cucumber cups with deviled-egg centers, courtesy of the flock. Our wheat beer had nice fizz and flavor. The Chardonnay was tart, clean, and incredibly refreshing, like biting into a cold green apple.

Next came corn soup, cold and smooth, each bowl sprinkled with crunchy diced trombetta zucchini, spicy chopped poblanos, and crumbled oregano cheese, with a zucchini blossom laid on top. For the main course, we ate golden wedges of potato cake; pattypan squashes, each cupping a baked egg; and our tomato salad, with homemade chive cheese and the most labor-intensive vinaigrette we had ever made, even though it was just salt, olive oil, red-wine vinegar, and a drop or two of honey. We finished with sorbets made from nothing but melons and honey, and little glasses of warm peppermint-lemongrass "tea."

It had taken us a year and a half to make this dinner. And in only a year and a half, we had learned to make wine, beer, cheese, olive oil, salt, and vinegar; grown thirty different herbs, fruits, and vegetables; successfully raised chickens and bees; and come to count on one another in ways we had not before. We would never again take any of these foods for granted. And we were all hungry for more. Fall lay ahead; we could live a whole new menu.

THE SUMMER GARDEN

Juicy tomatoes and supersweet corn are warm-season edibles, meaning they need warm soil and air temperatures to grow steadily and produce crops. We grew these, and other heat lovers for our summertime feast, in a spot that gets full sun for at least six hours per day. The edamames and squashes are really easy to grow from seed. Other crops, including tomatoes, are easier and bear more plentifully if grown from nursery transplants.

Potatoes grown in "towers" made of reed screens (see page 35)

Barley 'Lacey'

This high-yield, low-protein, six-row malting-type barley was developed for the brewing industry. We planted it in a 5-by-10-foot bed, with high hopes for harvesting the 9 pounds of barley we needed for making beer. Unfortunately, squirrels found our patch and ripped up a bunch of plants—we think to use for building their nests. We ended up with just 2 pounds of barley!

BEST SITE Full sun and well-drained soil.
DAYS TO HARVEST 90 to 120 days from seed.
PLANTING AND CARE Plant in November or December in moist, not wet, soil. Sow seeds 1 to 2 inches deep and about 3 inches apart. Space rows 7 inches apart. Water regularly.
HOW TO HARVEST The following summer, when the stalks are thoroughly dry and golden brown, clip them off a couple of inches above the ground. For details about processing the barley, see the directions for making Belgian Abbey Ale (page 52).
SEED SOURCE Howe Seeds, www.howeseeds.com.

Basil 'Genovese'

We are constantly using the tender, spicy-sweet green leaves for flavoring tomato and Italian dishes. They make wonderful pesto and give a lift to salads. 'Genovese' is easy to grow from both seed and transplants and bees love it.

BEST SITE Full sun and well-drained soil enriched with compost.
DAYS TO HARVEST 88 days from seed. For the best harvest, allow the seedlings to at least double in size before picking any leaves, and then pick them sparingly, pinching tips to induce bushiness, until the plant fills out.
PLANTING AND CARE Sow seeds in batches every two weeks from midspring through early- to midsummer. Plant in rows 18 inches apart, placing seeds 2 to 3 inches apart in each row and 1/4 inch deep. Once seedlings sprout, thin to 12 inches apart. If starting from seedlings, plant 12 inches apart. Water as needed to keep soil evenly moist.
HOW TO HARVEST Pick leaves whenever you need them. To keep leaves coming, pinch off branch tips and flowers. To harvest lots of leaves for making pesto, cut plants back by half (they will regrow). Or, plant seedlings in succession every month and harvest the entire plant.
SEED SOURCE Stokes Seeds, www.stokeseeds.com.

Chile, Poblano

A staple in Mexican cooking, especially for chiles rellenos, these fleshy, broad-shouldered, mildly spicy peppers grow on multistemmed plants about 2 feet tall. Often called pasillas, especially in California, they are 3 to 6 inches long. Flowers appear 50 days after sowing seed, followed by fruits that ripen from dark green to red. When dried, poblanos are known as anchos and have a deep, fruity taste.

BEST SITE Full sun and well-drained soil amply amended with compost.
DAYS TO HARVEST 100 days from seed.
PLANTING AND CARE Plant nursery seedlings when soil is warm in spring, placing the plants 18 to 24 inches apart. In containers, one or two plants are plenty. To start from seed, sow seeds indoors 6 to 8 weeks before the last spring frost. Let the soil dry out between waterings, and cut back on water as the chiles mature to concentrate their flavor.
HOW TO HARVEST Poblanos are almost always harvested green; their flavor mellows as they ripen. Snip pods off with scissors or pruners.
SEED SOURCE Tomato Growers Supply Co., www.tomatogrowers.com.

Chile, Serrano

About as long as your index finger, serranos start out green, then turn red as they mature. Hotter than jalapeños, they are extremely versatile in the kitchen, where they are added to everything from guacamole to stews. Plant heights vary from 1 1/2 to 5 feet tall; each plant produces about 50 pods.

BEST SITE Same as for Chile, Poblano, above.
DAYS TO HARVEST 75 to 80 days from seed.
PLANTING AND CARE Same as for Chile, Poblano, above.
HOW TO HARVEST Harvest serranos in the green or red stage. They are usually harvested green, when their heat has a lively, almost citrusy zing, but they are just as good red, when their flavor turns warm and ripe.
SEED SOURCE Same as for Chile, Poblano, above.

Chive

Chives are related to onions and garlic. They grow in delicate-looking clusters of narrow, slender green leaves that are loaded with flavor—like a green onion, but more intense. In midspring, they produce round clusters of lilac-pink blossoms that look like puffballs. The flowers are edible and are pretty in green salads. *(continued)*

BEST SITE Full sun or partial shade and fairly rich, well-drained soil.

DAYS TO HARVEST Leaves can be harvested any time, once the plants begin to fill out.

PLANTING AND CARE Grow from seed in spring or from nursery plants. Sow seeds 1/8 to 1/4 inch deep and 8 to 12 inches apart. Space nursery plants 8 to 12 inches apart. Water regularly to keep soil evenly moist.

HOW TO HARVEST Chives will send up pickable leaves from early summer until first frost. If you start from seed, harvest lightly in the first year, snipping stems near the base from the outside of the clump. For a more concentrated flavor, cut flowers while still in bud.

SEED SOURCE Renee's Garden, www.reneesgarden.com.

Corn 'Honey Select'

Triple-sweet types like this one combine great corn flavor with especially sweet, tender kernels. 'Honey Select' hybrid sweet corn is so good you can even eat it uncooked, fresh off the stalk. If you are grilling, boiling, or steaming it, however, cook it for no more than a few minutes to preserve its juiciness and crunch.

BEST SITE Full sun and moist, deeply cultivated, well-drained soil. Fertilize and cultivate prior to planting.

DAYS TO HARVEST 80 days from seed.

PLANTING AND CARE Start in spring after soil has warmed in moist, not wet, soil. Plant in blocks of at least 16 plants, in 4 rows of 4 plants each, planting in batches every 2 weeks. Sow seeds 4 to 6 inches apart and 1 to 2 inches deep in rows 2 to 3 feet apart. Thin to 8 to 12 inches apart when seedlings are 6 inches tall. Water regularly and deeply.

HOW TO HARVEST When silks start to turn brown (about 3 weeks after they first appear), pull back the husk and try popping a kernel with your thumbnail. If the juice is milky, it's time to pick. (Clear juice means the corn isn't ripe yet; pasty means it's overripe.)

SEED SOURCES Ed Hume Seeds, www.humeseeds.com; Park Seed, www.parkseed.com.

Cucumber 'Diva'

A vining type that reaches 5 to 6 feet tall and 1 to 2 feet wide, 'Diva' is very productive. Its cukes are sweet and crunchy, with no hint of bitterness. They also have no spikes on the skin, common in other varieties, which makes harvesting them a pleasure. We tried to trellis the plants, but they still flopped over and required tying. In the end,

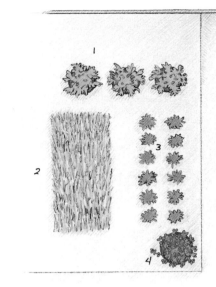

our best method was to plant them in hills or rows and let them ramble over the ground.

BEST SITE Full sun and moist, well-drained soil.

DAYS TO HARVEST 58 days from seed; 32 days from seedlings.

PLANTING AND CARE Sow seeds in spring after the last frost date, or start seeds indoors 4 weeks before the last frost date. Space rows 3 to 6 feet apart, then sow seeds 8 to 12 inches apart and 1 inch deep, in clusters of 2 or 3 seeds. When seedlings are a few inches tall, thin them to a single seedling per cluster. Alternatively, you can grow plants in hills; make soil mounds 4 to 6 feet apart, and sow seeds 1 inch deep in each hill, in clusters of 4 to 6 seeds. When seedlings are a few inches tall, thin them to 2 or 3 per hill. Water cukes regularly through the growing season, especially when the fruits begin to swell.

HOW TO HARVEST For cucumbers of supreme crunch and sweetness, harvest them while they are still young and no more than 6 to 8 inches long. To keep new cukes coming, harvest 3 to 4 times a week.

SEED SOURCE Park Seed, www.parkseed.com

Edamame 'Sayamusume'

Soybeans are nutty, buttery, and high in protein, and we grew them to add substance to our summer table. We chose 'Sayamusume' for its plump beans; its sturdy, well-filled pods; and its high yield. Despite its productivity, we didn't grow nearly enough to satisfy our appetite. We would have welcomed double or even triple the harvest we got from

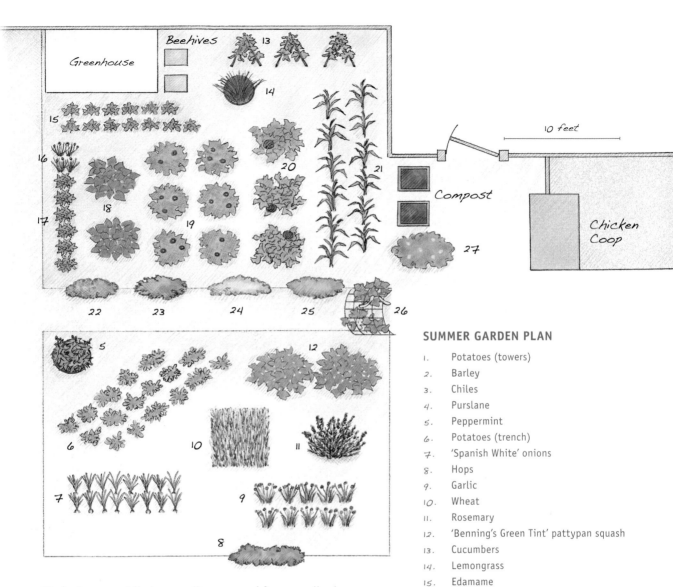

SUMMER GARDEN PLAN

1. Potatoes (towers)
2. Barley
3. Chiles
4. Purslane
5. Peppermint
6. Potatoes (trench)
7. 'Spanish White' onions
8. Hops
9. Garlic
10. Wheat
11. Rosemary
12. 'Benning's Green Tint' pattypan squash
13. Cucumbers
14. Lemongrass
15. Edamame
16. Chives
17. Basil
18. 'Sunburst' pattypan squash
19. Tomatoes
20. Melons
21. Corn
22. Parsley
23. Thyme
24. Oregano
25. Marjoram
26. 'Trombetta di Albenga' zucchini
27. Lemon tree

10 plants—especially because 'Sayamusume' freezes well (we defrosted some in winter, and they were delicious).

BEST SITE Full sun and well-drained soil.

DAYS TO HARVEST 85 days from seed.

PLANTING AND CARE Plant in spring after weather warms and night temperatures are consistently above 50°F. Moisten the soil thoroughly before planting. Sow seeds 1 inch deep and 3 inches apart in rows 2 feet apart, and do not water again until seedlings have emerged; once growth starts, keep soil moist. Soybeans ripen all at once, so sow them in batches every few weeks for a continuous crop. When seedlings are several inches tall, thin to final spacing of 6 inches apart.

'Sayamusume' Edamame   'Nugget' hops

HOW TO HARVEST Pluck off pods when they are nice and swollen (that means the beans have reached full size) but are still green.

SEED SOURCE Renee's Garden, www.reneesgarden.com.

Garlic 'Spanish Roja'

This heirloom "hard-necked" variety (meaning it develops large outside cloves and no inner cloves) is a Rocambole type known for its purple-blushed skin. The large, crisp, juicy cloves peel easily. Their flavor is pungent, though not bitingly so, and they turn buttery soft when cooked.

BEST SITE Full sun and rich, well-drained soil (where soils are poor, grow it in raised beds).

DAYS TO HARVEST Set out cloves in fall for an early-summer harvest.

PLANTING AND CARE Plant cloves with pointed tops up, placing them 1 inch deep, 4 to 8 inches apart, in rows 16 to 18 inches apart. In cold-winter climates, mulch heavily at the onset of winter to help prevent soil heaving, which can force the cloves out of the ground. Irrigate evenly and weed regularly or mulch. Rake back mulch in spring and pinch off any blossoms that develop. Once the leaf tips start to turn yellowish brown, stop watering.

HOW TO HARVEST When green leaves begin to turn yellow around July, stop irrigating for about 2 weeks, then carefully lift the bulbs out of the ground with a garden fork. Pulling by hand may crack the bulbs and decrease shelf life. Hang the bulbs in bundles to dry in a dry, well-ventilated area until skins are papery, about 3 weeks. Brush off the dirt, cut off most of the roots, and clip off the tops to 1 inch (unless you want to braid them). Store bulbs in mesh bags or paper bags in a cool (around 50°F), airy place out of direct sunlight for 4 to 6 months.

CLOVE SOURCES Irish Eyes Garden Seeds, www.gardencityseeds.net; and Peaceful Valley Farm & Garden Supply, www.groworganic.com.

Hops

The pretty little cone-shaped flowers grow on a mammoth climbing vine 12 to 18 feet tall, often much taller. They provide a key flavoring ingredient in beer, which is why we grew them. We chose 'Centennial' for its slightly bitter edge and 'Nugget' for its spicy and herbal notes. We lost most of the 'Centennial' to some sort of dieback. But 'Nugget' thrived, and donated the hops for making our beer. Our total bounty, from the single 'Nugget' rhizome we planted, was about 1 pound, and when you consider that you need only 2 to 3 ounces of hops to brew a 5-gallon batch of beer, that's a lot—more than enough for a party!

BEST SITE Full sun and light, well-drained soil. You must have a strong trellis for the vine to climb (for details on our trellis, see the directions on page 53). Plant your hops at the base—and the vines will race right up and attach themselves.

DAYS TO HARVEST 150 days from rhizome.

PLANTING AND CARE Plant in spring once the last frost date has passed. Hops of the same variety can be planted 3 feet apart; space different kinds at least

5 feet apart to keep them from becoming entangled. Plant the rhizomes vertically, about 2 inches deep, with the bud pointing up. Mulch the soil and keep it moist. Hops need watering three times per week to almost daily when weather is hot, windy, and dry.

HOW TO HARVEST Flowers will be ready to harvest between July and September, though your first year's yield will probably be tiny. Harvest the flower cones when they turn pale green and the yellow lupulin glands are visible underneath the bracts. When squeezed, the cones should feel slightly papery and have a pronounced odor: 'Nugget' is woodsy, and 'Centennial' has a citrusy, floral smell.

RHIZOME SOURCES Freshops, www.freshops.com; Nichols Garden Nursery, www.nicholsgardennursery.com.

Lemon 'Eureka'

A good all-around lemon tree, 'Eureka' yields fruits that are large, tart, juicy, and versatile. The tree is aptly named: It bears fruit year-round in mild climates.

BEST SITE Full sun and rich, fast-draining soil. Before planting, dig in a 4- to-6-inch layer of compost to a depth of 1 foot.

DAYS TO HARVEST Depends on the age of the plant you buy. Fruit production generally begins when a tree is 3 or 4 years old. Ours was 5 years old when we started the project.

PLANTING AND CARE Plant in spring after all danger of frost is past. Remove any fruit from the tree before planting from a nursery container. Add a 2-inch layer of mulch to help keep moisture in the soil and to prevent weeds. If your area is hot, wrap trunks of the newly planted trees with paper bands (available from nurseries) to prevent sunburn. Water consistently (twice a week in normal summer weather), and apply citrus fertilizer several times during the March to October growing season.

HOW TO HARVEST When fruit feels heavy in your hand, looks fully formed, and is yellow (not green), pick it and try it. Citrus won't ripen off the tree, so you need to sample to know when to pick. Ripe lemons can hang on the tree for months and be fine, but if they get puffy, they are too old.

PLANT SOURCES Sold as grafted plants in 2- to 15-gallon cans in almost every nursery; Four Winds Growers, www.fourwindsgrowers.com.

Lemongrass

Intensely aromatic and citrusy, this grasslike plant is a key ingredient in many Southeast Asian cuisines. We used it to make a wonderful end-of-dinner drink (page 80) and a hauntingly delicious dessert custard (page 79).

BEST SITE Full sun and rich, well-drained soil.

DAYS TO HARVEST The flavor is best when the bulbous leaf base swells to about $1/2$ inch in diameter. Plants grow fastest in tropical weather, so our stalks had relatively slender bases. It took 4 months for ours to produce harvestable stems.

PLANTING AND CARE Buy a potted plant and repot in a larger pot or in the ground in spring once all danger of frost is past. Eventually it will grow into a multi-stem clump 3 to 4 feet tall and equally wide. During the growing season, water well and feed monthly with half-strength fish emulsion. Lemongrass is sensitive to frost, so in winter, move potted plants to a bright spot indoors or cover in freezing weather.

HOW TO HARVEST Push an outside stem to the side, then twist and pull it off. Cut off and discard the leaves (or twist into knots and steep in boiling water for tea).

SEEDLING SOURCE Nichols Garden Nursery, www.nicholsgardennursery.com.

Marjoram, Sweet

Sweet marjoram (known just as "marjoram" in the culinary world) bears a strong resemblance to its kin, oregano. But its little leaves are softer and finer textured than those of oregano, and the plant has a tingly, spicy flavor, like a blend of mint, cloves, and cinnamon. We grow it along gravel paths and as a pretty edging for our vegetable beds.

BEST SITE Full sun and soil that drains especially well, or in a container indoors on a sunny windowsill.

DAYS TO HARVEST About 70 days (leaves can be picked any time once plants are established and growing).

PLANTING AND CARE Buy nursery plants in spring and plant them 9 inches apart. Keep the soil moist, not soggy, until the plants are established, then water less. Mature plants thrive on little water. Or, to plant from seed, sow in spring after the soil has warmed. Till the soil well, rake it smooth, then sow the seeds thinly and cover them lightly. Keep the seedbed moist and well weeded while seedlings are young.

HOW TO HARVEST Pinch off leaves. For a stronger flavor, cut stems when they are in bud (the blossoms are edible, too).

SEED SOURCE Renee's Garden, www.reneesgarden.com.

'Eureka' lemon   'Gigante Italian' parsley   'Sunburst' pattypan squash

Melons

We grew luscious, fragrant, cream-colored 'Sharlyn' melon, which tastes like a cross between a honeydew and a cantaloupe; seedless 'Sugar Baby' watermelon, a small, crisp, juicy melon that won't take up an entire shelf in the fridge; and deep orange, meltingly soft 'Ambrosia' cantaloupe (cantaloupes are also known as muskmelons). All these melons need plenty of heat in order to sweeten.

BEST SITE Full sun and rich, well-drained soil.

DAYS TO HARVEST 85 days from seed.

PLANTING AND CARE Plant outdoors in spring after the soil has warmed to at least 60°F (raised beds warm up faster than flat ground). Mix a 2- to 3-inch layer of compost into the soil. Plant seeds 1 inch deep and 4 inches apart, in rows 4 to 6 feet apart. As seedlings grow, thin them to 10 inches apart. Use drip irrigation or a soaker hose to avoid wetting the foliage, and water often. When the melons reach full size but are not yet ripe, cut back on watering to keep the fruits from splitting and to concentrate their flavors.

HOW TO HARVEST When fully ripe, cantaloupes slip off the vine easily. 'Sharlyn', a honeydew cross, is ready when the fruit has a strong, fruity fragrance and there's an orange tone to the skin beneath the tan-colored netting. For watermelons, wait for the tendril next to the stem to wither and the "resting spot" on the underside of the melon to turn creamy yellow. Avoid twisting the melons as you check them. It can damage the stem and thus their nutrient supply.

SEED SOURCE Seeds of Change, www.seedsofchange.com.

Onion 'Spanish White'

Large and evenly spherical, with good steady onion flavor, 'Spanish White' won't turn sweet when cooked. We planted in fall with high hopes for a good crop. But by the following April, our plants weren't looking so good. The bulbs didn't swell; many just produced flowers. We wondered whether temperatures or erratic watering was the cause. By summer, half our plants had not produced bulbs. Luckily, the rest of them finally matured.

BEST SITE Full sun (or light shade) and fine-textured (well-raked), loose, rich, well-drained soil.

DAYS TO HARVEST 150 says from seed; 100 days from sets.

PLANTING AND CARE Plant from seeds or sets (miniature, dormant onions). Sow seeds when the soil has warmed to at least 35°F and preferably 50°F, setting them about 1/4 inches deep in the soil, in rows 15 to 18 inches apart. Thin seedlings to 4 or 5 inches apart. Put out sets in spring, 4 to 6 weeks before the last frost date. Sets are easiest and produce quick results, but they may bolt into flowers, rendering the onion inedible. Select the smallest sets available, because they are less likely to bolt than large ones. To plant, push the sets under the soil, aligning their pointed ends with the soil level; space 4 to 5 inches apart. Water plants—whether from sets or seeds—regularly when green tops are growing. Weed regularly but carefully, because bulbs are easily damaged.

HOW TO HARVEST Water less frequently toward the end of the growing cycle. When 25 to 50 percent of the foliage in your onion patch has fallen over, the onions are nearly ready. Stop watering, bend the rest of the green tops to the ground, and let the bulbs harden and cure in the soil for 3 weeks before you pull them. Store the bulbs in a cool, dry spot.

SEED/SETS SOURCE Gurney's Seed & Nursery, www.gurneys.com.

Oregano, Italian

A familiar seasoning for bean dishes, pastas, and vegetables, Italian oregano (*Origanum* x *majoricum*) grows about 30 inches tall, producing tiny, pointy green leaves with an intense, spicy flavor. It is used in Mexican recipes, too, which means we relied on it a lot in our one-block cooking.

BEST SITE Full sun and soil that drains especially well, or in a container indoors on a sunny windowsill.

DAYS TO HARVEST Leaves can be picked any time once plants start to fill out.

PLANTING AND CARE Buy nursery plants in spring and plant them 18 inches apart. Keep the soil moist, not soggy, until the plants are established, then water less. Mature plants thrive on little water.

HOW TO HARVEST Pinch off leaves any time; for a stronger flavor, cut stems when they are in bud (the flowers are edible).

SEEDLING SOURCE Mountain Valley Growers, www.mountainvalleygrowers.com.

Parsley 'Gigante Italian'

Most chefs prefer to cook with Italian flat-leafed parsley (*Petroselenium crispum neapolitanum*), which has a more robust flavor than the curly-leafed types once commonly used as garnishes. Flat-leafed parsley is also very easy to grow in a pot or in the ground. We grew 'Gigante Italian', which has large, crisp, mellow-tasting leaves that we used all kinds of ways, including whole in salads.

BEST SITE Full sun or part shade (afternoon shade in the hottest climates) and rich, well-drained soil that's been well amended with compost.

DAYS TO HARVEST 80 days from seed, or, from seedlings, any time after plants have filled out.

PLANTING AND CARE Start seeds in the spring when the weather is settled but still cool (or in fall in hottest desert climates). Scatter seeds thinly over the soil, then cover them with 1/4 inch of soil. Parsley tends to germinate unevenly over several weeks, but don't be discouraged! Just keep the soil evenly moist. When the seedlings have a few fully formed leaves, thin them to 18 to 24 inches apart. Water regularly through the growing season and feed plants occasionally with liquid fish emulsion. If you would rather take the easy route, plant seedlings in containers (at least 12 inches wide and 10 inches deep) or in the ground.

HOW TO HARVEST Start picking leaves when the plants are 8 to 10 inches tall and relatively full. Harvest entire stems from the base to encourage growth.

SEED/SEEDLING SOURCE Renee's Garden, www.reneesgarden.com.

Pattypan Squash

We grew disk-shaped, scalloped-edged 'Benning's Green Tint' (lime green) and 'Sunburst' (brilliant yellow) for their tender skins, delicate flavor, and few seeds. Plus, they are small and perfect for stuffing.

BEST SITE Full sun and rich, well-drained soil.

DAYS TO HARVEST 50 days from seed.

PLANTING AND CARE Sow seeds indoors in a warm place in spring 1 week or so before the last frost date, or wait until the soil has warmed (at least 2 weeks after the last frost date) and sow seeds outdoors. To sow outdoors, plant seeds 12 inches apart and 2 to 3 inches deep in rows 3 to 5 feet apart. Once seedlings have several sets of leaves, thin them to 2 to 4 feet apart. Water regularly and deeply. Avoid splashing water on leaves, stems, and flowers.

HOW TO HARVEST Cut stems close to the fruits with a sharp knife (wear gloves; those stems are prickly). Unless you need larger squashes for stuffing, harvest them when they are 2 to 3 inches across—they taste best as tender "babies." Regular harvesting keeps the plants producing through September.

SEED SOURCES For 'Benning's Green Tint', Baker Creek Heirloom Seeds, www.rareseeds.com, and Southern Exposure Seed Exchange, www.southernexposure.com; for 'Sunburst', Park Seed, www.parkseed.com.

Peppermint

Peppermint has dark, slender, smooth-edged leaves and purplish stems. We love it for its almost shocking mintiness—it makes the best cup of mint tea ever. Like all mints, it spreads rapidly by underground stems and can be invasive in a kitchen plot. To keep it in bounds, we always grow it in a pot and set the pot atop paving (it can even root through the drainhole!). *(continued)*

BEST SITE A large container filled with potting soil, in a sunny or partially shaded location—mint is not fussy.

DAYS TO HARVEST Leaves can be picked any time.

PLANTING AND CARE Set out young nursery plants in spring, spaced at least 6 inches apart, in containers. For best growth, keep the soil moist. After 3 years, plants become bare in the center, so you need either to replace them or to dig them up, divide each plant, and replant a few of the pieces with roots.

HOW TO HARVEST Snip sprigs of new growth.

SEEDLING SOURCE Mountain Valley Growers, www.mountainvalleygrowers.com.

Potato 'Yukon Gold'

The best all-purpose potato, this spud has buttery, sweet flesh that is equally suited to boiling and baking. We hung onto our harvest for as long as we could, using it into the winter. A pretty plant with lightly fragrant flowers, the potato is a cinch to grow. But knowing when the spuds are ripe for digging is another matter. Our best advice: Watch for foliage to die back, then pull one up.

BEST SITE Full sun and fertile, fast-draining soil high in organic matter and with a pH on the acid side (below 5.5).

DAYS TO HARVEST 90 to 120 days after planting for fully mature potatoes. You can dig potatoes when they are small and tender (when plants begin to bloom), or when fully mature (when plants die down). For long-term storage, dig only mature potatoes. To store potatoes, see Our Makeshift Root Cellar, page 82.

PLANTING AND CARE Plant seed potatoes in spring 4 to 6 weeks before the last frost date, around mid-March in our area. Two days before planting, cut them into chunks about $1^{1}/_{2}$ inches square, each with two "eyes" from which sprouts will emerge, and leave them to dry (callus) in a dry area, either inside or outside, to help prevent rotting.

How to plant in furrows Dig furrows 6 to 8 inches wide and 4 inches deep, spacing them $2^{1}/_{2}$ to 3 feet apart. (Closer spacing will result in higher yields of smaller potatoes.) Then set the chunks 12 to 18 inches apart in the furrows and cover with 2 inches of soil. After sprouts emerge, add another 2 inches of soil, leaving the foliage tips exposed. As the vines grow, continue adding soil, mounding until you have ridges 4 inches high and 18 inches wide. The soil cover keeps the tubers at the right temperature, with the right amount of moisture. It also protects them from the sun, which can raise levels of solanine, a toxic compound. (The sun also turns potato skins green, which is usually a good indicator of toxin development.)

Keep soil uniformly moist during the growing season. Weed and watch for pests.

When most of the foliage has turned yellowish brown, water the plants for the last time, wait for 14 days, and then cut away the vines. This "sets," or hardens, potato skins so they won't peel or bruise easily. If you dig them up without hardening them, the skins will be as fragile as tissue paper and the potatoes will be moist, sweet, and highly perishable.

'Yukon Gold' potatoes   Purslane   'Tuscan Blue' rosemary

Harvest these "fresh" potatoes carefully and cook them the same day or the next.

How to plant in towers (See photo, page 26.) To save space and make potatoes a snap to harvest, plant them in towers made of wire and reed screening (find materials in a hardware or home supply store). Loosen the soil with a spading fork, then rake it smooth. Using a trowel, trace a circle about 3 feet in diameter in the prepared soil, then place seed potato pieces (see Planting and Care, opposite) about 5 inches apart within the circle. Bend a piece of welded wire into a cylinder 3 feet in diameter and 3 to 4 feet tall; secure the cut ends together with wire. Put the "cage" on top of the soil circle around your newly planted potato sets. Wrap a piece of reed screening (we bought a 12-foot privacy screen and cut it to fit) around the wire cage, then tie its ends together with twine. Pour a 3-inch layer of compost and another 3 inches of straw into the cylinder. Hand-water the potato sets every other day or so.

Once foliage appears (be patient; ours didn't show up for several weeks), continue adding compost and straw, leaving about 6 inches of green stem and leaves on top exposed to sunlight. Nearing the tower's top, just add straw.

HOW TO HARVEST

How to harvest furrows Within 5 to 7 days of cutting away the vines, preferably when the weather is cool and overcast, dig up the plants carefully with a spading fork, keeping it 10 inches away from the plants to avoid injuring the potatoes. Lift each plant gently, shake off the loose soil, and pull the potatoes from the vines. Gather them in burlap bags or baskets and keep out of strong sunlight.

If you are planning to store the potatoes long-term, it is vital that the air temperature be cool when you harvest, so do it early in the morning (see Our Makeshift Root Cellar, page 82).

How to harvest new potatoes in towers After the plants flower, open and remove the reed screening, then poke your hand through the welded wire and feel around for potatoes. Pick some small, tender, thin-skinned "new" potatoes. Replace the screening.

How to harvest mature potatoes in towers After the plants flower, withhold water for 2 to 3 weeks, or until the entire plant dies back. Then pull up the towers. All the potatoes will spill out in a perfect cascade—no digging required, and no spade damage to the potatoes.

SEED POTATO SOURCES The Cook's Garden, www.cooksgarden.com; Gurney's Seed & Nursery, www.gurneys.com; Henry Fields Seed & Nursery, www.henryfields.com; Irish Eyes Garden Seeds, www.irisheyesgardenseeds.com; Wood Prairie Farm, www.woodprairie.com.

Purslane

Okay, we know what you're thinking: Why would anyone in their right mind want to plant a weed in their summer garden—especially when it seems to pop out of the soil all by itself? Here's why: Purslane's rounded, succulent leaves add a citrusy zip and juicy texture to salads and stir-fries, and they're high in vitamin C. The little yellow-flowered green plant (*Portulaca oleracea*) is eaten with relish in many countries, including France (where it's called *pourpier*), Mexico (*verdolaga*), Holland (*postelein*), and Turkey (*semizotu*). We used it in a delectable Turkish-style salad with garlic, chiles, and mint (page 70).

BEST SITE Full sun and loose soil that's been enriched with compost.

DAYS TO HARVEST 60 to 70 days from seed.

PLANTING AND CARE Sow seeds after last frost date (in our area, April, when weather warms up to 68°F or more, is a good time). Sow the seeds $1/4$ inch deep in warm soil and rake the seeds in lightly. Keep the bed well watered. Seeds germinate quickly (7 to 10 days).

HOW TO HARVEST Once plants are growing well (June to October), pick tender tips and shoots as you need them. To preserve juiciness, harvest in early morning when temperatures are cool.

SEED SOURCE Seeds of Change, www.seedsofchange.com.

Rosemary 'Tuscan Blue'

We like this plant, sometimes sold under the name 'Blue Spires', for its sturdy good looks—it's an upright variety with broad leaves and dark blue flowers; its piney, intense, uplifting fragrance when you rub it between your fingers; and its versatility in the kitchen. Plus, the plant is tough, standing up to wind, salt spray, heat, and poor soil.

BEST SITE Full sun and soil that drains especially well, though it will tolerate poor, dry soil.

DAYS TO HARVEST Leaves can be picked any time.

PLANTING AND CARE Set out small nursery plants in early spring (the typical kitchen garden will need only a few of these vigorous plants), spacing them at least 24 inches apart. Water the plants regularly until they are established, then only enough to keep them from drying out. Rosemary often fails in soggy soil.

HOW TO HARVEST Snip branch tips with scissors or pruners.

SOURCES Plants are widely sold at nurseries.

Thyme, French

Like rosemary and oregano, thyme grows well in our Mediterranean climate, and we constantly make use of its tiny, aromatic leaves in our cooking. Plus, it looks gorgeous in the garden, clustered at the end of a row and nearly always shooting up at least a few pretty little blossoms. Our bees like it, too.

BEST SITE Full sun and light, well-drained soil, though it will tolerate poor, dry soil.

DAYS TO HARVEST Seedlings appear 14 to 21 days after sowing, and need at least a month to fill out before you start picking. Once mature, leaves can be picked any time.

PLANTING AND CARE Set out small nursery plants in early spring, 8 to 12 inches apart. Water regularly until the plants are established, then only to keep the plants from drying out completely. Or, to plant from seed, wait until the soil has warmed, then sow thinly 1/2 inch deep in a fine-textured (well-raked) bed and cover the seed lightly. Keep the seedbed moist and well weeded while seedlings are young.

HOW TO HARVEST Snip branch tips (the flowers are edible, too).

SEED/SEEDLING SOURCES Seedlings are sold in almost every nursery, or order seeds from Renee's Garden, www.reneesgarden.com.

Tomatoes

We grew five different tomatoes: deep yellow 'Sungold' cherry tomatoes, for their fabulous flavor and juiciness; prolific 'Sweet Million' red cherry tomatoes; dependable red 'Early Girl'; citrusy, tart 'Green Zebra'; tender, yellow-and-red-streaked 'Marvel Stripe'; and succulent, magenta-purple 'Brandywine'. We loved them all. But we grazed most often on 'Sungold', popping the juicy, sun-warmed fruits into our mouths like candy, right off the vine.

BEST SITE Full sun (at least 8 hours a day) and fertile, well-drained soil rich in organic matter.

DAYS TO HARVEST 50 to 90 days after setting out plants.

PLANTING AND CARE Plant seedlings as soon as the danger of frost has passed. Remove the lowest leaves, then plant them deeply, burying at least half of the stem to encourage vigorous root growth. Space the seedlings widely, at least 24 inches apart, and support them with sturdy stakes or wire cages to help prevent rot. If starting from seed, sow indoors in a warm place 5 to 7 weeks before setting them out (at least 10 days after the last frost). Water often enough to keep soil damp but not soggy, and keep water off the leaves. Tomatoes need lots of fertilizer. In rich soils that have been well amended with compost, they don't need anything. But if you have unamended soil, dig a single application of controlled-release fertilizer into the soil at planting time. Or feed plants lightly with a dilute liquid fish emulsion every two weeks from blossom set until harvest.

HOW TO HARVEST Snip fruit from the stem with scissors or pruners or gently pull by hand. Tomatoes ripen best on the vine. If your plants still have green tomatoes hanging on them after the weather starts turning cold, pick them from the vine and bring them indoors to ripen.

SEED/SEEDLING SOURCES For seeds, Seeds of Change, www.seedsofchange.com, or Renee's Garden, www.reneesgarden.com; for seedlings, Laurel's Heirloom Tomato Plants, www.heirloomtomatoplants.com.

Wheat

Initially, we grew wheat for brewing our beer: The carbohydrates in wheat convert to sugars when the grain is malted (sprouted), then, during fermentation, the sugars convert to alcohol. Once our one-block project progressed, we realized we could not have a year's worth of menus without a loaf of bread, crackers, or a crust of any kind. So, we chose a soft white wheat, which produces golden "berries" with a nutty, sweetish flavor.

BEST SITE Full sun and well-tilled, good-draining soil with plenty of compost mixed in. Till in blood meal and bonemeal (about 1 pound each per 100 square feet) along with the compost.

DAYS TO HARVEST 130 to 150 days from seed.

PLANTING AND CARE In January, scatter seeds over prepared soil (about 6 handfuls, or 1/4 pound, per 100 square feet), then rake seeds in so they are buried to a depth about three times their diameter. After planting, soak soil thoroughly, then water as needed to keep moist (every week in dry weather; we tend to get lots of rain in January, so we didn't need to water at all). Weed regularly. When the wheat starts turn-

'Early Girl' tomatoes

'Trombetta di Albenga' zucchini

ing brown, stop watering; when your tooth can no
longer dent the berries, the crop is ready to harvest.

HOW TO HARVEST Snip the seedheads from the stalks
with scissors or pruners. For details about processing
the wheat, see How to Make Beer (page 54).

SEED SOURCES Homegrown Harvest, www.homegrown
harvest.com; for 'Sonora' soft white wheat, contact
Pie Ranch, www.pieranch.org; Full Belly Farm,
www.fullbellyfarm.com; EatWell Farm, www
.eatwell.com); or Whole Grain Connection, www
.sustainablegrains.org.

Zucchini 'Trombetta di Albenga'

Probably the most captivating plant of our summer menu,
'Trombetta di Albenga' is an extremely vigorous climbing
vine with big, fan-shaped leaves and huge, pale green zucchini that can curve like trombones. They taste sweet and
mild, stay crunchy even when cooked, and all the seeds are
concentrated in the bulbous end, so most of what you get
is seed free. We grew ours over an arbor (one plant on each
side), so we could look up at the pretty squashes as they
ripened and to give their voluptuous shapes room to dangle.

BEST SITE Full sun and rich soil amended with aged
manure or compost.

DAYS TO HARVEST 85 days from seed.

PLANTING AND CARE Sow seeds indoors in a warm
place in spring 1 week or so before the last frost date.
Or, wait until the soil has warmed, at least 2 weeks
after the last frost date, and sow seeds outdoors. Sow
3 or 4 seeds 1 to 2 inches deep about 4 inches from

a vertical support (you will want to save space by
growing this vigorous vine on a sturdy trellis, fence,
or stakes). Thin to the strongest seedling for each
stake or 12 to 24 inches apart. Water deeply.

HOW TO HARVEST The fruits are best when they are
10 to 12 inches long, though they are usually still
tender up to 30 inches. Use pruners to cut the
fruits—with a bit of stem attached—from the vine.
Pick flowers in the morning, snipping them off the
vine when they're cool and fresh and still open; eat
that day if possible and no later than the next. Keep
in the refrigerator in a plastic bag until ready to use.

SEED SOURCE Renee's Garden, www.reneesgarden.com.

—*Kathleen N. Brenzel*

THE "IMPORTS"

We went outside our garden for these local foods:
milk, whole and unhomogenized (for cream, and for
cheese; page 46); olives (for olive oil, page 130);
seawater (for salt, page 172); wine grapes (for wine,
page 105); brewing kit (as a backup for our beer crops,
page 49); mother of vinegar (for vinegar, page 113)

THE SUMMER PROJECTS

HOW TO RAISE
HONEYBEES
(AND MAKE HONEY)

We began our bee adventure in part because we needed honey to sweeten our summer feast. But we also did it for the love of bees.

You have probably heard the statistic: bees, traveling from plant to plant and pollinating as they go, are responsible for producing about one-third of our country's food supply. Unfortunately for them and for us, they have been dying in huge numbers over the past several years. No one has conclusively figured out what causes colony collapse disorder, as it has been termed.

We figured that by raising bees, we would contribute, in at least a small way, to the overall population of bees. We also thought it would be easy. Plus, we have plenty of plants for them to browse, and conditions that are relatively benign (good weather, lots of well-watered suburban gardens). Life should be great for bees at Sunset.

Now, having seen our bees battle ants, bluejays, wasps, buckeye poisoning (the pollen is toxic to bees), varroa mites, tracheal mites (probably), hive beetles, wax moths, and American foulbrood, we understand just what these hardworking little creatures are up against (for a running diary of our life with bees, see http://one blockdiet.sunset.com/team_bee). And it's deepened our appreciation for what marvelous, interesting creatures they are (see Amazing Bees, page 45).

The stings? Well, working in the hives is not the killer-bee kind of drama you might see in a late-night horror movie. Bees only sting in self-defense and when they are protecting the hive. If you have calm, docile bees, and move slowly as you work the hives, you can hold them in your bare hands. Even with care, of course, we have been stung a few times, and for the most part it was no big deal.

Raising bees has been and continues to be an incredible experience. We will never taste honey again without a sense of gratitude.

2 COLONIES OF HONEYBEES

Both of our hives are filled with European honeybees (*Apis mellifera ligustica*), known for their gentleness and productivity. We recommend asking your neighbors whether they'd be comfortable with hives next door (promise them honey!) before you actually go out and buy bees. Also, check with your city to see if local regulations allow you to keep bees.

WHAT TO USE

Unless otherwise noted, our beekeeping supplies came from Dadant & Sons (www.dadant.com or 217/847-3324). We also recommend Mann Lake Ltd. (www.mannlakeltd.com or 800/880-7694) for beekeeping equipment. Prices do not include shipping.

2 MASTER POLLINATOR KITS

Each kit ($310 each) includes:

1 telescoping outer cover with galvanized metal top and an inner cover The inner cover helps insulate the box. The outer cover provides weather protection. Used together, they prevent the bees from gluing the hive shut with propolis (a sticky substance they collect from plants to bond parts of the hive) and wax.

2 hive bodies These are the "brood" boxes, deep boxes that the bees fill with brood (bee larvae), honey, and pollen. Each box has 10 frames loaded with Plasticell foundation (a thin sheet of plastic molded into hexagonal cells and coated with beeswax to make it easier for the bees to build the honeycomb).

1 bottom board We did not use this, preferring the "Country Rubes" bottom board (page 40), which helps you screen for mites.

1 metal hive tool This 10-inch-long tool is used to pry apart frames and to scrape off propolis and extra comb.

1 bee brush A gentle sweep with this brush removes bees from the surfaces of combs and frames.

1 smoker A small metal can with bellows that puff smoke when the fuel inside is lit. Smoke calms the bees, making working in the hive easier for the beekeeper.

Hives Veronica and Betty on a sunny day

Our caged queen, Califia (with packaged bees)

2 pounds smoker fuel We have had the best luck with KwikStart Smoker pellets (about $8 for 100) and cotton fuel (about $2) from Mann Lake Ltd. We have also used eucalyptus leaves, dead grass, pine needles—anything that will provide long-lasting, cool smoke.

1 entrance feeder Warned that these encourage robbing by intruder bees, we made our own feeders (see Other Equipment, opposite).

1 zipper veil suit We chose large, to fit the largest member of Team Bee, but it became hazardous to the smallest members of our team, because the loose pant legs allowed bees to crawl into the suit. We ultimately bought suits that fit Team Bee regulars.

1 plastic helmet and veil that zips to the suit A zipped-on veil keeps bees from sneaking under the helmet.

1 pair leather beekeeping gloves The gloves come in small, medium, large, and extra large. Most of the women on Team Bee found small to be the best size.

2 books These guides proved invaluable: *The Hive and the Honey Bee,* edited by Joe M. Graham (Dadant & Sons, 1992); and *First Lessons in Beekeeping,* by Keith S. Delaplane (Dadant & Sons, 2007).

A year's subscription to the American Bee Journal

1 medications brochure We found sound advice for dealing with bee diseases and problems in these pages.

NOT INCLUDED IN THE KIT

2 queen excluders, one for each hive An excluder is a screen with a mesh small enough to prevent the queen (larger than the rest of the bees) from crawling up into the "honey super" (a box designated for honey collection) and laying eggs there. About $11.50 each.

2 "Country Rubes" bottom boards, one for each hive A bottom board is a small box on which the hive rests. Designed to help manage varroa mites (see Pest Control, page 43), it has an open, screened bottom and a removable plastic board. $39 each from www.country rubes.com.

2 honey supers (unassembled), one for each hive A honey super is a box that is smaller than the brood box and is set on top of it. It is normally used with a queen excluder to get clean honey. Each measures $6\,5/8$ inches tall, with frames. $22.75 each.

20 Plasticell foundations Plastic sheets, $5\,1/2$ inches by $16\,3/4$ inches, used for filling the frames in the supers. About $0.75 each.

2 drone frames, one for each hive These are used to combat varroa mites (see Pest Control, page 43). $3 each.

3 vented helmets Much more comfortable than the plastic helmets from Dadant. A helmet paired with a round veil (see below)—plus a white, long-sleeved shirt, light-colored pants, and closed shoes—works fine as a basic beekeeping outfit, with gloves for heavy or prolonged work or for days when the bees are grumpy. About $14 each from Mann Lake Ltd.

3 round veils with string tie-ons These are not quite as secure as zip-on veils, but they are fine for working with gentle bees like ours, and you can put them on faster. About $12 each from Mann Lake Ltd.

BEES

You can get bees three ways:

Packaged bees and caged queen It takes time to build up the colony this way, but it's the least-expensive choice. You can usually order packaged bees through your local beekeepers' guild. Preorder as early as the fall and certainly no later than early spring, as bees are only available for a short time in spring. About $65.

Nuc (short for "nucleus") A nuc is a young hive, usually covering no more than 5 frames of comb, with a newly laying queen. Starting this way helps you get a jump on honey production. Buy from a reputable beekeeper to avoid getting diseased equipment or sick bees. We ordered two nucs from master beekeeper

Randy Oliver and drove to his location in Grass Valley, California, to pick them up. $90 for each nuc, queen included; www.scientificbeekeeping.com.

Well-established swarms or colonies Large colonies can be daunting if you've never kept bees before, and beginning beekeepers shouldn't try to capture a swarm. Leave that to a more experienced beekeeper (contact your local beekeepers' guild to find such a person), and perhaps he or she will help you start a hive with the captured swarm.

OTHER EQUIPMENT

2 hive stands, one for each hive The stands raise the hives off the ground. Made from scrap two-by-fours, each is 16^1/$_4$ inches wide, 20 inches long, and 1 foot tall and has an open top. We painted our stands with white latex paint.

8 sturdy square plastic food containers 32-ounce size. About $4 for 4 containers at a grocery store.

Terro ant bait About $7 for a package of 3 units at a nursery, garden center, or hardware store.

Apiguard For treating varroa mites. About $31 (enough for 10 individual treatments).

Formic acid Also for treating varroa mites. About $40 (enough for 10 treatments) from Mann Lake Ltd.

2 feeder tops, one for each hive These boards hold upended jars that dispense sugar syrup down into the hive to feed the bees.

To make a board, trim a thin piece of plywood to fit on top of the hive. Then cut a hole with a diameter slightly smaller than that of the feeder jar lid (see below). Put the board on top of the hive. Set a filled jar over the hole, lid down, so that it completely covers the opening.

2 (1-quart) glass jars and lids Punch several small holes in each lid with a nail to create feeder lids, fill the jars with sugar syrup, and then screw the lids on the jars. Any large clean glass jar will do.

10 cups (about 4^1/$_2$ pounds) granulated sugar You need this sugar to make the sugar syrup for the feeder jars. About $7.50 for a 5-pound bag at a grocery store.

Powdered sugar Used to control mites. You will need 1 cup per brood box per hive per week for as long as you are dusting for mites (see Pest Control, page 43). About $2 for 2 pounds at a grocery store.

Wooden spoons About $2 each at a cookware store.

Bench scraper Also known as a pastry scraper. From $8 online or at a cookware store.

Large glass bowl About $9 online or at a cookware store.

Preparing the smoker

Cheesecloth About $4.50 for 2 square yards at a hardware store or cookware store.

Large stainless-steel strainer About $25 for a good sturdy one (we like OXO brand) at a cookware store.

Honey jars and lids About $9 per 24-count box of 3-ounce hexagonal jars and about $6 per 12-count box of 6-ounce hexagonal jars from Mann Lake Ltd. (We used 5 boxes of the small jars and 2 boxes of the larger jars to bottle 31 pounds of honey.)

5-gallon food-grade plastic bucket with $1^1/_2$-inch honey gate Bubbles and foam rise to the surface and the pure honey settles to the bottom, where it can be drawn from the honey gate (a kind of faucet). About $19 from Mann Lake Ltd.

Comb from our top-bar hive

HOW TO DO IT

1. Choose the location Bees need four things. First, they need **sun**, or afternoon shade if your weather is hot. Second, they must have access to fresh **water** near the hive. We used a large plant saucer with stones in the center for the bees to land on and refreshed the water every day. A shallow bubble fountain would work well, too. Third, the hive must be **protected from wind**, which can blow rain (or snow) into the hive, making it harder for the bees to keep the hive warm. Finally, bees need **privacy**. Don't put the hives near high-traffic areas, play areas, swimming pools, or pet areas. Give each hive plenty of space—50 feet from high-traffic areas is ideal, but if space is limited, position the hive so the entrance is near a tall fence or hedge. This will force their flight path overhead to minimize contact with people and pets. And screening them from view will keep bees and people happy.

2. Prepare the location Hives should face south, if possible, and they need to be kept off the ground to protect them from dampness and critters. After clearing the brush and leveling the ground, we poured a cement pad to make care easier.

3. Install the bees Spring, when blooming flowers furnish a food supply, is the time to put your bees in their hives. Once you've chosen how to buy them, the best bet is to rely on your source for installation instructions.

Here is what happened when we picked up our bees from Randy Oliver at his property in Grass Valley: He gave us an introductory class in beekeeping, showing us how to use the hive tool and the smoker, handle bees, and check for eggs, brood (larvae), and queen—all vital signs of a colony's health. Randy loaded 5 frames of his gentle hybrid bees and a queen into each of our two brood boxes and sealed the openings by stuffing them with our beekeeping gloves. We used ratchet straps to secure the boxes in the back of our truck. When we got back to Sunset, we positioned the brood boxes in their designated locations and removed the gloves from the entrances. One hive we named Betty; the other, Veronica.

4. Feed the bees Young colonies have a lot of work to do—storing pollen and nectar, sealing all the cracks and seams in their new home, and taking care of the queen and new brood. To make their adjustment easier, we fed them a "nectar." Here is how to make it: Dissolve equal parts granulated sugar and water and use to fill the quart jars. Top with the feeder lids and invert the jars into the holes. The lids should not drip; they should be barely moist. The bees will drink what they need from the lids.

In the beginning, our nucs drank about three-fourths of a quart jar per day. Over the next 3 weeks or so, it tapered off to the point where we realized sugar water was no longer necessary. The bees were finding their nutrition in flowers. Plus, sugar water makes for insipid honey and should not be continued if it is not needed.

5. Inspect the hives inside and out Much of beekeeping is simple observation and response. If you are a novice beekeeper, inspect the hive about once a week for a couple of months so that you can learn. Once you feel comfortable, adjust your routine to every two weeks. Make sure the outside of the hive is clean and free of bee poop, the landing board is free of litter, and there are no ants on the hive. Open the hives and check frames for larvae and eggs (on warm days only). If the queen is healthy, you will see plenty of larvae in various stages of development.

If you don't see evidence of a healthy queen, consult an expert. Your local beekeeping guild is a good source.

Ultimately, the less often you inspect the hive, the better for its health. Opening the hives and thoroughly checking them requires smoking to keep the bees calm. This stresses the bees and it takes them about a day to recover. As you learn more, you will find you won't need to pull many frames to know what is going on inside. And you will figure out a lot simply by observing the bees as they come and go from the hive.

6. Check regularly for pests and diseases Varroa mites are the pest most typically found in hives. Left unchecked, they can cripple and eventually kill the hive (see Pest Control, below, for hints about checking for mites and mite control). Other pests you need to watch for include the small hive beetle and the wax moth. Diseases you need to be on the lookout for are American and European foulbrood. Early intervention can often mean the difference between a healthy hive and a dead hive.

7. Expand the hive when necessary Start with one deep hive body-brood box. When the bees have filled it with 7 or 8 frames of bees and brood, top it with a second brood box. Let the bees build up brood cells in the second

brood box, too. When the second brood box is well filled (7 or 8 frames of bees), top it with a queen excluder, if you choose to use one, and, finally, the honey super (the box from which you will collect most of your honey).

PEST CONTROL

Bees are like flying balls of delicate spun sugar filled with honey. Everything wants to eat them. Here are three of the worst pests we battled, and the tactics we used.

Ants Argentine ants can kill a hive by robbing honey and eating the brood. We couldn't spray to kill the ants, since that would also kill the bees. We tried Terro ant bait—little containers filled with boric acid mixed with a sweet substance ants like—with some success. In the end, we were most successful with a physical barrier. We placed each leg of the hive stands in plastic tubs filled with water that the ants could not cross.

Small hive beetles Hive beetle larvae will eat all parts of the hive, including the baby bees. We kill the beetles on site, and have been experimenting with traps like AJs Beetle Eater ($5.25) from Dadant.

Varroa mites The most damaging pests a beekeeper has to deal with are these mites, as they threaten the survival of a hive once they become established. They suck

Cutting the honeycomb off the foundation

Crushing the comb

the blood of adult bees and lay their eggs in brood cells, where their larvae feed off bee babies, infecting them with viruses and weakening and even killing them. To save their bees, beekeepers use a variety of methods:

1. Monitoring A 24-hour count of a natural mite fall will give you a good idea of a hive's infestation. Coat the bottom of your Country Rube board with petroleum jelly or cooking spray (to trap the mites), slide it into the lower part of the bottom board, wait for 24 hours, and then pull it out and count the mites. Anything more than 10 mites per brood box indicates you have a problem.

2. Sugar dusting The powdered sugar method lets you both count the mites and control them. Sift powdered sugar, 1 cup per brood box, over the tops of the frames and brush it into the hive. The powdered sugar makes the mites lose their grip on the bees and fall off; plus the bees groom the sugar off their bodies, dislodging more mites. Again, use the bottom board to capture the fallen mites. You should not see more than a few mites 10 minutes after dusting. If there are more, you have a problem.

3. Mite trapping Drone frames will also help trap varroa mites. These frames are designed to encourage bees to make drone comb cells, which are larger than worker comb cells. Since varroa mites prefer drone brood 10 to 1, the drone comb makes a great mite trap. Just before the drones hatch (24 days after the eggs were laid), destroy the drone comb (you can freeze it and return it to the hive, or simply cut it out), and replace the drone frame for the next cycle. (Since our queens have already mated and have a lifetime's supply of sperm inside of them, they do not need the drones in order to reproduce.)

Brushing powdered sugar into a hive

4. Apiguard A gel infused with thymol, made from the oils of thyme plants. It works well, but it makes the honey stored during the treatment taste like mouthwash.

5. Formic acid More toxic than thymol, formic acid kills the mites by gassing them. It makes the honey inedible for humans, so it is applied in the fall and winter, when the nectar flow is slow or stopped. You need to wear a respirator when applying it.

For more information on mite control, see the sources listed under Helpful Information, opposite.

HONEY COLLECTION

We were lucky to collect honey the first summer. Typically, during the first year the bees build up their hive, and if they overwinter well, you can begin harvesting in the late spring or early summer of the second year.

Three months after bringing our bees home, we had 4 frames packed with honey, each weighing about 8 pounds. Lacking a professional extractor, we used the following low-tech method.

1. Cut and crush Using the bench scraper, we cut the honey—wax and all—off the foundation into a bowl, balancing the frame on a wooden spoon set across the bowl like a bridge. Then we used a wooden spoon to crush the honey and wax in the bowl.

2. Straining and settling We poured this slurry of wax and honey through a double layer of cheesecloth and the stainless-steel strainer into our food-grade plastic bucket. Then we left it to drain and settle for a couple of days (bubbles and foam rose to the surface).

3. Bottling We covered the floor with newspapers and got our jars ready. Then we loosened the honey gate (the stopper at the bottom of the bucket) to release the honey into each jar. In went the honey, on went the lids. It was as simple as that. From 4 full frames of honeycomb, we reaped 12 pounds, 10 ounces of honey. We rinsed the leftover wax and froze it. Later, we rendered the wax in a solar wax melter and used it for craft projects like lip balm and hand salve (for more information, see http://oneblockdiet.sunset.com/team_bee.) We had a second surprise harvest later in the summer, bringing our total to about 31 pounds of pure, fragrant honey.

Worker bees—all females—work hard their whole lives. That's not true for the males, known as drones. They lounge about stealing honey until it is time for them to fly out and look for a queen to mate with. But only a day or two after a working girl pulls herself from her six-sided cell, she begins contributing to the health of the hive.

As they age, worker bees take on a series of jobs (although tasks sometimes overlap, depending on the needs of the hive). At five to ten days, they are house bees, cleaning the hive (bees are very clean), tending the brood (baby bees), taking care of the queen, and unloading nectar from the foraging bees and storing it in the wax combs. (The foragers take in the rest of the groceries—the pollen—themselves.) As they age, house bees start taking on other tasks, like guarding the hive and ventilating it by fanning their tiny wings across the comb. At two to three weeks, they become foragers, flying up to three miles away to find suitable blooming plants. Even as foragers they will help build comb, ventilate the hive, and protect it from honey-hungry animals.

Bee colonies are adaptable, and every worker can switch jobs when needed.

In the summer, the worker bees work so hard they just wear out after about thirty-five to forty days. The queen, no slacker herself, lays up to 1,500 eggs a day during the spring and summer brood buildup to provide a constant supply of new workers. In the winter, bees live longer—140 days or more—keeping the hive and queen warm, dry, and safe until spring, when the season begins again.

Queen (in center)

Workers

Drones (in center)

HELPFUL INFORMATION

GENERAL WEB SITES

- www.scientificbeekeeping.com
- www.sanmateobee.org
- www.sfbee.org
- www.beesource.com
- www.beginningbeekeeping.com
- www.caes.uga.edu/departments/ent/bees/beekeeping.html

WEB SITES ABOUT HOW TO CONTROL VARROA MITES

- www.caes.uga.edu/departments/ent/bees/disorders/honey-bee-parasites.html#varroa
- www.countryrubes.com/information/informationandpictures.html
- www.scientificbeekeeping.com
- www.dadant.com/Apiguard-Howtouse_003.htm

BOOKS AND PUBLICATIONS

- *The Hive and the Honey Bee*, edited by Joe M. Graham (Dadant & Sons, 1992).
- *First Lessons in Beekeeping*, by Keith S. Delaplane (Dadant & Sons, 2007).
- *The Backyard Beekeeper*, by Kim Flottum (Quarry Publishing Group, 2010).
- *American Bee Journal*, $24.95 per year (monthly publication); 51 South 2nd Street, Hamilton, IL 62341, 217/847-3324.
- *Bee Culture: The Magazine of American Beekeeping*, $25 per year (monthly publication); 623 West Liberty Street, Medina, OH 44256, 800/289-7668.

—Margaret Sloan and Kimberley Burch

HOW TO MAKE
CHEESE (PART I)

Milk needs very little encouragement to become cheese. Add heat and coagulant (like vinegar or lemon juice) and curds separate from whey to create, tah-dah, cheese.

Our first cheeses, for our summer feast, couldn't have been simpler, because we restricted ourselves to what we could get from our garden: lemons for coagulation and herbs for flavoring, plus salt, which we made from seawater, and milk, from a Bay Area dairy (eventually we found our own cow). But even with our supersimple cheeses, the results were slightly different depending on how we adjusted the variables: temperature, time, amounts, and technique.

BEFORE YOU START

Sanitize All kinds of bacteria love the warm, nourishing medium of milk. To keep bad bacteria from messing with the good, scrub your work surface with antibacterial soap. Boil utensils—ladle, whisk, measuring cups, and so on—for 10 minutes in an 8-quart pot before you use them. Wash everything else with antibacterial soap and let air-dry. After you finish making cheese, wash your equipment and let it air-dry.

Check your thermometer If the recipe calls for a dairy thermometer, check that it is calibrated correctly, or you might ruin your cheese. It's easy to check. As you're sterilizing it (submerging only the stem) with your other utensils, check the readout: It should be 212°F, the temperature of the boiling water. If it isn't, hold the face and adjust the pointer by turning the washer underneath the face with small pliers.

FRESH CHIVE CHEESE

MAKES 18 ounces (7-inch log; 28 servings)
TIME about 2½ hours, plus about 2 hours draining and chilling time

This recipe is based on one for *chenna*, an Indian cheese, in Ricki Carroll's *Home Cheese Making*. Making it involves kneading the curds into a satiny, moist "dough" that you then roll into a log, chill, and slice to use. We added it to our Tomato and Herb Salad (page 69).

WHAT TO USE

Milk Lacking a cow, goats, or sheep here at Sunset, we had to go outside our one-block parameter for milk. (Later, we bought a dairy cow; see page 213.)

Both pasteurized and raw whole milk will work in any of our cheese recipes. The only milk that will not work is ultra-pasteurized milk; the extreme heat of the pasteurizing process (at or above 280°F for 2 seconds) damages proteins in the milk and makes it harder for curds to form. Ultra-pasteurized milk and cream also have an unpleasant "cooked" flavor.

We used cream-top organic whole milk from Straus Family Creamery (www.strausfamilycreamery.com), near Tomales Bay in Marin County. It's sold in San Francisco Bay Area stores, starting at about $4.50 per gallon; 1 gallon yields about 1 pound cheese.

Lemons We used plain old 'Eureka' lemons—in our case, from our garden—squeezed and the juice strained.

Sea salt Salt is key for flavor development. It also extracts moisture from the curd and helps preserve the cheese. We used salt extracted from seawater (see How to Make Salt, page 172). Any good fine sea salt will work.

Herbs You can use any herbs that appeal to you, from parsley to tarragon to mint. We chose chives, because we like their sharp, oniony flavor and emerald color against the white cheese.

8-quart heavy-bottomed stainless-steel pot For heating the milk. From $60 at a cookware shop.

Large colander

Cheesecloth Lining the colander with a finely woven cheesecloth prevents any small curds from tumbling through the holes. About $4.50 for 2 square yards at hardware stores or cookware shops.

Stainless-steel perforated cheese ladle A cheese ladle has a large, flat surface that stirs milk and curds efficiently; you can also use a large slotted spoon. About $7.

Dessert or salad plate

5-pound weight Anything will do, from a barbell to heavy cans. We used round kitchen-scale weights.

Stand mixer with dough hook attachment (optional)

HOW TO DO IT

1 gallon whole milk, pasteurized or raw
¹/₂ cup freshly squeezed lemon juice
(4 to 5 large lemons)
2 tablespoons coarsely snipped fresh chives
³/₄ teaspoon fine sea salt

1. Separate the curds and whey Pour the milk into the 8-quart pot and bring to a gentle boil over medium-high heat, stirring often to prevent scorching (this will take about 30 minutes, so have a book handy). As soon as the milk boils, remove from the heat and slowly drizzle in the lemon juice while stirring slowly and gently with a rubber spatula. Keep stirring until solid white curds separate from greenish white, translucent liquid whey. This happens within seconds. If the curds have separated but the whey is still milky instead of clear, return the pot to low heat and cook until the whey is clear, then remove from the heat. Let sit until the curds have settled below the whey, about 15 minutes.

2. Drain the curds While the curds are settling, line the colander with a double thickness of cheesecloth and set it in the sink. Ladle the curds into the colander and rinse gently with lukewarm water for 5 seconds. Gather the cheesecloth into a knot over the curds and twist gently to squeeze out some of the liquid (the "bundle" should still be dripping after you have done this). To save the whey left in the pot for making ricotta (page 117), strain it through a cheesecloth-lined strainer into a container and chill until ready to use (up to 1 day).

3. Press the curds Place the dessert plate on the cheesecloth-wrapped curds and top with the 5-pound weight. Let drain for 45 minutes. At this point, the curds may still be dripping a bit, but that's okay. You want some moisture in the cheese.

4. Knead the curds Unwrap the curds and put them in the bowl of the stand mixer fitted with the dough hook. Add the chives and salt and beat on low speed until the cheese looks silky, 10 to 12 minutes. It should be as moist and smooth as cream cheese. Or, combine the curds, chives, and salt in a large bowl and knead by hand for about the same amount of time. The hand-kneaded cheese will be denser and more tightly grained than the machine-beaten cheese.

5. Shape and store the cheese Roll the cheese into a log about 2 inches in diameter. Wrap in waxed paper and then plastic wrap. Refrigerate until cold and firm, at least 1 hour, before using. It will keep for up to 3 days.

PER ¹/₄-INCH SLICE: 86 cal., 49% (42 cal.) from fat; 4.6 g protein; 4.7 g fat (2.9 g sat.); 6.9 g carbo (0 g fiber); 103 mg sodium; 20 mg chol.

Sanitizing the equipment   Field trip to Cowgirl Creamery   Tasting curds in the Sunset kitchen

●●

OREGANO QUESO BLANCO

MAKES about 2 cups (10½ ounces)
TIME about 2 hours

Crumbly and mild, this cheese reminds us of fresh Mexican *queso blanco*, or "white cheese," which is often also called *queso fresco*. It is based on the recipe for lemon cheese in Ricki Carroll's *Home Cheese Making*, but we more than doubled the lemon juice of the original, and we whisked the curds before draining them. The result: tart, moist, fluffy small curds that are good on soups, salads, or pizza. We sprinkled the cheese on our corn soup (page 70).

WHAT TO USE

Same as for Fresh Chive Cheese, page 46.

HOW TO DO IT

2 quarts whole milk, pasteurized or raw
½ cup plus 1 tablespoon freshly squeezed lemon juice
    (4 to 5 large lemons)
1½ tablespoons fresh oregano leaves, minced
1 teaspoon fine sea salt

1. Separate the curds and whey Pour the milk into the pot and bring just to boiling over medium-high heat, stirring often to prevent scorching. As soon as the milk looks as though it is about to boil, remove the pot from the heat and drizzle in the lemon juice while whisking briskly. Cover and let sit for 10 minutes.

2. Drain the curds Meanwhile, line the colander with a double thickness of cheesecloth and set the colander in the sink. Pour in the curds. Tie two opposite corners of

the cheesecloth into a knot over the curds, then repeat with the other two corners. Hang the cheesecloth sack from the sink faucet until the curds have stopped draining, 1 to 2 hours.

3. Flavor and store the cheese Transfer the curds to a bowl and mix in the oregano and salt with your fingers, breaking up the curds into small grains. Cover tightly and refrigerate. It will keep for up to 1 week.

PER TABLESPOON: 38 cal., 47% (18 cal.) from fat; 2 g protein; 2 g fat (1.3 g sat.); 3.2 g carbo (0 g fiber); 91 mg sodium; 8.5 mg chol.

HELPFUL INFORMATION

WEB SITE

- The Pacific Northwest Cheese Project, www.pnwcheese.typepad.com.

CHEESE-MAKING SUPPLIES

- The Beverage People (wine-, beer-, and cheese-making supplies), www.thebeveragepeople.com or 800/544-1867.
- Hoegger Supply Company, hoeggergoatsupply.com or 800/221-4628.
- New England Cheesemaking Supply, www.cheesemaking.com or 413-397-2012.

BOOKS AND DVDS

- *Home Cheesemaking: Recipes for 75 Homemade Cheeses,* by Ricki Carroll (Storey Books, 2002). First published in 1982, this little book has been reissued three times and has guided many a beginner to professional success.
- *The Cheesemaker's Manual*, by Margaret Peters-Morris (Glengarry Cheesemaking Inc., 2003). From a guru of the cheese-making world and the owner of Glengarry Cheesemaking Inc, in Lancaster, Ontario (Canada), this concise, well-organized book is a bit dry but packed with helpful information for home cheese makers, plus about fifty recipes for soft, hard, and washed-rind cheeses. Glengarry also sells a DVD, *Home Cheesemaking with Margaret Morris*, in which Ms. Morris calmly and cheerfully demonstrates how to make feta, Gouda, Camembert, and Cheddar (about $38).

HOW TO MAKE
BEER

Making home-brewed beer doesn't take long. You can make ale, the easiest type, in only four to six weeks. Also, you can play around with all sorts of ratios and roasts to make exactly the kind of beer you like. The biggest challenge is becoming familiar with the process and with the key pieces of equipment.

Most home brewers use brewing kits to make beer, and that's how we started, too. For our second batch in the spring, we made beer totally from scratch—as in, we used the wheat and barley that we had planted, threshed, winnowed, and malted (sprouted) ourselves, and grew hop flowers (called cones) for flavoring and preserving the brew. We were in a little over our heads, but we had expert advice and fun doing it.

We recommend that you start with a kit and either brew with a friend who has made beer before or take a class. Once you're comfortable with the process, progress to partial mash brewing (making beer from malted grain steeped in malt extract; we plan to do this next, and will write about it on our Team Beer blog, http://oneblockdiet .com/team_beer). Then try making all-grain brews, first from pre-malted grains, then from grain you malt yourself, and ultimately—if you're so inclined—from grain you grow, for a beer that is as personal as it gets.

Barley

SUMMER WHEAT BEER
(from a kit)

MAKES 48 (12-ounce) bottles
TIME about 1 month

Fresh and light, yet flavorful, this beer went well with the round, ripe flavors of our summer feast.

WHAT TO USE

All of our materials, unless otherwise mentioned, came from William's Brewing Company, 2594 Nicholson Street, San Leandro, California; www.williamsbrewing .com or 800/759-6025.

Honey wheat brewing kit A beginner-level kit contains one 6-pound pouch wheat extract, one 2-pound pouch blackberry honey, 2 ounces flavoring hop pellets (pulverized and compressed hop cones), 1 ounce aromatic hops, one 125-milliliter packet liquid yeast, and 1 packet corn sugar (fine, white and powdery; also called priming sugar) for carbonation. About $36.

Saniclean Safe for septic systems and does not stain; good for sanitizing your chiller, fermenters, ladle, tubing, and bottles. Use 2 ounces for 5 gallons of water. About $13 for a 1-quart bottle.

7-gallon boiling pot Also known as a brewing pot or brew kettle. A large, sturdy stockpot, available at any cookware or housewares store, will do. Or, you can use the 8-gallon boiling pot with spigot that we used for our Belgian Abbey Ale (page 52).

Medium plastic ladle

Long-handled plastic stirring spoon

Immersion chiller or plate chiller A coil of copper tubing, the immersion chiller is placed in the hot wort (the sweet liquid, made from malted grains, that will become beer) and then flushed with cold water to cool the wort rapidly. You can also put the pot in a sink full of cold water and change the water when it gets hot, but the chiller works much faster. The plate chiller, also known as a Shirron heat exchanger, is a slender metal box that brings in the cold tap water and the hot wort at the same time through separate tubes, instantly chilling the wort to about 70°F. The chiller costs about $55, the heat exchanger about $87.

Brewer's thermometer Indispensable for measuring the temperature of the new wort. If the wort is too hot, it will destroy the yeast. Brewer's Edge makes a thermometer with a large, easy-to-read face and a 12-inch probe stem. About $12.

Primary fermenter Also called a siphonless fermenter, this 7-gallon food-grade plastic bucket with a spigot is used for the fermenting stage. We've also used a 5-gallon carboy, but this is cheaper. About $30.

Strainer Choose a sturdy one that fits into the top of the primary fermenter. About $15.

Hydrometer A hydrometer measures the specific gravity (density) of the wort relative to water. Dissolved sugars make up the density of the wort, and the sugars are what ferment into alcohol, so the hydrometer measurement is a good indicator of the potential alcohol level of your beer. The MT300 hydrometer from www.morebeer.com has a potential alcohol scale. About $6.

Hydrometer jar A plastic tube with a flat base, sized to fit the hydrometer; used for holding the beer sample. $4.75 from www.morebeer.com.

Rubber stopper This almost fully seals the opening at the top of the primary fermenter. A small perforation in the middle accommodates the airlock (see below). $1.00 to $1.50, depending on size.

Airlock You fill this small plastic cylinder with water and insert it into the rubber stopper. This keeps bacteria from entering the new wort. It also allows the carbon dioxide in the fermenting beer to find a way out, so your container doesn't explode. About $1.

Large, dark cloth

Secondary fermenter Also known as a priming tank, this second 7-gallon, food-grade plastic bucket with a spigot is similar to the primary fermenter, but the spigot is placed lower on the bucket. This bucket is also used for bottling; it includes a small length of tubing, one end of which attaches to the spigot. The other end fills the bottles. About $20.

3-foot length food-grade vinyl tubing Clear vinyl, with a $3/8$-inch interior diameter, used to siphon the beer from one vessel to another. About $0.30 per foot at a home wine-making or plumbing-supply store.

Bottles You'll need 48 pry-top bottles (screw-top bottles are harder to seal) in dark green or brown glass (sunlight shining through clear glass can stimulate the growth of bacteria). We scrounged ours from various sources, namely friends, family, and colleagues. Free.

Jet bottle washer This fits on any outdoor hose thread faucet, such as those on a garage sink. About $12.

Bottle tree Invert your newly washed and sterilized bottles on this multipronged "tree" to dry. We like the 81-bottle model. About $30.

Beer caps A pack of 320 pry-type caps costs about $6.

Capper We like the easy-to-use Emily capper; $14.

Or, get a complete kit William's Brewing also offers a "home brewery," which includes most of the tools above (excluded are the bottles, caps, and boiling pot) and the ingredients for your beer of choice (from $110). The company also throws in a beginner's home-brewing book and a DVD guide.

HOW TO DO IT

BREWING (about 3 hours, plus up to 3 days for the yeast to swell)

1. Get the yeast going Pop the puffy center of your liquid-yeast packet and shake the packet. That bubble contained your yeast, and surrounding the bubble is wort for the yeast to feed on and multiply. Let the packet swell; this takes at least a day and up to three. Do not start the beer until the yeast packet is at least $1^1/_2$ inches thick.

2. Prepare your boiling pot Sterilize it with Saniclean solution, rinse with water, and fill the pot with 5 gallons of water. Add 2 teaspoons gypsum to the water to harden it.

3. Mix the wheat extract with the hot water Cover the pot and bring the water to a full boil over high heat. (That much water can take a long time to boil, so don't be in a hurry.) When the water boils, turn off the heat and squeeze the wheat extract into the water. Use the ladle to scoop hot water into the pouch to remove the residual extract, and then use your stirring spoon to mix the extract with the water. Now the mixture is considered wort.

4. Bring the wort to a boil When the extract is well mixed, cover the pot partially and bring the wort to a boil over high heat. Then uncover and keep the wort at a rolling boil. Be careful not to let it boil over the top of the pot, because it is a very sticky mess to clean up.

5. Add the flavoring hops Five minutes after the wort has begun to boil, add the flavoring hops. Boil for 45 minutes.

6. Add the honey Squeeze in the honey as you did the wheat extract, ladling some of the hot wort into the pouch to loosen any honey residue. Boil for 3 minutes.

7. Add the aromatic hops Stir in the aromatic hops and boil for 2 minutes more. Remove the wort from the heat.

8. Chill the wort Use the immersion chiller or plate chiller, or put the pot in a cold-water bath in the sink, to cool down the wort to the yeast's ideal fermentation temperature. The yeast packet will note the temperature; ours listed a range of between 58° and 74°F. Depending on which method you use, the chilling process can take anywhere from a few minutes (the plate chiller) to 30 minutes (immersion chiller) to more than 1 hour (the sink).

9. Start fermenting Pour the wort through the strainer into the primary fermenter, add the yeast, and give the wort a good stir with the stirring spoon.

10. Measure the original specific gravity (density) of the wort Insert the hydrometer into the hydrometer jar, drizzle in enough beer from the fermenter's spigot to make the hydrometer float, and read off the original specific gravity (OG) and the potential alcohol. Make a note of the OG. Although the precise figure isn't as important when you're using a kit, it will tell you how dense the wort is and will give you a way to measure the progress of the fermentation (as the sugars in the wort convert to alcohol, the mixture will become less dense).

11. Set up the beer for primary fermentation Put the fermenter lid on and insert the rubber stopper into the hole in the lid. Insert the airlock into the stopper, and then fill the airlock one-third full with water. Leaving only the airlock exposed, wrap the fermenter in the dark cloth. This blocks sunlight, which can stimulate the growth of bacteria. Keep the wort at the yeast's ideal fermentation temperature (see step 8). You can use an electric heating pad under the fermenter if the room gets too chilly.

FERMENTATION (2 to 4 weeks)

1. Primary fermentation After a day or two, the wort should start to ferment. As the carbon dioxide escapes, the airlock will start to sputter, bubble, and hiss vigorously. Once it has calmed down, generally within a few days, the primary fermentation is complete.

2. Secondary fermentation and racking Let the beer keep on fermenting for the time specified by the kit. In our case, this was 12 more days (for a total fermentation time of 16 days). Even though the airlock may not be sputtering, carbon dioxide is still forming and quietly seeping out through the airlock.

Meanwhile, the dead yeast cells are slowly filtering to the bottom, creating sediment (or trub). Moving the beer off the trub into a clean container (racking) helps to clarify it as it ferments. To rack your beer, set the primary fermenter on a countertop and the secondary fermenter on the floor below. Remove the airlock from the primary fermenter. Work one end of the 3-foot vinyl tubing onto the spigot of the primary fermenter, put the other end in the open secondary fermenter, and let the beer flow down. Shut off the spigot when you see sediment starting to enter the tube. Remove the vinyl tubing, snap the lid on the secondary fermenter, and seal it with the stopper and airlock. Wrap it up in the dark cloth to keep out light, and re-wrap after subsequent rackings (below).

When another layer of trub forms on the bottom of the secondary fermenter, usually in about a week, rack the beer again the same way, this time returning it to the primary fermenter.

At the end of this secondary period, check the final gravity again with your hydrometer (see Brewing, step 10).

Carbonating

Our kit specified a reading of 1.017 or less. If the reading is higher than that, let the beer ferment for another few days.

3. Clean your bottles At least a day before you think you will be bottling, start getting the bottles ready. Mix up a bucketful of Saniclean solution and put a batch of bottles in it for a few minutes, making sure the solution fills them completely. Then empty out the sanitizer back into the bucket and rinse the bottles with hot water using the jet bottle washer. Invert the bottles onto the bottle tree to drain. Sanitize the rest of the bottles the same way.

BOTTLING DAY (about 3 hours)

1. Carbonate the brew If the beer is not already in the secondary fermenter, siphon it in there. Stir in the corn sugar, which the surviving yeast will gobble up, releasing carbon dioxide—in other words, carbonation.

2. Bottle the beer Dunk the bottles in Saniclean solution and drain them on your bottle tree. Put the end of the secondary fermenter's tubing into your first empty bottle, holding it below the fermenter. Open the fermenter's valve and fill to within 1 inch of the neck bottom.

3. Cap the bottles Put a cap on the bottle, place the capper over it, and push down on the capper's arms to seal.

CARBONATION IN BOTTLE (1 to 2 weeks)

1. Let the beer rest Store in a cardboard box at room temperature (68°F or above) for a week. Then try a bottle: If it's fizzy, chill the beer and drink as soon as possible. If it is not fizzy enough, let it go for another week. When you like it, chill it.

This beer tastes best when it is freshly made. Ours kept well in the refrigerator for months, but the fizz and flavor were at their peak right after bottling.

BELGIAN ABBEY ALE
(from barley, wheat, and hops)

MAKES 48 (12-ounce) bottles
TIME 1^1/$_2$ years

Our aim was to make a combination barley-wheat beer, totally from scratch.

WHAT TO USE

All-grain brewing requires a few more pieces of equipment than kit-brewing does, but if you have already brewed using a kit, you can use the same equipment and just add to it. All of our materials, unless otherwise mentioned, came from nearby William's Brewing Company, 2594 Nicholson Street, San Leandro, California; www.williamsbrewing.com or 800/759-6025.

2 hop rhizomes ('Nugget' and 'Centennial') for planting The rhizome, the main stem of the hop vine, is sold cut into small pieces that look like little brown sticks.

3 pounds barley seed for planting, to yield 9 pounds malted, prepped barley Barley is the main grain used in beer. We planted 'Lacey', a malting type (versus a cereal type) developed for brewing (see page 27). About $5 per pound from Howe Seeds, www.howe seeds.com.

Our total yield was about 2^1/$_2$ pounds of grain, after winnowing and threshing (squirrels carried away most of the crop). The total yield after malting (sprouting) was 2 pounds. We needed about 9 pounds malted, prepped barley to make one 5-gallon batch of beer, so we had to supplement with 7 pounds store-bought malted barley. If we do this again, we'll grow more barley, as insurance. About $2 per pound for whole malted grain, $2.25 per pound for crushed malted grain.

2 pounds wheat seed for planting, to yield 6 pounds malted, prepped wheat We planted organic soft white wheat (see page 36). It is high in carbohydrates, which convert to sugars and then alcohol. About $5 per 2-pound bag from Homegrown Harvest, www.home grownharvest.com.

Those same marauding squirrels caused us to lose a lot of wheat. Our total harvest was about 1^1/$_2$ pounds. Our total yield after malting (sprouting) was 1 pound. We needed 6 pounds for our 5-gallon batch of beer, so, as with the barley, we had to supplement with 5 pounds of store-bought malted seed (wheat malt). About $2 per pound for whole wheat malt, $2.25 per pound for crushed wheat malt.

Trellis for growing hop vines Hop vines can reach upward of 30 feet, so we had to get creative. The lower part was a 5-by-10-foot piece of rigid ¹/₄-inch wire mesh. With deck screws, we attached four wooden blocks to a section of our garden fence (one block for each corner of mesh), screwed a lag hook into each block, and fitted the mesh over the hooks. Above the trellis and about 3 feet below the top of the fence, we attached two 2-inch-square wooden poles, each 8 feet tall. We attached them with deck screws to the fence and spaced them 10 feet apart. We ran several lengths of electrical wire between the poles, so the hops could grow across as well as up. The trellis cost $60 at a scrap metal shop. Everything else came from Home Depot: 6-inch-square wooden blocks (cut from an 8-foot board), about $8.50; 8-inch lag hooks, about $1.50 each; 8-foot poles, about $5 each; outdoor deck screws, about $8.75 for a 1-pound box of 75 screws; and uncoated electrical wire, from $0.25 per foot.

Hop-drying frame We built a 2-by-4-foot wooden frame from two-by-fours, and then nailed a piece of fine wire mesh to the bottom, sized to fit the frame. About $15 for all supplies at Home Depot.

Vacuum food sealer We vacuum-sealed our dried hops for storage. (You can also store your hops in two heavy-duty resealable plastic bags, one set inside the other.) Seal-A-Meal VS230 Vacuum Food Sealer, about $71 from www.amazon.com.

Several ordinary kitchen colanders for separately draining the soaked barley and wheat.

Grain mill The Barley Crusher MaltMill, with a 15-pound hopper, for use with a standard ³/₈-inch power screwdriver. $138 from www.barleycrusher.com.

Abbey Ale yeast Fruity and rich, this distinctive yeast is used in two of the world's six Trappist breweries. Like many Belgian yeasts, it is capable of continuing to ferment even when alcohol levels are high (high alcohol kills many yeasts). We had a lot of malted grain in this recipe (that is, potential sugars and therefore alcohol), so we thought it would be the right choice. About $6 for a 1-ounce tube from www.morebeer.com.

Corn sugar Also known as priming sugar, this fine, white, powdery sugar (sometimes available granulated) feeds the yeast, which unleashes the carbon dioxide that carbonates the beer. About $2 per pound.

Food-grade gypsum A blend of powdered calcium and sulfur, gypsum is used to harden the water. Hard water makes for clearer beer by helping coagulate malt proteins and encouraging the sedimentation of yeast. You will need only 1 teaspoon gypsum for each 5-gallon batch. About $3 for an 8-ounce bag.

8-gallon boiling pot with spigot This big, stainless-steel vessel is also known as a brewing pot or brew kettle. About $85.

5-gallon all-grain mash tun A Rubbermaid beverage cooler with a spigot attached and a fine-mesh screen laid over the bottom to keep the grains from clogging the spigot. About $125 from www.morebeer.com.

5-gallon all-grain hot liquor tank A Rubbermaid beverage cooler with a spigot attached. About $48 from www.morebeer.com.

Sparger Also known as a sparge tip, this plastic water dispenser has a central tube and four arms to keep it balanced atop the mash tun. Its job is to dribble water through the tube and arms very slowly and evenly into the mashed grain to rinse off residual sugar. About $25 from www.morebeer.com.

Two 3-foot lengths food-grade vinyl tubing Made of clear vinyl, and with a ³/₈-inch interior diameter, the

Belgian Abbey Ale

Hop rhizomes

Hop harvest

tubing is used to connect the hot liquor tank to the sparger and to let the wort flow from the mash tun into the boiling pot. It is also used later to siphon the beer into bottles. About $0.30 per foot online or at a home wine-making or plumbing-supply store.

Immersion chiller or plate chiller, Saniclean, stirring spoon, brewer's thermometer, primary fermenter, strainer, hydrometer, hydrometer jar, rubber stopper, airlock, secondary fermenter, bottles, jet bottle washer, bottle tree, beer caps, capper See the What to Use list for Summer Wheat Beer on page 49.

Or, get an All-Grain System kit The kit includes the mash tun, hot liquor tank, and sparger, plus tubing. $219 from www.sanfranciscobrewcraft.com; $235 from www.morebeer.com.

HOW TO DO IT

GROWING THE CROPS

1. Plant the hops In April, 18 months before we would savor our brew, we planted the rhizome pieces (we knew that the first season would yield few, if any, flower cones, so we had to plan for a second-season harvest). Because of the hop vine's prodigious size and abundance, we planted the pieces about 6 feet apart, right beneath the metal trellis that would support their fast-growing shoots (see page 30).

2. Plant the barley In November (for Northern California; for other regions, see planting calendars, page 250), plant the seed and care for the crop as directed on page 27.

3. Plant the wheat In January (for Northern California; for other regions, see planting calendars, page 250), plant the seed and care for the crop as directed on page 36.

HARVESTING, THRESHING, AND WINNOWING THE BARLEY AND WHEAT

1. Harvest the barley After the barley forms seeds in the spring, wait for the stalks to dry; they should be golden brown. If the weather is hot, this won't take long (we harvested in mid-May). Use hand pruners to clip a couple of inches below the seedheads.

2. Dry the barley Lay a tarp out indoors and spread the freshly harvested stalks in a single layer on the tarp. When the color of the barley changes from golden brown to grayish brown, it is fully dried. This takes about a month, depending on the heat and humidity.

3. Harvest the wheat Like the barley, the wheat seedheads should dry on the stalk to a golden brown before harvesting. We harvested our wheat a bit early because our crop was being devoured by squirrels. Harvest the wheat the same way you harvested the barley.

4. Dry the wheat Dry it the same way you dried the barley. It will take about the same amount of time.

5. Thresh and winnow the barley and the wheat Keeping the barley and wheat separate, thresh (loosen the grains from the stalks and the papery casings surrounding each grain, called chaff) and winnow (separate the seeds from the stalks and chaff) them. Each member of Team Beer tried a different tactic, but most ended up laboriously hand-peeling the casings from the grains and then either blowing off the chaff or soaking the grain and skimming the debris.

What we should have done, we've since learned, is thresh by banging the seedheads against the inside of a clean metal trash can to get them off the stalk. Then we should have stuffed the loosened seeds into a sturdy, thickly woven pillowcase or sack (clean of course) and walked in place on it, twisting our feet over the grain to rub off those papery bracts. As for winnowing, it's apparently easiest done in front of a floor fan turned to the lowest setting. You put a large sheet pan (or maybe a sheet itself) on the ground and then let loose handfuls of grain above the fan's windstream. The grains drop and the chaff flies away.

If we grow grain again, we'll try these methods.

HARVESTING AND DRYING THE HOPS

1. Harvest the hops 'Centennial' succumbed to fungus and bugs, so we were left with 'Nugget'. By September, the resiny balls called lupulins, found at the base of the flower cones, had turned golden yellow and were quite bitter, a sign of ripeness. (The lupulins, along with alpha acids in the flower, contribute a spicy, herbal, pleasingly bitter note to beer.) Harvesting was easy: We just snipped the cones from the vine with scissors.

2. Dry the hops We spread a carpet of newspapers on the floor and set our hop-drying frame on top, with a couple of bricks under each corner so air could circulate underneath. We placed the hop cones on the screen, spreading them out in a single layer. After about a week of drying, the hops were still green, but sprang back when pressed—a sign that they were dry enough. We kept small vacuum-sealed bags in the freezer. For our Belgian Abbey Ale, we used 3 ounces of hops.

MALTING THE GRAIN (at least 6 days)

This involves converting the barley and the wheat from a starch storage unit (a seed) to a slightly sweet, crunchy grain that can be further converted, through the brewing process, into the fermentable sugary solution known as wort (pronounced "wert").

1. Soak the grain Put the 2 pounds homegrown barley and 1 pound homegrown wheat seeds in separate bowls. Add water to cover by at least 2 inches, then leave the seeds to soak for 8 hours. Drain them separately in colanders, and let them dry in the colanders for 8 hours (if they are drenched for longer than 8 hours at a time, they will be deprived of oxygen and will die). Soak the seeds separately again the same way for another 8 hours. At this point, the seeds should have begun to swell and turn white, a sign that they are about to germinate (sprout). If they haven't, drain, dry, and soak them again the same way until they appear about to germinate.

2. Sprout the grain Line large rimmed baking sheets with paper towels. Keeping the wheat and barley separate, spread the swelled seeds in a single layer on the lined baking sheets. The paper towels absorb moisture and so maintain humidity, which is essential to helping the seeds germinate.

Put the pans in large, dark garbage bags and tie the ends closed. Let the seeds sit at room temperature until they sprout. Barley seed takes 4 to 7 days; wheat seed takes about 3 days. Note that each seed will put out root hairs (each finer than a root) and shoots. The shoots are much larger than the root hairs, and each seed has just one shoot but several root hairs. When the shoot has grown to one-half to three-fourths the length of the seed, stop the germination by baking the seeds.

3. Bake the grain Preheat the oven to between 100° and 125°F (if your oven has a pilot light, just turning the pilot light on may bring the oven to the perfect temperature). Remove the baking sheets from the plastic bags and slip them into the oven. Bake the seeds for about 1 hour, then take them out of the oven. Remove the towels from the pan (you will yank off some roots and shoots, too, but that's fine), spread the seeds evenly on the pans, and bake the seeds for 24 hours. Move them around with a spatula every 30 minutes for the first 4 to 6 hours, to help them dry evenly.

When the seeds are fully dried, bite into one. If it is rock hard, it is still a starch storage unit and won't make beer. Put the seeds back in the oven for another 30 minutes and test again. When they are crunchy and slightly sweet, the germination has converted the starch to sugar, and you have malt—the key to making beer.

4. Clean the grain One last step in the malting process: rub the fine dried root material off the grains. This will give you a clearer beer.

BREWING DAY (about 3 hours)

We brewed under the guidance of our friend Chuck Schwalbach, who is married to Sunset's manufacturing manager, Diane Schwalbach. Chuck, a product designer for Apple, really knows his way around all-grain home brewing and helped us each step of the way. We highly recommend that you make your first all-grain batch with a knowledgeable friend, or that you take a class.

Hoping to create a particularly fresh-flavored beer, we decided to roast and grind the grain the same day we brewed the beer.

1. Roast the grain Light 20 to 30 charcoal briquettes in the fire grate of your grill and let them burn until they are covered with ash. Push them into two small piles on either side of the grate. Put 8 ounces of the malted barley in an aluminum pie pan and place the pan on the cooking grate over the cleared space. Roast the grain, shaking the pie pan often, until about two-thirds of the grains are black. The timing will depend on the intensity of the fire; plan on about 20 minutes. Don't roast more than 1 pound of grain for a 5-gallon batch of beer, or your beer may turn out grainy and bitter.

2. Grind the grain Pour all of the grain—malted wheat, malted barley, and roasted barley—into the hopper of the grain mill, turn on the mill, and let it rip.

3. Prepare your boiling pot Sterilize your boiling pot with Saniclean solution. Rinse off the sanitizer with clean water.

4. Mash (hot-soak) the malted grain The key here is to mash the grain at just the right temperature for the grain's starches to convert to sugar. Chuck measured the temperature of our grain and calculated that we'd need the mash water to be 172°F when poured into the mash pot. As soon as the water and grain mingled, the temperature would drop to 152°F. The mash conversion temperature can range from 150° to 158°F, depending on the style of beer you want. (For more on this, see www.howtobrew.com, an excellent in-depth online brewing guide from beer guru John Palmer; refer to Sections 2 and 3 to learn about all-grain brewing.)

Fill the boiling pot with 13 quarts water, add 1 teaspoon gypsum, set the pot on the stove top, and heat the water to 180°F (measure it with your brewer's thermometer). Meanwhile, set your mash tun (the cooler fitted with the mesh bottom) on a nearby countertop. Attach one of your vinyl tubes to the spigot of the boiling pot, put the other end in the mash tun, and open the spigot to let the hot water flow into the mash tun. Then let the water in the mash tun cool to 172°F. (It's easier to start with hotter water and cool it down than have to pour the water back into the boiling pot and heat it up again.)

Pour the ground grain into the mash tun. Using the stirring paddle, mix well. The temperature of the mash should immediately decrease to 152°F. Let the mash rest for 1 1/2 hours.

'Nugget' hops   Malted grain   Adding grain to the mash tun

Sparging   Chilling (with a plate chiller)   Measuring original gravity

5. Sparge (rinse) the mash About 30 minutes before the mash has finished resting, start heating up 4 1/2 gallons of water in the boiling pot. Bring it to a boil to evaporate the chlorine in the water.

Remove the pot from the heat and let the water cool to 172°F. Transfer the hot water to the hot liquor tank (the cooler without the mesh bottom) and elevate the tank at least 1 foot above the mash tun. (We hoisted the tank onto the top of a wall oven, for example.) Set the sparger over the mash tun.

Place the now-empty boiling pot at least 1 foot below the mash tun. Attach one end of a length of vinyl tubing to the spigot of the mash tun, and put the other end in the empty boiling pot.

When the water registers 172°F (you can add ice to cool it down quicker), it is cool enough so that it won't leach tannins from the grain husks into your beer. Attach a second vinyl tube to the spigot of the hot liquor tank and the other end to the top of the sparger. Open up the spigot and let the water flow down through the sparger into the mash. (The point of sparging is to rinse off the residual sugar that adheres to the grain.)

At the same time, open up the spigot of the mash tun and let the sweet brown liquid—the wort—flow into the boiling pot. One hand will be monitoring the hot water flow from above, into the sparger, and the other hand will be monitoring the flow from the mash tun into the boiling pot below. You want the inflow to be at about the same pace as the outflow. Try to keep the grain covered by 1 to 2 inches of water, so that when the water drizzles down from the sparger arms, it hits water and does not

displace the grain at all or create channels, which can cause uneven rinsing. Properly done, sparging should take about 30 minutes for a 5-gallon batch of wort.

6. Boil the wort and add the hops Measure the wort to be sure you have 5 gallons. If you don't, add water to make up the difference. Bring the wort to a boil over high heat and boil for 1 1/2 hours.

After the wort has boiled for 30 minutes, add 1 ounce hops. At the 1-hour mark, add another 1 ounce hops; at the 1 1/4-hour mark, add 1/2 ounce hops; and at the end of 1 1/2 hours of boiling the wort, add the last 1/2 ounce hops. The early additions will give the beer bitterness (the hops release alpha acids, which contribute more bitterness the longer they boil), and the later additions will add aroma.

7. Chill the wort Use the immersion chiller or plate chiller, or put the pot in a cold-water bath in the sink, to cool down the wort to 68°F, the ideal fermentation temperature for Abbey Ale yeast (the temperature will be specified on the yeast label). Depending on which method you use, the chilling process can take anywhere from a few minutes (the plate chiller) to 30 minutes (the immersion chiller) to an hour or more (the sink).

8. Start fermenting Pour the cooled wort through the strainer (to remove the spent hops) into the primary fermenter, add the yeast, and give the wort a good stir with the stirring spoon.

9. Measure the wort's original specific gravity Insert the hydrometer in the hydrometer jar, drizzle in enough beer from the fermenter's spigot to make the hydrometer float, and read off the original specific gravity (OG) and the potential alcohol. Make a note of the OG. For this beer, our OG was 1.062 degrees; the corresponding readout of potential alcohol, marked on the hydrometer, was about 7.84 percent. The OG tells you how dense the wort is and will give you a way to measure the progress of the fermentation (as the sugars in the wort convert to alcohol, the mixture will get less dense).

10. Set the beer up for primary fermentation Put the fermenter lid on and insert the rubber stopper into the hole in the lid. Insert the airlock into the stopper, then fill the airlock one-third full with water. Leaving only the airlock exposed, wrap the fermenter with the dark cloth. This blocks sunlight, which can stimulate the growth of bacteria. Keep the wort at 68°F, the ideal fermentation temperature for this yeast. You can use an electric heating pad if the room gets too chilly.

FERMENTATION (2 to 4 weeks)

Follow the fermentation instructions for Summer Wheat Beer (page 51), but try to keep the beer at around 68°F. In Step 2 (secondary fermentation and racking), let the beer settle for 3 weeks. The final specific gravity for this beer should be 1.021 (and the corresponding alcohol content should be 7.65 percent). Surprisingly, our final specific gravity reading was 1 (the specific gravity of water), an indication that something had gone very wrong.

BOTTLING DAY (about 3 hours)

Follow the bottling instructions for Summer Wheat Beer (page 52).

CARBONATION IN BOTTLE (at least 3 weeks)

Let the beer rest Store in a dark cardboard box at room temperature (68°F or above) for 3 weeks. Then try a bottle: If it's fizzy, chill the beer and drink it as soon as possible. If it is not fizzy enough, let it go for another week or two, then try it again. When you like it, chill it.

After all our work, the Belgian Abbey Ale was, unfortunately, kind of funky. The final specific gravity did not lie. We think the brew got contaminated at some point during primary fermentation. Or, possibly our yeast was bad. We hope we have better luck next time.

HELPFUL INFORMATION

- John Palmer's easygoing yet detailed introduction to making beer at home: www.howtobrew.com.
- *The Complete Joy of Home Brewing,* by Charlie Papszian (Harper Paperbacks, 2003).
- American Homebrewers' Association, www.homebrewersassociation.org.
- Product questions section on William's Brewing Company site, www.williamsbrewing.com.
- *The Home Brewer's Answer Book,* by Ashton Lewis, (Storey Publishing, 2007) columnist for *Brew Your Own* magazine, www.byo.com.
- Helpful and lively forum for makers of AG (all-grain) brews on www.homebrewtalk.com, www.realbeer.com, and www.onebeer.net.
- Forums on www.forums.morebeer.com.

—Rick LaFrentz

HOW TO RAISE
CHICKENS

What could be more idyllic than a flock of hens happily clucking in your backyard? We got six baby chicks in August 2007 and raised them to provide eggs, not meat. (We wanted protein we wouldn't have to kill.) They yielded a side benefit, too: their droppings, which make great fertilizer for our garden (see Cultivating Compost, page 10, for more on this). Plus, chickens are unexpectedly entertaining.

They're not like other pets, however. For one thing, you probably eat others of their species. Some people who raise backyard chickens find they lose interest in eating meat. Others, after observing their chickens' behavior and getting to know them, decide that they feel okay about chickens as meat.

In our experience, chickens do not have the emotional range of cats or dogs. If you are looking for a cuddly creature with whom you will have an emotional relationship, chickens may not be the most rewarding option.

This is not to say that we don't like our chickens. We enjoy watching them scratch around, and we like feeding them treats. We feel the obligation to make them safe and comfortable and healthy. And we like their eggs a lot.

Before you get your baby chicks (adorable balls of fluff), evaluate your space and your lifestyle.

Does your city allow you to keep chickens? Every city has its own rules. Our municipality (Menlo Park, California) lets residents keep hens, but not roosters. That's fairly common in cities: Many have no problem with a few quiet hens (usually classified as pets), but they ban noisy roosters. Check your local regulations before picking out your flock. It would be dreadful to get them and then have to get rid of them.

Do you have space? Each chicken should have at least 10 square feet to run around in, plus 4 square feet of house.

Can you keep them safe? Making their digs secure is extremely important, especially at night. Chickens are prey, and they sleep so soundly that they seem unconscious—morsels waiting to be devoured. They are vulnerable to attack by raccoons, skunks, foxes, weasels, and other predators. Raccoons are particularly nasty, and they're particularly clever about using their little nasty hands to get into your coop. Also, keep in mind that your other pets (cats, dogs) may be predators. (Read more about chicken coops on page 60.)

Carmelita (at left) and Ruby

One of our baby Buff Orpingtons

What will do you with them when they stop laying eggs?
Hens lay best in the first year, and may lay sporadically for four or five years, but they can live for eight years (or longer). After their prime egg-laying years are over, will you be happy to keep caring for them?

What will you do if one gets injured or sick? Before you acquire your flock, and regardless of your philosophical feelings about whether your chickens are pets, you must make sure you have a plan for what to do in case something happens to one of them. If you choose to take your chickens to a vet, locate an avian vet in your area in advance, preferably one familiar with chicken health problems.

   Not everyone who raises chickens chooses to treat them when they get sick. Some people will euthanize a sick or injured animal; others have a friend, family member, or neighbor willing to do it in an emergency.

Can you afford it? You'll be getting good fresh eggs for free, but setting up a coop can cost a few hundred dollars, depending on the materials you use, and chicken food is an ongoing expense. If you decide to visit the vet, those bills can add up quickly.

ONE FLOCK OF 6 CHICKENS

2 Ameraucanas (Ophelia lays blue eggs, Alana green)
2 Buff Orpingtons (Honey and Charlotte; buff-colored eggs)
2 Rhode Island Reds (Carmelita and Ruby; deep brown to bronze eggs)

WHAT TO USE

The coop Most of the work in raising chickens is setting up their space. Chickens need a box to lay their eggs in (plan on one or two boxes for half a dozen hens), a secure house with a roost for them to sleep on, and a place to run around and do their chicken thing. "The coop" refers to both the house and the enclosed run where chickens scratch around and spend the day.

   We got our 4-by-6-foot henhouse from Wine Country Coops, whose houses are both luxurious (glass windows! high-quality wood! beautiful construction!) and pricey ($1,300 and up; www.winecountrycoops .com or 707/829 8405). Ours is built on stilts with an open-mesh floor, which lets droppings fall through to the ground below. You can get a less posh chicken house at a feed store, or you can build one yourself. Find inspiration at www.backyardchickens.com.

The yard Allow 10 square feet per hen. (You can give your chickens less room if you let them range freely outside their yard. We don't, because they like to eat the seedlings in our garden.) We marked the boundaries of our yard with wooden posts; stretched chicken wire between the posts and buried it 12 inches into the ground to keep digging predators at bay; and then topped the yard with a corrugated, translucent plastic roof to allow light in but keep the chickens dry in foul weather. (Note: If raccoons are a problem in your area, you should use $1/2$-inch hardware cloth instead of chicken wire, since raccoons can reach right through the wire and grab; they can also pull it apart if sufficiently motivated.) The door of our chicken house opens right into the yard, so the coop is completely enclosed and protected. The yard also has a human-size door—made of two-by-fours, more chicken wire, and a hinge—so that we can easily get in and out to feed and visit the chickens. (About $200 in supplies from a hardware store.)

Unless otherwise mentioned, we purchased everything below from a local feed store, Half Moon Bay Feed & Fuel (650/726-4814). McMurray Hatchery sells a starter kit for about $65 (www.mcmurrayhatchery.com). Many supplies can be purchased from a pet store, such as Petco (www.petco.com) or Petsmart (www.petsmart.com).

FOR CHICKS

A warm indoor location We used a storage shed on the Sunset grounds.

Heat lamp, reflector, bulb, and clamp Until they have feathers, chicks need to be kept very warm. About $20.

Wire cage or enclosure This houses the chicks for the first few weeks of their lives. It is a few feet in length and the heat lamp hangs above it. We prefer the type with a door at the top, because it makes reaching in easier. You can use a cardboard box, but it's more difficult to clean and may not be escape-proof. From $50.

1-gallon plastic water fount A narrow lip keeps the chicks from tumbling into the water. Buy one with a wide base so it won't tip easily. $5 to $10.

Chick feeder Make sure your feeder has a top, or the chicks will scratch their food right out of it. About $5.

Chick starter and grower food A finely ground, high-protein (20 to 22 percent) mixture of grains. This is what a chick should eat until it is 18 weeks old. (Some brands sell separate starter and grower crumbles; in that case, feed the chicks starter until they are 8 weeks old, then switch to the grower food until they start laying.) Medicated chick starter helps stave off the nasty parasitic infection called coccidiosis; alternatively, you can buy chicks that have been vaccinated for coccidiosis. Don't do both. $30 to $40 for a 50-pound sack of organic starter and grower food.

Electrolyte powder Dissolve this in the chicks' water according to package instructions. It will shore up their frail systems with nutrients, and is especially important to use if the chicks are sick or stressed from traveling. Stop adding it when the chicks are 10 weeks old. $8 for an 8-ounce packet; a single packet is enough to raise at least a dozen chicks.

FOR ADULT CHICKENS

5-gallon water and food dispensers Galvanized steel dispensers hang from the roof of the coop and provide the chickens with a steady source of food and water. $40 to $50 each.

Large covered trash can If rats are a problem in your area, stow the food dispenser in a trash can at night. Make sure the can has a sturdy lid that snaps closed securely. About $15 from a home supply store.

EGGS: QUESTIONS AND ANSWERS

Q: Do you need a rooster for eggs?
A: Chickens lay eggs with or without the presence of roosters. Since we don't have a rooster (they are not allowed in Menlo Park), the eggs are not fertilized, so they will never hatch into chicks. (This is just as well, because we're not in the market for more chickens.) If we did have a rooster, the eggs would be fertilized while they were, ahem, still in the hen. The rooster doesn't do anything to eggs once they have been laid.

Q: Do colored eggs taste different?
A: Different varieties of chickens lay different colors of eggs. Our Ameraucanas lay blue and green eggs; the other four lay brown eggs of varying shades. All of them taste exactly the same, and wonderful.

Q: How many eggs do you get a day?
A: Chickens usually lay one egg a day. When they get to be two or three years old, this drops off, and the eggs become more sporadic. Many chickens on large industrial farms lay two eggs a day.

FOODS TO AVOID

Eggshells (can encourage them to peck their own eggs), citrus (weakens shells), onions and garlic (can impart a funny flavor to eggs), and legumes (some uncooked beans are toxic for birds). We avoided giving them meat so as not to attract rats—and because we think it's creepy—but chickens will eat just about anything.

"The acme of food packaging."
—Alan Davidson, *The Oxford Companion to Food*

Every day, our chickens deliver eggs to us—anywhere between two and six, depending on the weather (in winter, they slow down). Each egg is slightly different in shape, in color, and in thickness of shell.

If you have a day job, it's hard to catch a chicken in the act of laying an egg. The thing pops out in less than a minute. Within the chicken, it takes only about a day for the egg to form.

Here's how it works.

Every female chick is born with thousands of undeveloped yolks, or ova, grouped together near the middle of her backbone in a large cluster, the ovary.

When a hen is old enough to lay, these ova begin to mature. At any given time within an adult hen's body, her ova are in various stages of development: Some are tiny yellow bubbles, others are the size of marbles. Every twenty-four to twenty-six hours, one ripens fully and is released into the instant grip of the waiting oviduct. As the egg moves down this tube, sperm from the rooster, if there is

any, attempts to penetrate the egg; most eggs proceed down the oviduct unfertilized.

Next, the egg is coated with layers of gel-like albumen (the egg white) and wrapped in a thin, translucent, antimicrobial membrane. At this point, the egg is only about half its final size. Time elapsed: about four hours.

The soft, shell-less egg then moves into the thickest part of the oviduct, the shell gland (uterus). For five hours or so, water and salts pump up the albumen to full size. Now a floating cloud of calcite (calcium carbonate) begins to swirl around the egg. Precisely spaced protein points on the membrane's surface attract the calcite particles, which build up in geometric columns to form a thin, smooth crystal: the shell.

The shell-encased egg is just centimeters from the exit. The oviduct releases a coating that both blocks bacteria and colors the egg—blue, green, brown, or white—which seems like a lovely bit of primping on nature's part just before the egg emerges.

Finally, the hen gets an urge and climbs into the nest box. After a bit of heaving, out pops the egg. There it is, protein rich, marvelous, ready to go. We take it away to eat, and the hen starts making another one, as if it were the most ordinary thing in the world.
—Margo True

Ophelia

Layer pellets These pellets have less protein and a coarser formulation than chick starter. Begin feeding them to your hens at 18 weeks or when they start laying. This is the chickens' main food for life. If you like, you can give it to them in crumble form instead, but the pellets are less messy. We order Purina organic layer pellets through our closest pet-supply store, San Mateo Pet Supply (www.sanmateopet.com or 650/365-6738). About $40 for a 50-pound sack.

Coarse-ground oyster shells Strew a couple of handfuls on the floor of the yard a few times a week for your chickens to peck up. The crushed shells supply calcium to strengthen eggshells, which can otherwise be weak and rubbery. $12 for 50 pounds.

Treats from the garden and the kitchen Chickens love leafy greens, chile seeds, weeds picked from the garden (especially anything in the dandelion family and wild grasses), plain yogurt, leftover bread and cooked pasta, apple cores, overripe strawberries and other fruits, and insects and worms they find in the dirt. If your hens aren't roaming all over the garden during the day, though, they can become overweight. This means that you need to restrict treats for cooped chickens to greens and maybe a little fruit, with the occasional dish of yogurt. Give them only as much as they'll eat within a 15-minute period.

HOW TO DO IT

1. Buy the chicks Some companies will mail you chicks (newly hatched, they can survive for 2 days without food or water), but for beginning chicken raisers, we recommend buying them at a local feed store. Not only is it reassuring to pick up your cheeping chicks in person, but feed stores also have knowledgeable employees who can be valuable resources. Plus, mail-order shipping can be hard on chicks, and getting a package that contains a dead chick or two can be traumatic for first timers.

We got our hens as sexed 2- and 7-day-old chicks from Half Moon Bay Feed & Fuel (650/726-4814). "Sexed" means the store's staff were pretty sure that they were girls. They came vaccinated for Marek's disease, a fatal poultry disease, and cost $4.50 each. We chose them because they were the kind the feed store happened to have that day. That said, Rhode Island Reds are good, old-fashioned layers, as are Buff Orpingtons. Our Amer-aucanas proved to be fine layers, too.

2. Raise the chicks indoors Keeping the chicks alive for the first few weeks was a fun kind of bustle. We kept them in a warm shed in their wire cage, with the heat lamp suspended above, until they started to feather out. We visited them several times a day, making sure that the heat lamp was the right distance from the cage to maintain the ideal temperature (90° to 100°F for the first few weeks, and then decreased by 5 degrees per week after that). We made sure that food and water were always available, and we cleaned the cage every few days. Also, we gently picked them up to get them used to people. It worked: As adults, they are friendly and easy to handle.

3. Move the flock outdoors At 5 weeks, the chicks were fully feathered, the sign that they were ready to leave the nest, so to speak. It was September and balmy when we took them out to their coop in our test garden. During the cold months, we kept the heat lamp inside their house for extra warmth at night. This was probably unnecessary; chickens huddle together for warmth, and

Ruby the chicken

supplemental heat really isn't needed unless nighttime temperatures go below freezing.

4. Encourage and collect eggs Most chickens will begin to lay when they are somewhere between 18 and 24 weeks, depending on the chicken and the weather. Moderate warmth and 14 hours of daylight encourage laying. We put a marble egg in the nest box when the girls were of age, hoping it would give them the right idea (a "decoy" is supposed to help). Our first egg, a long-awaited event, appeared in January, courtesy of our Ameraucana Ophelia. Over the next several weeks, the other hens followed.

5. Routine maintenance Adolescent and adult chickens don't require much care. Feeding and watering, cleaning the coop, and collecting the eggs pretty much sums up what you need to do.

The hens must be fed daily, and clean water must always be available. If a chicken goes thirsty for even a few hours, she may temporarily stop laying.

Whatever you use as flooring in your coop must be scooped out and replaced about once a month, more often if it gets smelly faster. We initially used straw as bedding and on the floor of the coop, but we don't recommend it.

How to Raise Chickens 63

Ophelia ate it and got it knotted up in her crop. Now we use pine bark, which is sturdy enough not to blow away, but easy for the hens to move around so they can dig in the dirt. We hose out the house about four times a year, and we compost the droppings (see page 10 for details).

We collect the eggs every day, not only because we want to eat them, but also because egg buildup can encourage broodiness (a condition in which a hen refuses to get off the nest in the hope of hatching chicks).

Beyond this basic care, we recommend daily visits because it's enjoyable to go see the ladies. Plus, bringing them treats and petting and picking them up helps them get used to human presence and makes it easier to handle them if you've got a sick chicken you need to check out.

HELPFUL INFORMATION

- **Your local feed store:** Often, this will be the place that supplied your chicks, and someone on the premises will know quite a bit about chicken care. At our store, we were given an informative how-to-raise-chicks handout and told about a condition we hadn't known of until that moment: pasty butt. This is basically a clogged vent, which can be deadly for a little chick. Pasty butt is easily resolved with cotton balls dipped in warm water and gently applied to get the crud off.
- **The forum at www.backyardchickens.com:** No matter what weird problem you're having, someone else has had it first. If you're looking for practical advice and real anecdotes, this is the best resource on the Web. Sifting through the active message board will get you up to speed on what to worry about, what not to worry about, and what to do next.

BOOKS

Every month, a few more books on chicken raising seem to hit the shelves. These are some of our favorites.

- *Creating Your Backyard Farm*, by Nicki Trench (Cico Books, 2010). Good introduction to keeping hens, including how to deal with health problems.

- *The Backyard Homestead*, edited by Carleen Madigan (Storey Publishing, 2009). A substantial section on raising chickens offers great-looking coop designs. This is a terrific all-around raise-your-own-food book.
- *The Chicken Health Handbook*, by Gail Damerow (Storey Publishing, 1994). Packed with technical (and often grisly or terrifying) information, but also extremely useful; reading it will help you prevent sickness in your flock.
- *The Joy of Keeping Chickens: The Ultimate Guide to Raising Poultry for Fun or Profit*, by Jennifer Megyesi (Skyhorse Publishing, 2009). A heartfelt guide to the pleasures of the backyard flock by the owner of Fat Rooster Farm, in Royalton, Vermont. With artful photographs of chickens and humans by Geoff Hansen.
- *Keep Chickens! Tending Small Flocks in Cities, Suburbs, and Other Small Spaces*, by Barbara Kilarski (Storey Publishing, 2003). Geared toward absolute beginners and inspiringly enthusiastic.
- *Keeping Chickens with Ashley English*, by Ashley English (Lark Books, 2010). A slim volume with helpful advice on topics such as how to choose a good layer, plus interviews with chicken keepers.
- *Minnie Rose Lovgreen's Recipe for Raising Chickens*, by Minnie Rose Lovgreen (NW Trillium Press, 2009). This friendly little book, dictated by the eighty-six-year-old Minnie Rose to her friend Nancy Rekow in 1974, reads as though Minnie herself were sitting at your kitchen table, giving you advice.
- *Raising Chickens for Dummies*, by Kimberly Willis with Rob Ludlow (Wiley Publishing, 2009). Willis, a poultry breeder, and Ludlow, owner of the excellent Web site www.backyardchickens.com, include a section on how to butcher and process chickens.
- *Storey's Guide to Raising Chickens*, by Gail Damerow (Storey Publishing, 1995). Technical and thorough, it's great for those who have had some experience and are looking for more extensive information.

—*Elizabeth Jardina*

Opposite page: Our henhouse arrives (top);
Honey, brooding (bottom right)

THE SUMMER RECIPES

❋ SKILLET-ROASTED EDAMAME

Smoky, salty, and addictive, these soybeans were inspired by a recipe for griddle-roasted peas in Niloufer Ichaporia King's *My Bombay Kitchen: Traditional and Modern Parsi Home Cooking* (University of California Press, 2007). To eat them, pop the peas out of the pod with your fingers—or, if you like the salt and char, with your teeth.

MAKES about 4 cups TIME about 10 minutes

1 pound fresh or frozen edamame (soybeans) in the pod
Fine sea salt

1. If using fresh edamame, bring a large pot of salted water to a boil. Add the edamame and boil for 2 minutes. Drain and let cool. If using frozen edamame, skip this step.

2. Heat a large, heavy skillet or a wok over high heat. Toss in half of the edamame and cook, turning with tongs, until blackened in several spots, 5 to 8 minutes. Pour into a bowl. Repeat with the remaining edamame.

3. Toss the edamame with salt to taste.

PER 1/2 CUP SERVING 65 cal., 38% (25 cal.) from fat; 6 g protein; 2.8 g fat (0 g sat.); 5 g carbo (2.8 g fiber); 18 mg sodium; 0 mg chol.

❋ DEVILED CUCUMBER CUPS

These pretty little bites show off the bright color of eggs from pasture-raised chickens. If you want the cups to have fluted edges, you will need two round, fluted biscuit cutters, each at least 3/4 inch high: one 1 1/2 inches in diameter, for the narrower parts of the cucumber, and the other 2 inches in diameter, for the fatter sections. A melon baller is useful, too, for removing the seeds.

MAKES 24 cucumber cups, or 8 servings
TIME about 1 hour

3 large eggs
Ice cubes
4 cucumbers, each at least 7 inches long
2 1/2 tablespoons Green Chile Mayonnaise (page 73)
2 1/2 tablespoons minced red onion, rinsed
About 1 teaspoon freshly squeezed lemon juice
1/2 teaspoon fine sea salt, plus more to finish
1 to 2 red or green serrano chiles, seeded and slivered, for garnish

1. Put the eggs in a small saucepan and fill with water to cover by 1 inch. Bring to a boil; immediately reduce the heat to a simmer and cook, uncovered, 10 minutes. With a slotted spoon, transfer the eggs to a bowl of water and ice cubes and let cool for 1 minute, then crack all over and put back in the ice water for 5 minutes to help loosen the shells. Lift the eggs out of the water, peel, and pat dry.

(continued)

2. Meanwhile, cut the cucumbers crosswise into 24 rounds, each 3/4 inch thick (you will have some cucumber left over). For fluted edges, cut out fluted rounds, using a biscuit cutter in the size that works best (see headnote). Using a melon baller or small spoon, scoop the seeds from the center of each cucumber round, leaving at least a 1/4-inch-thick layer of cucumber on the bottom and sides. Set the rounds on a baking sheet.

3. Shred the eggs with a razor-sharp grater (such as a Microplane) or against the finest slatted holes of a box grater, and put in a bowl. Add the mayonnaise, onion, lemon juice, and salt. Mash the mixture together with a fork.

4. Fill the cucumber cups with the egg mixture, mounding it slightly. Sprinkle each filled cup with salt and a few drops of lemon juice. Top each with a sliver of serrano.

MAKE AHEAD You can make both the filling and the cucumber cups up to 1 day ahead and cover and refrigerate them separately. Blot the cups dry just before filling.

PER CUCUMBER CUP 24 cal., 58% (14 cal.) from fat; 1.1 g protein; 1.7 g fat (0.35 g sat.); 1.4 g carbo (0.36 g fiber); 61 mg sodium; 29 mg chol.

TEMPURA SQUASH BLOSSOMS

We came up with this recipe as a way to control the crazy productivity of our pattypan squash plants: If you eat the blossoms, the squashes can't form. The dish is just as tasty and works just as easily with zucchini blossoms.

MAKES 4 to 6 servings TIME about 20 minutes

Extra virgin olive oil for deep-frying
1/2 cup plus 2 tablespoons Summer Wheat Beer (page 49) or other wheat beer
1/2 cup 'Sonora' white whole-wheat flour,* whole-wheat pastry flour, or a mix of all-purpose flour and cake flour
1/4 teaspoon fine sea salt, plus more for sprinkling
12 small pattypan squash blossoms or blossoms from 'Trombetta di Albenga' or other zucchini, about 3 inches long
1/4 cup Fresh Chive Cheese (page 46) or fresh goat cheese mixed with 2 teaspoons minced chives

1. Pour the oil to a depth of 2 inches into a medium saucepan and heat to 350° to 375°F on a deep-frying thermometer. Meanwhile, in a small bowl set in a larger bowl of ice and cold water, whisk together the beer,

flour, and salt, stopping when the batter is almost but not quite smooth.

2. Brush any debris or insects off the blossoms (check inside, too). Gently open the petals and stuff each blossom toward its base with about 1 teaspoon cheese, depending on the size of the blossom. Leave enough room for the petals to close easily over the cheese.

3. Dip a few stuffed blossoms in the batter to coat. One at a time, lift the blossoms from the batter, allowing the excess batter to drip back into the bowl, and slip them into the hot oil. Fry the blossoms, turning them occasionally, until golden and crisp, about 1 minute. Transfer with a slotted spoon to paper towels to drain. Repeat with the remaining blossoms, dipping and frying only a few at a time. Sprinkle the blossoms with salt, if you like, and serve immediately.

* *We used finely milled 'Sonora' wheat flour because it makes a delicate, crisp batter. See "The Allure of Local Wheat," page 156, for more on local flours.*

PER 3-BLOSSOM SERVING 146 cal., 58% (85 cal.) from fat; 4.1 g protein; 9.8 g fat (2.6 g sat.); 12 g carbo (1.3 g fiber); 152 mg sodium; 11 mg chol.

❊ TOMATO AND HERB SALAD WITH FRESH CHIVE CHEESE

This is the salad to make with dead-ripe tomatoes from your backyard. The surprise is the easy homemade cheese.

MAKES 8 servings TIME about 20 minutes

2 pounds assorted vine-ripened tomatoes
12 to 14 slices Fresh Chive Cheese (page 46)
    or fresh mozzarella
1 teaspoon fine sea salt, plus more to finish
1/2 teaspoon honey
1 1/2 tablespoons Syrah Vinegar (page 113) or other
    red-wine vinegar
1/4 cup extra virgin olive oil
2 or 3 sprigs marjoram, plus flowers if any
10 to 12 fresh basil leaves, plus flowers if any

1. Slice large tomatoes; leave small tomatoes whole, or cut into wedges or halves. Arrange on a platter with the cheese.

2. In a small bowl, whisk together the salt, honey, and vinegar until the salt has dissolved; whisk in the oil. Spoon the dressing over the tomatoes and cheese.

3. Strip the leaves and flowers from the marjoram sprigs onto the salad. With kitchen scissors, snip the basil leaves and flowers over the tomatoes. Sprinkle with salt.

PER SERVING 227 cal., 59% (135 cal.) from fat; 8.5 g protein; 15 g fat (5.8 g sat.); 17 g carbo (1.5 g fiber); 424 mg sodium; 32 mg chol.

WATERMELON-CHILE SALAD

If you have ever had a cold slab of watermelon sprinkled with salt, chile, and lime on the streets of a Mexican town, you'll recognize the roots of this salad.

MAKES 4 to 6 servings TIME about 15 minutes

4 teaspoons freshly squeezed lemon juice
1/2 teaspoon fine sea salt
2 to 2 1/2 teaspoons minced green serrano chile
2 teaspoons finely chopped fresh chives
2 tablespoons extra virgin olive oil
6 cups cubed watermelon (1-inch cubes)
1/3 cup loosely packed small flat-leaf parsley leaves
    (chop coarsely if large)

(continued)

1. In a large bowl, whisk together the lemon juice, salt, chile, chives, and oil to make a dressing.

2. Add the watermelon and parsley to the dressing and toss gently to coat evenly.

PER SERVING 86 cal., 49% (42 cal.) from fat; 1.1 g protein; 4.9 g fat (0.7 g sat.); 11 g carbo (0.79 g fiber); 191 mg sodium; 0 mg chol.

PURSLANE-CUCUMBER SALAD

What better way to control the weeds in your garden than to eat them? And you can definitely eat purslane. It is pleasantly lemony and its fat little leaves have a juicy crunch. This Turkish-style salad is one of our favorite ways to get rid of purslane.

MAKES 4 to 6 servings TIME about 20 minutes

1 large cucumber, about 7 inches long
2¹/₂ cups lightly packed purslane or watercress sprigs
2 teaspoons finely chopped fresh peppermint
1 clove garlic
¹/₄ teaspoon fine sea salt
2 tablespoons Crème Fraîche (recipe follows)
¹/₂ teaspoon crushed dried red serrano chile
  or red chile flakes
3 tablespoons extra virgin olive oil
1 tablespoon freshly squeezed lemon juice

1. Peel the cucumber, halve lengthwise, and remove the seeds. Cut into ¹/₂-inch cubes and put in a serving bowl. Add the purslane and peppermint.

2. Mince the garlic, sprinkle it with the salt, and mash to a paste with the flat side of a big chef's knife. In a small bowl, whisk together the garlic paste, crème fraîche, chile, oil, and lemon juice to make a dressing.

3. Pour the dressing over the salad and toss to coat evenly.

PER SERVING 90 cal., 87% (78 cal.) from fat; .86 g protein; 9 g fat (2.2 g sat.); 2.5 g carbo (0.4 g fiber); 107 mg sodium; 4.2 mg chol.

CRÈME FRAÎCHE

In France, this luxuriously thick, tangy, slightly nutty-tasting cream is often made with unpasteurized cream, and naturally occurring bacteria do the work of thickening. If you are using pasteurized cream, you have to add a fermenting agent to the milk to get it to thicken. Even so, homemade crème fraîche is wonderful stuff, and less expensive than store-bought. There are many ways to make it. This is our favorite.

MAKES about 1 cup TIME about 5 minutes, plus at least 8 hours to ripen

1 cup heavy cream
2 tablespoons buttermilk

1. Pour the cream and buttermilk into a small bowl and stir to combine. Cover tightly with plastic wrap and let sit at room temperature until thickened, at least 8 hours or up to overnight.

2. Stir well, re-cover, and refrigerate. It will keep for up to 1 week.

PER Tablespoon 53 cal., 94% (50 cal.) from fat; 0.4 g protein; 5.6 g fat (3.5 g sat.); 0.5 g carbo (0 g fiber); 7.4 mg sodium; 21 mg chol.

❖ CORN SOUP WITH ROASTED POBLANOS AND ZUCCHINI BLOSSOMS

The essence of sweet, just-picked summer corn, this soup lends itself to a gardenful of garnishes. It is equally good hot or cold.

MAKES 8 servings TIME about 1 hour

3 large poblano chiles
10 freshly picked ears corn,* any variety
2 tablespoons olive oil
1 large white onion, chopped
1 to 2 green serrano chiles, finely chopped
2 teaspoons fine sea salt
4 large cloves garlic, minced
1 'Trombetta di Albenga' zucchini (7-inch-long piece)
  or 1 medium regular zucchini, seeded and cut into
  ¹/₄-inch dice (about 1 cup)
8 'Trombetta di Albenga' zucchini blossoms or other
  zucchini blossoms, brushed clean and halved
  lengthwise
1 cup Oregano Queso Blanco (page 48), crumbled
  store-bought queso fresco,* or crumbled mild feta,
  homemade (page 120) or store-bought

(continued)

1. Preheat the broiler. Put the poblanos on a rimmed baking sheet. Broil about 4 inches from the heat source, turning as needed, until blackened all over, at least 15 minutes. Drape the pan with a sheet of aluminum foil and let the chiles stand until cool enough to handle. Gently pull off and discard the blackened skins. Stem and seed the chiles, then cut into 1/2-inch dice.

2. Meanwhile, remove the husks and silk from the corn. Working with 1 ear at a time, stand it on one end in a deep, wide bowl. Using a sharp knife and starting at the top of the ear, cut off the kernels.

3. Heat the oil in a large, wide pot over medium heat and add the onion, serranos, and salt. Cook, stirring occasionally, until the onion and chiles have softened, about 5 minutes. Stir in the garlic and corn kernels and cook for 3 minutes more.

4. Pour just enough water into the pot to cover the corn. Cover, bring to a simmer over medium heat, and cook for 15 minutes. Remove from the heat and let cool slightly.

5. While the corn mixture is cooking, put the diced zucchini in a small saucepan with salted water just to cover. Bring to a simmer and cook until tender-crisp, about 2 minutes. Drain.

6. In batches, whirl the corn mixture in a blender until very smooth. Strain through a fine-mesh strainer into a bowl, mashing with the back of a spoon to press out as much liquid as possible. Thin the soup with water if you like. To serve the soup hot, return it to the pot and reheat gently (don't boil). To serve the soup cold, cover and chill for at least 2 hours. Just before serving, season with salt if necessary.

7. Divide the soup among 8 bowls. Top each bowl with 2 tablespoons diced poblanos, 2 tablespoons diced zucchini, and 2 zucchini blossom halves. Sprinkle each serving with 1 tablespoon cheese, and pass the remaining cheese at the table.

* *Just-picked corn is much juicier than corn that has been sitting around for a while, so if you are using older, chewier, starchier corn, you may need to add more water to the pot when simmering the corn. Queso blanco, also known as queso fresco, is a mild, fresh white Mexican cheese with a moist, crumbly texture.*

MAKE AHEAD You can make the soup through step 6 up to 2 days ahead, cover its components seperately, and refrigerate.

PER SERVING 238 cal., 34% (80 cal.) from fat; 9.2 g protein; 8.9 g fat (3.2 g sat.); 36 g carbo (4.3 g fiber); 695 mg sodium; 17 mg chol.

'TROMBETTA' ZUCCHINI AND ITS FLOWERS

Our 'Trombetta' zucchini plants produced big, curving, crisp, pale green zucchini and enormous blossoms, both of which worked perfectly for this recipe. But you can use any kind of zucchini—or squash, actually—and its flowers for this dish. If you have two big frying pans, use them both to cook all the zucchini at once. Otherwise, cook the dish in two batches. It does not need to be served piping hot.

MAKES 4 to 6 servings TIME about 20 minutes

2 tablespoons extra virgin olive oil
2 pounds 'Trombetta di Albenga' or other zucchini, cut on the diagonal into 1/2-inch-thick slices
1 teaspoon fine sea salt
2 1/2 teaspoons minced fresh marjoram
30 'Sungold' or other yellow cherry tomatoes
4 cloves garlic, thinly sliced
2 to 3 teaspoons freshly squeezed lemon juice
8 to 10 'Trombetta di Albenga' or other zucchini blossoms

1. Heat 1 tablespoon of the oil in a large nonstick frying pan over medium heat. Add half of the zucchini slices and cook, without stirring, until the slices on the bottom begin to brown, 2 to 3 minutes. Sprinkle with 1/2 teaspoon of the salt and 1 teaspoon of the marjoram. Using a thin spatula, turn the zucchini so the bottom slices are on top.

2. Add half of the tomatoes and half of the garlic and cook, stirring gently every now and then, until most of the zucchini slices have browned a little, about 10 minutes, and the tomatoes are hot. Transfer to a bowl.

3. Return the pan to medium heat and heat the remaining 1 tablespoon oil. Add the remaining zucchini and cook the same way with the remaining salt, tomatoes, garlic, and 1 teaspoon marjoram. Return the first batch of zucchini to the pan and sprinkle with lemon juice to taste. Tear all but 3 blossoms into petals and fold into the zucchini.

4. Turn the zucchini out onto a platter or into a wide serving bowl and sprinkle with the remaining 1/2 teaspoon marjoram. Tear the remaining 3 blossoms into petals and scatter over top.

PER 1-CUP SERVING 84 cal., 56% (47 cal.) from fat; 4.6 g protein; 5.4 g fat (0.81 g sat.); 7.6 g carbo (2.1 g fiber); 398 mg sodium; 0 mg chol.

•
OVEN-BAKED STEAK FRIES WITH GREEN CHILE MAYONNAISE

We didn't have steak, but managed to eat plenty of these regardless, especially dunked in the mayo—and washed down with cold, fizzy homemade beer.

MAKES 4 servings TIME about 45 minutes

1 pound 'Yukon Gold' potatoes, cut into 1/2-inch-thick
**   wedges**
2 tablespoons extra virgin olive oil
1/2 teaspoon fine sea salt
Green Chile Mayonnaise (recipe follows)

1. Preheat the oven to 425°F. Place the potato wedges on a rimmed baking sheet, drizzle with the oil, and sprinkle with the salt. Toss the potato wedges to coat evenly.

2. Roast, turning the wedges halfway through, until golden and crisp, about 35 minutes.

3. Transfer the fries to a platter, spreading them out evenly (they will stay crisp longer on a platter than heaped in a bowl), and season with more salt, if you like. Serve with the mayonnaise.

PER SERVING 153 cal., 39% (60 cal.) from fat; 2.7 g protein; 7 g fat (1 g sat.); 20 g carbo (1.3 g fiber); 287 mg sodium; 0 mg chol.

✤ GREEN CHILE MAYONNAISE

A fiesty spread that's good on sandwiches, too. Have ingredients at room temperature to help the mayonnaise thicken. (If the egg is straight from the refrigerator, put it in warm water for several minutes before you use it to help it warm up.) Seed the chile if you want less kick. You can also leave out the garlic and serrano entirely for a mild mayo; see page 241.

MAKES About 1 cup TIME 5 minutes

1 large egg
2 garlic cloves, minced
1/2 to 1 red or green serrano chile, finely chopped
1 1/2 to 2 teaspoons fine sea salt
2 tablespoons lemon juice, plus more to taste
1 cup extra-virgin olive oil

In a blender, whirl together the egg, garlic, chile, 1 1/2 teaspoons of the salt, and 2 tablespoons lemon juice until the mixture thickens slightly, about 1 minute. With the motor running, add the oil through the top of the blender in a slow, steady stream, whirling until all of it has been incorporated and the mayonnaise is thick. Whirl in more salt and lemon juice to taste, if you like.

MAKE AHEAD: Up to 4 days, covered and chilled.

PER TABLESPOON 87 cal., 95% (83 cal.) from fat; 0.55 g protein; 9.7 g fat (1.5 g sat.); 0.4 g carbo (0.02 g fiber); 52 mg sodium; 18 mg chol.

✦ ROSEMARY POTATOES ANNA

A thin, golden brown "cake" of sliced potatoes cooked in a heavy skillet, potatoes Anna typically calls for butter. We used our own olive oil instead. This recipe works best with potatoes that you have allowed to cure (see page 82). If they are freshly dug, they will be too moist. (All potatoes in grocery stores and most potatoes in farmers' markets are cured.)

MAKES 8 servings TIME about 1 hour

3 pounds 'Yukon Gold' potatoes
1 tablespoon extra virgin olive oil
1/2 teaspoon fine sea salt
2 teaspoons minced fresh rosemary

1. Preheat the oven to 375°F. Peel the potatoes and cut into 1/8-inch-thick slices.

2. In a 10-inch ovenproof nonstick frying pan, heat 2 teaspoons of the oil over medium-high heat. When the oil is hot, arrange about one-fifth of the potatoes in the pan in concentric circles, starting from the outer edge, covering the bottom completely. The potatoes should sizzle when you put them down on the hot pan. If they don't, wait for the pan to get hot enough. Mix together the salt and rosemary in a small bowl, and sprinkle the potatoes in the pan with about one-fifth of the mixture. When the potatoes begin to brown around the edges, reduce the heat to low. Top the first layer of potatoes with 4 more layers, arranging them the same way and sprinkling each layer with the salt mixture. Before you sprinkle the final layer, brush the remaining 1 teaspoon oil over the potatoes.

3. With a heatproof spatula, gently pull back the edge of the layered potatoes to see if the bottom layer is starting to brown. If it is, transfer the pan to the oven and bake until the potatoes are tender when pierced with a fork, about 45 minutes. If it isn't, increase the heat to medium-high and cook until the bottom layer begins to brown, then transfer the pan to the oven. Check the potatoes occasionally, and if they start to look dry or begin to curl, cover the pan with aluminum foil.

4. Remove from the oven. Run the spatula between the layered potatoes and the pan sides. Invert a flat, round plate or platter over the pan and invert the pan and the plate together, releasing the potatoes onto the plate. Serve hot or warm, cut into 8 wedges with a serrated knife.

MAKE AHEAD The finished dish can be kept warm in a 200°F oven for up to 2 hours.

PER SERVING 141 cal., 11% (15 cal.) from fat; 3.6 g protein; 1.7 g fat (0.2 g sat.); 27 g carbo (1.8 g fiber); 154 mg sodium; 0 mg chol.

GRILLED SUMMER SUCCOTASH

Succotash usually involves a mixture of boiled corn, lima beans, and bell peppers. We had the corn, no problem. Instead of limas, we used edamame. And our poblano chiles stood in for the bells. Then, because every summer needs a grilled salad, we grilled the corn and chiles—and threw in a few ripe cherry tomatoes for sweetness at the last minute.

MAKES about 5 cups, or 4 to 6 servings
TIME about 45 minutes

4 large ears corn
1/4 cup extra virgin olive oil, plus more for brushing
3/4 teaspoon fine sea salt, plus more for sprinkling
3 poblano chiles

1 cup shelled fresh or frozen edamame (soybeans)
2 cloves garlic
2 teaspoons freshly squeezed lemon juice
1 1/2 cups 'Sweet Million' or other red cherry tomatoes,
    cut in half
About 1/2 cup heavy cream (optional)

1. Prepare a grill for medium-hot cooking (350° to 450°F; you should be able to hold your hand above the cooking grate for only 5 to 7 seconds). Strip the husks and silk from the corn, brush the ears with oil, and sprinkle with salt.

2. Arrange the corn and chiles on the cooking grate. Grill the corn, turning often, until lightly browned, 10 to 15 minutes. Grill the chiles, turning as needed, until completely blackened on all sides, about the same amount of time.

3. Meanwhile, bring a pot of well-salted water to a boil. Add the edamame, bring back to a boil, and cook for 2 1/2 minutes if fresh or 4 minutes if frozen. Drain and set aside.

4. Mince the garlic, sprinkle it with the 3/4 teaspoon salt, and mash to a paste with the flat side of a big chef's knife. In a small bowl, whisk together the garlic paste, lemon juice, and the 1/4 cup olive oil to make a dressing.

5. Let the corn and chiles cool until they can be handled. Then, stand 1 ear on end in a deep, wide bowl and, slicing downward, cut off the kernels.* Repeat with the remaining ears. You should have about 3 cups kernels. Peel the blackened skin from the poblanos. Holding each poblano over the bowl of corn kernels, slit the chile and let the juices drain into the bowl. On a work surface, stem and seed the chiles and cut into 1/2-inch dice. Add the diced chiles to the corn.

6. Add the tomatoes and edamame to the corn and chiles, drizzle with the vinaigrette, and toss together gently to coat evenly. Eat drizzled with cream if you like.

*   *Save the corn cobs for your chickens. They'll love them.*

PER SERVING 217 cal., 49% (106 cal.) from fat; 6.6 g protein; 12 g fat (1.6 g sat.); 25 g carbo (5.4 g fiber); 296 mg sodium; 0 mg chol.

❊ PATTYPAN SQUASH WITH EGGS

Harvest or buy the squashes when they are 4 inches across. We found that this was the perfect size for holding a single large egg. Since our chickens had just started laying, their eggs tended to be small, so some of our squashes held two eggs. (If the egg won't quite fit, scoop out a little of the white with a spoon.)

MAKES 8 servings TIME about 1 hour

8 pattypan squashes, yellow or green or a combination,
    each 4 inches across
About 3 tablespoons extra virgin olive oil
3/4 teaspoon fine sea salt, plus more for sprinkling
1 white onion, finely chopped (about 3/4 cup)
4 large cloves garlic, minced
1 1/4 teaspoons minced fresh thyme
8 large or 16 small eggs, at room temperature

1. Preheat the oven to 375°F. Cut off the top (stem end) of each squash and reserve. Using a small spoon, scoop out and discard the flesh (or reserve for another use) from each squash, leaving a shell at least 1/4 inch thick. Brush

(continued)

the squashes and their tops all over with about 2 tablespoons of the olive oil, and set, cut side up for squashes and stem side up for tops, on a rimmed baking sheet.

2. Bake until tender when pierced with a sharp knife, 20 to 30 minutes. The tops will cook more quickly, so check them after 15 minutes and remove them when they are done. When the shells are ready, remove from the oven and sprinkle the insides of the shells and the tops with salt. Set the tops aside; leave the shells on the baking sheet.

3. While the squash shells are baking, heat the remaining 1 tablespoon oil in a large frying pan over medium-high heat. Add the onion and the 3/4 teaspoon salt. Cook, stirring occasionally, until the onion is very soft and starting to brown, 8 to 10 minutes. Add the garlic and cook, stirring, until fragrant, about 30 seconds. Add the thyme and stir until combined. Keep hot.

4. Divide the hot onion mixture among the squash shells, spreading it over the bottom and up the sides to form a thin coating. Crack 1 large egg or 2 small eggs into each squash and drizzle with a little more oil. Cover the baking sheet with aluminum foil and bake until the egg whites are firm but the yolks are still loose, 15 to 20 minutes.

5. Sprinkle each egg with a pinch of salt and serve immediately, with the squash tops replaced or set to the side.

MAKE AHEAD Bake the squash cups up to 4 hours ahead, cover, and keep at room temperature. Rewarm the cups in the oven before adding the onion mixture and the eggs.

PER SQUASH 165 cal., 48% (80 cal.) from fat; 10 g protein; 8.9 g fat (2.1 g sat.); 14 g carbo (3.9 g fiber); 366 mg sodium; 212 mg chol.

● ●

WHOLE-WHEAT PIZZAS

If we had known more about wheat when we started our project, we would have grown high-protein hard red wheat for breads and pizzas in addition to our low-protein soft white wheat. The soft wheat was excellent for beer making and for pastries and crackers, but made gummy bread and crackerlike pizza dough. So, after some exasperating dough experiments, we found a great locally grown and milled hard wheat flour called 'Expresso' and used it for this recipe (see The Allure of Local Wheat, page 156, for more on local flours). The crust is reasonably puffy, and it has a nutty, wholesome flavor that is great with toppings of fresh vegetables and cheeses.

If your pizza dough balls are fully proofed (puffy and ready to be stretched into pizza crusts), but you are not yet ready for them, punch them down and form them into tight little balls, then let them rise for an hour. They will puff up again and be good to go.

We tried to make a whole-wheat starter from just wheat and water to use as leavening, but we couldn't get it to work consistently. So, in the interest of creating a reliably delicious pizza dough, we ended up with packaged yeast. However, we'll keep exploring a way to grow a good starter on http://oneblockdiet.sunset.com/team_kitchen.

MAKES 6 pizzas, or 6 servings TIME about 1 1/2 hours

1 package (2 1/4 teaspoons) active dry yeast
1 teaspoon honey
3 1/2 to 4 cups 'Expresso' whole-wheat flour* or other
    whole-wheat flour, plus more for sprinkling
1 1/2 tablespoons extra virgin olive oil
1 teaspoon fine sea salt
Topping of choice (recipes follow)

1. Put the yeast, honey, and 1 3/4 cups warm water (100° to 110°F) in the bowl of a stand mixer fitted with a dough hook. Let stand until the yeast dissolves and bubbles appear, 5 minutes. Add 1 cup flour and mix with the dough hook on low speed until combined. Gradually add 2 1/2 cups more flour and mix for 8 minutes to thoroughly combine.

2. Add the oil and the salt and mix on low speed for 7 minutes more. The dough should feel elastic—when you poke it, it should spring back—and only slightly sticky. If it is quite sticky, mix in more flour, 1 tablespoon at a time, until the stickiness subsides.

3. Turn the dough out onto a floured work surface and cut into 6 equal portions. Roll each portion into a tight ball and place on a well-floured tray. Dust the tops with flour.

4. Cover the tray loosely with plastic wrap and a kitchen towel. Let the dough balls rise at warm room temperature until they are soft, pillowy, and full of air, 1 to 1 1/2 hours. (Alternatively, cover the tray as directed and refrigerate overnight. Let come to room temperature for at least 1 hour before continuing.)

5. Place a pizza stone or baking sheet on the lowest rack of the oven and preheat the oven to 500°F (or as high as your oven will go) for at least 30 minutes. *(continued)*

Corn and Zucchini Pizza (bottom);
Fresh Chive Cheese and 'Sweet Million' Pizza (top)

The One-Block Feast

6. Working with 1 dough ball at a time (keep the others covered), set the ball on a well-floured pizza peel or baking sheet. Tap the center of the ball first to deflate it, then stretch and pat the dough out from the middle with your fingers into a 7- to 8-inch round, leaving the outer rim untouched (the dough will not be very stretchy, so be careful not to tear it). Add the toppings.

7. With a quick thrust of the peel (set the tip of the peel or sheet on the stone first to make it easier), shove the pizza onto the stone. Bake until the crust is puffy and browned, 8 to 12 minutes, or follow baking directions in the topping recipe. Repeat with remaining dough balls and toppings.

* *'Expresso' has a protein content of 12.3 percent, which we needed to give our pizza crust a good soft, chewy texture. See "The Allure of Local Wheat," page 156, for more on local flours.*

PIZZA TOPPINGS

We borrowed from future seasons to come up with these pizza toppings; in the summer, we had only the first one.

FRESH CHIVE CHEESE AND 'SWEET MILLION' TOMATO SAUCE

Parbake the pizza crusts until firm and dry but not browned, about 3 minutes. Spread with a thin layer of 'Sweet Million' Tomato Sauce (at right) or other pizza sauce. Top with thin slices of Fresh Chive Cheese (page 46) or fresh mozzarella sprinkled with chopped chives, and bake until the crust is puffy and browned, 3 to 4 minutes more. Finish with a drizzle of extra virgin olive oil, a sprinkle of sea salt, and chopped fresh thyme.

PER 1/4 PIZZA (APPROX.) 202 cal., 45% (91 cal.) from fat; 7.5 g protein; 10 g fat (3.7 g sat.); 22 g carbo (2.6 g fiber); 425 mg sodium; 20 mg chol.

CORN AND ZUCCHINI

Heat extra virgin olive oil in a frying pan over medium heat, add slivered white onion, diced zucchini, minced garlic, chopped fresh marjoram, and fine sea salt to taste and cook until tender. Mix in fresh corn kernels. Mix fromage blanc, homemade (page 118) or store-bought, with enough heavy cream to create the consistency of softened cream cheese. Spread the cheese mixture onto the pizza crusts, spoon the zucchini-corn mixture evenly over the cheese layer, and top with a few more spoonfuls of the fromage blanc mixture. Bake as directed in step 7. Halfway through baking, sprinkle with Oregano Queso

Blanco (page 48) or crumbled feta, homemade (page 120) or store-bought and mixed with minced oregano.

PER 1/4 PIZZA (APPROX.) 164 cal., 40% (66 cal.) from fat; 4.9 g protein; 7.5 g fat (2.7 g sat.); 21 g carbo (3.1 g fiber); 234 mg sodium; 13 mg chol.

CHERRY TOMATO, RICOTTA, MINT, AND CHILE

Top pizza crusts with generous smears of ricotta cheese, homemade (page 117) or store-bought, mixed with crushed dried serrano chiles or red chile flakes and a little fine sea salt. Cover with whole cherry tomatoes. Sprinkle with more chile flakes, if you like, and drizzle with extra virgin olive oil. Bake as directed in step 7. Finish with torn fresh peppermint leaves and a sprinkle of sea salt.

PER 1/4 PIZZA (APPROX.) 122 cal., 43% (53 cal.) from fat; 3.7 g protein; 6.1 g fat (1.4 g sat.); 15 g carbo (2.6 g fiber); 148 mg sodium; 4 mg chol.

POTATO, ONION, AND GOUDA

You won't need a baking stone or preheated baking sheet for this Roman-style pizza. For 6 pizzas, peel 1 3/4 pounds 'Yukon Gold' potatoes and slice as thinly as possible on a mandoline. Place the slices in a very large bowl of well-salted water and let soak for at least 1 hour at room temperature (or several hours if chilled). Drain and pat dry, then toss with 2 cups finely chopped white onion and about 1/2 cup extra virgin olive oil.

For each pizza, oil a large rimmed baking sheet, then gently stretch and flatten each dough ball into a thin rectangle (about 10 by 7 inches). Brush with more oil, then cover the surface of the dough with no more than a double or triple layer of the potato-onion mixture.

Bake as directed in step 7 until the potatoes are just beginning to turn brown, about 10 minutes. Remove from the oven, sprinkle with shredded Gouda cheese, homemade (page 122) or store-bought, and with chopped fresh rosemary. Return to the oven and bake until the crust is browned, the edges of the potato slices are crisp, and the cheese is bubbling, about 5 minutes more.

PER 1/4 PIZZA (APPROX.) 197 cal., 47% (92 cal.) from fat; 6 g protein; 11 g fat (2.8 g sat.); 21 g carbo (3 g fiber); 271 mg sodium; 11 mg chol.

'SWEET MILLION' TOMATO SAUCE

We created this recipe especially for our red 'Sweet Million' cherry tomatoes, but you can use any small, tender cherry or pear-shaped tomato. The sauce has a rustic character and nice crunch from the tomato seeds and skins.

MAKES about 1¾ cups TIME about 1 hour, 10 minutes

1 quart 'Sweet Million' tomatoes
1 tablespoon minced garlic
1 tablespoon extra virgin olive oil
1 teaspoon honey
¹/₂ teaspoon crushed dried red serrano or árbol chile
¹/₂ teaspoon fine sea salt
1 teaspoon chopped fresh basil
1 teaspoon chopped fresh oregano

1. Pulse the tomatoes in a food processor to chop coarsely. Heat the garlic and oil in a medium saucepan over medium heat, stirring, 1 minute. Stir in the tomatoes, honey, chile, and salt. Bring the mixture to a boil over high heat. Reduce the heat to low and simmer uncovered, stirring often, until very thick, 50 to 60 minutes.

2. Stir in the basil and oregano and use right away, or cool, cover, and refrigerate.

MAKE AHEAD Refrigerate, tightly covered, for up to 3 days. Or, pack into a sturdy plastic container or resealable plastic bags and freeze for up to 5 months.

PER ¹/₄-CUP SERVING 42 cal., 50% (21 cal.) from fat; 0.78 g protein; 2.3 g fat (0.29 g sat.); 4.7 g carbo (1.1 g fiber); 164 mg sodium; 0 mg chol.

···

SUMMER LEMONGRASS CUSTARDS

Silky and delicate in texture, with a surprising little zing from the lemongrass, these custards are lovely on their own. But a pouf of whipped cream puts them over the top.

MAKES 6 servings TIME about 1¹/₂ hours, plus at least 1¹/₂ hours to steep

4 large stalks lemongrass
2 cups whole milk
2 large eggs
¹/₃ cup plus 2 teaspoons honey
¹/₃ cup heavy cream

1. Trim the tough outer layers from the lemongrass stalks, then slice the core. In a small saucepan over medium-high heat, combine the milk and lemongrass, stirring, until small bubbles form, 5 minutes. Let cool, stirring often, for 20 minutes. Cover and refrigerate for at least 1¹/₂ hours or up to overnight.

2. Preheat the oven to 350°F. In a bowl, whisk together the eggs and the ¹/₃ cup honey until well blended. Strain the milk mixture into the egg mixture (discard the lemongrass) and whisk again. Divide the custard among six 5-ounce ramekins.

3. Set the ramekins in a 9-by-13-inch baking dish. Pull out the oven rack halfway and put the baking dish on the rack. Pour boiling water into the baking dish to come halfway up the sides of the ramekins. Carefully slide the rack into place. Bake until the custards jiggle only slightly when ramekins are gently shaken, about 30 minutes.

4. Using a wide metal spatula, transfer the ramekins to a cooling rack. Let cool for at least 15 minutes.

5. In a bowl, whisk together the cream and the remaining 2 teaspoons honey until thick. Serve the custards warm or chilled, with spoonfuls of cream on top.

MAKE AHEAD Cover tightly and refrigerate for up to 1 day.

PER SERVING: 184 cal., 45% (83 cal.) from fat; 5 g protein; 9.2 g fat (5.1 g sat.); 22 g carbo (0.04 g fiber); 64 mg sodium; 97 mg chol.

HERB BLOSSOMS ON THE TABLE

One of the loveliest aspects of growing your own herbs is that you have access to their flowers, which you rarely see in grocery stores because they are so fragile. Even farmers' markets can have trouble keeping them fresh. When herbs are a few feet from your kitchen door, you can pick them minutes before you need them and scatter the blossoms over salads or soups. (They taste like the herbs themselves, only spicier.)

Beyond cooking, the blossoms make unusual, fragrant bouquets for your table, and because they are short, they don't block the view of diners sitting across from each other. We like to put bunches of them, along with the leafy sprigs, in small glasses all over the table.

2. In a saucepan, bring ¹/₂ cup water to a boil. Remove from the heat and stir in the honey. Pour into a bowl and chill until cold. Strain into the melon puree.

3. Freeze in an ice cream maker according to the manufacturer's directions. Serve immediately.

PER ¹/₂-CUP SERVING 87 cal., 5% (4.5 cal.) from fat; 1.6 g protein; 0.5 g fat (0.1 g sat.); 22 g carbo (1.4 g fiber); 17 mg sodium; 0 mg chol.

PEPPERMINT-LEMONGRASS TISANES

Herbal infusions, or *tisanes* (the French term), make a soothing, caffeine-free finish to dinner. We paired this zingy mentholated one with our melon sorbet (at left), and liked the way it brought out the ripe flavors of the fruit. This is an especially enjoyable tisane to make, because the peppermint leaves release an intoxicating aroma as you crush them. You can use ordinary spearmint, but it won't be nearly as fragrant.

MAKES 8 servings TIME about 10 minutes

12 stalks lemongrass
6 cups loosely packed peppermint sprigs, plus 8 small
    sprigs or leaves
2 tablespoons honey (optional)

1. Bring 8 cups water to a boil in a medium pot over high heat. Meanwhile, peel 2 or 3 tough outer layers off each lemongrass stalk, then mash the core with a meat mallet or the bottom of a small, heavy frying pan. Cut the stalks into 2-inch lengths.

2. Remove the boiling water from the heat, add the lemongrass, cover, and steep for 2 minutes. Crush the 6 cups mint sprigs in your hands and add to the pot. Re-cover and let steep for 5 to 8 minutes.

3. Pour through a strainer into a large, heatproof pitcher and stir in the honey. Divide among 8 small tea glasses or cups and top each serving with a mint sprig.

MAKE AHEAD The tisane can be made through step 2 a day ahead; once strained, cover and refrigerate. Reheat to a simmer before serving (don't allow it to boil).

PER 1-CUP SERVING 61 cal., 15% (9 cal.) from fat; 4.5 g protein; 1 g fat (0.3 g sat.); 12 g carbo (fiber n/a); 41 mg sodium; 0 mg chol.

❋ WATERMELON, CANTALOUPE, OR HONEYDEW SORBET

This sorbet is only as good as your melon, so use the best fruit you can find (or grow). We especially loved the flavor of our sweet, honeyed 'Ambrosia' cantaloupes in this sorbet, but the greenish 'Sharlyn' melons and 'Sugar Baby' watermelons were good too. The sorbet is best when eaten as soon as possible after freezing, because the lack of refined sugar makes it turn icy as it sits in the freezer. The good news is that any leftover sorbet makes an excellent granita: Turn it into a square baking pan, rake it with a fork until fluffy, cover, and freeze. To serve, let the granita sit at room temperature for 5 minutes, then rerake with the fork until fluffy.

MAKES 1 quart, or 8 servings TIME about 1 hour, plus at least 20 minutes in an ice cream maker

8 to 10 cups ripe cantaloupe, honeydew, or watermelon
    chunks (1-inch chunks)
3 tablespoons honey

1. Whirl the melon in a blender or food processor until smooth. Pour into a bowl, cover, and chill until cold.

SUMMER PRESERVED

Throughout the summer, we put up some of what we'd grown, to make cooking more exciting for the rest of the year. Four tools were our best friends in these undertakings:

1. **A boiling-water canner** You can use the canner for tomatoes and for jams and lots of other preserves. Use it once and it's no longer intimidating.

2. **A dehydrator** Haul out that 1970s dehydrator (or go get a new one) and put it to work. It's the coolest and most efficient way to dry herbs and chiles, and you can use it to dessicate any fruit or vegetable into a fine snack for hiking or biking. The dehydrator is ridiculously simple to use: Cut up your food, spread it on the dehydrator tray, and plug in the dehydrator. During the next day or two, your food will dry in a gentle waft of warm, recirculating air, without a chance of molding or bug infestation.

3. **The freezer** We forget that the freezer can be a second pantry for fruits and vegetables. The two main tips we can give you: Pack your food into doubled resealable plastic bags or an airtight sturdy plastic container to prevent freezer burn, and label the bag or container with the contents and the date. We always think we'll recognize a food down the road, and then find ourselves puzzling over dark, icy blobs, wondering what they are and how long they've been in the freezer.

4. **A "root cellar"** This is in quotes because we don't actually *have* a root cellar. Few Californians—or anyone living in a warm place—do. If you live in a cold climate and have a basement, the basement will work. For specifics on this, we recommend the excellent and venerable *Root Cellaring,* by Mike and Nancy Bubel (Storey Communications, Inc., 1979, 1991), and *The Complete Root Cellar Book*, by Steve Maxwell and Jennifer Mackenzie (Robert Rose, 2010). To see what we used instead to store our potatoes (essential for year-round cooking), refer to "Our Makeshift Root Cellar," page 82.

Clockwise from top right: dried poblano (ancho) chiles; canned 'Marvel Stripe' tomatoes; dried corn; dried peppermint; dried rosemary; dried flageolet beans; dried serrano chiles

We wanted to preserve our onions and garlic, too, because they are also indispensable in year-round cooking, but unfortunately we grew the wrong varieties for long-term storage. So, after the last onions and garlic were eaten in the fall, we had to buy them for winter and spring, because frankly we can't cook without them. We will plant at least two varieties next time—one each for "keeping."

CANNED HEIRLOOM TOMATOES

Can your own ripe tomatoes, and you'll thank yourself all winter long for bottling up the essence of summer. For this easy recipe, adapted from the "USDA Complete Guide to Home Canning" (www.uga.edu/nchfp/index.html), you just squish raw skinned tomatoes into jars. This cold-pack technique may cause the fruit and liquid to separate a bit during processing, but the results still taste delicious.

When working with tomatoes, it's essential for food safety that you acidify them as noted in the recipe, and that you do not increase the amount of herbs or add any other ingredients. Look for canning jars, rings, and lids in a hardware store or a well-stocked grocery store.

MAKES 6 to 7 quarts TIME about 3 hours

17 pounds ripe red or yellow heirloom tomatoes
14 tablespoons lemon juice*
7 teaspoons fine sea salt (optional)
7 sprigs thyme, each 3 to 4 inches long (optional)

1. Fill a 20-quart boiling-water canner half full with water. Set the rack so it rests on the pan rim, cover, and bring the water to steaming over high heat. While the water is heating, wash 7 wide-mouthed quart jars, screw rings, and flat lids in hot, soapy water and rinse and drain. Nest the lids inside the rings, place in a medium saucepan, and cover with water. Heat until small bubbles form (do not boil). Remove the pan from the heat, cover the pan, and set aside until the lids and rings are needed. No need to dry before using.

2. Meanwhile, peel the tomatoes: Fill a large saucepan three-fourths full of water and bring to a boil over high heat. Add only enough tomatoes to make a single layer and leave them in the water just until the skins split and will peel easily with a knife, 20 to 40 seconds. Using a slotted spoon, lift out the tomatoes and let cool until they can be handled. Working over a bowl to catch the juices, core the tomatoes, pull off the skins, and trim any browned areas. Repeat with the remaining tomatoes.

3. Put 2 tablespoons lemon juice and 1 teaspoon salt into each jar. Add the tomatoes to the jars, cutting them first if needed to make them fit. Push down on the tomatoes to ensure a compact fit, making sure the tomatoes are covered with juice and leaving 1/2-inch headspace. If the tomatoes are not covered with juice, add the juice from the bowl as needed to cover. Using the handle of a fork, poke 1 thyme sprig down the side of each jar. Release air bubbles by gently running a table knife around the inside of jars. Wipe the rim of each jar clean with a damp cloth. They must be clean for the lids to seal.

4. With tongs, lift the rings and lids from the hot water. Center a flat lid on each jar, making sure the sealing

OUR MAKESHIFT ROOT CELLAR

We planned how to store our spuds with help from Greg Lutovsky, who owns Irish Eyes Garden Seeds in Washington State and specializes in potatoes.

First, choose unbruised, unblemished potatoes for storing. After harvest (see page 35 for tips on how to harvest), let the potatoes cure, spread out in a single layer, at room temperature in a dark, well-ventilated place for about 2 weeks. This will toughen their skins and make them last longer.

Arrange the potatoes in single layers in slatted stackable boxes (we used clear acrylic letter trays from an office supply store). Slide the boxes into a clean, empty fridge set to between 40° and 42°F. The beat-up old "extra" fridge some people have in their garages is great for this. (Don't store apples or alliums like garlic, onions, or shallots in the same space, adds Lutovsky, because all of them emit ethylene gas, which will make the potatoes sprout.) Unscrew the fridge's lightbulb, so the potatoes don't develop toxins (which they do if exposed to light).

Besides cold temperatures and complete darkness, storage potatoes like extremely humid conditions—in the neighborhood of 90 percent; otherwise, they shrivel. To boost moisture, put a couple of wide deep pans filled with water next to the potatoes. Also, remove the shelf that covers the crisper drawers and fill the drawers with water. To monitor the humidity and temperature inside the fridge, set a combination hygrometer (moisture meter) and thermometer on a shelf. It costs about $10 at a hardware store.

The last requirement: ventilation. Set a small desk fan on one of the fridge's shelves to keep the air circulating. Plug the fan's power cord into an electrical socket near or behind the fridge (the fridge shuts easily over the cord). Refill the water once a week or so. The potatoes should last for at least 3 months and, depending on variety and your maintenance of the storage conditions, up to 6.

compound is resting on the jar rim. Screw the metal rings on firmly, but do not overtighten.

5. Put the jars on the canner rack and lower the rack into the water. The water should cover the jars by at least 1 inch. If necessary, add more hot water now and during processing. Cover the canner, bring the water to a boil, then boil for 1 hour and 25 minutes (add 5 minutes for every 3,000 feet in altitude above sea level). The jars may leak a little; this is okay.

6. Turn off the heat and let the jars stand in the water in the canner for 5 minutes. Line a work surface with kitchen towels. Then, using the tongs and a hot pad, lift the rack with the jars onto the edge of the canner. With a jar lifter or hot pads, remove the jars from the rack and set them upright on the towels. Do not tighten the rings. Let the jars cool completely at room temperature. You may hear a satisfying "ping" as the lids form a vacuum seal.

7. Press on the center of each lid. If it stays down, the jar is sealed; if it pops up, it isn't. You can still eat the tomatoes if the seal did not form, but you have to keep the jar refrigerated and finish its contents fairly quickly (within a week). Remove the rings. Wipe the jars and lids with a clean, damp cloth. Replace the rings, if you like.

8. Label the jars and store in a cool, dark place for up to 1 year.

* *The USDA recommends that you acidify tomatoes with bottled ReaLemon lemon juice, which has a standardized acidity of pH 2.5, or that you use 1/2 tsp. citric acid (Fruit Fresh) per quart jar instead of lemon juice. We used juice from our own lemons, but tested the pH using acid test strips (0 to 2.5 pH range) from www.indigo.com to verify that the pH was 2.5.*

PER 1/2-CUP SERVING 23 cal., 10% (2.4 cal.) from fat; 1.1 g protein; 0.26 g fat (0.04 g sat.); 5.2 g carbo (1.5 g fiber); 7.1 mg sodium; 0 mg chol.

DRIED HERBS

Preserving your herb harvest is as simple as hanging up bunches and waiting for them to air-dry, or, even simpler, spreading the sprigs on racks and drying them in a dehydrator for several hours. They will keep for a year.

TO AIR-DRY

Immerse the herbs in a sinkful of water and give them a good rinse. Shake off as much water as you can (you may want to go outside for this). Tie handful-size bunches at the cut end with kitchen string, leaving some string hanging.

Select a spot away from the sun (which will darken the herbs) and dust to hang the bunches. We used thumbtacks to attach them by their strings to walls around the office. Also, leave enough space for air to flow freely around each bunch. The herbs are ready when the leaves are completely dry and crumbly, 1 to 2 weeks. Some herbs may darken; this will not affect the flavor.

Working over a large bowl, strip the leaves from the stalks, discarding the stalks and allowing the leaves to drop into the bowl. Sort through the bowl and remove any stems. Crumble the leaves with your hands. (Chives are a little more difficult to crumble; you may need to chop them.) Pack into airtight containers and store at room temperature in a dark place for up to 1 year.

TO DRY IN A DEHYDRATOR

Rinse the herbs and shake them dry in the same way as for air-drying. Break off and discard any large stems. Arrange the herbs in a single layer (do not crowd them, or they will take longer to dry) on one or more dehydrator trays, and dehydrate until dry and crumbly, 8 to 24 hours. Store as directed for air-dried herbs.

DRIED CHILES

For spicing up our cooking all year, we relied heavily on dried serrano and poblano chiles, picked from our bushes when fully ripe and at their fruitiest. Rinse the chiles and pat them dry before using either of the following methods.

TO AIR-DRY

Using a needle and strong thread (fishing line works well, too), pierce red, fully ripe chiles through the base of the stem and space out along the length of your thread. (The beautiful New Mexican *ristra* style—chiles threaded so they overlap—works well in that state's arid climate, but in more humid areas, the chiles rot.) Leave enough thread on either end to tie to shelving or some other support, so the chiles hang like a necklace. Hang the necklace in a well-ventilated spot out of the sun and let the chiles dry until they have withered. Serranos are ready when they are brittle, at least 2 weeks. Poblanos (called anchos in their dried state) should be taken down when they are evenly darkened, fully wrinkled, and leathery but still supple, 2 to 3 weeks. Put both types in airtight containers. They will keep, stored at room temperature, for up to several months.

TO DRY IN A DEHYDRATOR

Arrange rinsed, dried whole chiles in a single layer on one or more dehydrator trays. Because poblanos are thick, you may have to invert the tray above them for the first day to accommodate their girth. Once they have shrunk, you can stack the trays normally. Dehydrate the serranos until they are brittle, 1 to 2 days. The anchos should be leathery but still supple, which will take 2 days.

DRIED CORN

We ate most of our corn fresh off the cob, but dried some of it for use later in the year (we put it into stuffed poblano chiles, page 142). Using a dehydrator (page 81) is the simplest and fastest approach.

Remove the husks and silk from the ears. Cut each ear into 2-inch lengths and set the pieces in a single layer on

the dehydrator trays. Dehydrate until just dried, about 36 hours. Rub the dried kernels off the ears.

Two ears will yield about 1 1/4 cups fresh kernels or 1/3 cup dried kernels. Store the dried kernels in airtight containers at room temperature for up to several months.

PER 1/4-CUP SERVING 150 cal., 12% (18 cal.) from fat; 4 g protein; 2 g fat (0 g sat.); 31 g carbo (6 g fiber); 15 mg sodium; 0 mg chol.

ROASTED POBLANOS FOR THE FREEZER

When chiles are in season, we like to roast lots of them and stash them away in bags in the freezer. Then when we want to make chiles rellenos, a salsa, or a stew, we just pull out a bag. We freeze the chiles whole with the seeds, so they can be prepped in a number of different ways.

MAKES 8 roasted chiles TIME about 45 minutes

8 poblano chiles, about 2 pounds total

1. Preheat the broiler. Put the chiles on a rimmed baking sheet lined with aluminum foil. Place in the broiler about 4 inches from the heat source and broil, turning as needed, until blackened all over, at least 15 minutes.

2. Remove the poblanos from the broiler, cover with a kitchen towel, and let cool until they can be handled. Gently pull off and discard the blackened skins. Let the chiles cool completely, then arrange them in a single layer in a 1-gallon resealable plastic bag. Seal the bag closed, pressing out the air. Seal the first bag in a second bag.

3. Freeze for up to 6 months.

PER CHILE 33 cal., 45% (15 cal.) from fat; 1.7 g protein; 0.17 g fat (0.02 g sat.); 7.8 g carbo (1.2 g fiber); 5.8 mg sodium; 0 mg chol.

SLOW-ROASTED TOMATOES FOR THE FREEZER

These slow-roasted tomatoes freeze well and add deep, tomatoey flavor to any dish long after summer has gone. Any variety or size of tomatoes will work, but in our climate, tomatoes seldom get much bigger than 3 inches in diameter. Roast tomatoes of the same size together so they cook evenly.

MAKES 8 cups TIME about 8 hours

10 pounds tomatoes
1/2 cup extra virgin olive oil
3 cloves garlic, finely chopped
2 teaspoons fine sea salt
1/4 cup chopped fresh oregano

1. Preheat the oven to 250°F. Core all tomatoes except cherry tomatoes. Cut small tomatoes in half, keep cherry tomatoes whole, and cut medium and large tomatoes into 1 1/2-inch-thick wedges. Arrange the tomatoes, cut side up and packed tightly together, on rimmed nonreactive or aluminum foil–lined baking sheets.

2. In a small bowl, mix the oil and garlic, then drizzle over the tomatoes. Sprinkle with the salt and oregano.

3. Roast the tomatoes, switching the pans to a different oven rack every 2 hours, until they have wrinkled and shrunk by more than half but are still slightly moist, 6 to 8 hours. If roasting cherry tomatoes, begin checking after 5 hours.

4. Let the tomatoes cool completely, then transfer to a sturdy airtight container and store in the refrigerator for up to 1 week or in the freezer for up to 5 months.

PER 1/4-CUP SERVING 54 cal., 59% (32 cal.) from fat; 1.2 g protein; 3.8 g fat (0.54 g sat.); 5.2 g carbo (1.6 g fiber); 147 mg sodium; 0 mg chol.

SPOTLIGHT: COMMODITIES

	Type	YTD	1 Yr	5 Yr	Ratio	(mil $)	Fund Name (Ticker)
	SH	+12.2	-4.8	+5.5	0.29	10,891	**LEADERS**
	SN	+21.5	-37.0	+1.8	0.74	7,843	Dryden Financial Serv
	EE	+23.7	-27.2	+14.7	0.28	5,917	First Small Cap Financial
	LO	+5.6	-8.4	+9.0	1.11	5,233	Tocqueville Gold (TGLDX)
	SP	+49.8	-31.1	+16.3	0.66	4,214	Dreyfus Commodity Trends
	SN	+30.3	-33.1	+19.9	0.30	3,066	First Eagle Gold A (SGGDX)
	LO	+2.9	-27.8	+2.8	0.94	2,829	OCM Gold (OCMGX)
	SR	+12.3	-29.2	+0.7	0.21	2,821	JPMorgan Market Neutral Instl (JMNIX)
	SP	+18.4	+10.4	+18.3	0.86	2,470	Franklin Gold and Precious Metals Adv (FGADX)
	SN	+50.4	-35.4		1.40	2,412	USAA Precious Metals and Minerals (USAGX)
	ST	+9.5	-5.2	+9.9	1.52	2,309	Rivernouse Precious Metals & Mining A (RPMIX)
	SU	+12.4	-31.4	+7.3	0.81	2,281	Fidelity Select Gold (FSAGX)
	ST	+48.9	-11.1	+3.7	1.00	2,137	Evergreen Precious Metals A (EGNAX)
	SR	+12.8	-30.5	-0.2	0.88	1,975	
	SN	-2.3	-0.4		NA	1,711	**LAGGARDS**
	SH	+21.1	-9.9	+7.5	0.86	1,948	Oppenheimer Commodity Strat Total Ret (QRACX)
	ST	+29.2	-5.4	+9.9	1.32	1,931	Guinness Atkinson Alternative Energy (GAAEX)
	EE	+28.1	-38.2	+11.8	0.83	1,914	Fidelity Select Energy Service (FSESX)
	SU	+20.9	-15.6	+12.1	1.04	1,734	BlackRock Energy & Resources Inv C (SSGDX)
	SP	+11.2	-30.2	+0.2	0.33	1,710	Fidelity Advisor Energy C (FANCX)
	LO	+5.9	+2.9	+4.3	1.47	1,661	Fidelity Select Energy (FSENX)
	SR	+12.5	-30.9	+0.7	0.75	1,651	SSgA Tuckerman Active REIT (SSREX)
	SP	+13.3	+1.4	+19.5	1.19	1,551	American Century Real Estate A (AREEX)
							U.S. Global Investors Global Res (PSPFX)
			+27.8	-16.2	+5.0		PIMCO Commodity Real Ret Strat B (PCRBX)
			364	364	329		PIMCO Real Estate Real Return Strategy (PR...)
							Spirit of America Real Estate Inc & Gr (SOA...)

BM-Real Market **CD**-Consumer Discretionary. **CC**-Consu...
EE-... **ID**-Equity Energy **IM**-Commodities Indu...
SN-... **SP**-Equity Precious Metals **SR**-Real Esta...

MORE PRICES AND ANALYSIS

Existing Home Prices
Median, in thousands
of dollars

July '09   178.3
June '09   181.4

...plus bonds, mutual funds, commoditi...
nytimes.com/markets

FALL

Our cornstalks were dried out and toppling over. The lovely trombetta zucchini vine had just a few withered fruits left. The pattypans, so verdant and green a month before, had splotchy mildew all over their leaves, and we'd all eaten way too many squashes—even the chickens were sick of them. It was time to move past summer.

Johanna Silver, our new test-garden coordinator, waded into the pattypan patch one late August day and started vigorously ripping out the monster vines. A former city kid from Denver, she's a girl who loves the physical exercise of gardening, and she threw her whole body into it. By the end of the day, a big swath of the garden had been cleared, ready to be planted with new crops for our fall feast.

This time the Food and Garden teams had formed a plan well in advance. In went seeds and seedlings for radicchio and fennel, to be thrown on the grill for a salad; plenty of sage, because it is indispensable in fall cooking; Swiss chard, for the same reason; and squat, juicy little cipollini onions, as a backup for our already-harvested 'Spanish White' onions. (We had discovered, belatedly, that this variety—and our sweet, juicy 'Spanish Roja' garlic—weren't the right kind for storing, and had both of them stashed away in a cool, dry spot, hoping they would survive long enough to use for the dinner.) I tried to persuade Team Garden to plant more garlic, but it just couldn't be done. If it were started now, in late summer for a fall harvest, the cloves wouldn't form.

Some crops, needing a longer spell in warm weather, had already been planted: Three kinds of beans, to be shelled and dried, and a butternut squash vine. Along with our cipollini onions, they would go into a big vegetable cassoulet-type dish, our main course. Johanna had the brilliant idea of planting quinoa, one of the fabled "ancient grains" of the Andes, and now it stood in a thick patch about five feet tall, with colossal yellow-orange seedheads. It was close to our grapevine, and looking at them together inspired our first course: quinoa-stuffed grape leaves! The quinoa would be cooked with raisins from the same grapevine, of course. This made us instantly want to have nuts, to add to the stuffing, but we had not a single nut tree on the grounds. Even if we bought a baby tree immediately, it would take years to bear fruit. Nuts seemed crucial to a fall feast, so we added

The One-Block Fall Feast

Quinoa Bites with Walnut Romesco (page 138)
Pickled Cocktail Mushrooms and Onions (page 137)
Creamy Flageolet Dip with Red Pepper Sticks (page 139)

❖

Grilled Radicchio and Fennel Salad with Apples and Toasted Walnuts (page 141)
Butternut Squash Gnocchi with Chard and Sage Brown Butter (page 145)

❖

Cheese platter: Gouda and feta with fresh honeycomb, walnuts, pineapple guava slices, Last-Minute Pineapple Guava Preserves (page 155), and Whole-Wheat Rosemary Shortbreads (page 149)
Honey Ice Cream (page 150)

❖

Chardonnay (page 110)

---

walnuts to our list of "imports" and hoped we could soon plant a couple of our own trees.

Apples also seemed indispensable for a fall menu. We did have a dwarf apple tree, but it had pooped out the year before and was still standing around doing nothing. So apples went on the imports list, too.

We chose to use them in salad instead of in something sweet, because we had a grand plan for dessert. Fabulous, nectarlike Calimyrna figs grew on one straggly old vine near our test kitchen. We'd dry them at their peak, in September, and simmer them with our raisins in a Syrah syrup, until they turned into a dark, velvety, sophisticated compote, which we would lavish with dollops of homemade crème fraîche.

❖

With our menu set and our garden growing, we figured we might as well take Team Cheese to the next level. After our bumbling experiments with making cheese from a book, we needed expert help. We found it at Bellwether Farms, in the rolling, green hills of Sonoma County. In Bellwether's warm, milk-scented cheese-making room, Liam Callahan showed us how to turn milk into ricotta, one of the glories of Italian gastronomy. We saw how

gently he handled the curds to make them fat and fluffy, using nothing more than vinegar (although we would use lemon juice), salt, and heat. We spooned up the sweet new ricotta right out of the mold, and tried to commit its taste and texture to memory—our cheese lodestar.

At Cowgirl Creamery, up in cool, foggy Marin county, co-owner Sue Conley and cheese maker Jonathan White explained how to make their award-winning fromage blanc, a luxuriously smooth, rich, spreadable cheese that can be used umpteen ways in cooking. It was a breakthrough for us. Mysterious ingredients that only real cheese makers seemed to understand, like cheese culture and rennet, were just ingredients, we realized. They were no harder to add to milk than cocoa, although it took longer to taste and see their full effects.

These lessons inspired us to go even further. We pored through home cheese-making catalogs and bought cheese molds, a few different types of cultures, our own little bottle of rennet, and even a small cheese press. In a fit of ambition, we decided we would do a full-out cheese course for our fall feast and make Gouda and feta. Each of these took several days to finish (and the Gouda then had to age for months). It took many tests to get them both right, which led to our coining a new term: cheese slave. Finally, we managed to produce cheeses that tasted surprisingly good, like actual, bona fide Gouda and feta, and our pride blocked out our pain.

✤

Our gorgeous eggs, on which we had come to be utterly dependent, would, of course, be a main ingredient in our fall feast. Then, suddenly, the chickens stopped laying. Not only that, they were shedding feathers like crazy. The infamous annual chicken molt had arrived.

Once a year, usually when the weather starts to turn cold, chickens drop their old feathers to make way for strong new ones, and their energies go into producing feathers, not eggs. This went on for several weeks, threatening to leave us eggless for our dinner. Plus, the chickens looked freaky, as though they had been mauled. So many feathers were strewn around the coop that Jim, our Team Chicken leader, said it looked like the scene of a pillow fight.

We had an even bigger chicken drama to deal with, though. Nugget, our adopted chick, had gotten nasty, nipping at us when we came into the coop. Nugget's red feathers had grown unusually long and glistening. Nugget had a suspicious upright stance. . . . We hadn't heard

Nugget the rooster

actual crowing yet, but Johanna, who had been in charge of chickens at a farm, said it out loud: "Guys, Nugget is a dude."

That meant we had to get rid of him. Roosters are illegal in our city, as they are in many others, because they're noisy. And even if keeping Nugget hadn't been against the law, we knew he had to go. We couldn't handle an explosion of chicks.

Some of us on Team Chicken voted for eating him, in time-honored chicken-raising fashion. Plus, as Elizabeth pointed out, we publish chicken-dinner recipes in the magazine all the time. "If we're chicken eaters, why not eat this chicken?" But others argued that we weren't exactly running a farm, that Nugget had a name, and we should find him a home.

We tried, we really did, but had zero luck. Finally, we decided to take him to the feed store where we had bought our chicks. We'd noticed cages of half-grown roosters there, and the clerk had said that sometimes people "adopted" them. Sure, it was a euphemism, but we had no choice. To the feed store he would go.

I wrote about our decision on our one-block blog, and late one night, when Nugget was groggy and unsuspecting, my valiant boyfriend, Peter—who'd dealt with roosters at his grandparents' farm—and I crept into the coop and nudged Nugget into a big, sturdy box. We taped it and left him boxed up till dawn—and his ride to the feed store.

That morning, I happened to check my e-mail before hopping in the car. A woman named Tina had sent me an urgent message. She had read my blog post and was aghast. Her e-mail sat atop a chain of other e-mails from bird rescuers all around the Bay Area, discussing how to save Nugget. It was amazing. Upshot: Tina urged me to call a number in San Juan Bautista, belonging to a person who would possibly take Nugget.

So I did, and the very next day, Nugget was off to an entirely different fate. He rode south to join an extended family of other rescuees: emus; chinchillas; a hedgehog; many, many rabbits; and about thirty other roosters who lived in a fenced-in orchard, eating bugs, and—due apparently to the absence of hens—not ripping one another to shreds. It was too good to be true.

And it got even better. When Nugget's new owner extracted him from the box, he behaved so beautifully (possibly stunned by the car ride?) that she decided to put him with her own backyard flock of hens. So Nugget, twice rescued, ended up with a harem.

While Nugget began his new, charmed life, our luck had turned sour in the garden. The perfectly ripe, green-gold Calimyrna figs had been gobbled up by squirrels, right through the bird netting. In other words, those cursed fur-balls ate our dessert. It is hard to dream about a dish for weeks on end and then have it chewed to bits in one day.

Then the mother of one of our interns came for a tour of the garden. A discerning cook of Palestinian and Syrian background, she nibbled a grape leaf from our vine, since it was an ingredient she knew well—and immediately spat it out. Apparently, we should have picked in spring, when the leaves were tender and sweet, rather than waiting till fall, when they were leathery and disgusting. Also, the grapes, which we had imagined would automatically turn into plump raisins, had molded. Good-bye, first course.

Team Kitchen had an emergency powwow. Instead of our figgy compote, we would use what we had lots of—honey—and make ice cream. Then, to replace our stuffed grape leaves, we decided to create a trio of appetizers—which lacked only one ingredient: mushrooms.

And so Team Mushroom was born. The easiest and quickest way to get a good variety of fungi is to order "logs," which we soon discovered looked like misshapen loaves of bread. Mainly they were sawdust and bran, held together with threadlike mycelium, the main body of the mushroom.

Within a week of their arrival, our logs sprouted a miniforest of oyster, shiitake, and poofy, white pom pom mushrooms. It was immensely gratifying. "When I have a kid and he needs a science project that works, I'm getting one of these," said Brianne McElhiney, assistant to the editor-in-chief. She became the main mushroom-log caretaker, and whenever she went on vacation, the logs would send up crazy, deformed shapes—almost as if they sensed her absence.

Spooky or no, mushrooms cast an undeniable spell. Once we began to learn about them, we felt as though we had gone down a rabbit hole and emerged in the marvelous world of fungi. Did you know that the largest organism on earth is a four-square-mile fungus in eastern Oregon? And that it is at least twenty-four hundred years old? These were the kinds of factoids we now sprinkled into party conversation.

When we found morel spawn for sale, we couldn't resist. Morels are incomparably tasty and usually harvested wild. If we could grow them, well, that would be

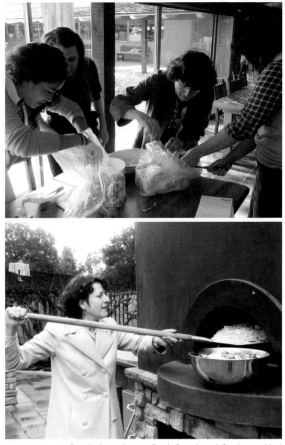

Top: Mushroom harvest (logs); Scooping ash for the morel bed

close to miraculous. Elaine Johnson, our associate food editor, serious mushroom-lover, and co-captain of Team Mushroom, guided the adventure. In a damp patch of soil near the redwood trees, we dug in the spongy white threads—essentially the baby fungus, from which morels would soon sprout like crazy, we hoped. We would get morels in anywhere from three months to two years, said the seller. We fed the bed with a steady diet of fresh compost and Elaine tenderly showered it with ash from the pizza oven, and we waited. It's been six months, and so far *nada*, but we are patient. Perhaps also a tiny bit obsessed.

❖

Besides the butternut squash, we had one other phenomenally successful crop: our 'Nugget' hop vine, which had shot right up its fourteen-foot trellis over the summer and then sideways, too. It hadn't been ready to pick for our summer beer, but was now loaded with pale green flowers. We picked pounds of the slightly sticky blossoms, dried them, and stashed them in the freezer until we were ready to make beer again.

The other components of our beer were wheat and barley. Earlier in the summer, we had harvested what was left of both after the squirrels had ripped through, and, since we had already made a backup beer, spread the stalks of grain on a tarp inside to fully dry. Now it was time to thresh, an ancient and picturesque-sounding activity that brings to mind charming villagers rhythmically beating golden sheaves of grain against stone floors.

We couldn't have been less picturesque if we had tried. To thresh properly, you have to convince each tiny grain to let go not only of the stalk, which isn't so hard, but also of the papery envelope—the chaff—that tightly encloses it. Nothing we did, not rubbing the grains together in a bowl or mashing them against the bottom of a perforated bucket, seemed to loosen the envelopes. (Then again, we hadn't actually gotten around to researching how to thresh; there was so little left, after the squirrels' rampage, that it seemed easier to just wing it.) Stephanie Dean, our test-kitchen coordinator, bent over her portion of wheat and barley at her desk, peeling the envelope from each

Threshing quinoa

seed. Then she took it home and talked her relatives into helping. It was torture.

As we were thinking that perhaps what we should have done was bag up the grain and whack it like a piñata, or maybe run it over with a car, we found out—from a grain historian who threshes her own heritage wheat—that we should have put the seedheads in a large, strong sack and then danced the twist on it with rubber-soled shoes. Seriously. If you don't have an actual threshing machine, the twist is the way to go. Afterward, the winnowing—getting rid of the bits of envelope—is relatively easy, and we had done it correctly, more or less: You let the grains fall into a bowl in a light breeze, and the breeze whisks away the chaff. The picturesque villager would have a broad woven winnowing basket, for tossing the grain. We had metal mixing bowls, but it still worked.

In the end, we had about three pounds of wheat and barley combined, ready to be stored until we made our next beer. If nothing else, it made us deeply appreciate the people who grow our grains and mill them into flour.

Compared to the wheat and barley, the quinoa was a cinch to thresh. We just stripped the dusty dried seeds (blessedly unenclosed by papery envelopes) off the seedheads into bags. Then, on the advice of Seeds of Change, who sold us our quinoa to plant, we figured out a better way to winnow. In the test kitchen, we draped a big sheet over some chairs and a table to create a kind of giant catcher's mitt, positioned a small fan opposite it, and put a baking pan in front of the fan. Then we rubbed handfuls of the quinoa in midair above the baking sheet. The wind blew the chaff into the sheet and the heavier seeds fell onto the baking pan—more or less. We had to winnow each batch a few times to get it completely clean, but it did work. The kitchen acquired a fine layer of quinoa dust, however. Next time, we'll do it outside.

❖

By early October, well past the usual honey season, hive Veronica had produced nearly twenty more pounds of honey. This bonanza, after the twelve pounds we had collected in August, seemed remarkable, especially because new hives, just building up their colonies, often yield no honey at all their first year. The women of Team Bee were beaming as they carried in the heavy golden frames. Over the months, they had grown even more entranced by the bustling of the hives, by the way the bees took care of and communicated with one another—licking each other clean, for instance, and clustering around the queen on cold days to keep her warm. "I like the honey, but I like the bees better," said Margaret. Sometimes, when she was stressed, she would take not a coffee break but a bee break, and go out to sit with the hives for a while. Brianne, a new member of Team Bee, was so inspired that she set up her own hives at home. By this time, all three of them could point out the queen bees within a humming mass of workers in only a few seconds.

Kimberley deepened her bond with bees one day when she found one flying around inside the test kitchen. Not wanting any of our allergic coworkers to possibly be stung, she dipped a finger in honey—we were still processing the harvest, so had plenty sitting around—and held it out to the bee, who landed and began lapping it up. "I could feel a little tickle. She didn't move at all, and I was able to walk her out." The girl hand-fed a *bee*.

❖

It was mid-October now, and almost time for the feast. The hens had sprouted new feathers and resumed laying, so at least we had eggs. But we were having major problems with the main course. In the test kitchen, Amy Machnak had been doing her best to make a knockout vegetable cassoulet using all our pretty beans, plus mushrooms, peppers, squash, and onions. But no matter what she tried, it kept turning out gloppy. "It's just a big pot of mess!" she moaned. She abandoned cassoulet and experimented with individual potpies, draping a sort of biscuity wafer over each. They looked sweet, but did not taste exciting. She fooled around with a vegetable terrine next, but it didn't hold together. We realized we were trying to cram all our crops into a single dish, and we had to simplify. Time was running out.

With days to go, Amy focused on our garden savior, the butternut squash. From it she made a glowing orange gnocchi, lightened with the ricotta we had recently learned to make, and scattered with Swiss chard and the seeds from the squash, roasted till crunchy. The finishing touch: a drizzle of sage browned butter. It was delicious. Our menu had an anchor.

❖

This time, we set the table in our outdoor kitchen, at dusk. Candles twinkled down the center, and the light from inside the building shone onto us as we stood around in chatty clusters, eating tiny quinoa cakes with a spicy red pepper sauce, pickled mushrooms and onions, and a creamy dip made from the flageolet beans. We had our crisp Chardonnay again, but we were still waiting for the Syrah. It had tasted wild and thorny and not completely

drinkable when we'd sampled it a few days before. We were betting it would mellow by the time our next feast rolled around, though.

It felt so refreshing to be at the table not as seasoned coworkers who knew how to put out a magazine together, but as people who had collectively decided to make something happen, despite our not knowing how. Everything we ate—the grilled radicchio and fennel salad, Amy's triumphant gnocchi, the go-for-broke cheese platter, the rich honey ice cream—tasted great, but it meant so much more. Not that we were consciously thinking this (mostly we were just enjoying catching up with one another), but on some level we knew how much each bite had cost us, and also given us, and that made us happy.

THE FALL GARDEN

As with our summertime garden, most of the crops we planted for our fall menu thrive in a spot that gets full sun for at least 6 hours per day. Some plants, such as beans and winter squashes, are easily started from seed. Others, like peppers and tomatoes, fare better when started from nursery transplants. For planting tips, see page 11.

Bean 'Cannellini'

Most beans are frost-sensitive heat lovers, easy to grow from seed. Gardeners can choose from many types, but 'Cannellini' is one of our favorites. A mainstay in Italian cuisine, this pearly white bean, a cousin to the kidney bean, cooks up rich and meaty. It's wonderful in soups and stews, or all by itself with just a little olive oil and fresh herbs. The beans grow on bush plants to 26 inches tall.

DAYS TO HARVEST 85 days from seed.
HOW TO HARVEST Pick pods in the green "wax" stage to use fresh, and at the dried stage for shelling and storage. For dried beans (which was how we used them), let the pods completely dry out on the bush through October, then pick and shell.
SEED SOURCE Gourmet Seeds, www.gourmetseed.com.

Bean, Flageolet

This pretty little kidney-shaped, bush-type, pale green bean comes from southern France, where it is traditionally served with lamb. We used it for a creamy bean dip (page 139) and in a vegetarian shepherd's pie (page 186).

DAYS TO HARVEST 90 days from seed.
HOW TO HARVEST Pick these shelling beans in fall after the pods have matured and the leaves have dried and dropped off. For dried beans (which was how we used them), let the pods completely dry out on the bush through October, then pick and shell.
SEED SOURCE Seed Savers Exchange, www.seedsavers exchange.com.

'Scarlet Emperor' beans, freshly opened (right), 2 hours after opening (center), and dried (left).

ALL BEANS

BEST SITE Full sun and well-drained soil.
PLANTING AND CARE Sow seeds as soon as the soil is warm. Heavy seed leaves must push through the soil, so be sure the soil is reasonably loose and open.
For vining types: Insert poles 1 to 2 feet apart in rows, and sow seeds 1 inch deep and 1 to 3 inches apart. Or, sow along a sunny wall, fence, or trellis and train vines on a web of light string supported by wire or heavy twine.
For bush types: Plant seeds 1 inch deep and 1 to 3 inches apart, allowing 2 to 3 feet between rows. With both types, moisten the soil thoroughly before planting, then do not water again until the seedlings have emerged. Keep the soil moist throughout the growing season. Fertilize after the plants are in active growth and again when the pods start to form, working a 5-10-10 fertilizer into the soil along the row.

Bean 'Scarlet Emperor'

A stunner in the garden, this vine grows to 8 to 10 feet tall. Its scarlet-orange flowers give way to velvety green pods that turn plump and juicy as they grow to 8 inches long. The beans themselves are large, like big limas, and a shocking lipstick pink color that quickly darkens to purple.

DAYS TO HARVEST 75 days from seed.
HOW TO HARVEST To eat fresh, harvest when beans are fully formed and starting to pull away from the pod (you'll see the bulge of the developing bean through the shell) but before pods start to change color and the beans inside start to rattle when you shake them. Remove the beans from the pods and seal them in

FALL GARDEN PLAN

1. Pineapple guava
2. Fennel
3. Quinoa
4. Peppers and chiles
5. Beans
6. Parsley
7. Chives
8. Rosemary
9. Radicchio
10. Tomatoes
11. Cippolini onions
12. Swiss chard
13. Sage
14. Thyme
15. Oregano
16. Butternut squash
17. Lemon tree

10 feet

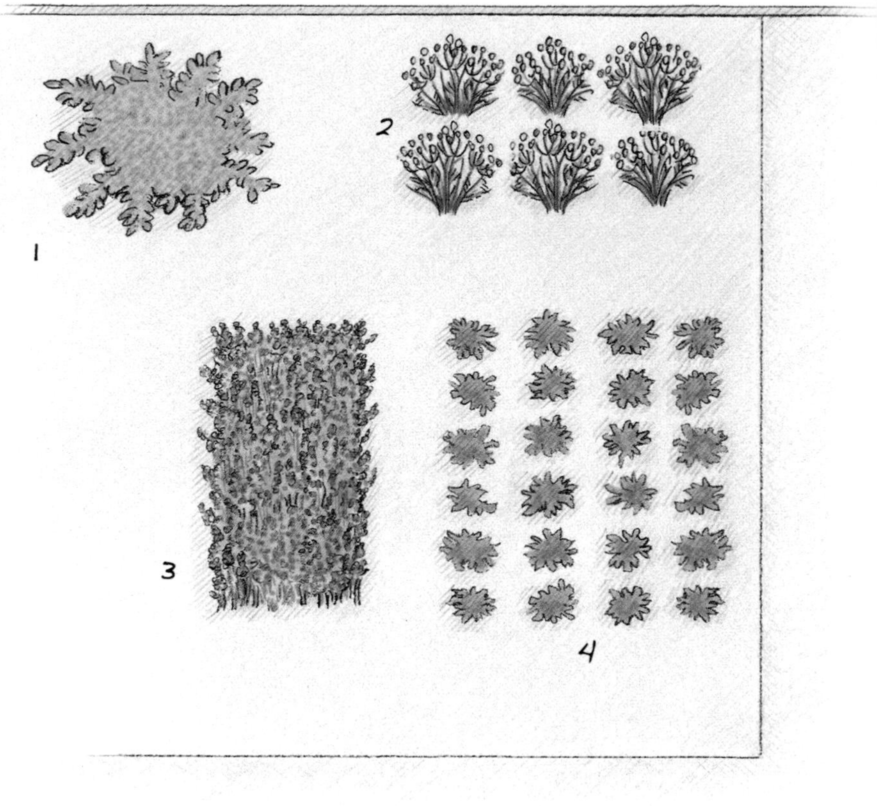

plastic bags to store in the refrigerator for 10 to 14 days (you can also freeze them for longer storage). For dried beans (which was how we used them), let the pods completely dry out on the bush through October, then pick and shell.

SEED SOURCE Territorial Seed Company, www.territorial seed.com.

Butternut Squash

Like all winter squashes, butternuts have a hard rind and a firm, dryish flesh. They are excellent for baking and store well, too. The plant pumps out delicious fruits on a tall vine, and it was by far our most successful fall crop. We loved how

pretty it looked, rambling up a sturdy metal arbor over a gravel path, with most of the fruits dangling downward like piñatas.

BEST SITE Full sun and rich, well-drained soil. Give the vine plenty of room to sprawl, unless you are training it up a trellis or arbor, as we did.

DAYS TO HARVEST 75 to 80 days from seed.

PLANTING AND CARE When soil temperatures warm to about 50°F, sow seeds directly in the ground 1 inch deep, spacing them 2 to 4 feet apart in rows. Or plant seeds on mounds or hills of soil about 8 to 12 inches across and 4 to 6 feet apart, spacing seeds on each hill 4 inches apart. Once plants reach 4 inches tall, thin to 3 seedlings per hill. Water at planting time,

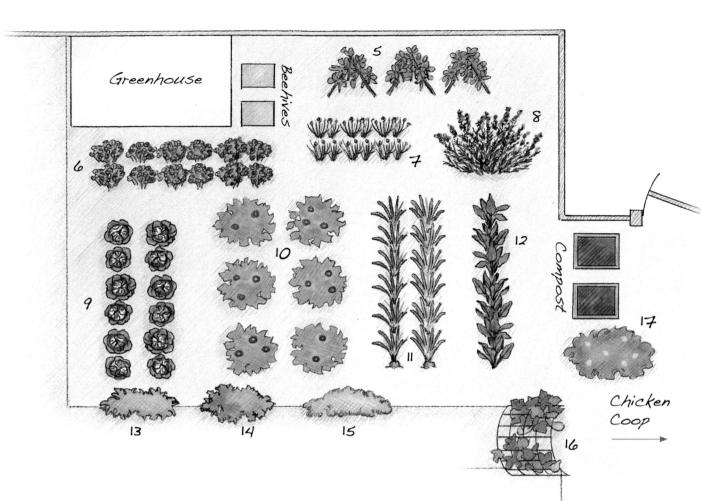

then every 2 or 3 days until seeds germinate. As the plants grow, give the roots plenty of water, but keep the leaves dry to avoid mildew. Feed the plant regularly by working a complete fertilizer into the soil around the mounds or along rows.

HOW TO HARVEST Allow a squash to ripen on the vine until it has thoroughly hardened, then cut it from the vine with 1 inch of stem attached.

SEED SOURCE Burpee, www.burpee.com.

Chiles

We picked the last of our summer garden poblanos and serranos for our October feast. See the Summer Garden, page 27.

Chive

See the Summer Garden, page 27.

Fennel, Florence or Finocchio

Cooks prefer this annual fennel *Foeniculum vulgare azoricum* over the perennial common fennel (*F. vulgare*) for its larger, thicker leafstalk bases. These bulbous bases, which have a celerylike crunch and a sweet, light anise flavor, can be steamed, sautéed, baked, grilled, simmered in soups and stews, or eaten raw. The feathery leaves resemble those of dill, but have a coarser texture, and make good garnishes and seasonings. The seeds are a staple "spice" in our pantry. *(continued)*

Butternut squash

Harvesting Florence fennel seeds

BEST SITE Full sun and well-drained soil rich in organic matter.

DAYS TO HARVEST 90 to 100 frost-free days from seed.

PLANTING AND CARE Sow seeds directly in the ground, $1/4$ inch deep and 4 to 6 inches apart. Thin seedlings to 1 foot apart. Keep the soil moist until the first leaves appear. As they grow, water the plants regularly, but don't overwater. To make the bulb more tender, sweeter, and extra white, try "blanching" it: When the bulb is about the size of an egg, pile up compost around it.

HOW TO HARVEST Snip off fronds as you need them. Cut whole stalks by slicing them off where they join the bulb. As for the bulb itself, wait for it to gain some girth: at least 3 inches end to end and a couple of inches wide (ours were most flavorful at about 5 inches wide). Then harvest by slicing horizontally through the bulb just above the root line. This leaves the base of the bulb behind, from which new sprouts will often shoot. Or, pull up the bulb, roots and all.

Even though Florence fennel is grown for its bulb rather than its seeds, you can still harvest seeds from it to use in cooking. They are less plump than seeds from common fennel, but they are still very flavorful, especially when fresh. To harvest the seeds, wait until the plant sends up its giant flower stalks (they can grow up to 6 feet tall) and then blossoms, sometime in fall. The flower clusters will eventually produce pale green seeds. When they are plump and swollen, cut the stalk from the plant (the seeds won't fall off), rinse off the aphids if you have them, and let the clusters dry on paper towel–lined baking sheets inside at room temperature, uncovered, until the seeds are completely hard (4 to 5 days; bite into one to check). Each large cluster will yield about 1 teaspoon seeds, so just one plant will yield around $1/4$ cup fennel seed. Store in a tightly closed glass jar; for maximum freshness, keep in the fridge.

SEED SOURCE Burpee, www.burpee.com.

Lemon 'Eureka'

See the Summer Garden, page 31.

Mushrooms

See How to Grow Mushrooms, page 126.

Onion, Cipollini

These 2- to 3-inch, flattish bulbing onions are Italian heirlooms—so special they are usually listed in their own class in catalogs. They come in red, straw yellow, and white and have a mild, sweet flavor. You'll need patience to grow them, though; to form bulbs, they need long days (typical of northerly climates from Bakersfield, California, north to Alaska), and they take more than 4 months to mature. We think they are worth the wait. We used them to make a melt-in-your-mouth cocktail pickle (page 137) and also added them to a rich bean ragoût (page 142).

BEST SITE Full sun and warm, fast-draining soil that has been amended with compost.

DAYS TO HARVEST About 105 days from seed.

PLANTING AND CARE We planted sets as soon as the ground warmed up. Plant seeds a bit later in spring (March or April), $1/2$ inch deep in rows 18 inches apart, then thin seedlings to 2 or 3 inches apart. Water regularly to keep soil moist just below the surface.

HOW TO HARVEST Pull up the onions in late summer after the tops have died down, then store them in a cool, dry place.

SEED/SEEDLING/SET SOURCES Gourmet Seed International, www.gourmetseed.com; Territorial Seed, www.territorialseed.com; Northwest Seed & Pet, www.nwseed.com.

Oregano, Italian

See the Summer Garden, page 33.

Parsley 'Gigante Italian'

See the Summer Garden, page 33.

Peppers 'Carmen' and 'Mariachi'

'CARMEN' An early-maturing Italian sweet pepper, 'Carmen' has horn-shaped, 6-inch-long fruits that taste great whether grilled or sautéed. As they mature from green to red, they get even sweeter. That's when they are best sliced fresh for salads. The plants grow to 28 inches tall.

'MARIACHI' These cone-shaped beauties deliver a blast of color and a hint of heat—spicy but only mildly hot. They change from creamy yellow to bright red all summer on plants 18 to 24 inches tall. The plants produce 4-inch fruits well into fall (although you can start harvesting them in the summer).

BEST SITE Full sun and fertile, well-drained soil.

'Mariachi' pepper

DAYS TO HARVEST 65 days for 'Mariachi' to 75 days for 'Carmen' from seed.

PLANTING AND CARE Sow seeds indoors 6 to 8 weeks before the last spring frost. Plant seedlings only after the soil is warm in spring (peppers are heat lovers). Place the seedlings 18 to 24 inches apart. One or two plants in a container (at least 14 inches wide and 12 inches deep) are plenty. Let the soil dry out between waterings, and cut back on water as the peppers mature to concentrate their flavor.

HOW TO HARVEST Harvest at the red or green stage. Snip off pods with scissors or pruners.

SEED/SEEDLING SOURCES 'Carmen', Tomato Growers Supply Co., www.tomatogrowers.com; 'Mariachi', Burpee, www.burpee.com. Check your local nursery for seedlings of these varieties.

Pineapple guava

The hardiest of subtropical fruits, pineapple guava (*Feijoa sellowiana*), also called feijoa, blooms in late spring or early summer. Showy, inch-wide white flowers with big tufts of red stamens are edible, too—crisp, succulent, and sweet: Toss them into fruit salads or use them to top cakes and cupcakes. The oval, gray-green fruits that follow have dense, sweet, slightly grainy flesh that tastes a bit like pineapple. They grow on evergreen, multistemmed shrubs (10 to 15 feet tall and wide).

BEST SITE Full sun and well-drained soil.

DAYS TO HARVEST Fruits are ready to harvest 4 to 5½ months after flowering in warm climates, 5 to 7 months after bloom in cooler areas. Plants can take 2 to 3 years to bear fruit.

PLANTING AND CARE Set out nursery plants (gallon size or larger) in spring if you are in the mildest climates of California, Arizona, or Hawaii; give them room to spread and water regularly to start. Once established, pineapple guava needs only occasional watering, although fruiting is best with deep regular waterings. Feed lightly with a complete fertilizer such as 8-8-8 once every 2 months during the spring and summer growing season. The plant can take almost any amount of training (in late spring) to shape it as an espalier, screen, hedge, or small tree.

HOW TO HARVEST To harvest lots of fruits at a time, wait until the first ones drop, then spread a tarp underneath the tree and give the trunk a shake. Repeat every few days. Or, gently squeeze a fruit to see whether it is ripe. If it gives to the touch, pick by hand. Ripe pineapple guavas, which are green (sometimes with a red blush) when mature, can be stored in the refrigerator for up to a month and frozen for up to a year.

PLANT SOURCES Look for plants in garden centers, or ask your nursery to order it for you from a wholesaler such as Monrovia Nursery, www.monrovia.com.

Quinoa 'Faro'

Grown mostly for its edible seed, quinoa (say it: "keen-wa") has an unusually high protein content—16 to 23 percent—and contains all eight essential amino acids. We grew 'Faro', a variety bred to thrive at sea level, and loved its statuesque height (nearly 5 feet) and its big, heavy, golden orange seedheads. Having gotten so little from our summer planting of wheat and barley, we wondered how much this next grain experiment would yield. But we're always willing to grow anything once. After threshing and winnowing, which was a pain but not nearly as bad as threshing the wheat and barley, we were rewarded with about 15 quarts of quinoa from just a couple of tablespoons of seed.

BEST SITE Full sun and loose, well-drained soil.

DAYS TO HARVEST 100 to 110 days from seed.

PLANTING AND CARE Sow seeds in midspring when soil is warm (at least 65°F) by scattering them over soil that's been raked smooth, then watered lightly with a hose. Cover them lightly with ¼ to ½ inch of soil. (We raised 54 plants in a 4-by-8-foot raised bed.) Keep the soil moist until the seeds germinate and the first two or three leaves appear, then let them get super-thirsty. You want to give them just 10 to 12 inches of water for the entire season.

HOW TO HARVEST The crop is ready in September or so, when it looks dry, starts to flop over, and the seeds barely dent when you push into them with a fingernail. Cut off the seedheads, lay them flat indoors, and let them dry completely (including stems and leaves) until the stalks are brittle. This takes about 2 weeks. Next, roughly remove the seeds from the stems—that's the threshing part—and then comes the "fun" part: winnowing to separate the seeds from the rest of the particulate matter. It's a messy process, best done outdoors. Set up a small fan and put a tray in front of it to catch the seeds. Then rub the quinoa between your hands in front of the fan. The heavier seeds drop onto the tray, while the featherlight chaff blows away.

HOW TO RINSE FOR COOKING Quinoa seeds are coated with a bitter, soapy substance called saponin, which has to be rinsed off before cooking. (Store-bought quinoa is prerinsed, but still benefits from a dunk in water.) Because our sea-level quinoa was a particularly bitter variety, we were extra-thorough when it came to cleaning. We soaked the seeds for a few hours in warm water, changing the water often. Then we rinsed them several times, rubbing the grains between our fingers, until the water was no longer cloudy. We did big batches at once and thoroughly dried the seeds on kitchen towels before storing them in airtight containers in the freezer.

SEED SOURCE Seeds of Change, www.seedsofchange.com.

Opposite page: 'Faro' quinoa (top); quinoa laid out to dry; then, threshing the seeds (bottom)

The Fall Garden

Radicchio 'Palla Rossa Ashalim'

The radicchio we grew is really a red-leaved Italian chicory (*Cichorium intybus*) that forms a lettucelike head. The stunning purple-red leaves with bright white veins taste sharp and spicy, with a hint of bitterness that adds a pleasing bite to mixed salads. Radicchio is a bit trickier to grow than lettuce: It takes slightly longer to mature, doesn't tolerate heavy frost (mild frost is fine, and gives it a wonderfully sweet flavor), and needs to be monitored, much like cabbage, to determine when to harvest.

BEST SITE Full sun and compost-rich, well-drained soil.

DAYS TO HARVEST 65 days from seed.

PLANTING AND CARE Plant in midspring or early summer for a fall harvest; in mild winter climates, plant in fall for a winter harvest. Sow seeds $1/4$ to $1/2$ inch deep in rows spaced 18 inches apart, then thin seedlings to about 12 inches apart. Protect from frosts with floating row covers. Keep soil evenly moist during the growing season, and apply a 10-10-10 fertilizer after growth starts.

HOW TO HARVEST When the heads start feeling firm to the touch, slice them from above the crowns with a sharp knife, then peel away the outer leaves to reveal the white-veined leaves inside. (If enough time remains before a frost, the crowns may resprout and develop second heads.) Heads are past their prime for harvest when they turn hard and their leaves turn tough and bitter.

SEED SOURCE Botanical Interests, www.botanical interests.com.

Rosemary 'Tuscan Blue'

See the Summer Garden, page 35.

Sage

Common sage (*Salvia officinalis*) is a kitchen garden essential—one we would never be without. You can use its soft, aromatic gray-green leaves fresh or dried to flavor everything from soups, stews, and egg dishes to vegetables and vinegar. A small perennial subshrub (1 to 3 feet tall), it comes in many forms; our current test-garden favorites include 'Icterina', whose leaves are edged with yellow, and 'Tricolor', whose new leaves are flushed with purple.

BEST SITE Grow it in full sun in cool climates, afternoon shade in hot climates, in a spot with loose, well-drained soil.

'Palla Rossa Ashalim' radicchio

DAYS TO HARVEST Any time after the plants have filled out.

PLANTING AND CARE Set out plants from nursery containers with the crown (the thickened area at the stem base) slightly above the surrounding soil. Space several at 12- to 24-inch intervals in garden beds (they make pretty edgings). Or, grow a single plant in a 16-inch-wide container. Water once a week or so (more in hot, windy weather) for the first year, then taper off to occasional irrigations (once a month during the warm season if leaves look droopy). Apply a granular 10-10-10 fertilizer once a year in spring when new growth begins.

HOW TO HARVEST Pick leaves as needed.

SEEDLING SOURCE Mountain Valley Growers, www.mountainvalleygrowers.com.

Swiss chard

Grow this form of beet for its leaves and stalks rather than its roots. It's one of the easiest vegetables you can grow, and you can harvest leaves all summer (and, in mild climates, into fall and even spring, depending on when you plant). We grew both green-and-white chard and 'Bright

Sage

Swiss chard

Lights'—with leaves ranging from green to burgundy and stalks in various shades of yellow, orange, pink, purple, and red.

BEST SITE Full sun and fertile, well-drained soil.

DAYS TO HARVEST About 60 days from seed.

PLANTING AND CARE Sow the big, tan, crinkly seeds $^1/_2$ inch deep and 2 inches apart in spaded soil any time from spring to early summer. Gardeners in mild winter climates (like us) can plant it in the late summer to early fall for harvest starting in the late fall through winter. As seedlings appear, thin them to 12 inches apart. Keep the soil evenly moist. Feed with a 10-10-10 fertilizer after plants are established and again 6 weeks later.

HOW TO HARVEST When the plants are 12 to 18 inches tall, begin cutting the outer leaves, keeping the core of the plant intact to continue growing.

SEED SOURCES Nichols Garden Nursery, www.nichols gardennursery.com; Renee's Garden, www.renees garden.com; and Territorial Seed International, www.territorialseed.com.

Thyme, French

See the Summer Garden, page 36.

Tomatoes

At this point in the year, our summer garden was still producing 'Sungold', 'Sweet Million', and 'Brandywine' tomatoes. See the Summer Garden, page 36.

—*Kathleen N. Brenzel*

THE "IMPORTS"

We went outside our garden for these local foods: milk, whole and unhomogenized (for cream; butter and buttermilk, page 154; and for cheese, pages 117 to 125); walnuts; Honey Crisp apples; whole-wheat flour ('Sonora' and 'Expresso,' page 156)

Crushing and destemming Syrah grapes

THE FALL PROJECTS

HOW TO MAKE
WINE

Wine making is like following a very large, very slow recipe, with strange and fascinating moments along the way. At the end of the process, with luck (as Team Wine seems to have had), you'll have pretty decent stuff to proudly call your own.

If you can, pick your own grapes. We considered quitting our day jobs after our October 2007 experience of harvesting dusty, juicy Syrah grapes in Thomas Fogarty Winery's remote and gorgeous Fat Buck Ridge Vineyard in California's Santa Cruz Mountains.

The home wine-making journey will get under your skin and give you a huge appreciation for the quality in the bottles you buy. Just remember to keep a record of everything you do to your wine and to sanitize everything every step of the way. Then celebrate the chance to use that high-school chemistry.

· ·

SYRAH

Ours is an inky, deep purple wine. Blueberries and blackberries mingle with leather, smoke, and bacon. To make the journey worthwhile, you should make at least four cases (twelve bottles per case); we made sixteen cases.

WHAT TO USE

Clipboard, pencil, and log sheet You need to record your wine's progress, additions you make (such as yeast), and any preventative or preservative measures you take. We downloaded a free "log chart" from *WineMaker* magazine (www.winemakermag.com).

Wine grapes To make four cases of wine, you need about 125 pounds of grapes. Make sure you can get your hands on the wine grapes before you buy or rent any equipment. By midsummer, look into harvesting grapes in early fall at a U-pick vineyard (try El Dorado County, California's www.edc-farmtrails.org

and search for "wine grapes"). PickYourOwn.org (www.pickyourown.org) lets you search for U-pick farms near you, with grape growers posting when vines are ready to harvest.

You could put dibs on grapes in summer for fall delivery by mail or special truck shipment (both methods are fairly expensive). But if you live near a grower with excess grapes, you can load up for less by cruising by with your own van or truck (this is primarily an option in California, Oregon, and Washington). At MoreGrapes! (www.moregrapes.com), growers on the West Coast and beyond list available grapes, including Syrah from about $1 per pound. And many wine-making association Web sites dedicate a page to "grapes available" (check out the El Dorado Wine Grape Growers Association's comprehensive site: www.eldoradograpes.com).

A good first stop is to ask about grape options at your local home wine-making shop. To find one, go to www.winemakermag.com and click "Resource Guide" and then "Supplier Directory." Many homebrew beer shops have wine contacts, too. They will likely refer you to small local growers or to largely Web-based enterprises like F. Colavita & Son (www.cawinegrapes.com) that cater to home winemakers.

Potassium metabisulfite The industry-standard chemical for equipment sterilization and protecting finished wine from spoiling. Buy it in powdered form, not Campden tablets (for which you have to take the extra step of crushing). We used 1/2 teaspoon per 5-gallon carboy (water cooler–style glass jugs) of Syrah. We sprinkled some into each piece of equipment we needed to sterilize, then added some water, sloshed it around every inner surface, and rinsed liberally. We also mixed some with water to create our airlock solution and to sterilize bottles before filling and corking them. About $5 per 1/2 pound (you shouldn't need more than this, for everything) online or at a home wine-making store.

Large plastic garbage can For stomping grapes with your feet, after which you'll have to pick through the must (the newly crushed grapes) to remove the stems.

About $10 at a hardware store or home-improvement center. Or, use a hand-cranked **crusher-destemmer** (like a large trough with a rotating screw in the middle), which gives you relatively stem-free must. Rent this from a home wine-making store; buying one will cost at least $450.

5-gallon food-grade plastic buckets For schlepping grapes, must, and wine and for sanitizing tubing. About $7 at a hardware store.

Two 32-gallon food-grade plastic drums with lids For your must's first (primary) fermentation. About $70, including lid, at a home wine-making store. Or, you can use two **large plastic garbage cans** (if you bought one for crushing and destemming, just pick through the must to remove the stems, then add yeast to start fermentation). About $10 each at a hardware store or home-improvement center.

Cheesecloth For keeping bugs out of your fermenter. About $4.50 for 2 square yards at a hardware or cookware store.

Garden hose and sprayer For making quick work of cleaning equipment at the end of a messy day. About $30 at a hardware store or home-improvement center.

Wine yeast For starting your fermentation to convert your grape-juice must to wine. We used a strain called ICV-D80. About $1.50 for an 8-gram packet online or at a home wine-making store; for most wines, you need 1 gram of yeast per 1 gallon of must.

Wooden or stainless-steel wine-cap punch-down tool For punching down the cap of skins and seeds, which gives red wine its beautiful color and contributes flavor and tannins. Or, with some basic lumber and tools, you can make a wooden "plonker" (for project directions, visit www.winemakermag.com/component/resource/article/107-build-3-wine making-projects). At least $80 for a stainless-steel model at home wine-making stores.

Hydrometer For measuring the sugar level of your fermenting must. About $6 from www.morebeer.com.

Hydrometer jar A plastic tube for holding the wine sample you're measuring with the hydrometer. Some hydrometers come with their own jars. About $5 online or at a home wine-making store.

Floating thermometer For taking the temperature of your fermenting must. About $10 online, or at a home wine-making store.

Malolactic bacteria For prompting a secondary fermentation. $15 to $20 for 2.5 grams (enough for 66 gallons of wine) online or at a home wine-making store.

Bladder press For pressing your young wine off the skins and seeds. Rent this at a home wine-making store; buying one will set you back at least $1,500. Or, you can use a **basket press**. Again, rent this at a home wine-making store; buying one will run at least $275.

5-gallon glass carboys Surrogate barrels—buy one for every 5 gallons of wine you are making, plus one extra for the racking stage. From $20 to $30 at a home wine-making or home-brewing shops.

Airlocks For keeping oxygen and bugs out of your wine while allowing carbon dioxide to bubble out. Buy one for each carboy. About $1.50 each online or at a home wine-making store.

Rubber stoppers Aka bungs with small holes in the center, for sealing your carboys while accommodating the airlocks. About $1.50 each online or at a home wine-making store.

Two 3- to 5-quart nonreactive mixing bowls For sterilizing stoppers, tubing, and corks. Stainless steel is ideal (don't use aluminum or copper). Borrow them from your kitchen, or buy them for as low as $10 each online or at a cookware store.

Wine thief A glass tube for extracting wine from a carboy for tasting and testing. From $25 online or at a home wine-making store. We resorted to a **plastic turkey baster**. From $5 online or at a cookware store.

Plastic funnel For pouring wine into carboys. Choose an asymmetrical one with a high side to avoid splash back. From $3.50 online or at a home wine-making or cookware store.

6- to 8-foot lengths of food-grade vinyl tubing For siphoning wine. We used two tubes with a $^3/_8$-inch interior diameter: one could be siphoning while the other soaked in sanitizer. About 30¢ per foot online or at a home wine-making or plumbing-supply store.

Sturdy worktable For elevating the full carboys when racking. From $75 at a home-improvement center.

Oak chips or cubes For barrel flavor substitute. We used small cubes—26 grams per 5-gallon carboy of Syrah. $10 to $30 per pound; buy online or at a home wine-making store.

Digital kitchen scale For weighing the oak chips. From $30 at a cookware store.

Wine bottles Reuse empty wine bottles (you'll need to scrub off the original labels and sanitize the bottles) or buy new ones (sanitize these, too). Consider a Rhône-style bottle (with sloping shoulders) if you want your Syrah to look authentic. From $15 per dozen at a home wine-making store; you'll need

Fogarty Winery's Fat Buck Ridge

26 standard (750-milliliter) wine bottles for each 5-gallon carboy of wine you're making.

2 bottle rinsers and 1 "bottle tree" drying rack For sanitizing the insides of the bottles. You just slip a rinsed wine bottle over the sprayer nozzle and pump it up and down on the nozzle a few times, then drain each bottle on the drying rack, which is shaped like a tall, spiky tree trunk. Each bottle rinser runs about $20, and a drying rack starts at about $40; both can be purchased at a home wine-making or home-brew store.

Manual bottle filler For controlling the bottle-filling process. You attach the plastic rod with a spring-loaded tip to your plastic tubing. About $6 online or at a home wine-making or home-brew store.

Corks Price depends on quality. Natural cork is divided into several grades. Flor corks are the finest grade (about $150 for 250 corks), but we decided to go with similarly top-quality 1³/₄-inch "overrun" corks left over from bottling runs at Napa wineries (we paid

$19 per 100 corks at MoreWine in Los Altos, California; www.morewinemaking.com or 800/600-0033). Buy corks online or at a home wine-making store.

Corker Rent a "floor corker" at a home wine-making store, or buy time on a vacuum corker at a home wine-making or home-brew store. Hand corkers are available and cost less, but they limit your ability to move between bottling elements. Buying a floor corker at a home wine-making store will cost at least $85 and more along the lines of $850 for a really sturdy one (the $85 version should be fine).

Labels You can use a design-graphics program like Adobe Illustrator, or you can work with your local home wine-making or home-brew store to create a label on their software. Conveniently, we had designers down the hall.

HOW TO DO IT

Wine is a living, changing thing, and your timeline will vary based on environmental factors like temperature, starting sugar level, and yeast health. Here is the timeline we followed. Consult the resources listed in Helpful Information (page 112) for more general guidance.

OCTOBER 4, 2007

Harvested 500 pounds of Syrah grapes We picked our grapes at Thomas Fogarty Winery's Fat Buck Ridge Vineyard in the San Francisco Bay Area's Santa Cruz Mountains. After hauling the grapes back to our office, we crushed them, both by foot in sanitized garbage cans and with a hand-cranked crusher-destemmer. Then we put the destemmed must (crushed grapes, skins, seeds, and juice) into two food-grade plastic drums, covered each with cheesecloth and drum lid, and allowed the must to cold-soak (to extract color and flavor) for 4 days.

OCTOBER 8

Added yeast Following the package directions, we added the yeast to start primary fermentation.

OCTOBER 12–28

Punched down the "cap" Two or three times a day, we used our punch-down tool to push the cap of skins and seeds that continually formed on our fermenting must back down into the juice. The cap was thick and radiated heat,

and we had to stand on a chair to get enough leverage to punch through it for the first few strokes.

Every afternoon during this period, we took two measurements: The wine's temperature (with the floating thermometer), to make sure the wine was warm and fairly constant (it hovered around 78°F), and the wine's sugar level (a Brix scale reading with the hydrometer), to check that the yeast continued to eat up the sugar, converting it into alcohol.

OCTOBER 22

Started malolactic fermentation This secondary, bacterial fermentation—ML for short—converts harsh malic acids into softer lactic ones. It's as simple as sprinkling the powdery bacteria into the wine (following the package directions, of course).

OCTOBER 29

Pressed the wine off its pomace The pomace is the skins, seeds, and other solids that form the cap. We used the bladder press, catching the "free-run" wine (what naturally spilled through the slats of the press and out through the spigot with only gravity's assistance). This was followed by the "press-run" wine, which was coaxed off the pomace by inflating the bladder of the press with a garden hose to 15 psi—pounds (of pressure) per square inch.

As the wine streamed from the press, we ran a bucket brigade from the spigot over to sanitized 5-gallon carboys, each topped with a plastic funnel. Then we outfitted

Pushing grapes into the crusher-destemmer

Crushing by foot

Pressing the Syrah

Shin-deep in grapes

each carboy with an airlock filled about halfway with "meta" solution (2¹/₄ teaspoons potassium metabisulfite dissolved in 1 quart water; we made our meta solution once and stored it in a sterilized gin bottle) and stuck the airlock in a bung to create a seal on top of the carboy, keeping oxygen (the enemy of wine) and bugs (we don't like to share, and we didn't want to risk bacteria from their tiny legs) out of the wine while allowing carbon dioxide to bubble out.

NOVEMBER 2007–APRIL 2008

Periodically checked airlocks Every two weeks or so, we checked the airlocks (refilling them with new meta solution if wine had burbled into the lock or if the meta level was looking low) and tasted our wine. In mid-February, we gave some wine samples to Fogarty winemaker Michael Martella to test pH and total acidity (TA) to make sure things were on track. Our pH was 3.8 (a little high; Martella thought it would come down), and our TA was .64 (which Martella said was fine).

Each time we pulled wine out of a carboy with our wine thief (okay, our turkey baster) to sample it, we "topped off" the headspace (the air between the wine level and the airlock) with more Syrah (because, as mentioned above, oxygen is the enemy of wine). The extra Syrah came from smaller glass jugs, also topped with airlocks, that we had set aside for this purpose.

APRIL 29, 2008

Racked the wine We siphoned our wine off the lees (the spent yeast and other sediment that drops out as fermentation ends) into fresh carboys. Here's how: Put a full carboy on top of your worktable and position an empty, sterilized carboy on the floor under it. Remove the airlock and set it upright in a sterilized container to save for the carboy you are about to fill up. Put one end of the sterilized vinyl tubing in the full carboy (don't let the tubing end get too close to the lees at the bottom of the carboy), then gently suck the open end of the tube until wine is flowing toward it. (Be prepared to quickly pinch the open end and stop the wine with your index finger.) Put this open end into the clean carboy and let gravity do the rest of the work for you. Keep pushing the tubing in the full carboy lower and lower toward the lees to keep the wine flowing, but don't let it dip into the lees. Ask a friend or two to help you out for this step.

Once the wine was racked, we added oak chips for body and rounded flavor: 26 grams of small, medium-toast oak cubes in each 5-gallon carboy.

We also added ¹/₂ teaspoon powdered potassium metabisulfite per 5-gallon carboy to protect our finished wine from spoilage by microbes. We filled the headspace with more Syrah, and then topped the new carboys with the meta-filled airocks. Finally, we moved them into a cool, temperature-controlled environment (our basement, which is a steady 56°F).

LATE FALL 2008 (A YEAR AFTER WE STARTED)

Created labels In anticipation of bottling, we got our label design ready and printed it (see page 165).

JANUARY 30, 2009

Bottled our Syrah With a drain and a hose-rigged spigot nearby for easy cleaning and cleanup, we dragged out the worktable; stainless-steel bowls for sterilizing our siphon tubing, bottle filler, and corks; two bottle rinsers; and our "bottle tree" drying rack.

Sterilized bottles We whipped up a batch of bottle wash (4¹/₂ teaspoons potassium metabisulfite dissolved in 1 gallon water) and split this solution between our two bottle rinsers. We gave each bottle a rinse with bottle wash: two pumps on one spring-loaded bottle rinser to wash away any dust, followed by two pumps on our second rinser to complete the sterilization. Then we placed each bottle onto the tree for 10 to 15 minutes of drying.

Place a full bottle on the spring-loaded platform of the corker, position a sanitized cork in the jaws of the "compression chamber," or iris, then brace the corker with your foot and use your hands to pull down the handle. In one fluid motion, the cork gets squeezed on four sides and a metal rod comes down to plunge the compressed cork into the bottle.

Once in a bottle, the cork expands to create a tight seal. Place the bottles upright (cork side up) for 24 to 48 hours, then flip them upside down in a case or store them horizontally, either in a wine rack or by tilting a full case of bottles on its side, so the wine stays in contact with the cork.

A FEW DAYS LATER

Labeled our Syrah It was just a matter of lining the label up straight while pressing the label onto a clean, dry bottle.

But don't start pulling corks and sharing your wine with friends immediately. Your living wine is adapting to its new life in a bottle and could be experiencing bottle shock. Give your wine a few weeks to settle into its smaller confines, then uncork away.

CHARDONNAY

Our Chardonnay has a touch of creaminess to it, but with the vibrant, juicy acidity of crisp Granny Smith apples and none of the caramel and toast you would get from new oak barrels.

In terms of home wine making, the biggest differences between white and red wine are that for white, the juice is pressed off the skins before you start fermentation, and the fermentation takes place right in the glass carboys. Since pressing white grapes takes special equipment, we started with juice, not grapes.

WHAT TO USE

To make Chardonnay, follow the What to Use list for Syrah (page 105). If you are starting with pressed juice, you won't need these items from the Syrah list:

Large plastic garbage can or crusher-destemmer
Food-grade plastic drum with lid or large plastic
garbage can
Cheesecloth
Punch-down tool
Bladder press or basket press

Siphoned wine into bottles Here's how we did it: Stick one end of vinyl tubing into a carboy (as close to the remaining sediment as you dare), then put the other end in your mouth. Start sipping, as you did for racking, keeping a hand near to pinch off the tubing. Grab your bottle filler, and gently but firmly slide the rod into the tubing. As long as you keep the rod end lower than the carboy that's up on the table, your siphon is ready whenever you are.

Take a bottle off the tree, place it at your feet, and poke the bottle filler into the empty bottle. Depress its tip against the bottom of the bottle, and the rod will let wine flow in. Fill the bottle until it is approaching full, pausing to let it foam as needed. When the wine crests the top of the bottle neck, gently lift the rod out.

Corked the bottles Even though they're natural, corks still need sterilizing before being put in contact with wine (which remains alive, even when bottled). Prep another sanitizing solution (for corks, use $1/2$ teaspoon potassium metabisulfite dissolved in 1 gallon water) in one of your stainless-steel bowls. To keep the corks from bobbing up in the solution, nestle a smaller nonreactive bowl on top of the corks.

After 20 minutes, they're ready to use. Leave them bathing until you need them; just set the bowl at the base of the floor corker for easy access.

You'll also need:

Juice (or wine grapes) In midsummer, you can put dibs on pressed juice. We bought 20 gallons of freshly pressed Chardonnay—enough to make just over 100 standard (750-milliliter) bottles of wine—from Thomas Fogarty Winery.

Oak chips or cubes We used small cubes, adding a small handful per 5-gallon carboy of Chardonnay (we oaked only half of our 20 gallons). See our Syrah guide for where to buy.

Rubber stoppers (bungs) without holes For "stirring" the lees (rolling the carboys to add character and complexity). You need one for each carboy. About $1.25 each online or at a home wine-making store.

Duct tape For securing the stoppers when rolling the carboys. About $4 at a home-improvement center.

Thick cardboard or a thick old rug For rolling the carboys.

Wine bottles Consider a Burgundy-style bottle (sloping shoulders and a relatively wide base) if you want your Chardonnay to look authentic. See our Syrah bottle-buying advice for more tips and how to calculate the number of bottles you'll need.

HOW TO DO IT

The process of Chardonnay making is much the same as for Syrah. Check our step-by-step guide for Syrah for more details on any of the phases described.

OCTOBER 4, 2007

Brought home our Chardonnay juice We split the 20 gallons among four 5-gallon carboys. Then we started fermentation by adding yeast to each carboy. Finally, we outfitted the carboys with airlocks filled about halfway with meta solution.

OCTOBER 11

Added oak chips We put them in half of our carboys, placing just a small handful in each one.

OCTOBER 16

Took two measurements We noted both the wine's temperature and its sugar level.

OCTOBER 17

Started malolactic fermentation.

MID-OCTOBER 2007 TO MARCH 2008

Periodically tasted We sipped our Chardonnay over the months to see how it was evolving. Also, in mid-February, we gave some wine samples to Fogarty winemaker Michael Martella to test pH and total acidity (TA) to make sure things were on track. The pH was 3.2 (low, which means our acidity is high, which is an excellent thing, we think, for a Chardonnay). The TA was .68 (great).

Each time we pulled wine out of a carboy, we had to "top off" the vacant headspace with more Chardonnay. We

Yeast slurry   Adding the slurry to Chardonnay juice   Fitting airlocks into carboys

Corking Chardonnay

opened bottles of other West Coast Chardonnays for this purpose. Or we could have added marbles to the carboy.

MARCH 3, 2008

Stirred the lees We swapped each carboy's airlock and stopper for a stopper without a hole, duct-taped it down, and rolled each carboy on a thick rug until all of the sediment that was lodged on the bottom had been mixed back up into the wine. Then we added $1/3$ teaspoon powdered potassium metabisulfite (swirled in a little Chardonnay and slightly heated in a microwave to dissolve the powder) per 5-gallon carboy to protect our wine. Finally, we retopped each carboy with a meta-filled airlock.

MARCH 27

Rolled the carboys We took our Chardonnay out on the rug again and retopped it with meta-filled airlocks.

APRIL 29

Ditto.

MAY 13

Rolled the carboys One last time, the carboys took a spin. Then we moved them to our basement.

JULY 8

Racked the Chardonnay We siphoned the wine off its lees it into fresh carboys. Then we added $1/4$ teaspoon powdered potassium metabisulfite per 5-gallon carboy, filled the headspace with Chardonnay, and topped the new carboys with meta-filled airlocks.

OCTOBER 1, 2008

Bottled, corked, and labeled After letting our Chardonnay rest for nearly three months, we bottled, corked, and labeled it. Beyond wanting to let the wine settle, we were waiting for cooler weather so as not to expose the wine to the heat.

HELPFUL INFORMATION

WEB SITES

- For general and specific advice, plus free charts and sulfite calculator, check out www.winemakermag .com.
- For general advice, visit www.grapestompers.com.

BOOKS AND OTHER PUBLICATIONS

- *The Way to Make Wine: How to Craft Superb Table Wines at Home* by Sheridan Warrick (University of California Press, 2006).
- *The Wine Maker's Answer Book: Solutions to Every Problem, Answers to Every Question* by Alison Crowe (Storey Publishing, 2007).
- *WineMaker Beginner's Guide* (Battenkill Communications, no date).
- *WineMaker* magazine (available at home winemaking shops; find subscription information and many articles on www.winemakermag.com).

HOME WINE-MAKING SHOPS

- Find a home wine-making or home-brew shop near you: go to www.winemakermag.com and click "Resource Guide" and then "Supplier Directory."
- Our favorite local shop, MoreWine in Los Altos, California, also has an online shop (great for yeast, malolactic bacteria, and most equipment and materials); www.morewinemaking.com or 800/600-0033.
- An excellent Web-based store for equipment, materials, and kits is E.C. Kraus, www.eckraus.com or 800/353-1906.

—Erika Ehmsen

HOW TO MAKE
VINEGAR

Delicious, fancy vinegars are easy to find in the United States. Go to a well-stocked grocery store and you can get everything from French Banyuls to Spanish sherry to Italian balsamic.

What is harder to find is good ordinary red-wine vinegar. Most of what is available commercially for a couple of bucks a bottle is thin and flavorless. Some of it is laboratory-produced acetic acid, diluted with water and dressed up with coloring. Slightly better, though only marginally, is vinegar made using a speeded-up fermentation process (anywhere from one to three days). Traditional red-wine vinegar, left to ferment naturally on its own, takes about seventy-five days and results in a much richer texture and flavor.

The good news is that "slow vinegar" is easy to make at home, tastes wonderful, and is cheap to produce (it feeds on leftover wine). We have two crocks going in our kitchen that yield a constant supply for salad dressings, sauces, and gifts.

• •

SYRAH VINEGAR

Because we were already making Syrah wine, we decided to divert some of it to making vinegar. The result was a deep purple-red vinegar, intensely fruity and sharp and fresh.

WHAT TO USE

Avoid aluminum or iron kitchen tools for making vinegar, because they can impart off flavors. We used plastic, glass, and wood.

A notebook and a pencil It's easy to lose track of when and how much you fed your vinegar, unless you record the dates and amounts. This is most important when the vinegar is newly establishing itself.

A good mother In the world of vinegar, a "mother" is a live starter, similar to a sourdough starter for bread. It is home to acetic acid–producing bacteria of the *Acetobacter* genus that convert wine to vinegar. The mother will form a not-unpleasant and actually quite fascinating thin, somewhat firm gelatinous layer on the surface of your vinegar crock. This is a sign that the bacteria are alive and well and doing their work.

Decanting aged vinegar

You can either get your mother from a vinegar-making friend, as we did (see How to Do It, step 1), or buy it from a vinegar-supply shop, which more often than not will also be selling wine and/or beer supplies (typically about $12.50 per 8-ounce jar).

Leftover red wine We used our own Syrah, but you can use any decent, fruity red wine. It's a great use for that half bottle you didn't finish at dinner.

1- to 1½-gallon fermenting container The best fermenting containers allow for a wide surface area and have an open top, so that the bacteria have enough oxygen, and are enclosed to keep out light, which slows down the bacteria's progress. A 1-gallon glass iced-tea jar can work (keep it in a cardboard box), but Mason jars are too narrow. We had our best results with 5-liter Italian demijohns enclosed in mesh holders ($37.50 each from Oak Barrel Winecraft, Inc., www.oakbarrel.com) and with gorgeous 1-gallon clay crocks ($80.00 each, from Clay Coyote Pottery, www.claycoyote.com).

A simple countertop thermometer *Acetobacter* bacteria prefer the 70° to 90°F range.

1-gallon aging container New vinegar is very sharp, almost feisty. To let your vinegar mellow, age it for at least a month in a separate, sterilized, lidded container after straining and pasteurizing.

Clay crocks (see page 113) produce a fine, soft vinegar and were our favorite aging containers. French oak crocks are pricey (6-liter crock, $160 from Oak Barrel Winecraft), but they impart a lovely mellow toasty flavor to the vinegar and look stunning.

Cheesecloth It keeps out fruit flies and dust, yet allows oxygen to reach the bacteria. About $4.50 for 2 square yards at a hardware or cookware store.

1- to 1¹/₂-foot length of plastic tubing This is what you will use to feed your vinegar. $1 per foot at a hardware store.

Plastic funnel Make sure the funnel is narrow enough to fit securely into your tubing and bottles. From $3.50 online and at a cookware store.

Large plastic colander sized to fit the top of the pot, below. From $6 at a cookware store.

Coffee filters About $3.50 for 40 filters at a grocery store.

8-quart stainless-steel heavy-bottomed pot for pasteurizing the vinegar. From $60 at a cookware store.

Candy or deep-fry thermometer with bracket so you can clip it to the side of the pot. From about $6 online or at a cookware store.

Storage-serving bottles and corks The Olive Oil Source, www.oliveoilsource.com, sells bottles by the case, in various sizes; 200-milliliter bottles with corks are about $19.50 for a case of 12.

21-quart boiling-water canner with canning rack Handy for sterilizing your bottles and for pasteurizing the vinegar. From $16 online and at a cookware store.

Jar lifter For gripping steaming, slippery bottles, draining them, and positioning them for filling. Use it for canning and jam making, too. About $9 at a cookware store.

HOW TO DO IT

1. Find the mother We got our mother for free, from cookbook author and vinegar maven Paula Wolfert. Paula was given hers several years ago by her friend Abra Bennett, a food writer from Bainbridge Island, Washington. She thinks it's at least forty years old.

Paula cut 5 playing card–size pieces from a mother fished out of one of her crocks, slipped each piece into a small glass jar, and fed it with just enough diluted red wine (1 cup wine and ¹/₂ cup water) for it to travel safely back to our offices. "Start small," she advised us. "Swamp it, and it'll be dead."

2. Start the mother Pour each jarful of mother into a fermenting container and add more diluted wine: 2 cups wine to 1 cup water. Cover the open top of each container

with a double layer of cheesecloth and roll a rubber band down around the rim to keep it in place (or screw on a jar ring). Put the containers in a warm place out of direct sunlight.

3. First feedings: a set of 3 Once the bacterial conversion has begun, which will be about 1¹/₂ weeks after you have started the mother, you will need to start feeding your vinegar. Add 2¹/₂ cups Syrah to each container three times over a period of 1¹/₂ weeks.

How to feed your vinegar: Sometime into the first-feeding period, a mother will form on the surface of your vinegar. To avoid "swamping" it, slide one end of the plastic tubing underneath the edge of the mother, then fit the funnel into the other end and pour in the wine. Work on a surface that's easy to wipe clean.

Your vinegar is ready when it smells and tastes like vinegar. It is possible to do a titration test to figure out just how acidic the mixture is, but this is unnecessary unless you're using the vinegar for pickling food (you will need 4 percent acidity for pickling); for details, see Fresh Pickled Beets, page 230. We dipped clean plastic spoons into our vinegar, took thoughtful sips, and if it tasted like vinegar—tart, sharp, strong, delicious—we either pasteurized, aged, and bottled it (steps 5, 6, and 7), or continued feeding it (step 4) to increase the volume. If it tasted more like wine than vinegar, we left it alone until it was ready.

Warning sign: If your vinegar ever starts to smell like furniture polish, throw it away. It has been contaminated and can't be saved. Always taste a bit of the wine before you feed it to your vinegar.

4. Maintenance feedings Once the *Acetobacter* bacteria have established themselves vigorously, add 1 to 2 cups of wine every few weeks or so. When the vinegar is at a vinegary moment (taste it to see), you can pasteurize and age it.

Every now and then, the mother will wear out and sink to the bottom, and a new mother will take its place. This doesn't harm your vinegar, but after a while the old mothers will start to absorb the vinegar in the crock. Every month or so, using clean hands or plastic or wooden salad tongs, gently push aside the nice firm top mother, fish out any settled mothers, and throw them away.

5. Pasteurize the vinegar This step ensures that a mother won't grow in the bottle or, if you decide to age your vinegar, the aging vessel. However, you can keep a mother from growing if you store the vinegar in the refrigerator (the bacteria go dormant). To age vinegar, though, you have to pasteurize or the mother will form again.

Fill the canner with hot water up to the first ring from the bottom, insert the canning rack upside-down (handles down), and bring it to a boil, covered. Meanwhile, line the colander with a few coffee filters and place it over the 8-quart pot. With a plastic ladle, scoop the vinegar into the lined colander. Homemade vinegar is exhilaratingly strong, and because it will evaporate as you heat it, you may want to add from 1 to 3 cups water to the pot. Keep tasting until it reaches the strength you like.

Position a clean candy thermometer in the vinegar and clip it to the side of the pot. Ease the pot into the boiling water, turn the heat off, and heat the vinegar to 155°F; hold it there for 30 minutes. If it climbs above 155°F, lift the pot out and let it sit near the stove until the temperature drops to 155°F. If it drops below, turn the burner on to give it a boost. You can now let your vinegar age for a while (step 6) or you can bottle it (step 7).

6. Age the vinegar Let the pasteurized vinegar cool, then pour it into the aging vessel. Store in a dark, quiet, cool (50° to 75°F) place. Taste periodically to see how the flavor is developing. After a couple of weeks, you should start to notice the mellowing. During aging, solids fall to the bottom of the vessel, so the vinegar not only mellows but also becomes beautifully bright and clear.

When you like what you taste, sterilize a batch of bottles and bottle your vinegar, bearing in mind that some aging will continue in the bottle. You can also keep topping up your aging vessel with newly pasteurized vinegar for as long as you like.

7. Bottle the vinegar Wash the bottles, corks, a plastic ladle, and a plastic funnel in hot, soapy water, then rinse. To sterilize the bottles, immerse them in the canner, cover with water by one inch, bring to a boil, and boil for 10 minutes. Remove the bottles carefully with a jar lifter (or tongs) and tip out the hot water. Using the ladle and funnel, fill each bottle with hot pasteurized vinegar or room-temperature aged vinegar, leaving 1/2-inch headspace. Stopper the bottles with the clean corks.

A bottle of unpasteurized vinegar is a form of insurance for vinegar making. If something goes wrong with your current batch of vinegar, your unpasteurized vinegar can be used to start a new one. A bottle of this "live" vinegar is also a great gift for friends interested in developing their own stash of flavorful homemade vinegar.

HELPFUL INFORMATION

- *Homemade Vinegar: Make Your Own with Mother of Vinegar*, by Patrick and Carole Watkins (A-Printing Publishing, 1995).
- *Making Vinegar at Home*, by Frank Romanowski, Mark F. Larrow, and Gail Canon; revised by Mark F. Larrow (Beer & Winemaking Supplies, Inc., 1994).
- *Vinegar: The User-Friendly Standard Text Reference & Guide to Appreciating, Making, and Enjoying Vinegar*, by Lawrence J. Diggs (Quiet Storm Trading Co., 1989; iUniverse, 2003).

A piece of the mother in its traveling jar   Covering the vinegar with cheesecloth and a jar ring   Feeding the vinegar

CHEESE (PART II)

As our one-block project continued, we kept making cheeses using just milk, lemon juice, salt, and herbs, but we also learned to use cheese cultures (freeze-dried packets of microorganisms that give acidity, flavor, and texture) and rennet (enzymes that help coagulate milk). Most of the world's great cheeses—all the soft-ripened, oozy beauties and the long-aged hard cheeses—depend on cultures for their identities, and many need rennet to form curds. We never seemed to make exactly the same cheese twice, although they were similar. And once we started playing around with presses and brines, the chances for variation only multiplied. So far, we have made six cheeses, with more to follow, which we'll write about on http://oneblockdiet.sunset.com/team_cheese.

At this point, we like the fact that our cheeses are one of a kind. Their mutability helps us understand why some of our favorite artisanal cheeses differ from time to time. It also puts us in awe of the discipline, knowledge, and skill required to make a consistently great cheese.

BEFORE YOU START

Two basic rules apply to all our cheese making: sanitizing all your equipment and making sure your thermometer is accurate. For details, see Before You Start, page 46. As for equipment for the four cheeses that follow, most of what you'll need is available at a good grocery store, cookware store, or hardware store. (We haven't included ordinary cookware like saucepans, baking sheets, or measuring cups in the lists, assuming those would already be in your kitchen.) For specialized cheesemaking tools and ingredients, we turned to the Beverage People, in Santa Rosa, California (www.thebeveragepeople.com or 800/544-1867), unless otherwise mentioned.

· ·

RICOTTA

MAKES 1¹/₄ to 1¹/₂ cups (3¹/₂ cups if you use all milk)
TIME about 1¹/₂ hours

Ricotta, which means "recooked" in Italian, is essentially a thrifty way to squeeze more cheese out of what another cheese left behind (usually with some milk added for richness). Bellwether Farms, in Sonoma, California, is famous for its sweet, light, delicious ricotta, and cheese maker

Liam Callahan showed us how to make it at home. "It takes a little bit of practice," he says, "but the results are worth it.

WHAT TO USE

Fresh whey We used leftover whey from making Fresh Chive Cheese (page 46) and Feta (page 120). We have also used whey from Fromage Blanc (page 118), but its acidity causes the curds to form almost as soon as the milk heats. Our Gouda (page 122) does not yield enough whey. Use the whey right away or chill for up to 1 day.

Milk, sea salt, and lemons For more on these ingredients, see page 46. You can also make this recipe using 1 gallon whole milk instead of the whey-milk combination. It won't technically be ricotta, but it will taste similar, just less delicate.

21-quart boiling-water canner with canning rack Large and lightweight, an aluminum canner filled with hot water makes a great water bath for your milk pot. The water bath helps keep the temperature steady and prevents the milk pot from scorching. From $16 at www.amazon.com.

8-quart heavy-bottomed stainless-steel pot, colander, cheesecloth See page 46 for more about these tools.

Dairy thermometer Unlike a candy thermometer, it measures low temperatures. Get the kind with a bracket so you can clip it to the side of the pot. About $25.

Stainless-steel perforated cheese ladle You can use a slotted spoon, but a cheese ladle's large, flat surface makes stirring the milk and curds more efficient. $7.

1 ricotta mold (4¹/₂ inches wide; about $9 each; product code CH87). A small, open-weave basket made of food-grade plastic, it gives the cheese a pretty shape. Or, substitute the basket from a small salad spinner (8 inches in diameter or smaller works best).

2 or 3 cookie or biscuit cutters without handles These are used to elevate the mold to let the whey drain freely (from $2 each at a cookware store). Or use small empty cans with the tops and bottoms removed.

HOW TO DO IT

10 cups fresh whey

6 cups whole milk, pasteurized or raw (or 1 gallon whole milk if not using whey)

2 teaspoons fine sea salt

3¹/₂ tablespoons freshly squeezed lemon juice if using whey (or 4¹/₂ tablespoons if using only milk), from 2 to 3 large lemons

Cheesemaking supplies   Heating milk for ricotta   Draining ricotta curds

1. Heat the milk Put the canner on the stove and insert the canning rack upside down (handles down). Fill the canner with water to 1 inch below the top ring. Cover the canner and bring the water to a boil over high heat. Meanwhile, fill a sink with cold water. This will be your cool-down spot should you need it.

Uncover the canner and set the empty 8-quart pot on the upturned rack (it will float a little). Pour the whey, milk (or milk only), and salt into the pot and insert the tip of the thermometer into the whey mixture. With the cheese ladle, stir the mixture 20 times with a gentle surface-to-bottom circular motion to evenly distribute the heat.

Re-cover the canner and heat the mixture over high heat, undisturbed, until it registers 192° to 194°F (the water will be boiling) on the thermometer, 30 to 40 minutes. Adjust the heat if necessary to maintain the temperature. If the mixture starts to get too hot, immerse the pot in the water-filled sink.

2. Acidify the milk Slowly pour the lemon juice over the hot milk while stirring it with the cheese ladle. (The acid coaxes the remaining proteins in the whey to come together.) Stir 20 times with a gentle surface-to-bottom circular motion. Small curds will begin to form (they may have already). Re-cover the canner and leave the mixture undisturbed over high heat for 25 minutes to allow the curds to finish forming. The temperature should stay between 192° and 194°F; check occasionally and adjust the heat as needed. Meanwhile, line the mold with a double thickness of cheesecloth, trimmed to hang slightly over the rim. Set cookie cutters in the stainless-steel bowl.

3. Drain the curds Lift the cheese pot out of the water bath and put it next to the sink. Hold the mold over the sink and gently ladle the curds and whey into the mold. Allow the mold to drain until the whey flow slows to a trickle. This usually happens within a couple of minutes. Smooth the cheese in the mold so it's level, then set the mold on top of the cookie cutters in the bowl.

Cover the bowl with plastic wrap and chill right away to preserve the ricotta's delicate sweetness. Let the curds drain until there are no visible pockets of liquid (curds should still be moist). This will take up to 30 minutes. Your ricotta is ready to eat. You can either invert the mold onto a plate, or just spoon the cheese out of the mold.

4. Store the cheese Wrap the mold airtight with plastic wrap. Or, if you haven't used a mold, transfer the cheese to an airtight container. It keeps, chilled, for up to 4 days.

PER 1/4-CUP SERVING 108 cal., 66% (71 cal.) from fat; 7 g protein; 8.1 g fat (5.2 g sat.); 2 g carbo (0 g fiber); 52 mg sodium; 32 mg chol.

• •

FROMAGE BLANC

MAKES about 4 cups cheese and 10 cups whey
TIME about 20 minutes, plus 16 to 18 hours
to culture and drain

Smooth, creamy, and delicately tangy, fromage blanc is a lot more sophisticated than its French name—"white cheese"—lets on. It's very versatile in the kitchen, and we've used it in a number of recipes in this book.

Sue Conley, co-owner of Cowgirl Creamery, in Petaluma and Point Reyes Station, California, taught us the Cowgirl way to make fromage blanc. She prefers to start with raw milk and use a gentle pasteurizing method, rather than the more intensive one typical for store-bought pasteurized milk. "The less aggressive method maintains the integrity of the milk and allows it to form a strong curd," she explained. "It also allows the culture to more fully express the flavors inherent in the milk as it ripens." (If you would like to use raw milk and gently pasteurize it yourself, see page 214.) If the milk is homogenized, the fat globules are much smaller and are difficult to retain in the curd; they escape into the whey, compromising the flavor, texture, and yield of the cheese. You can make a fine fromage blanc with pasteurized milk, but avoid homogenized milk if possible.

For specialized cheesemaking tools and ingredients, we turned to the Beverage People, in Santa Rosa, California (www.thebeveragepeople.com or 800/544-1867), unless otherwise mentioned.

WHAT TO USE

Milk and sea salt For more on these ingredients, see page 46.

Farmhouse culture (MA4001). Freeze-dried microscopic bacteria (it looks a lot like the freeze-dried yeast used for baking) that, once revived in warm milk, give the cheese both its flavor and texture—and acidify the milk so that curds develop properly. Fromage blanc may be made with other cultures, but the Beverage People carries this one, and we liked the results. $10 per packet; each packet can make at least 12 batches of fromage blanc. Store it in the freezer in a resealable plastic bag.

Calcium chloride (optional) A type of salt added as a liquid brine, calcium chloride helps firm up the curds (particularly useful with most commercially pasteurized and homogenized milk, which has a weaker structure than raw milk). Use it if your fromage blanc is not as thick as you'd like. $6.50 for a 120-milliliter (about 4-ounce) bottle.

Vegetarian rennet A lab-created version of the natural enzymes that coagulate milk, this rennet is fine for any young cheese, but can give a bitter flavor to aged cheeses. That's why some cheese makers prefer using animal rennet, a group of enzymes derived from the stomachs of calves, lambs, or sheep, for making aged cheeses. $10 for a 60-milliliter (about 2-ounce) squeeze bottle.

Crème fraîche This enhances the smoothness to the cheese and rounds out its flavor. See the recipe on page 70.

8-quart heavy-bottomed stainless-steel pot, colander, cheesecloth For more on these, see page 46.

Dairy thermometer See page 117.

Stainless-steel perforated cheese ladle You can use a large slotted spoon you already have, but a cheese ladle has a large, flat surface that makes the stirring of the milk and curds more efficient. $7.

Cheese bucket A 5-gallon, food-grade plastic bucket to capture whey. From about $7 at a housewares stores.

HOW TO DO IT

1 gallon whole milk, pasteurized or raw
1/8 teaspoon farmhouse culture (MA4001)
2 drops (0.2 milliliter) calcium chloride, if needed
1 drop (0.1 milliliter) vegetarian rennet
1/2 cup crème fraîche, homemade (page 70) or store-bought
3/4 to 1 teaspoon fine sea salt

1. Heat the milk Pour the milk into the 8-quart pot and insert the tip of the dairy thermometer. Heat the milk over medium-high heat until it registers 85°F on the thermometer, stirring often with the cheese ladle to prevent scorching. This takes about 5 minutes.

2. Add the culture Remove the pot from the heat and remove the thermometer. Sprinkle the culture as evenly as possible over the milk and let sit for 10 minutes. Using the ladle, stir the milk 20 times to incorporate the culture, using a gentle, surface-to-bottom circular motion.

3. Add the calcium chloride and rennet Dilute the calcium chloride in 2 tablespoons cool water. Pour the calcium chloride mixture evenly all over the milk and, using the ladle, stir the milk for 1 minute to get it moving in a circular direction. Dilute the rennet in 2 tablespoons cool water, pour it into the still-moving milk, and stir gently a couple of times in the same direction. (Rennet is extremely sensitive to trace minerals found in water and to agitation—so don't dilute it until you're ready to add it, and incorporate it very gently.) Stir once in the opposite direction to stop the movement of the milk. Cover the pot with a double layer of cheesecloth and let rest overnight on the counter (the temperature can be anywhere between 60° and 85°F). The milk will ripen and set dur-

Sprinkling fromage blanc culture   Draining fromage blanc curds   Adding crème fraîche and salt

ing this time, creating curds (your future cheese, full of proteins and enzymes) and whey.

4. Drain the curds Line the colander with a double thickness of cheesecloth and set the lined colander over the cheese bucket. Ladle the curds out of the pot into the colander. Drain the curds, scooping and turning them with a soup spoon every hour or so to help them dry evenly, until the mixture resembles thick sour cream. This will take 6 to 8 hours. The whey will drain into the bucket throughout this period. If you'd like to use it for making Ricotta (page 117), periodically transfer it to a bowl, cover, and refrigerate. Use the whey within a day.

5. Add the crème fraîche and salt When the cheese is ready, turn it into the large bowl and stir in the crème fraîche and the salt to taste. The cheese is now ready to eat. It will keep in an airtight container in the refrigerator for up to 1 week.

PER OUNCE (ABOUT 2 TABLESPOONS) 45 cal., 60% (27 cal.) from fat; 2 g protein; 3 g fat (2 g sat.); 2 g carbo (0 g fiber); 40 mg sodium; 15 mg chol.

• •

FETA

MAKES 2 small (4½-inch) wheels
(about 1½ pounds total)
TIME about 6 hours, plus overnight to drain, at least
3 hours to brine, and at least 1 day to dry

Tangy, crumbly feta can be made many different ways. We've based our method on one developed by Margaret Morris, a well-known Canadian cheese maker and owner of Glengarry Cheesemaking and Dairy Supply, who documented it on her DVD *Home Cheesemaking with Margaret Morris* (see Helpful Information, page 48, for details). This recipe demonstrates the amazing ability of milk to maintain a stable low temperature. Once you heat it up to 85°F, it's likely to stay there for several hours.

For specialized cheesemaking tools and ingredients, we turned to the Beverage People, in Santa Rosa, California (www.thebeveragepeople.com or 800/544-1867), unless otherwise mentioned.

WHAT TO USE

Milk and sea salt For more on these ingredients, see page 46.

Feta cheese culture (ChoozitMT1) This mixture of four different freeze-dried microscopic bacteria (it looks a lot like the freeze-dried yeast used for baking) is what gives the cheese both its flavor and texture; it also acidifies the milk so that curds develop properly. $13 per packet; each packet can culture about 6 gallons of milk, or 6 batches of cheese. Store it in the freezer in a resealable plastic bag.

Lipase powder One of the enzymes found in a calf's stomach, lipase breaks down the fatty acids in the milk into pleasingly tangy compounds. It makes cow's milk taste more like sheep's or goat's milk, the more traditional milks for making feta. $11 for 26 grams (just under 1 ounce).

Calcium chloride and vegetarian rennet For more on these ingredients, see page 119.

21-quart boiling-water canner with canning rack, dairy thermometer, 2 ricotta molds See page 117. You can also use a small salad spinner insert (see photos, page 122) if you don't have the molds.

8-quart heavy-bottomed stainless-steel pot, colander, cheesecloth For more on these, see page 46.

Stainless-steel perforated cheese ladle See page 119.

Wooden spoon with a round, narrow handle

Thin metal spatula (at least 8 inches long)

Cheese bucket A 5-gallon, food-grade plastic bucket to capture the whey. From about $7 at a houseware store.

HOW TO DO IT

1 gallon whole milk, pasteurized or raw
1/4 teaspoon feta cheese culture (ChoozitMT1)
1/4 teaspoon lipase powder
3/4 teaspoon calcium chloride
1/4 teaspoon vegetarian rennet
1/2 cup fine sea salt
1 1/2 teaspoons freshly squeezed lemon juice

1. Heat the milk Put the canner on the stove and insert the canning rack upside down (handles down). Fill the canner with water up to the first ring from the bottom. Bring the water to a boil, covered, over high heat. Meanwhile, fill a sink with cold water. This will be your cool-down spot should you need it.

Turn off the heat, uncover the canner, and set the empty 8-quart pot on the upturned rack (it may float a little). Pour the milk into the pot and insert the tip of the thermometer into the milk. Stir the milk with the cheese ladle 20 times in a gentle surface-to-bottom circular motion until it registers 85°F. This will take only a couple of minutes.

Make sure the milk stays between 85° and 88°F for the duration of the cheese making. If it starts to climb above 86°F, lift the pot from the canner and set it in the sink of cold water until the temperature returns to 85°F; then return the pot to the water bath. If the temperature of the milk sinks, set the canner with the milk pot over medium-high heat, stirring gently every minute or so, until the milk once again registers 85°F.

2. Add the culture Measure the feta culture into a measuring cup, add a big spoonful of warm milk from the pot, and stir to dissolve. Pour the mixture into the milk pot and, using the cheese ladle, stir 20 times with a gentle

surface-to-bottom circular motion. Cover the canner and let the milk sit for 45 minutes to ripen.

3. Add the lipase, calcium chloride, and rennet Put the lipase in a measuring cup, add a big spoonful of warm milk from the pot, and stir to dissolve. Pour the mixture into the milk and, using the ladle, stir 20 times with a gentle surface-to-bottom circular motion. Put 1/2 teaspoon of the calcium chloride in the measuring cup, add 1/4 cup cool water, and stir to dissolve. Add the mixture to the milk the same way you added the lipase mixture. Put the rennet in the measuring cup, add 1/4 cup cool water, stir to dissolve, and add to the milk the same way. Cover the canner and let the milk sit for 1 1/2 hours to set. Check every now and then to be sure the temperature stays at 85°F.

4. Check the curd set Resting your hand on the edge of the pot, insert the tip of the wooden spoon handle at a 45° angle into the middle of the pot and slowly lift it straight up. If the curd is ready, it will break cleanly over the rising handle. If it leaves lots of soft, milky residue on the handle, it is not. Re-cover, let rest for another 30 minutes, and check again. Repeat once more if the curds still haven't set. (If they are *still* too soft, the milk may be weak or not properly acidified; or possibly the culture, lipase, or rennet is too old; or the temperature wasn't right. Drain the curds, add salt, and eat them like cottage cheese instead.)

5. Cut the curds With the spatula, rapidly cut the curd into 1-inch slices, cutting all the way to the bottom of the pot. Then cut the curd again, perpendicular to the first direction, to create 1-inch cubes. Now slash the cubes on a diagonal, again spacing the cuts about 1 inch apart. The curds should look like soft tofu.

Let the curds sit for 1 hour, covered, stirring every 10 minutes with the cheese ladle to break up large

Feta—our first attempts, using a salad spinner

chunks (the curds should look like rough cottage cheese). Be sure the curds' temperature is still 85°F.

6. Drain the curds Lift the stockpot from the canner and set it on the counter. Remove the thermometer. Line the colander with a double thickness of cheesecloth and set the lined colander over the cheese bucket. Drain the sink of water and put the bucket-colander setup in the empty sink. Put 1 mold in the lined colander and carefully ladle curds into the mold, filling it about halfway. When the mold is filled, transfer it to the rack set inside the baking sheet and fill the second mold. Even out the curds between the molds.

Empty the whey from the bucket (or save it for making ricotta cheese, page 117: put it in an airtight container, chill, and use within a day.) Let the cheeses drain for 30 minutes, then invert them into your clean hands and ease them back into the molds so that their bottoms are now facing up. Over the next 2 hours, invert them twice more; then let them drain overnight at room temperature, loosely covered with plastic wrap.

7. Brine the cheese Meanwhile, in a saucepan, bring 4 cups water and $^1/_3$ cup salt to a boil, stirring until the salt dissolves. Remove from the heat and let cool to room temperature. Stir in the remaining $^1/_4$ teaspoon calcium chloride and the lemon juice to create a brine.

Unmold the cheeses onto a clean work surface and cut into quarters. Put into a glass or ceramic bowl and pour in the brine. Let the cheeses pieces float in the brine, cov-

ered with plastic wrap and chilled, $1^1/_2$ hours. Turn the cheeses over and cure for $1^1/_2$ hours longer.

8. Dry the cheese Transfer the cheese pieces to the cooling rack in the baking pan. Chill, turning them a couple of times a day, until their surfaces are dry and hard, for at least 1 day and up to 3. The feta is ready to eat.

9. Store the cheese Make a storage brine with remaining $2^1/_2$ tablespoons sea salt dissolved in 4 cups water. Put the cheeses in an airtight container, pour in brine, and store, chilled, for up to 3 months. Whenever the brine starts forming a cloud on the surface, replace it with a fresh batch of brine. If you find the cheese too salty, soak it in cold water for 15 minutes before eating.

PER 2-OUNCE SERVING (about $^1/_4$ cup crumbled) 150 cal., 73% (109 cal.) from fat; 8 g protein; 12 g fat (8.5 g sat.); 2 g carbo (0 g fiber); 632 mg sodium; 50 mg chol.

GOUDA

MAKES one 2-pound wheel
TIME about 5 hours to set, cut, and wash the cheese; 6 to 8 hours to press; 3 to 4 days to dry; 4 hours to coat; and about 30 minutes to wax, plus between 2 and 6 months to age

Mild and creamy, Gouda gave us the "melting cheese" we needed for a number of different dishes in this book. As we did for our feta, we've based our method on one developed by Canadian cheese maker Margaret Morris, who calmly and cheerily demonstrates it on her *Home Cheesemaking with Margaret Morris* DVD (see Helpful Information, page 48).

For specialized cheesemaking tools and ingredients, we turned to the Beverage People, in Santa Rosa, California (www.thebeveragepeople.com or 800/544-1867), unless otherwise mentioned.

WHAT TO USE

Milk and sea salt For more on these ingredients, see page 46.

Annatto (sometimes called "butter color") A natural dye often used to color butter, annatto is made from the orange-red (achiote) seed. About $10 for 60 milliliters (about 2 ounces).

Mesophilic type III culture A mixture of two strains of freeze-dried microscopic bacteria (it looks like the freeze-dried yeast for baking) that help create flavor and texture; it also acidifies the cheese so that curds develop properly. $11 for 10 grams, enough for 8 batches of cheese. Store in the freezer in a resealable plastic bag.

Calcium chloride and vegetarian rennet For more on these ingredients, see page 119.

21-quart boiling-water canner with canning rack, dairy thermometer, cheese bucket See page 117.

10-quart heavy-bottomed stockpot For setting the curd. About $60 at IKEA.

Colander, cheesecloth, cheese ladle For more on these, see page 46.

Wooden spoon with long, round, narrow handle

Stainless-steel wire whip The whip, designed specifically for cheese making, is 20 inches long and is sturdy enough to cut curds evenly. $8.25 from Hoegger Supply Company (www.hoeggergoatsupply.com or 800/221-4628). A large standard wire whisk (not a balloon whisk) will also work, but not quite as well.

2-pound cheese press Made of solid hardwood, it comes with a 1-pound press as part of the Hoegger's Deluxe Two Hoop Cheese Press. About $90 from Hoegger Supply Company (above). We used the 2-pound press instead of a pricier, single Gouda mold (the 1-kilogram Dutch Kadova mold, $82, from Glengarry Cheesemaking and Dairy Supply, www.glengarry cheesemaking.on.ca). The Hoegger mold works well, but produces a Gouda with sharp edges rather than the classic, round-shouldered shape.

Cheese-press pressure scale This handy tool tells you how much pressure you're putting on the cheese. About $40 from Hoegger Supply Company (above).

Cheese draining/ripening mat A nylon grid that allows air to circulate underneath the cheese as it dries. $3.

Cheese coating (cream wax) A liquid wax coating that you apply to your new cheese with a pastry brush; it quickly sets into a flexible rind that keeps the cheese moist and helps prevent mold. $19 for a 500-gram (17½-ounce) jar.

New pastry brush

Red cheese wax This paraffin-based wax is melted and used for dipping your new cheese into after you have sealed it with cheese coating (or, use your own beeswax, as we did; see above). About $6 per 1-pound block.

Small deep saucepan At least 4 inches deep, for melting wax, and wide enough to dip the finished cheese.

HOW TO DO IT

2 gallons whole milk, pasteurized or raw
2 drops annatto
¹/₄ teaspoon mesophilic type III culture
¹/₂ teaspoon calcium chloride
³/₄ teaspoon vegetarian rennet
¹/₂ cup fine sea salt

1. Heat the milk Put the canner on the stove and insert the canning rack upside down (handles down). Fill the canner with water up to the first ring from the bottom. Bring the water to a boil, covered, over high heat. Meanwhile, fill a sink with cold water. This will be your cool-down spot should you need it.

Remove the canner from the heat and set the stockpot on the upturned rack inside it. The water should come 2¹/₂ inches up the sides of the stockpot; add more hot water as needed. (Some stockpots have handles that rest on the edge of the canner, preventing the pot from sitting fully on the rack.) Pour the milk into the pot and insert the tip of the thermometer into the milk. Stir the milk with the cheese ladle 20 times in a gentle surface-to-bottom circular motion to distribute the heat evenly.

Watch for the thermometer to register 85°F; this will take only a couple of minutes.

The milk should be held at about 85°F for the duration of the cheese making. If it starts to climb above 86°F, lift the pot from the canner and set it in the sink of cold water until the temperature returns to 85°F; then return the pot to the water bath. If the temperature of the milk sinks, briefly set the canner with the milk pot over low heat until the milk again registers 85°F.

2. Add the annatto and culture Add the annatto to 1/4 cup cool water and stir with a soup spoon to dissolve. Pour the mixture into the milk and, using the ladle, stir 20 times with a gentle surface-to-bottom circular motion. Immediately sprinkle the culture as evenly as possible over the milk and let rest for 10 minutes.

3. Add the calcium chloride and rennet Place the calcium chloride in a measuring cup, add 1/4 cup cool water, and stir to dissolve. Pour the mixture into the milk and, using the ladle, stir 20 times in the same way as before. Place the rennet in a measuring cup, add 1/4 cup cool water, and stir

OUR LITTLE CHEESE CAVE

Although it would be very romantic if we had a cool, stone-lined cave dug into a mountain for aging cheeses, or even a modern cheese maker's walk-in cooler "cave," our cheese cave is cheap and humble: a dorm fridge with its thermostat rejiggered to allow temperatures above 40°F. The living bacteria in cheeses are what ripen it, and they shut down when the temperature is too low. On the other hand, if the temperature shoots high, as room temperatures can, the cheeses may spoil; that's why they need to age in an atmosphere that can be controlled.

To override the fridge's normal temperature settings, we bought a Controller external thermostat (from Williams Brewing, www.williamsbrewing.com, about $60). It permits a range of temperatures from 37° to 80°F, adjustable with a knob, and is easy to install. We also put in a tiny electric desk fan (from about $9 at hardware stores) for air circulation—its cord snakes out through the fridge's door seal and into a nearby plug—and shallow pans of water, for humidity. Lastly, we bought a combination thermometer and hygrometer (from about $9 online or at hardware stores), and set it next to our cheese so we could monitor the temperature and humidity.

to dissolve. Stir the mixture into the milk the same way you did the calcium chloride. Cover the canner and let the milk sit for 1 hour to set. Check the temperature occasionally to make sure it remains at 85° F and correct if needed as described in step 1.

4. Check the curd set Resting your hand on the edge of the pot, insert the tip of the wooden spoon handle at a 45° angle into the middle of the pot and slowly lift it straight up. If the curd is ready, it will break cleanly over the rising handle. If it leaves lots of soft, milky residue on the handle, it is not. Re-cover, let rest for another 30 minutes, and check again. Repeat once more if the curds still haven't set. (If they are *still* too soft, the milk may be weak or not properly acidified; or possibly the culture, lipase, or rennet is too old; or the temperature wasn't right. Drain the curds, add salt, and eat them like cottage cheese instead.)

5. Cut the curds Drag the wire whip rapidly but evenly through the entire mass of curd once, breaking it into roughly 1/2-inch bits. Repeat the motion, this time dragging perpendicular to the first direction. Then drag the whip through the curd on a diagonal.

Using the ladle, stir the curd for 5 to 10 minutes, using surface-to-bottom strokes in a circular motion. Let the curds settle into the whey for 5 minutes. Meanwhile, start heating 7 cups of water to 175°F in a saucepan.

6. Wash the curds Lift the stockpot from the canner and set it on a work surface. Remove the thermometer. Line the colander with a double thickness of cheesecloth and set the lined colander over the cheese bucket. Drain the sink of water and put the bucket-colander setup in the empty sink.

Scoop out all the curds into the lined colander and let drain until the whey has almost stopped dripping. Pour the whey in to a large stainless-steel bowl. Return two-thirds of the whey and all of the curds to the pot.

Measure 3 cups of the 175°F water (you may need to heat the water a bit) and add to the curds and whey. Scoop the ladle down one side of the pot and lift the curds, jiggling the ladle to separate them. Using a surface-to-bottom motion, keep lifting and jiggling the curds until they begin to shrink, 10 to 15 minutes. Let the curds settle to the bottom of the pot, about 10 minutes.

7. Wash the curds a second time Scoop out the whey down to the level of the curds and pour into the colander. Return any curds in the colander to the pot and discard

Applying cream wax to Gouda

the whey. Add enough of the 175°F water (2 to 3 cups) to the curds to heat them to 100°F, and stir and shake the curds with the ladle as before for about 10 minutes. Let the curds settle for another 10 minutes.

Scoop up a spoonful of the curds and squeeze them gently. If they're springy and moist, they're ready to be pressed. If they feel soft, let them sit in the hot water for several more minutes. When the curds are ready, pour them into the colander and let drain for 5 minutes.

8. Press the cheese Arrange a double thickness of cheesecloth on the base of the press and place the 2-pound hoop on the base (or set a 2-pound Gouda mold into the press). Set the press in a rimmed baking pan. Scoop the curds into the press, packing them down as evenly as possible. Cover the curds with another double thickness of cheesecloth and set the follower (the inset top) of the mold over the curds. Screw down the wing nuts on either side of the hoop simultaneously to distribute the pressure evenly. Screw in the central pressure-gauge screw and tighten to 35 pounds of pressure.

Leave the cheese in the press for 6 hours, checking the pressure every couple of hours and retightening the pressure-gauge screw as needed to register 35 pounds pressure. After 3 hours, turn the cheese over in the mold.

9. Brine the cheese Meanwhile, in a medium saucepan, bring 4 cups water and the salt to a boil over high heat, stirring until the salt is mostly dissolved. Let the brine cool to room temperature, then slip the cheese out of the mold and into the brine. Cover and brine the cheese in the refrigerator for 12 hours.

10. Dry the cheese Put the draining mat on a cake cooling rack and set both on the baking sheet. Remove the cheese from the brine, set it on the on draining mat, and let the cheese air-dry at room temperature, flipping it every several hours, until dry to the touch, 3 to 4 days.

11. Coat the cheese Using the new pastry brush, paint the top and sides of the cheese with the cream wax. Let the wax dry completely, about 1 hour. Turn the cheese over, paint the bottom, and let dry completely, about 1 hour. Coat the cheese again the same way and let dry completely.

12. Wax the cheese Line the small deep saucepan with heavy-duty foil. Put 1 pound cheese wax in the pan. Fill the roasting pan halfway with water and bring to a boil over medium-high heat. As it's heating, set the pan of wax in the roasting pan to melt. When the wax has melted, dip the cheese sideways into the wax to coat as completely as possible. Lift out, let harden (this takes only a couple of seconds), then dip the other side. Repeat at least twice, or until you have nice coverage. Set the cheese on the cooling rack (remove the mat first) to harden completely.

13. Age (ripen) the cheese Ripen the cheese at 50° to 55°F and about 75 percent humidity for at least 2 months and up to 6 months. Make sure the area is well ventilated. You can repurpose an old refrigerator for greater control when ripening cheese. See Our Little Cheese Cave, opposite, for directions. The longer you ripen the cheese, the stronger in flavor and drier in texture it will be.

PER 2-OUNCE SERVING 201 cal., 70% (140 cal.) from fat; 14 g protein; 15 g fat (9 g sat.); 1 g carbo (0 g fiber); 464 mg sodium; 64 mg chol.

HELPFUL INFORMATION

For information on web sites, cheese-making supplies, and books and DVDs, see page 48.

—Margo True and Elaine Johnson

HOW TO GROW
MUSHROOMS

We took both the fast route, raising mushrooms from logs that you purchase as kits, and the slow, planting a morel patch in our garden. The kits are as easy as growing a houseplant. The process is fun and encourages the mad scientist in you as you watch the logs that you purchase as kits sprout weird, Dr. Seuss-like fungi. Home-cultivated mushrooms have a delicious, mild flavor and tender texture, and you can experiment with several varieties.

Morels, on the other hand, are a long-term endeavor, with no guarantees that you will reap the rewards the first year (we are still waiting). But what rewards when they do come! Few treats compare with a panful of fragrant, earthy morels sautéed in butter.

SHIITAKE, OYSTER, AND
POM POM BLANC MUSHROOMS
(grown from a kit)

WHAT TO USE

Log kits Mushrooms are the fruit of a fungus whose body is the mycelium, a net of threadlike fibers. In a mushroom-log kit, the mycelium is distributed throughout a growing medium, such as sawdust mixed with rice bran. The log looks like a loaf of bread covered with a fine, soft mold. As the mushrooms grow, they sprout from the log. Although the kits come with instructions, they are fairly general, and we added a lot of extra notes based on our experiences.

From Far West Fungi (www.farwestfungi.com), we bought a shiitake minifarm kit ($19.50) and a tree oyster minifarm kit ($19.50). From Gourmet Mushrooms and Mushroom Products (www.gmushrooms.com), we purchased a shiitake kit ($20.00), plus kits for pom pom blanc mushrooms ($19.00) and brown oyster mushrooms ($17.00). Each kit comes with plastic bags, an important part of the mushroom-growing environment. The kits from Gourmet Mushrooms also include a sponge for the log to rest on, which allows the log to take up the moisture it needs without sitting in a pool of water.

Shiitake mushrooms

Extra materials Depending on the brand and type of kit, you may also need a spray bottle and a deep plate large enough to hold each log with a little water.

HOW TO DO IT

1. Prepare the log's environment For Far West Fungi kits, untie the twist tie and retie it at the top of the bag. Cut 10 to 20 (see package directions) small X-shaped holes in the upper part of the bag to allow the mushroom culture to breathe without drying out.

For Gourmet Mushrooms kits, leave the plastic covering on the logs. If shiitake logs have not started to sprout, they may need a pregrowing rest period of 7 to 12 days (see kit directions); ours didn't need this. Then rinse the log if the kit directs you to (it depends on the mushroom).

Next, cut two X-shaped openings through the plastic covering over the oyster or pom pom blanc mushrooms and into the log. Each opening should be about 1 inch deep and on either side of the log near the top. Gouge a 1-inch-wide, 1-inch-deep hole in the top of the shiitake log with a table knife. Set the log on its sponge in a large, rimmed plate and add cool water to a depth of $1/2$ to $3/4$ inch. Don't let standing water touch the log. Open the

Oyster mushrooms

Pom pom mushroom

perforated plastic sleeve (or for shiitakes, inflate the bag by blowing into it), and put the sleeve over the log so the bottom of it rests inside the water dish. The top of the sleeve should be closed.

2. Find a good spot Set the log indoors at room temperature or a bit cooler, away from the kitchen, which can foster mold growth (we learned this the hard way), and away from direct light and drafts.

3. Encourage growth For Far West Fungi kits, lightly mist the mushrooms once or twice a day, but not enough to cause water to collect in the bottom of the bag. Open the bag a little as needed so the environment stays humid but not wet. Within a week or two, you'll begin to see tiny knobs, or "pins"—the start of mushrooms—on the log. When these are about 1 inch long or $1/2$ inch across, remove the twist tie and open the bag slightly at the top to make room for the mushrooms to grow. Otherwise, you'll get strange, strangulated shapes.

For Gourmet Mushrooms kits, add water as needed to the plate to keep the water about $1/2$ inch deep. Every day until you see growth (2 to 21 days for pom poms or oysters, 5 to 9 days for shiitakes), open up the top of the plastic sleeve and either mist or drizzle a little water over

the logs (for pom poms or oysters) or pour water into the hole in the top (for shiitakes).

4. Let the mushrooms mature A few days after you see growth starting, the mushrooms will reach full size. As they grow, open up the sleeves a bit as needed to give them room, and continue to add moisture as before.

5. Harvest Shiitakes are ready when the white cottony veil beneath the cap has fully broken away from the stem but the caps still curl under slightly. Harvest oyster mushrooms when the caps have grown but before their outer edges begin to curl up. Pom poms are ready when the heads have formed and are still firm and white. Cut mushrooms at the base with a sharp knife. Cook them, or enclose them in paper bags (not plastic ones, which can trap moisture and make the mushrooms slimy), and refrigerate. You may get anywhere from 8 ounces to 2 pounds mushrooms per log.

6. Cook If consumed raw, these mushroom varieties can make some people ill.

7. Encourage additional mushrooms You should get three or four more "flushes" of mushrooms that are a week to a month apart before the mycelium runs out of food. To encourage additional growth, clean off any remaining mushroom stems from the log with a knife. Wrap the log in paper towels (for Gourmet Mushrooms kits) or a plastic bag (for Far West Fungi kits) and let rest for about a week at room temperature for oysters and pom poms, 2 to 3 weeks for shiitakes. Then repeat the steps to grow more mushrooms, using a clean plastic bag. We had only sporadic production from our logs after the first harvest.

8. Deal with moldy logs We had a little mold during our mushrooms' initial growth period, and simply scraped it off with a table knife, decreased the water, and opened the bags to let in more air. Between harvests, we got a lot of mold on a couple of the logs; we had some luck scraping it off with the knife, then cleaning the area with rubbing alcohol.

9. Recycle the logs Once they have stopped producing, add them to your compost pile.

MOREL MUSHROOMS (grown from spawn)

In the wild, morels grow in a number of different colors. We are raising common, or yellow, morels.

WHAT TO USE

Spawn This is mycelium in a wad of white, crumbly fiber that can be mixed straight into soil. As it grows, the mycelium spreads underground and produces mushrooms—the fruit—above ground when conditions are right. We bought our spawn from Gourmet Mushrooms and Mushroom Products (www.gmushrooms .com) for $30.

Soil You need a 4- to 16-square-foot patch of ordinary, well-drained garden soil, in the ground or in a raised bed (in contact with the ground). The area should be shaded at least half the day, with less than 3 hours of direct sunlight, and protected from wind (you can build a windbreak if needed).

Shovel

Compostables Fresh materials from your kitchen, such as vegetable trimmings, coffee grounds, eggshells, and the like. We also added ash from a wood fire, as morels in the wild grow well in areas where there has been a forest fire or controlled burn.

Water source Pick a spot within reach of a hose, or plan to make frequent trips with a watering can.

HOW TO DO IT

1. Let the spawn rest After the spawn arrives, it needs to sit in a cool (below 70°F), dark place for a couple of days. It will also keep in the refrigerator for up to 6 months.

2. Plant the spawn Morels can be planted any time of year as long as the soil isn't frozen.

3. Prepare the soil With a shovel, turn the soil to a depth of 6 to 12 inches to loosen it. Clear away any rocks or debris.

4. Scatter the spawn Crumple the spawn over the prepared soil, then turn the soil under. Rake it smooth on top.

5. Add compostables About once a week, dig in a bowlful of fresh food scraps, 9 to 18 inches deep. Water the soil so it stays damp. Continue this for at least 3 months.

6. Wait Now you need to let the soil rest so the mycelium can spread underground. Typically, it takes a full year before you'll see mushrooms, but depending on when you planted your spawn, you could get results in as soon as 2 months. As the soil rests, you may get plants sprouting from the compost. This is okay, and may even be helpful, as they will shade the area.

It's hard to predict exactly what month the mushrooms will pop above ground. They need the right conditions for a "morel spring," which can be any time of year, though more often in spring. Typically they appear when there has been a period of heavy rain followed by a period of light to no rain for a week or two, with the weather changing to highs in the upper 60s and 70s. This can be January to April in areas with mild climates and May or June in areas with colder climates. Also, the spawn we used produces a warm-weather morel that comes up later than wild morels.

7. Water regularly In warm weather, water your patch often enough to keep it damp.

8. Check for mushrooms Our morels did not emerge in May, as we had hoped, and they haven't appeared in the months since. When we finally spot them, it will be a happy day. Young morels look like small, white tooth-

Turning the morel bed   Raking it smooth   First fruits: shiitake and oyster mushrooms

picks poking out of the soil. We'll probably need to give them a week or two to reach full size.

9. Harvest We're planning to trim the mushrooms at the base without digging up the soil, which would disturb the mycelium. Gourmet Mushrooms tells us that the yield can vary from year to year—sometimes none, and sometimes as many as 50, but the mycelium may keep producing for up to 15 years.

10. Cook Since morels grow in dirt, they'll need a quick rinse to remove soil. They should only be eaten cooked. A word of caution: If the mushrooms you've picked don't look like morels, do not eat them until you've checked with an expert, such as someone at your local mycological society (see a couple of choices in Helpful Information, below).

HELPFUL INFORMATION

WEB SITES

- "6 Ways Mushrooms Can Save the World: Paul Stamets on TED.com." A dazzling 18-minute presentation from Stamets, an "entrepreneurial mycologist," on the potential that mushrooms have to transform biotechnology. Watch and be awed by the not-so-humble 'shroom. http://blog.ted.com/2008/05/06/paul_stamets.
- Fungi Perfecti LLC, www.fungi.com. A one-stop resource from Paul Stamets (see above) with indoor and outdoor mushroom kits, culinary mushroom products, dietary supplements, information for kids, recipes, articles, and books—including Stamets' *Mycelium Running: How Mushrooms Can Help Save the World* (Ten Speed Press, 2005).
- The Great Morel, www.thegreatmorel.com. Interactive site with stories, recipes, and photos, from fellow 'shroomers around the world.

BOOKS

- *Growing Gourmet and Medicinal Mushrooms*, by Paul Stamets (Ten Speed Press, 2000). An indepth resource for growing and learning about mushrooms.

ORGANIZATIONS

- Cascade Mycological Society, www.cascademyco.org. Based in Eugene, Oregon, the group promotes wild mushroom education and identification, leads wild forays, and hosts an annual wild mushroom feast.
- Mycological Society of San Francisco, www.mssf.org or 866/807-7148. Gives information on how mushrooms grow, how to cultivate mushrooms, mushrooms in the wild, and recipes.

—Elaine Johnson

HOW TO MAKE
OLIVE OIL

It was the sight of the olive trees all around Sunset that did it: tall, stately, and loaded with thousands of ripening olives. We needed some sort of cooking fat for our one-block feast, and after rejecting peanuts and corn for oil, we realized that our trees held the answer in their branches. Plus, we would be using a heretofore wasted resource—every fall, olives rained down onto the ground and into the bushes, feeding only the birds and insects.

Unfortunately, they were feeding the insects a little too well. Our olives, we learned, were thoroughly infested with the maggots of olive fruit flies. So we picked olives at a nearby, fruit-fly-free olive farm instead and drove them to a commercial olive press, where we had planned to press our olives anyway.

The actual making of olive oil is instantly gratifying. Unlike with wine, there are no months of fermenting and aging. It all happens in a single day. The thick, jewel green new oil is ready to taste immediately, mere hours after it was fruit hanging on a tree. This new oil—what

Harvesting olives in the Santa Cruz foothills

the Italians call *olio nuovo*—is the biggest perk of crushing olives yourself, since it's difficult to find in stores. The other big perk: a stock of your own good oil to give as gifts and use whenever you like.

We are still holding out hope that by next harvest season we will be able to use our own olives, which we believe are a combination of Mission and Redding Picholine. In fact, as this book went to press, we had just started spraying our trees with an organic control called GF-120 that has been recently approved for backyard trees. For more on this, see Our Future Plans (page 133) and see http://oneblockdiet.sunset.com/team_olive, where we will post ongoing updates of Our Battle Against the Olive Fruit Fly.

EXTRA VIRGIN OLIVE OIL

20 gallons, pressed from a blend of six Italian olives: Maurino, Leccino, Frantoio, Pendolino, Ascolano, and Taggiasca

WHAT TO USE

Olives To make 20 gallons of olive oil, you'll need about 800 pounds of olives. Because many growers worry about liability these days, finding a farm where you can pick your own fruit is difficult. We got lucky and were kindly allowed to pick at a ranch, but it was a one-time-only situation. You can order olives by mail, however, through the Olive Growers Council of California (559/734-1710 or adin@goldstate.net) and from La Conda Ranch (www.lacondaranch.com or 530/824-5946). Call to place your order starting in early September. Prices vary depending on variety and growing conditions. As an example, last season, La Conda Ranch sold their olives for $1.75 per pound (plus shipping.) All of these olive farms are in California—in fact, 98 percent of U.S. olive production is in the state.

Olive press We didn't buy one. They are expensive (upward of $200,000!) and we were already spending money on the olives themselves. A separator and a washing system boost the bill even higher. The home-version First Press, available through the Olive Oil Source (see Helpful Information, page 134), is a relatively reasonable $2,790 and includes all the machinery you need. The advantage is that you can run just a few buckets of olives through it and get oil, and do it fresh from your trees. It is slow and labor-intensive, however.

Our brand-new oil

The stone mill at Pietra Santa Winery

With a larger amount, at least a few hundred pounds, you can go to a communal mill: an olive-oil maker that rents its mill periodically to the public during harvesttime (and also takes care of the separating and washing). We took our olives to Pietra Santa Winery in Hollister, which makes its own superb olive oil ($525 minimum fee per ton or less; www.pietrasantawinery.com or 831/636-1991). Frantoio Ristorante & Olive Oil in Mill Valley (www.frantoio.com or 415/289-5777) will press a half ton for $250, which includes a $50 pomace disposal fee. If you want the skins and seeds yourself and can haul them away, you'll save $50. Frantoio will also press quantities less than a half ton, but they mix the olives with other small lots, so you'll end up with a blend. Other communal mills offer this small-lot service, too, on "community press days." One is McCauley Brothers Olive Groves, in Brentwood (www.mccauleyolivegroves.com or 925/754-6457); call for prices. For more communal presses and community press days, search the list of millers on the Olive Oil Source's website. It's usually about $450 per ton, depending on the mill, and less for smaller amounts.

A cool, dark place Where you keep your oil as it settles and once it is bottled is important. Olive oil needs to be kept at temperatures between 60° and 70°F, in as dark a place as possible. (Heat and light are the top degraders, along with oxygen.) We stored our olive oil in a temperature-controlled shed at Sunset, and laid big sheets of black plastic over the containers during the settling period to block the light completely.

5-gallon food-grade plastic drums with spigot You need these for storing the new oil. They're about $15 each from the Olive Oil Source. We bought seven, figuring we could always use the extra three for the next harvest. Stainless-steel containers are ideal as they block out all light and oxygen and are beautiful. They are also expensive (from $515 for a 50-liter tank). Plastic drums admit a small amount of oxygen, but not enough to affect the oil as long as the drums are filled to the top. The drums do need to be scrupulously washed with a food-grade degreaser for reuse, because even a trace of old oil will contaminate your nice fresh batch.

Power drill with a small bit You need to make a "breather hole" in each plastic drum when you are ready to bottle. From about $30 at a hardware store.

Bottles and corks Dark green or amber glass is best, to prevent light from spoiling the oil. We chose small bottles (250-milliliter/about 1-cup size) to give away as gifts and also because we could use up an opened bottle more quickly, with less chance of it oxidizing. Bottles sell out fast during harvest season in fall, so place your order well ahead of time. The Olive Oil Source sells bottles by the case, in various sizes; 200-milliliter bottles with corks in dark amber are about $19.50 for a case of 12. If you buy a minimum of 7 cases (over $100), the $20 handling fee is waived.

Plastic funnels Get at least two, and make sure they're narrow enough to fit securely into your bottles. From $3.50 online or at a cookware store.

Towels or rags For mopping up and wiping bottles.

Sturdy worktable Where you will set the containers of olive oil for bottling, with their spigots hanging over the edge. From $75 at a home-improvement center.

Plastic tarps As much as you'll try not to, you *will* splatter, making a tarp under and around the worktable indispensable. If you care about your worktable top, spread one there, too. About $40 for a 10-by-100-foot tarp at a home-improvement center.

Large aluminum pans Old turkey roasting pans or the like, placed beneath the spigots, work well for catching drips.

Mallet or small hammer For tapping corks into bottles. From $6 at a hardware store.

Hot, soapy water Mix up a batch in a bucket to use for cleaning slippery hands while bottling.

HOW TO DO IT

Given that our own olive trees were infested with olive fruit fly maggots, we didn't grapple with harvesting them. If you have a backyard tree or several, and are interested in learning how to harvest olives, control the olive fruit fly, or care for your trees, see Helpful Information (page 134).

NOVEMBER 29

Pick and press We drove to Valencia Creek Farms in Aptos (www.valenciacreekfarms.com), about 50 miles south of Sunset, and hand-picked olives. We put them in 23 plastic crates, each of which measured 3/4 by 16 by 9 inches and held 40 to 44 pounds of olives. Valencia Creek's Chris Banthien sells them for $1 per crate. Similar crates are available through the Fairfield, California, branch of MacroPlastics (www.macroplastics.com or 707/437-1200).

We immediately drove 30 miles south to Pietra Santa Winery to press the olives. Our 800 pounds were mechanically washed and then crushed in an Italian stone press (three enormous rotating stone wheels weighing a total of 7,000 pounds). The mush was separated, filtered, and poured into the 5-gallon plastic drums we had brought with us.

NOVEMBER 30

Settling Olive particles in oil makes it spoil faster (although it does taste delicious when fresh), so we needed to let the solids fall to the bottom of the drums. We reserved a small portion to use as *olio nuovo*, and then we put the drums in the Sunset prop shed and set them on their sides so they would be in the same position on bottling day, with the spigot facing down (if we stored them upright and then turned them, all the sediment would swirl back up into the oil). We draped them with black plastic to shut out light, and set the thermostat to 65°F to keep them properly cool.

FEBRUARY 6

Bottle After about 2 months of quiet resting, each drum had a layer of olive sludge on its bottom (settling usually happens within 30 to 45 days). It was time to bottle. Here's how:

- **First, taste it** You don't want to go through all that work of bottling if your oil is no good! We tasted the oil as best we could to make sure it hadn't acquired any of the flaws that can downgrade an extra virgin olive oil to just plain olive oil: fustiness, mustiness, vinegariness, muddiness, or just plain rancidity. Phew—it was still good. It was less "green" tasting and peppery than when just pressed, and the color had mellowed to a golden hue, but good.

- **Divide the labor** Put 1 or 2 people to work filling the bottles, another pushing in the corks, and a fourth wiping the bottles free of oil and putting them in storage boxes (we reused the boxes that the bottles came in).

- **Spread the tarp** Lay the tarp on the ground where you will be working. Set your worktable on top and cover it with a tarp, too, if it's a stainable surface.

- **Set the drums on the table** Position each so the spigot is hanging over the edge. Drill a small "breather hole" into the tiny cap opposite the spigot to release pressure and enable flow. (Once the drum is empty and cleaned, it can be reused for storage as long as the cap's cover is in place; it comes with the drum.)

- **Put the aluminum pans on the ground** Slip a pan under each spigot to catch drips.

- **Fill and cork the bottles** Slip a funnel into the neck of the first bottle, stick it under the spigot, open up the valve, and let the oil pour in, stopping within 1/2 inch of the rim to leave room for the cork. Close

Bottling olive oil

the valve, push in the cork, clean off the bottle, and put the bottle in the box. Keep going until you've bottled up all the oil.

APRIL 22

Store We moved our boxes of oil down into the Sunset wine cellar, where it's always cool and dark.

NOVEMBER

An anniversary taste One year had passed since the harvest. Some bottles were starting to lose flavor and turn bitter once they were removed from their cool home in the cellar. Others stayed stable.

FEBRUARY

A last taste Although our remaining couple dozen bottles tasted passable, the oil was no longer as flavorful as it was in November. We relegated these final bottles to cooking, rather than saving them for drizzling over dishes before serving.

OUR FUTURE PLANS

We have finally mounted a plan of attack against the olive fruit fly. By the time you read this, we hope to have executed the plan, harvested our olives, and pressed them into oil. (Check our blog to read all about it.)

IDENTIFY WHICH TREES TO TREAT

Short, or at least thinned in the canopy Olive trees for fruit production should be no more than 14 feet high, and/or pruned so that they are not densely foliaged. Big, full trees like ours are ideal habitats for the fruit fly. Our trees were planted decades ago as ornamentals, however, so they are now 40 to 50 feet tall and beautiful, and are part of the landscaping at Sunset. Team Olive can't go hacking away at them. But we don't want them to stand around spreading disease, either (untended, infested public and backyard trees pose a major problem for olive growers in California). One avenue we are exploring for most of these statuesque lovelies is spraying them with a plant growth regulator called FruitStop, which goes on at blossom time and prevents the baby olives from forming. This way we'll still have pretty trees. No olives to pick, but no olive fruit flies to contend with either—and we'll focus on treating the trees that we do hope to harvest.

In the meantime, we've decided to treat just four of our twenty-one olive trees—the shortest (25 to 30 feet) and relatively best-pruned ones.

Relatively free of surrounding bushes and other plants This makes harvesting and treating them easier and also means they're relatively pest-free (olives with larvae drop into bushes and can't be raked up; the larvae burrow into the ground and overwinter there).

CHOOSE THE WEAPONS

Organic spray The best organic control of the olive fruit fly is a spray called GF-120 NF Naturalyte, which contains a tiny amount of natural pesticide called Spinosad, plus a sticky, molasses-like substance (hydrolyzed protein). When you spray the stuff on the trees, it lands as gooey globs that act as bait. Ingesting GF-120 makes the insects' muscles contract, leading to paralysis—and, within a day or two, death. It doesn't hurt birds (even if they eat the bugs). It can harm honeybees that land directly on the globs, but according to olive ranchers we spoke to who also raise bees, the bees would much rather go for blossoms than for the GF-120, and don't seem affected at all by the spraying. Just in case, spray early in the morning, before the bees are up.

The price of GF-120 NF Naturalyte ranges from $100 to $150 per gallon. For sources, see Helpful Information, page 134.

Infested olive tree at Sunset

Hanging traps Also known as olipe traps. We're painting liter-size plastic bottles yellow, filling them with water, cutting a 1/4-inch hole in the top of each bottle, dropping 4 yeast tablets (available from Napa Valley Ag Supply, 707/963-3495; $59 for 180 tablets) into each bottle, and then hanging the bottles. The flies love the yeast. They'll fly into the bottles and never come out. Traps will also be a great indicator of just how infested our trees are. We plan to check them (and dump out the dead flies) once a week.

PICK UP FALLEN OLIVES

Olive fruit flies really like the olives they find on the ground. And any larvae laid inside burrow into the dirt and live there all winter long, to hatch as flies in the spring. So we will have to be diligent about picking up fallen fruit from last year, to help keep the olive fly population down (it would help to get all the old fruit off the tree, too). We do, of course, still have day jobs, but it looks like Olive Pick-Up might be the new lunch hour.

OUR WORRIES, OUR DOUBTS

Okay, we'll be honest here. Our number-one worry: Is this all for naught? Our trees have been infested for *years, probably decades*. (The olive fruit fly was discovered in California in 1998, and in our complete ignorance that we even had a problem, we have never sprayed our trees. And, like we said, we are only treating four of our twenty-one trees. That means that seventeen trees are going untreated. We can't imagine that these relentless olive flies will be afraid to cross the street to where the treated trees are. The Spinosad spray attracts flies from up to a couple of miles away! As Bill Krueger, an olive-tree expert from UC Davis, told us, "They're the superfly of fruit flies." Is this going to work? "Well . . . ," says Sunset's head gardener, Rick LaFrentz, "I wouldn't bet on it. But you have to try. You have to try." So, we're giving it our best shot.

HARVESTING

How we'll go about actually picking the olives from our tall trees is still somewhat up in the air. Ladders that tall, we're told, are pretty dangerous. It is more likely we'll stand on standard ladders and beat our trees with sticks. We hear that PVC pipes (a type of plastic, and the main kind of irrigation pipe buried underground) are good, too. Or, if we can get a hold of some mechanized rakes, that would be helpful. We'll definitely need tarps to spread out under the trees to catch the olives as they drop.

PLANTING NEW TREES

This is an idea we've been tossing around: planting a few short, high-density olive trees on trellises. It's the latest trend in the industry, and UC Davis has an exhibition planting near its Olive Center. High-density trees are easier to manage, harvest, and—best of all—are more likely to hold their own against the olive fly.

HELPFUL INFORMATION

ORGANIZATIONS

- The Olive Oil Source, based in Santa Ynez, California (805/688-1014 or www.oliveoilsource.com), sells everything from books to mills to bottles and has a trove of resources and links on its Web site, including information on how to grow and harvest olives.
- The new Olive Center at the University of California at Davis (www.olivecenter.ucdavis.edu) has horticultural information about raising olives for oil and

for the table. Also, the university harvests its own landscape olive trees and makes good oil, which it sells in the campus bookstore and through its Web site for $10 per bottle.

- The California Olive Oil Council (COOC) gives pointers and guidance to anyone interested in growing olives or learning about olive oil. From time to time, they hold informative olive oil–tasting workshops open to the public. They also certify extra virgin olive oils via an expert tasting panel, following the Italian model. Look for the COOC label the next time you buy oil and you won't be disappointed (www.cooc.com or 888/718-9830).

BOOKS

- *California's Olive Pioneers: Early Essays on Olives & Olive Oil*, foreword by Judith M. Taylor, MD (Robert Mondavi Institute for Wine and Food Science, 2009); available through the Olive Center (see opposite).
- *Olive Oil: From Tree to Table* by Peggy Knickerbocker (Chronicle Books, 1997). A gorgeous overview (photographs by Laurie Smith) of olive oil production around the world, with guidance on tasting and usage, plus recipes.
- *Olive Production Manual*, edited by Louise Ferguson and G. Steven Sibbett (A.N.R. Publications, 1994). A good introduction to olive growing.
- *Olives: The Life and Lore of a Noble Fruit*, by Mort Rosenblum (Absolute Press, 2000). A mesmerizing story of the olive and its deep, abiding roots in cultures around the Mediterranean, prompted by the author's quest to revive some ancient olive trees on his property in Provence.
- *The New American Olive Oil: Profiles of Artisan Producers and 75 Recipes,* by Fran Gage (Stewart, Tabori & Chang, 2009). Profiles of growers, with recipes, tips on choosing and storing extra virgin olive oils, and how to host an olive oil tasting.
- *The Olive in California: History of an Immigrant Tree*, by Judith M. Taylor, MD (Ten Speed Press, 2004). A richly detailed account of more than two hundred years of olive growing in the Golden State.

OLIVE FRUIT FLY CONTROL

The olive fruit fly invaded California more than ten years ago and has ruined many an olive crop. Here are some resources to help you battle the pest:

Tying olive traps in one of our olive trees

- "Controlling Olive Fruit Fly at Home," by Paul Vossen and Alexandra Kicenik Devarenne, two of California's leading olive fruit fly experts. www.ucce.ucdavis.edu/files/filelibrary/2161/28457.pdf.
- "Olive Fly Control," The Olive Oil Source, Santa Ynez, California. www.oliveoilsource.com/olive_fly.htm.
- University of California Cooperative Extension. www.ucanr.org (enter "olive fruit fly" in search field).
- "Pruning: Topping Tall or Neglected Olive Trees," by Paul Vossen. www.ucce.ucdavis.edu/files/filelibrary/2161/36224.pdf.
- Ernie's Pest Control, Orland, California; 530/865-9829. Sells GF-120 NF Naturalyte; specializes in olive fruit fly control.
- ISCA Technologies, www.iscatech.com. For yellow sticky traps.
- Wilbur-Ellis, St. Helena, California; 707/963-3495 (website is hard to navigate; it's easier to call). Sells GF-120 NF Naturalyte, yellow sticky traps, torula yeast tablets, and FruitStop.

—Rachel Levin

THE FALL RECIPES

FRESH APPLE CIDER AND APPLESAUCE

Not having a powerful juicer or a purpose-built press for creating cider from the apples, we came up with this twofer: a rather unorthodox way to make the cider, plus an applesauce bonus.

MAKES 2 1/2 to 3 cups cider and 3 1/2 to 4 cups applesauce TIME about 1 hour

8 or 9 large Honey Crisp or other favorite local apple (about 5 pounds total)

1. Peel, quarter, and core the apples, then cut the quarters in half crosswise. Put half the apples in a food processor and add 3/4 cup water. Whirl into a smooth puree.

2. Pour the puree into a medium-mesh strainer set over a bowl, and press and rub with the back of a spoon to extract the cider. Transfer the puree to a saucepan.

3. Process the remaining apples the same way, adding 3/4 cup of the cider instead of water. Add the puree to the saucepan.

4. Cover the pan and bring the puree to a gentle simmer over medium heat, stirring occasionally. Cook, stirring occasionally and reducing the heat if the sauce starts to stick, until very soft, 15 to 20 minutes.

5. Serve the applesauce warm or at room temperature. Serve the cider hot or at room temperature.

MAKE AHEAD Both the applesauce and the cider can be made up to 3 days in advance and refrigerated. Bring to room temperature before serving.

PER 1 CUP CIDER 120 cal., 0% from fat; 0 g protein; 30 g carbo (0 g fiber); 25 mg sodium; 0 mg chol.
PER 1/2 CUP APPLESAUCE 51 cal., 0.02% (1.1 cal.) from fat; 0.2 g protein; 0.1 g fat (0 g sat.); 13.8 g carbo (1.3 g fiber); 2.4 mg sodium; 0 mg chol.

Butternut Squash and Cipollini Onion Soup (page 140)

❋ PICKLED COCKTAIL MUSHROOMS AND ONIONS

These tangy, spicy, thyme-scented pickles would be great with a martini.

MAKES about 5 cups TIME about 40 minutes, plus at least 9 hours to cool and chill

4 tablespoons olive oil
4 cloves garlic, peeled and crushed
2 cups Chardonnay
6 to 8 sprigs thyme, plus a few small sprigs
2 dried red serrano or árbol chiles, finely chopped
1 teaspoon fine sea salt
1/2 pound small cipollini onions, peeled
1/2 pound medium-size shiitake mushrooms, stemmed
1/2 pound medium-size oyster mushrooms, stemmed
1 to 2 teaspoons freshly squeezed lemon juice

1. In a large frying pan, heat 1 tablespoon of the oil over medium-high heat. Add the garlic and cook, stirring, for 1 minute. Add the wine, thyme (the amount depends on your tastes), chiles, and salt. Reduce the heat to low, cover partially, and simmer for 5 minutes.

2. Add the onions, mushrooms, and the remaining 3 tablespoons oil. Cover and simmer until the mushrooms are barely tender, 10 to 15 minutes.

3. Remove from the heat, pour into a heatproof bowl, and let cool completely. Remove and discard the thyme sprigs and stir in the lemon juice to taste. Cover and refrigerate for at least 8 hours or up to 1 week.

4. To serve, bring to room temperature. Put the onions and mushrooms in a bowl, pour a little of the marinade over them, and add a few small thyme sprigs. Set out with toothpicks.

PER 1/4-CUP SERVING 56 cal., 45% (25 cal.) from fat; 0.7 g protein; 2.8 g fat (0.4 g sat.); 3.3 g carbo (0.7 g fiber); 116 mg sodium; 0 mg chol.

spoon 2 teaspoons of the quinoa mixture into the pan for each patty, spacing them about 1/2 inch apart. Cook until browned underneath, about 4 minutes. Turn the patties with a fork and cook until just browned on other side, about 3 minutes more. Transfer the patties to a plate lined with a paper towel to drain. Cook the remaining quinoa mixture the same way, adding more oil as needed.

3. Arrange the patties on a serving plate and top each with about 1/2 teaspoon romesco and a parsley leaf.

* *For instructions on how to rinse homegrown quinoa to rid it of bitterness, see page 100.*

MAKE AHEAD You can prepare the patties through step 2 up to 4 hours ahead and leave them at room temperature. To serve, reheat them at 350°F until hot, 10 minutes.

PER 3-BITE SERVING 96 cal., 52% (50 cal.) from fat; 2.7 g protein; 5.8 g fat (1 g sat.); 8.6 g carbo (0.9 g fiber); 53.8 mg sodium; 33 mg chol.

WALNUT ROMESCO

We eat this Spanish-style sauce (traditionally made with almonds and usually tomatoes) on everything from potatoes to toast to green beans to eggs. It's as versatile as pesto.

MAKES about 1 cup TIME about 30 minutes

2 'Mariachi' or 'Carmen' peppers or red bell peppers
4 tablespoons extra virgin olive oil
4 dried red serrano or árbol chiles
1/2 cup walnut pieces, lightly toasted
2 small cloves garlic
1/2 teaspoon fine sea salt
1 tablespoon red-wine vinegar

1. Preheat the broiler. Rub the peppers with 1 tablespoon of the oil and put on a rimmed baking sheet. Broil, turning as needed, until completely charred on all sides, 12 to 15 minutes. During the last minute, add the chiles to the baking sheet to warm and soften. Let the peppers and chiles cool until they can be handled. Stem the chiles, and stem, seed, and peel the peppers.

2. In a food processor, pulse the walnuts and garlic until coarsely chopped. Add the chiles, peppers, salt, vinegar, and the remaining oil and process until smooth.

MAKE AHEAD Keeps, covered and chilled, at least 3 days.

PER 2-TABLESPOON SERVING 114 cal., 85% (98 cal.) from fat; 1.4 g protein; 11 g fat (1.4 g sat.); 3.3 g carbo (1.2 g fiber); 141 mg sodium; 0 mg chol.

❋ QUINOA BITES WITH WALNUT ROMESCO

We liked these crisp-edged little nuggets so much that we made a bigger version as a main course (page 144).

MAKES about 40 patties TIME about 1 1/2 hours, plus 30 minutes to cool

1 cup quinoa*
2 large eggs, lightly beaten
1/4 teaspoon fine sea salt
About 4 tablespoons extra virgin olive oil
1 cup Walnut Romesco (recipe follows)
About 40 fresh flat-leaf parsley leaves

1. Fill a large bowl halfway with water. Add the quinoa and rub the grains briefly between your palms in the water. Drain in a fine-mesh strainer, then combine with 2 cups water in a medium saucepan. Bring to a boil, reduce the heat to a simmer, and cook until translucent in the center and a white ring appears, about 15 minutes. Transfer to a bowl and let cool. Stir in the eggs and salt.

2. In a large nonstick frying pan, heat 1 tablespoon of the oil over medium heat. Working in batches of 8 to 10,

❋ CREAMY FLAGEOLET DIP WITH RED PEPPER STICKS

With their elegant, oblong shapes and soft green color, flageolet beans look like bits of pale jade. They are sweet and mild and make a great bean dip.

MAKES about 2 cups TIME about 10 minutes

2 cups drained cooked flageolet beans (see method, page 142)
¹/₂ cup crème fraîche, homemade (page 70) or store-bought
2 tablespoons extra virgin olive oil
1 tablespoon freshly squeezed lemon juice
1 teaspoon finely shredded lemon zest
³/₄ teaspoon fine sea salt
2 tablespoons coarsely chopped fresh flat-leaf parsley
'Mariachi' and 'Carmen' peppers or other sweet red peppers, seeded and cut into narrow strips

In a food processor, whirl together the beans, crème fraîche, oil, lemon juice and zest, and salt until smooth. Transfer to a bowl and stir in the parsley. Serve with pepper strips alongside the dip.

PER 3-TABLESPOON SERVING 190 cal., 35% (67 cal.) from fat; 9 g protein; 8 g fat (3 g sat.); 22 g carbo (9 g fiber); 177 mg sodium; 10 mg chol.

❋ ROASTED SPICED BUTTERNUT SQUASH SEEDS

Next time you cut up a butternut squash, save the seeds for this tasty snack. The roasted seeds are good sprinkled over gnocchi (see page 145), soup, or salads, too.

MAKES about ³/₄ cup TIME about 1 hour

1 cup butternut squash seeds (from about 3 squashes), rinsed free of any squash flesh and patted dry (be patient; this takes a quite a while)
1 tablespoon extra virgin olive oil
About ¹/₂ teaspoon fine sea salt
¹/₂ teaspoon finely ground dried red serrano or árbol chile

1. Preheat the oven to 350°F. In a bowl, toss the seeds with the oil, salt, and ground chile until they are evenly coated. Spread the seeds on a rimmed baking sheet

2. Roast the seeds, turning them often with a spatula, until lightly golden and crunchy, about 15 minutes. Let them cool, then season with more salt, if you like. Store in an airtight container at room temperature for up to 2 weeks.

PER TABLESPOON 34 cal., 55% (19 cal.) from fat; 1 g protein; 2.2 g fat (0.4 g sat.) 1 g carbo (000 g fiber); 230 mg sodium; 0 mg chol.

ROASTED TOMATO-FENNEL SOUP

The velvety richness of this soup comes not from cream, but from the slowly roasted vegetables themselves—and plenty of good olive oil. We used the very last of our vine-ripened tomatoes for this soup, but you could easily use roasted tomatoes that you froze earlier in the season (see page 84); just thaw and reheat in the broth, then blend in with the fennel and onion.

MAKES about 6 cups or 4 servings TIME about 1¹/₂ hours

3 pounds ripe red tomatoes such as Brandywine, cored, halved, seeded, and cut into 1-inch wedges
2 fennel bulbs, trimmed and cut into 1-inch wedges
1 white onion, cut into slivers
1¹/₄ teaspoons fine sea salt
1 teaspoon dried thyme   *(continued)*

1/4 cup extra virgin olive oil, plus more for finishing
3 cups Herb Vegetable Broth (recipe follows), heated
　　to a simmer

1. Preheat the oven to 425°F. Combine the tomatoes, fennel, and onion in a roasting pan. Sprinkle with the salt and thyme, drizzle with the oil, and toss to coat evenly. Spread the vegetables in a single layer in the pan and roast them, turning once halfway through cooking, until very tender and collapsed, about 1 hour.

2. Remove from the oven, add the broth, and stir to scrape up any browned bits. Puree the soup in a blender.

3. Serve the soup with a drizzle of olive oil.

PER 1 1/2-CUP SERVING 277 cal., 56% (155 cal.) from fat; 4.3 g protein; 18 g fat (2.4 g sat.); 29 g carbo (7 g fiber); 1,404 mg sodium; 0 mg chol.

HERB VEGETABLE BROTH

Unlike some vegetable broths, which can be strong flavored, this one tastes light, sweet, and gentle.

MAKES 4 to 4 1/2 quarts TIME about 2 hours

1/4 cup extra virgin olive oil
2 1/2 pounds cipollini or white onions, loose peels
　　removed and coarsely chopped
2 cups coarsely chopped mushroom stems or whole
　　mushrooms such as shiitake and/or oyster
20 large sprigs flat-leaf parsley
16 large sprigs thyme
10 fresh sage leaves
2 sprigs rosemary, 6 inches each
2 tablespoons fine sea salt

1. In an 8- to 10-quart pot, heat the oil over high heat. Add the onions and mushrooms and sauté until the vegetables start to brown, 10 minutes. Add the parsley, thyme, sage, rosemary, salt, and 5 quarts water. Cover and bring to a boil. Reduce the heat and simmer about 1 1/4 hours.

2. Strain the broth through a colander set over another large pot. Discard the solids. For perfectly clear broth, strain again through a fine-mesh strainer.

3. Use the broth right away, or let cool, cover, and refrigerate for up to 1 week or freeze for up to 6 months.

PER 1-CUP SERVING 49 cal., 63% (31 cal.) from fat; 0.6 g protein; 3.6 g fat (0.5 g sat.); 4.3 g carbo (0 g fiber); 842 mg sodium; 0 mg chol.

BUTTERNUT SQUASH AND 'CIPOLLINI' ONION SOUP

Every cook's repertoire should include a good butternut squash soup. For this one, you roast a big batch of vegetables and puree most of them for the soup. A few choice pieces become the garnish, along with fried sage leaves and a drizzle of brown butter.

MAKES about 2 1/2 quarts or 6 servings
TIME about 2 hours

4 1/2 pounds butternut squash (from 1 large or
　　2 medium)
3 tablespoons plus 1/2 cup extra virgin olive oil
1 1/2 tablespoons fresh thyme leaves
1 1/2 teaspoons fine sea salt, plus more for sprinkling
1 1/3 pounds small cipollini onions, peeled
4 tablespoons unsalted butter
About 18 small fresh sage leaves, patted dry
About 7 cups Herb Vegetable Broth (at left), heated
　　until boiling

1. Preheat the oven to 425°F. Cut the ends off the squash and discard. Cut the squash in half lengthwise, then scrape out the seeds (save the seeds for roasting, page 139, if you like). Using a vegetable peeler, peel the squash halves, then cut the flesh into 1 1/2-inch chunks. Put the chunks on a large rimmed baking sheet and toss with 2 tablespoons of the oil, 1 tablespoon of the thyme, and 1 teaspoon of the salt. Spread in a single layer.

2. Place the onions on a second rimmed baking sheet. Drizzle with 1 tablespoon of the oil and sprinkle with the remaining 1 1/2 teaspoons thyme and 1/2 teaspoon salt. Toss to coat evenly, then spread in a single layer.

3. Roast the vegetables for 30 minutes. Using a wide spatula, turn over the onions and squash chunks and switch the pan positions. Continue to roast until the onions are very soft and golden brown all over, 10 to 15 minutes longer, and the squash is tender and beginning to brown, 20 to 25 minutes longer.

4. While the vegetables are roasting, melt the butter in a small saucepan over medium-low heat. Heat, shaking the pan occasionally, until the butter has turned a dark gold, 5 to 6 minutes. Pour into a heatproof bowl and set aside.

5. In another small saucepan, heat the remaining 1/2 cup oil over medium-high heat. Working in batches, add the sage leaves and cook, stirring occasionally, until their color fades to light olive, 20 to 30 seconds. With a slotted spoon, transfer to paper towels to drain. Sprinkle with salt.

6. When the vegetables are ready, remove the pans from the oven. Set aside 12 small squash pieces and 6 small onions for garnish. Working in batches, puree the remaining roasted vegetables in a blender with 6 cups of the broth until very smooth, then pour into a large saucepan. Divide about 1 cup broth between the vegetable-roasting pans. Stir to scrape up any browned bits, then add to the saucepan with the soup. Heat the soup over medium-low heat until piping hot. Add enough additional broth to create a velvety, pourable soup.

7. Ladle the soup into warmed bowls. Garnish each serving with the reserved whole onions, squash chunks, fried sage, and a drizzle of brown butter.

PER SERVING 493 cal., 66% (326 cal.) from fat; 5 g protein; 38 g fat (9 g sat.); 43 g carbo (12 g fiber); 1,609 mg sodium; 20 mg chol.

❈ GRILLED RADICCHIO AND FENNEL SALAD WITH APPLES AND TOASTED WALNUTS

Our radicchio took forever to ripen. It sat stubbornly in the ground, green as green cabbage, for months. Finally, tinges of red started to take hold. By the time we used it for this salad, its leaves were a beautiful streaky combination of green and red. It lasted well into winter, turning redder and sweeter after the first frost.

MAKES 4 to 6 servings TIME about 1 hour

3 small heads radicchio, about 1 1/2 pounds total
2 large fennel bulbs with stalks and feathery fronds
4 tablespoons extra virgin olive oil
About 1 1/2 teaspoons fine sea salt
1/4 cup Syrah Vinegar or other fruity red-wine vinegar
1/4 lemon
1 Honey Crisp or other firm, tart-sweet red apple
3/4 cup coarsely chopped toasted walnuts

1. Prepare a grill for medium-low heat (about 300°F; you should be able to hold your hand 5 inches above the cooking grate for only 7 to 9 seconds).

2. Cut the radicchio heads lengthwise into quarters. Trim the stalks from the fennel bulbs and cut the bulbs crosswise into 1/2-inch-thick slices. Snip enough fronds from the stalks to measure about 3/4 cup loosely packed fronds. Slice the stalks very thinly and set aside.

3. Put the radicchio quarters and fennel bulb slices on rimmed baking sheets and drizzle with 3 tablespoons of the oil, doing your best to keep their pieces together. Sprinkle lightly with 1/2 teaspoon of the salt.

4. Arrange the radicchio and fennel bulb slices on the cooking grate. Grill the radicchio, turning as needed, until the edges are crisp and browned on all sides, 15 to 20 minutes. As they are ready, return them to the baking sheet. Grill the fennel slices, turning as needed until browned on both sides and very tender, 20 to 25 minutes. (If the grate bars are widely spaced, grill the fennel on a baking sheet.) Return the slices to the baking sheet.

5. Meanwhile, in a small bowl, whisk together the remaining 1 teaspoon salt and the vinegar. Squeeze the lemon quarter into a medium-size bowl filled with water. Quarter the apple through the stem end and core with a melon

(continued)

baller or a knife. Slice the apple quarters thinly crosswise, and slip the slices into the lemon water.

6. Cut away the core from each radicchio quarter and separate the leaves. Slice the outer leaves in half lengthwise. Cut the grilled fennel into bite-size pieces. Drain the apple slices. Put the radicchio, grilled fennel, apple slices, and about three-fourths of the sliced raw fennel stalks in a large bowl. Whisk the remaining 1 tablespoon oil into the vinegar-salt mixture to make a vinaigrette. Pour all but about 1 tablespoon of the vinaigrette over the salad and toss gently to coat evenly.

7. Divide the salad among 4 to 6 plates. Top with the remaining sliced raw fennel and the walnuts, drizzle with the remaining vinaigrette, and garnish with the fennel fronds.

PER 2-CUP SERVING 251 cal., 68% (171 cal.) from fat; 5 g protein; 19 g fat (2 g sat.); 19 g carbo (6 g fiber); 640 mg sodium; 0 mg chol.

'SCARLET EMPEROR' RAGOÛT

'Scarlet Emperor' is a particularly pretty variety of scarlet runner bean. The flowers are a deep lipstick pink and, in summer, pop out all over the vine—which itself is a graceful, twirling, high-climbing plant. The bean inside the pod, when freshly picked, is the same color the flower was; then it quickly oxidizes to a shiny purple, then purple-black. This ragoût (a French style of stew) is simple yet incredibly flavorful, and we ate big bowls of it by itself with bread, or with braised greens.

MAKES 4 to 6 servings as a side dish
TIME about 1¹/₂ hours

2 tablespoons extra virgin olive oil, plus more for finishing
12 cipollini onions, peeled and halved
16 roasted tomato halves (see Slow-Roasted Tomatoes for the Freezer, page 84)
1 tablespoon minced garlic
2 cups drained cooked 'Cannellini' beans (method follows)
2 cups drained cooked 'Scarlet Emperor' beans (method follows)
1¹/₂ teaspoons fine sea salt
1 tablespoon chopped fresh rosemary

1. Preheat the oven to 350°F. In a Dutch oven or other heavy pot, heat the oil over medium heat. Add the onions and cook, stirring often, until browned and softened, 5 to 6 minutes. Add the tomatoes and garlic and cook, stirring, until fragrant, 1 minute. Stir in the beans and salt. Pour in just enough water to cover the beans.

2. Cover the pot, place in the oven, and bake for 30 minutes. Stir the ragoût, return the pot to the oven, uncovered, and cook for another 30 minutes to blend the flavors and reduce and thicken the liquid.

3. Remove from the oven and stir in the rosemary. Spoon into warmed bowls, and top each serving with a drizzle of oil.

PER 1-CUP SERVING 238 cal., 24% (58 cal.) from fat; 12.5 g protein; 6.4 g fat (0.9 g sat.); 33 g carbo (6.5 g fiber); 619 mg sodium; 0 mg chol.

HOW TO COOK DRIED BEANS

In general, 1 pound (about 2¹/₄ cups) dried beans yields 2 to 2¹/₂ pounds (about 6 cups) cooked beans.

In a large pot, combine the dried beans with water to cover by 2 inches, cover, and bring to a boil over high heat. Reduce the heat to a simmer and cook, occasionally skimming off any foam from the surface, until the beans are just tender, 45 minutes to 1¹/₂ hours. Add fine sea salt to taste (1 teaspoon for every 2 cups uncooked beans is about right) when the beans are still a little crunchy, about 15 minutes before they have finished cooking. For the most velvety texture, let the beans cool in their liquid. The beans can be stored, covered, in their liquid, in the refrigerator for up to 2 days and frozen (drained) for up to 1 month.

STUFFED POBLANOS WITH RED PEPPER SAUCE

With their filling of quinoa and dried corn, these stuffed poblanos are both earthy and light. We used the last of the fresh poblanos in our garden for this recipe.

MAKES 6 servings TIME about 1¹/₂ hours

²/₃ cup quinoa*
¹/₄ cup dried corn kernels**
6 poblano chiles
2 'Mariachi' or 'Carmen' peppers, or red bell peppers
3 cloves garlic, unpeeled
¹/₂ white onion, unpeeled
1 cup shredded Gouda cheese, homemade (page 122) or store-bought
1 large egg, lightly beaten

(continued)

2 tablespoons finely chopped fresh oregano
1 teaspoon fine sea salt
1/4 cup extra virgin olive oil
2 tablespoons freshly squeezed lemon juice

1. Fill a large bowl halfway with cool water. Add the quinoa and briefly rub the grains between your palms in the water. Drain the quinoa in a fine-mesh strainer, transfer to a saucepan, add 2 cups water, and bring to a boil. Reduce the heat and simmer until translucent in the center and a white ring appears, about 15 minutes. Let cool for a few minutes, then fluff with a fork.

2. In a small saucepan, combine the corn kernels with water just to cover. Bring to a boil, then reduce the heat and simmer until tender, about 2 minutes. Drain.

3. Preheat the broiler. Place the poblanos on a rimmed baking sheet lined with aluminum foil. Broil, turning as needed, until completely charred on all sides, 15 to 20 minutes. Cover the poblanos with a kitchen towel and let cool until they can be handled. Reduce the oven temperature to 425°F.

4. Put the red peppers, garlic, and the onion half, cut side down, on a rimmed baking sheet lined with foil. Roast until the peppers have blackened slightly, about 20 minutes. Let the vegetables cool until they can be handled. Leave the oven set at 425°F.

5. When the poblanos are cool enough to handle, peel off and discard the skins. Cut a lengthwise slit 2 to 3 inches long on one side of each poblano, and carefully scoop out the seeds with your fingers or a small spoon. Put the poblanos back on the baking sheet.

6. In a bowl, mix together the quinoa, 1/2 cup of the cheese, the egg, the oregano, 1/2 teaspoon of the salt, and the corn. Carefully spoon the mixture into the poblanos, dividing it evenly. Cover the poblanos with foil.

7. Bake the poblanos for 15 minutes. Uncover, sprinkle with the remaining cheese, and bake until the cheese has melted and has begun to turn golden, about 5 minutes.

8. While the poblanos are baking, peel the roasted garlic and onion and stem and seed the red peppers. Put them all in a food processor; add the oil, lemon juice, and the remaining salt; and puree until smooth. If the puree is cool, warm it in a small saucepan over low heat.

9. To serve, spoon the warm sauce into a serving dish and top with the hot stuffed poblanos.

* For instructions on how to rinse homegrown quinoa to rid it of bitterness, see page 100.
** We used corn from our summer garden that we dried ourselves (page 84). Feel free to use fresh corn kernels, if you like, increasing the amount to 1/2 cup.

PER POBLANO WITH 1/4 CUP SAUCE 286 cal., 52% (149 cal.) from fat; 10 g protein; 17 g fat (5 g sat.); 25 g carbo (4 g fiber); 548 mg sodium; 57 mg chol.

. . . .

QUINOA HUARACHES WITH EGG AND PARSLEY SALAD

In Mexico, *huaraches* is the word for sandals and also for the thick, oval tortilla-like cakes that resemble them. They are usually piled with lots of delicious toppings, and so are these.

MAKES 6 servings TIME about 1 1/2 hours

1 cup quinoa*
9 large eggs
1/2 teaspoon fine sea salt
4 tablespoons extra virgin olive oil
2 cups drained cooked 'Cannellini' beans (see method, page 142), warmed
2 cups Walnut Romesco (double recipe, page 138)
2 cups fresh flat-leaf parsley leaves
1 teaspoon freshly squeezed lemon juice
1/4 cup 1-inch-long fresh chive pieces

1. Fill a large bowl halfway with cool water. Add the quinoa and briefly rub the grains between your palms in the water. Drain the quinoa in a fine-mesh strainer, transfer to a saucepan, add 2 cups water, and bring to a boil. Reduce the heat and simmer until translucent in the center and a white ring appears, about 15 minutes.

2. Transfer the quinoa to a bowl and refrigerate 20 minutes. Meanwhile, put 6 eggs in another small saucepan and add water to cover. Bring to a boil over medium-high heat, remove from the heat, cover, and let stand for 15 minutes. Drain the eggs and rinse with cold water until cool. Peel the eggs and quarter lengthwise. Set aside.

3. Lightly beat the remaining 3 eggs, add to the cooled quinoa with 1/4 teaspoon of the salt, and stir to combine.

4. In a large nonstick frying pan, heat 1 tablespoon of the oil over medium heat. To make 2 *huaraches* at a time, spoon 2 ladlefuls (about 1/2 cup) of the quinoa mixture into the oil for each *huarache* and use a spoon or spatula to spread into 1/2-inch-thick oval patties. Cook the patties, turning once, until firm and golden brown, about 6 minutes. Transfer each patty to a plate and repeat with the remaining quinoa mixture, adding 1 tablespoon oil to the pan for each batch.

5. Top each patty with 1/3 cup beans. Then dollop 2 heaping tablespoons of the romesco onto each mound of beans. In a small bowl, gently mix together the parsley, the remaining 1 tablespoon oil, the lemon juice, the chives, the remaining 1/4 teaspoon salt, and the quartered eggs. Carefully set the salad mixture on top of the cakes.

* *For instructions on how to rinse homegrown quinoa to rid it of bitterness, see page 100.*

PER SERVING 685 cal., 61% (421 cal.) from fat; 23 g protein; 48 g fat (7.6 g sat.); 47 g carbo (10 g fiber); 808 mg sodium; 322 mg chol.

· ·

❋ BUTTERNUT SQUASH GNOCCHI WITH CHARD AND SAGE BROWN BUTTER

Unlike many of the vegetables we grew for our fall dinner, our butternut squash thrived. They bulged by the dozen from the vine, so we made the most of them, as in this radiant main course.

MAKES 4 to 6 servings TIME about 4 hours

GNOCCHI
3 pounds butternut squash (about 1 large)
1 1/2 teaspoons extra virgin olive oil
2/3 cup ricotta cheese, homemade (page 117) or store-bought
1 large egg, lightly beaten
1 1/2 tablespoons honey
3/4 teaspoon fine sea salt
About 3 cups sifted 'Expresso' whole-wheat flour* (to remove some of the coarse germ), plus more for sprinkling

SAGE BUTTER
1/2 cup unsalted butter
2 1/2 teaspoons freshly squeezed lemon juice
2 tablespoons thinly sliced fresh sage leaves

1 tablespoon extra virgin olive oil, plus more for oiling baking sheet
1 1/2 teaspoons minced garlic
9 to 10 ounces Swiss chard (about 1 bunch), stemmed and leaves chopped
About 3/4 cup Roasted Spiced Butternut Squash Seeds (page 139)

1. To start the gnocchi, preheat the oven to 350°F. Cut off the ends of the squash and discard. Cut the squash into large chunks, but do not peel. Scrape off the seeds and save them for roasting (see page 139) if you like. Rub the flesh sides of the squash chunks with the oil, set on a rimmed baking sheet, and cover with aluminum foil.

2. Roast the squash until tender when pierced with a knife tip and starting to brown, 45 to 60 minutes. Remove from the oven and let cool, then scoop the flesh from the skins into a medium-mesh strainer set over a bowl. Let the squash drain of any excess liquid, about 15 minutes. Reserve the squash and liquid separately and throw away the skins.

(continued)

3. In a food processor, whirl the squash flesh until smooth. If it's dry and not moving freely, add 2 tablespoons of squash liquid. Continue adding the liquid 2 tablespoons at a time, until the squash has the consistency of velvety mashed potatoes. Set the puree aside.

4. To make the sage butter, melt the butter in a large saucepan over high heat. Reduce the heat to medium and simmer until the butter darkens to a medium brown, about 10 minutes. Be careful not to let the butter get too dark. Remove from the heat and stir in the lemon juice and sage. Set the butter aside.

5. To finish the gnocchi, in a large bowl, combine 2 cups squash puree (save the extra for another use), the ricotta, egg, honey, and salt, mixing well. Gently stir in 2 to 3 cups of the flour in $1/2$-cup increments, adding just enough flour to form a very soft dough. It should still be quite wet.

6. Bring a large pot of salted water to a boil. Meanwhile, heavily dust a work surface with more sifted flour. Scoop about 1 cup of the dough onto the flour (the dough will be extremely soft) and sift a little more flour on top. Roll the dough with your hands into a rope 15 inches long. Cut the rope into 1-inch pieces, sprinkling the dough with more flour if it gets sticky. As the pieces are cut, transfer them to a rimmed baking sheet lightly dusted with sifted flour. Repeat with the remaining dough.

7. Reduce the heat under the boiling water to medium-low. Working in batches of 15 to 20 pieces, carefully drop the gnocchi into the water and cook until they are firm and float to the surface, about 5 minutes. With a slotted spoon, transfer the gnocchi to a large colander to drain, then to a lightly oiled rimmed baking sheet. Cook and drain the remaining gnocchi the same way.

8. To assemble the gnocchi, heat $1/2$ teaspoons of the oil in a large nonstick frying pan over medium-high heat. Working in batches, add the gnocchi to the pan and cook, stirring often, until browned, 5 to 8 minutes. Transfer to a warmed serving dish.

9. Add the remaining $1/2$ teaspoons oil and the garlic to the same pan over medium-high heat and cook, stirring, until the garlic is fragrant, 2 minutes. Add the chard and cook, stirring occasionally, until softened, 5 minutes. Gently combine the chard with the gnocchi.

10. Warm the reserved sage butter and drizzle half of it over the gnocchi. Sprinkle the gnocchi with the roasted squash seeds. Pass the remaining sage butter at the table.

* *We liked the nutty flavor of this freshly milled local flour, but any whole-wheat flour will work. See the Allure of Local Wheat, page 156, for more on local flours.*

MAKE AHEAD: You can prepare the gnocchi through step 6, cover tightly, and refrigerate for up to 3 days. Or, you can freeze the gnocchi on the baking sheet until solid, then transfer them to resealable plastic bags for up to 3 weeks. Cook directly from the refrigerator or freezer.

PER $1/2$-CUP SERVING 733 cal., 49% (366 cal.) from fat; 22 g protein; 41 g fat (15.5 g sat.); 77 g carbo (13 g fiber); 594 mg sodium; 91 mg chol.

....

ANCHO CHILE–SAUCED NOODLES WITH SHIITAKES AND BUTTERNUT SQUASH

We used a combination of flours to give these noodles a more supple, finer texture than they have when they are made from regular whole-wheat flour. If you like a rustic, hearty noodle, use just the regular whole-wheat flour.

MAKES 4 to 6 servings TIME about 3 hours

1 cup 'Sonora' whole-wheat flour* or whole-wheat pastry flour, plus more for sprinkling

1$1/4$ cups 'Expresso' whole-wheat flour* or other whole-wheat flour

1$1/2$ teaspoons fine sea salt

3 large eggs plus 2 large egg yolks

6 tablespoons extra virgin olive oil

1 butternut squash, 2 to 2$1/2$ pounds

4 small ancho chiles (about 1 ounce total)

$1/4$ white onion

3 cloves garlic, unpeeled

1 pound shiitake mushrooms, stems removed and caps sliced 1 inch thick

4 roasted tomato halves (about 2 tablespoons; see Slow-Roasted Tomatoes for the Freezer, page 84)

$1/2$ cup chopped fresh flat-leaf parsley

1. To make the noodle dough, in a large bowl, whisk together the flours and $1/2$ teaspoon of the salt. Form a well in the center and add the eggs and egg yolks to the well. Break up the eggs with a fork and mix in 1 table-

spoon of the oil. Gradually mix the flour from the sides of the well into the eggs. Stir until a dough forms.

2. Turn the dough out onto a well-floured work surface and sprinkle with a little more flour. Knead the dough, dusting it lightly with flour whenever it starts sticking to your hands, until it is smooth, 2 to 3 minutes. Cover with a damp kitchen towel and let rest for at least 30 minutes or up to 1 1/2 hours.

3. Meanwhile, preheat the oven to 450°F. Cut off the ends of the squash and discard. Halve the squash lengthwise and scrape out the seeds. Rinse any flesh off the seeds and pat dry on a kitchen towel. Using a vegetable peeler, peel the squash halves, then cut them crosswise into 3/4-inch-thick slices.

4. Start the ancho sauce: In a heavy frying pan (not nonstick), toast the chiles over medium-high heat, pressing down on them occasionally with tongs, until soft and pliable, 2 to 3 minutes. Transfer 3 of the chiles to a small heatproof bowl and pour 1 1/4 cups boiling water over them. Let soften for 20 minutes. Stem the remaining chile, break into pieces, and pulverize in a spice grinder or in a mortar with a pestle.

5. Add the onion and garlic cloves to the same frying pan over medium-high heat and toast, turning occasionally, until browned in several spots, 10 minutes. Transfer to a small bowl. Add 1 tablespoon of the oil to the same pan over medium heat, add the squash seeds, sprinkle with 1/2 teaspoon of the salt, and toast, stirring, until crisp, 5 minutes. Pour into a bowl.

6. Cook the vegetables: Arrange the squash slices in a single layer on a large rimmed baking sheet and arrange the mushrooms in a 9-by-13-inch baking dish. Sprinkle the squash slices and mushrooms with the ground chile, then sprinkle with the remaining 1/2 teaspoon salt. Add 1/2 cup water to the mushrooms, cover the dish tightly with aluminum foil, and braise in the oven until tender, about 30 minutes. Drizzle the squash slices with 2 tablespoons of the oil and roast, turning the slices halfway through cooking, until browned and tender, about 40 minutes. Set aside, covered.

7. Finish the sauce: Stem the soaked chiles and put in a blender. Add 3/4 cup of the chile soaking water and the toasted squash seeds and blend until smooth. Peel the toasted garlic and add to the blender along with the onion, tomatoes, and the remaining oil. Blend again until smooth.

8. Divide the dough into 4 equal portions and pat each into a square 1/2 inch thick. Put 1 square on a floured work surface (keep the others covered with the towel), and roll out 1/8 inch thick. Using a pizza cutter, cut the dough sheet into noodles 1/4 inch wide. Scoop up the noodles with a bench scraper or a large, wide spatula and lay them on a cooling rack. Repeat with the remaining dough. Let the noodles dry for at least 20 minutes or up to 1 day.

9. Bring an 8- to 10-quart pot of salted water to a boil. Add the noodles to the boiling water, shaking off excess flour. Cook until chewy-tender, 3 to 4 minutes. Drain the noodles, reserving 1/2 cup of the cooking water, and pour into a large bowl.

10. Add the ancho sauce to the noodles and toss to coat, adding as much of the reserved cooking water or remaining chile soaking water as needed to loosen the sauce a little. Add three-fourths of the parsley and toss again. Arrange the noodles on a warmed platter. Top with the roasted squash slices, the braised mushrooms, and the remaining parsley.

(continued)

* We used finely milled 'Sonora' white whole-wheat flour, because it behaves like commercial whole-wheat pastry flour. For the regular whole-wheat flour, we used 'Expresso', a hard red winter wheat. See the Allure of Local Wheat, page 156, for more on local flours.

PER SERVING 431 cal., 40% (172 cal.) from fat; 14 g protein; 20 g fat (3.6 g sat.); 58 g carbo (13 g fiber); 627 mg sodium; 177 mg chol.

. . . .

MEXICAN SKILLET EGGS

Our eggs seemed especially flavorful in this one-pan dinner, fortified with pureed 'Scarlet Emperor' beans (our substitute for black beans, because they have a similar starchy texture), intense oven-roasted tomatoes preserved from summer, and our last few fresh chiles. Once we ran out of fresh, we made it with frozen poblanos (see page 84 for a method) and dried serrano chiles (page 83).

MAKES 4 to 6 servings TIME about 30 minutes

2 tablespoons extra virgin olive oil
1/2 white onion, sliced
2 red or green poblano chiles, stemmed, seeded, and sliced

1 tablespoon minced garlic
1 tablespoon minced red serrano chile
1 1/2 teaspoons fine sea salt
3 cups drained cooked 'Scarlet Emperor' beans (see method, page 142)
8 roasted tomato halves (see Slow-Roasted Tomatoes for the Freezer, page 84), halved
4 to 6 large eggs
1 tablespoon fresh oregano leaves

1. In a large nonstick frying pan, heat the oil over medium heat. Add the onion and poblanos and cook, stirring often, until starting to soften, about 4 minutes. Add the garlic, serrano chile, and 1/2 teaspoon of the salt and cook, stirring, until fragrant, about 1 minute. Set aside off the heat and cover to keep warm.

2. In a small saucepan, combine the beans, 1/2 cup water, and the remaining 1 teaspoon salt over low heat and heat just until warm. Transfer to a food processor and puree until smooth and loose, adding more water as needed.

3. Return the frying pan to medium heat, pour the bean puree over the vegetables, and heat until the mixture begins to simmer. Scatter the tomato halves over the beans. Use a spoon to make 4 or 6 wells, depending on how many people you are serving, and crack an egg into each well. Cover the pan and cook until the eggs are just set but still a little runny in the center, about 5 minutes. Sprinkle with the oregano and serve.

PER EGG WITH 1/4 CUP BEANS 217 cal., 42% (93 cal.) from fat; 13 g protein; 10.5 g fat (20 g sat.); 18 g carbo (2 g fiber); 649 mg sodium; 211 mg chol.

. . . .

CREAMY SCRAMBLED EGGS WITH OYSTER MUSHROOMS

This recipe is based on one by Niloufer Ichaporia King, a wonderful Bay Area cook and the author of *My Bombay Kitchen: Traditional and Modern Parsi Home Cooking*.

MAKES 4 to 6 servings TIME about 30 minutes

2 tablespoons unsalted butter, homemade (page 154) or store-bought
7 ounces oyster mushrooms, stems trimmed if woody and any large caps halved
1 1/2 teaspoons fresh thyme leaves, minced
Fine sea salt

2 cloves garlic, minced
8 large eggs
1/2 cup whole milk

1. In a nonstick frying pan, melt the butter over medium heat. Pour about half of the melted butter into a medium bowl and set aside. Add the mushrooms, thyme, and 1/4 teaspoon salt to the frying pan and cook, stirring every now and then, until the mushrooms have softened and are starting to brown, about 5 minutes. Add the garlic and cook, stirring, for 1 minute more.

2. Add the eggs, milk, and a couple of pinches of salt to the bowl with the melted butter and whisk to blend. Pour the egg mixture into a medium saucepan and cook over low heat, stirring slowly with a rubber spatula and keeping contact with the bottom of the pan, until small, soft curds begin to form, 10 to 15 minutes.

3. Stir in the mushrooms and keep cooking and stirring until the eggs are just set, about a minute longer.

PER SERVING 151 cal., 63% (95 cal.) from fat; 10 g protein; 11 g fat (5 g sat.); 4 g carbo (0.7 g fiber); 222 mg sodium; 299 mg chol.

* *

❖ WHOLE-WHEAT ROSEMARY SHORTBREADS

We wanted some kind of buttery cracker to go with our fall cheese platter. These melt-in-your-mouth shortbreads are too fragile to be topped or spread with anything, but they taste wonderful with cheese and fruit.

MAKES about 12 shortbread squares
TIME about 30 minutes, plus 1 hour to chill

3/4 cup unsalted butter, homemade (page 154)
    or store-bought, at room temperature
1 teaspoon honey
1/2 teaspoon fine sea salt
1/2 teaspoon minced fresh rosemary
11/2 cups 'Sonora' whole-wheat flour,* plus more
    for sprinkling

1. In a medium bowl, using a mixer on medium speed, beat together the butter and honey until light and fluffy. Beat in the salt and rosemary. On low speed, gradually beat in the flour just until well combined.

2. Line a rimless cookie sheet with waxed paper and scrape dough onto the paper. Sprinkle the dough lightly with flour. With a floured rolling pin, roll out the dough to about 1/4 inch thick. Top with another sheet of waxed paper and refrigerate for at least 1 hour or up to 2 days.

3. Preheat the oven to 325°F. Using a 2-inch square cookie cutter (we used one with a scalloped edge), cut out as many squares as possible and place on 2 rimmed baking sheets, spacing them 1/2 inch apart. Gather up the dough scraps, reroll, cut out more squares, and add to the baking sheet. (If the dough gets too sticky to roll, chill and try again.)

4. Bake until set but not browned, 10 to 12 minutes. Let cool completely on the baking sheets set on wire racks.

* *We liked a medium-fine grind of this local flour, but regular whole-wheat flour works well, too. See the Allure of Local Wheat, page 156, for more on local flours.*

MAKE AHEAD Shortbreads keep, stored airtight, at room temperature, for up to 1 week.

PER SHORTBREAD 159 cal., 66% (105 cal.) from fat; 2.4 g protein; 12 g fat (7 g sat.); 12 g carbo (2 g fiber); 176 mg sodium; 31 mg chol.

* *

WALNUT-HONEY CRISPS

We started out trying to make *tuiles*, thin, blond, curvy French cookies that shatter when you eat them. Our sole sweetener, though, was honey—which is too moist to produce anything thin or crisp enough to hold a curve, and our wheat flour made the cookies dark. So these are *tuiles'* flat, homey, but very tasty cousins.

MAKES 10 cookies TIME about 30 minutes

1/3 cup unsalted butter
1/4 cup honey
1/8 teaspoon fine sea salt
1/4 cup finely chopped toasted walnuts
1/4 cup 'Expresso' whole-wheat flour* or other
    whole-wheat flour

1. Preheat the oven to 325°F. Line 2 rimmed baking sheets with parchment paper.

2. In a small saucepan, heat the butter, honey, and salt over medium heat until boiling, stirring often. Remove from the heat and whisk in the walnuts and flour. Continue

Fall cheese platter: Gouda (page 122) and feta (page 120) with fresh honeycomb, walnuts, pineapple guava slices, Last-Minute Pineapple Guava Preserves (page 155), and Whole-Wheat Rosemary Shortbreads (page 149)

to whisk until the mixture is very smooth and thick and no fat dots appear on the surface, about 3 minutes.

3. For each cookie, spoon 1 tablespoon batter onto the prepared sheets, spacing the spoonfuls about 3 inches apart (the batter will spread a lot).

4. Bake the crisps until dark golden brown, about 12 minutes. Halfway through baking, switch the pan positions and rotate the pans back to front to ensure the cookies bake evenly. Let cool completely on the pans on wire racks. Store in an airtight container at room temperature for up to 1 day.

* *We liked the nutty flavor of this freshly milled local flour, but any whole-wheat flour will work. See the Allure of Local Wheat, page 156, for more on local flours.*

PER COOKIE 95 cal., 78% (74 cal.) from fat; 3.4 g protein; 8.3 g fat (1.3 g sat.); 1.8 g carbo (0.5 g fiber); 97 mg sodium; 0 mg chol.

❈ HONEY ICE CREAM

We were knocked out by the intensely floral, seductive flavor of our honey all over again in this simple, lovely ice cream. Use your favorite honey when you make this.

MAKES 4 cups TIME about 1 hour, plus 6 hours to freeze

2 cups heavy cream
1 1/2 cups whole milk
4 large egg yolks
About 1 cup honey
Pinch of fine sea salt, plus more for finishing
Ice cubes

1. Pour the cream and milk into a medium saucepan and bring to a simmer over medium heat. Right before it comes to a simmer, in a medium heatproof bowl, whisk together the egg yolks, 3/4 cup of the honey, and the salt.

2. Immediately pour the cream and milk slowly into the yolk mixture while whisking constantly. Return the mixture to the pan and cook over medium heat, stirring constantly and adjusting the heat to prevent the mixture from boiling, until it begins to thicken, about 8 minutes.

3. Fill a large bowl with ice cubes and water, and nest a medium bowl in the ice water. Strain the custard mixture through a fine-mesh strainer into the medium bowl. Let cool completely, stirring occasionally and replacing the ice if needed.

4. Freeze in an ice cream maker according to the manufacturer's directions. Transfer to an airtight container and freeze until firm, at least 6 hours or up to 2 weeks.

5. To serve, scoop ice cream into bowls. Drizzle with more honey and top with a sprinkle of salt.

PER 1/2-CUP SERVING 390 cal., 60% (234 cal.) from fat; 4.1 g protein; 26 g fat (15.5 g sat.); 38.7 g carbo (0.1 g fiber); 328 mg sodium; 192 mg chol.

LEMON-THYME ICE CREAM SANDWICHES

Made with nutty whole-wheat flour and honey, the cookie part tastes like graham crackers, with the barest hint of thyme. The ice cream brings back summer, when we harvested the last of the heavy, dripping frames of honey.

MAKES 30 ice cream sandwiches (60 cookies)
TIME about 1 hour, plus about 1 3/4 hours to chill

1 cup butter, at room temperature
1/2 cup honey
Grated zest of 1 lemon
1 teaspoon minced fresh thyme
2 1/4 cups whole-wheat pastry flour*
About 1 pint Honey Ice Cream (opposite), frozen overnight

1. In a large bowl, using a mixer on medium speed, beat together the butter, honey, lemon zest, and thyme until smooth. On low speed, gradually beat in the flour until a smooth dough forms.

2. Divide the dough in half. Put each portion on a sheet of plastic wrap and pat into a rough log about 7 inches long. Move the logs, still on the plastic wrap, onto a

rimmed baking sheet and freeze until firm enough to shape, about 20 minutes.

3. Pat each log until it is smooth and reaches a uniform 1 1/2 inches in diameter, squeezing the dough together if it starts to crack. Wrap airtight in plastic wrap and freeze until firm enough to slice, 20 to 30 minutes.

4. Preheat the oven to 325°F. Line 2 rimmed baking sheets with parchment paper. Unwrap the dough. Using a thin, sharp knife, cut the logs into 1/4-inch-thick slices. Arrange the slices 1/2 inch apart on the baking sheets.

5. Bake the cookies until the edges are golden brown, 12 to 15 minutes. Switch the pan positions and rotate the pans back to front about halfway through baking so the cookies bake evenly. Let cool on the pans on wire racks for 5 minutes. Transfer to the racks to cool completely.

6. To make the sandwiches, put a baking sheet in the freezer until it is cold. Arrange 5 or 6 cookies, bottom side up, on a work surface. Put 1 tablespoon ice cream on each cookie, then top with a second cookie, bottom side down, and squish gently to spread the ice cream evenly. Put the finished sandwiches on the baking sheet in the freezer, then repeat with the remaining cookies and ice cream, working in batches. When all of the sandwiches are

made, wrap them individually in plastic wrap and freeze until the ice cream is firm, about 1 hour.

* *We used finely milled local 'Sonora' whole-wheat flour, but any whole-wheat pastry flour will work. See the Allure of Local Wheat, page 156, for more on local flours.*

MAKE AHEAD Plain cookies can be stored in an airtight container at room temperature for up to 2 days or in the freezer for up to 1 month. Ice cream sandwiches will keep in the freezer for up to 1 week.

PER ICE CREAM SANDWICH 156 cal., 56% (87 cal.) from fat; 1.5 g protein; 9.7 g fat (6 g sat.); 17 g carbo (1.2 g fiber); 88 mg sodium; 42 mg chol.

APPLE CHEESE PUFF

This pastry is all about layers: a thin, buttery crust, then a poufed circle of cream puff dough topped with creamy, sweetened cheese and caramelized apples. You can cook the apples a day ahead, but not the crust—it gets leathery as it sits. This is a dessert best eaten in one go.

MAKES one 7- to 8-inch pastry or 9 servings
TIME about 1½ hours

1/2 cup plus 3 tablespoons cold unsalted butter, homemade (page 154) or store-bought
1 cup 'Sonora' whole-wheat pastry flour*
1 large egg plus 1 large egg white, lightly beaten
4 Honey Crisp or other firm, tart-sweet apples
9 tablespoons honey
3/4 cup fromage blanc, homemade (page 118) or store-bought**

1. Preheat the oven to 350°F. Cut 1/4 cup of the butter into small cubes. Put 1/2 cup of the flour in a small bowl, scatter the butter cubes over the top, and mix the butter into the flour with a pastry blender or your fingertips until the mixture is the consistency of crushed crackers. Sprinkle in 1 tablespoon water and mix with a wooden spoon until the dough comes together. If the dough is not coming together, sprinkle in another 1 tablespoon water. Press the dough into a disk.

2. Put the disk on an ungreased rimmed baking sheet and pat into a round 8 inches in diameter and 1/8 inch thick.

3. In a saucepan, bring 1/4 cup of the butter and 1/2 cup water to a rolling boil. Remove from the heat and quickly stir in the remaining 1/2 cup flour with a wooden spoon.

Pour in the eggs and stir vigorously until smooth. With a wet soup spoon, spread the mixture over the dough disk, pushing it higher on the edge to form a narrow rim. Poke the center several times with a fork to keep the pastry from puffing up when it bakes.

4. Bake the pastry until crisp and brown, 45 to 55 minutes. Let cool completely on the pan on a cooling rack.

5. Meanwhile, make the toppings: Peel, halve, and core the apples, then slice 1/4 inch thick. In a large nonstick frying pan, melt the remaining 3 tablespoons butter over medium-high heat. Add the apples and cook, stirring occasionally, until they start to brown, about 8 minutes. Turn the heat to its lowest setting, cover, and cook the apples until they are very soft, about 20 minutes more. Add 6 tablespoons of the honey, raise the heat to medium-high, and cook, uncovered, until the apples are deep golden brown and most of the liquid has evaporated, about 20 minutes. Let cool until just warm.

6. In a small bowl, whisk together the fromage blanc and the remaining 3 tablespoons honey. Spread the mixture on the cooled pastry and top with the warm apples.

* *We liked this local finely milled soft whole-wheat flour for this recipe because its texture is great in pastries. Any whole-wheat pastry flour will work, however. See the Allure of Local Wheat, page 156, for more on local flours.*

** *Store-bought fromage blanc is often much drier than homemade fromage blanc. If you use it, stir in enough heavy cream (at least 3 tablespoons) to give it the consistency of softened cream cheese.*

PER SERVING 387 cal., 52% (200 cal.) from fat; 5.5 g protein; 22.5 g fat (13.8 g sat.); 43 g carbo (2.9 g fiber); 303 mg sodium; 91.5 mg chol.

BUTTERNUT SQUASH COMPOTE WITH HONEY AND TOASTED WALNUTS

A quick glance at the ingredients here might give you an unpromising impression, but this dessert is a standout: as the squash bakes slowly in honey, it takes on a deeply floral, slightly caramelized note. Resist the temptation to take it out of the oven once it is cooked. When left in the oven to cool, the squash becomes infused with the flavor of the honey, and its texture turns velvety. The recipe is

(continued)

the parchment, moisten it with water, and then flatten it on a work surface. Cover the squash with the parchment, tucking it around the inside of the dish to fit snugly.

3. Bake the squash, stirring every 30 minutes or so, until it is tender when pierced, 1³/₄ to 2 hours. Turn off the oven and leave the squash inside for about 3 hours to finish cooking evenly.

4. Meanwhile, in a small frying pan, melt the butter over medium heat. Add the walnuts and cook, stirring often, until the nuts are lightly browned, 3 to 4 minutes.

5. Spoon the slightly warm squash and honey syrup into bowls. Garnish each serving with a spoonful of crème fraîche and a scattering of the walnuts.

MAKE AHEAD The compote can be refrigerated for up to 2 days. Warm slightly in a microwave for about 1¹/₂ minutes or in a 300°F oven before serving.

PER SERVING 387 cal., 40% (156 cal.) from fat; 3.5 g protein; 17 g fat (8 g sat.); 60 g carbo (4 g fiber); 11 mg sodium; 27 mg chol.

based on one in *The Slow Mediterranean Kitchen: Recipes for the Passionate Cook* (Wiley, 2003) by Paula Wolfert.

MAKES 4 to 6 servings TIME about 2 hours, plus about 3 hours to stand

1 small butternut squash, about 1³/₄ pounds
1 cup honey
1 teaspoon salted butter, homemade (at right) or store-bought
¹/₂ cup walnut halves
³/₄ cup crème fraîche, homemade (page 70) or store-bought

1. Preheat the oven to 300°F. Cut off the ends of the squash and discard. Cut the squash in half lengthwise, then scrape out the seeds (save the seeds for roasting, page 139, if you like). Using a vegetable peeler, peel the squash halves, then cut the flesh into 1¹/₂-inch chunks. You should have 3¹/₂ to 4 cups.

2. Put the squash chunks in a deep 1- to 1¹/₂-quart baking dish such as a soufflé dish. Add the honey and stir to coat the squash chunks evenly. Cut a piece of parchment paper a few inches larger than the diameter of the dish. Crumple

HOMEMADE BUTTER AND BUTTERMILK

Here is your chance to ignore that rule about not over-beating cream and go straight for the clumps of butter. Unlike commercial butter, which has small amounts of culture added, homemade butter tastes extra sweet and fresh—and so does the buttermilk that's left over. (We use it to make Wheat Berry Ciabatta, page 182.)

MAKES 1 cup butter and ³/₄ cup sweet buttermilk TIME about 10 minutes

2 cups heavy cream
Fine sea salt (optional)

1. Whirl the cream in a food processor until it separates into buttermilk and clumps of butter that look like fluffy scrambled eggs. Then keep whirling until the butter forms bigger clumps. This takes 2 to 3 minutes total.

2. Set a fine-mesh strainer over a bowl. Pour the butter-milk and butter into the strainer and let drain briefly. Squeeze the butter with your hands to extract the remaining buttermilk (it's okay if a little is left).

3. Turn the butter into another bowl and stir in salt to taste, if you like. Both the butter and buttermilk will keep in the refrigerator for up to 1 week.

PER TABLESPOON BUTTER 101 cal., 100% (101 cal.) from fat; 0.1 g protein; 11.5 g fat (7.3 g sat.); 0 g carbo (0 g fiber); 1.5 mg sodium; 30.5 mg chol. PER 1/2 CUP BUTTERMILK 75 cal., 20% (14.5 cal.) from fat; 6 g protein; 1.5 g fat (1.2 g sat.); 9 g carbo (0 g fiber); 193 mg sodium; 7.5 mg chol.

. . . .

❋ LAST-MINUTE PINEAPPLE GUAVA PRESERVES

We wanted some sort of fruity component for our cheese course, and in the wake of the Fig Disaster, we scoured the garden for fruit, any fruit at all—and found some very ripe pineapple guavas still hanging on our tree.

We had not considered including guavas in the feast (we'd been focused on those figs), but suddenly they seemed perfect: We would make a classic Spanish-style membrillo (quince paste)—so good with cheese—only with pineapple guavas! Like quince, pineapple guavas are extremely fragrant and are used to make purees, pastes,

and preserves. Also known as feijoas, they have a wonderful flavor that combines pineapple, pear, and strawberry, and their flesh is slightly grainy, like that of a Bosc pear.

We ended up with both a thick guava jam (shown in photo, page 150) and, in later tests, a firm paste that can be cut into pieces. Both were delicious, and went well with the Gouda and feta.

MAKES about 2 cups TIME about 3 hours, plus 30 minutes to cool and 2 hours to chill

2 pounds ripe pineapple guavas (fejoias)
1 cup water
1 cup honey

1. Trim off the ends of the guavas, then chop coarsely, skins and all. Put the chunks in a large pot with the water. Cook over low heat, stirring occasionally, until the chunks are soft, about 1 hour.

2. Preheat the oven to 250°F if making a paste. Transfer the cooked fruit to a food processor and pulse until smooth. Strain the mixture back into the pot and add the honey. Cook over medium-low heat, stirring frequently with a rubber spatula and scraping the bottom of the pot to prevent the mixture from sticking, until it is very thick and bubbling, the consistency of mashed potatoes, about 1 hour. The color goes from green to light brown. If you want a firm paste, continue with the next step. Otherwise, let the preserves cool, then chill them until ready to serve.

3. Scrape the jam into a nonstick 9-inch square baking dish and bake, stirring occasionally, until dark brown and very thick, about 45 minutes. Remove the preserves from the oven, stir, and let cool 30 minutes. Chill until cold, then cut into pieces.

MAKE AHEAD The preserves can be made up to 2 weeks in advance and stored, tightly covered, in the refrigerator.

PER 2-TABLESPOON SERVING 85 cal., 3% (3 cal.) from fat; 0.05 g protein; 0.3 g fat (0 g sat.); 22 g carbo (2.2 g fiber); 2 mg sodium; 0 mg chol.

After we ran out of our own wheat, we decided to try to find the next best thing: locally grown whole-wheat flour.

At a farmers' market near our office, we found a finely milled soft white variety called 'Sonora', grown and milled by Full Belly Farm in Yolo County, to the northeast of us. At Pie Ranch in Pescadero, on the coast to the south, we found more 'Sonora', with a medium-fine texture. Eatwell Farm—in inland Solano County— sold several flours at San Francisco's Ferry Plaza Farmers Market; we tried 'Expresso', a hard red type.

When you're used to standard refined all-purpose flour, it's exciting to cook with flour made from nonstandard wheat varieties. They each have their own character and flavor, and you have to adjust your recipes to suit them. The 'Sonora' has a delicate, fresh taste, and, we discovered, works best as a pastry flour; it is very soft and doesn't develop the stretchiness needed for bread making. The very finely milled 'Sonora' sold by Full Belly Farm was great for tempura (page 68), which usually requires rice flour in order to be lacy and crisp. The protein content of 'Sonora' is typically 9 percent, about the same as pastry flour. The 'Expresso', at 12.3 percent protein, makes good, nutty-tasting bread with a fine rise. All three farms we bought from mill their grains every couple of weeks, so the flour is fresh and sweet—another big difference between the little guys and the big manufacturers.

Modern Wheat

As we cooked with the flours, we found out more about them. 'Expresso', developed by Arizona breeder Kim Shantz in 2005, is a thoroughly modern "inbred" variety created to fight off a common wheat disease called stripe rust. It is mainly grown in the Sacramento Valley. Its parent, 'Express', came from an international breeding program in Mexico. Neither had roots in California. "Breeders use varieties from around the world. You can't really regionalize any more," says Shantz. I asked him whether the fine flavor of 'Expresso' flour was making the wheat more popular. "Big producers don't care so much about that," he said. "They're looking at protein level and mixing qualities." (The term *mixing qualities* refers to the strength of the dough and how long it can be mixed without breaking down.)

Nigel Walker, of Eatwell Farm, bought the 'Expresso' originally to feed to his chickens. Then he heard that it made good bread, so he milled some, and now he sells all he can supply. "I know it's not an heirloom. But it makes really good baking flour and responds to organic methods," he says. Modern flours typically need heavy doses of herbicide to fight off weeds. But so far, Walker's 'Expresso' is doing fine on his organic farm.

Landrace Wheat

'Sonora' wheat comes from the other end of the wheat spectrum. It is a landrace variety, meaning it has adapted to its specific environment over many years. In the case of 'Sonora', that means centuries. Monica Spiller, the founder of Whole Grain Connection, in Mountain View, California, thinks its cultivation in California probably predates the Spanish missionaries. It is known to have existed in Sonora, in northern Mexico, since at least the early 1700s, hence its name. (The big white flour tortillas famous in that part of Mexico were once made with 'Sonora' wheat.)

In California, 'Sonora' thrived. Along with a few other wheat varieties, it made California the number one wheat producer in the country by the late 1800s. So much of it was grown in 1884—nearly three million acres—that it set the floor prices at the London International Wheat Exchange.

Unfortunately, its decline began immediately afterward, with the rise of hard red wheat from the Midwest, and the invention of the roller mill. Hard red was not only superprolific, but it could be put through a roller mill that sheared off the germ and bran to produce refined white flour, for which the public had an insatiable appetite. 'Sonora' didn't work well in the roller mills—it was best ground whole—and, not being quite as white as refined white flour, it floundered. By 1910, California's total wheat acreage fell to six hundred thousand, and gradually modern hybrids replaced the older strains.

Wheat Revival

It is thanks in large part to Spiller that 'Sonora' is back on the scene. A former chemist, she has spent the past thirty years researching which varieties do best in our area, and 'Sonora', which she found preserved at the United States Department of Agriculture's Small Grains Collection in Idaho, tops the list. Unlike hybrids, which tend to get knocked out by evolving strains of stripe rust, 'Sonora' is enduringly resistant to the disease, requires no chemical fertilizing, and needs very little water once it gets going, which makes it great for drought-prone California and also Arizona. The next time we plant wheat, we'll probably give both 'Sonora' and 'Expresso' a try.

HELPFUL INFORMATION
Whole-wheat flour

Oregon Tilth A good list of national producers who grow organic wheat (www.tilth.org/producer-search/producers).

Anson Mills, Columbia, South Carolina Owner Glenn Roberts grows a range of heritage wheats for flour, including colonial-era 'Red May' (www.ansonmills.com).

Bob's Red Mill, Milwaukie, Oregon
The whole-grain, stone-ground giant gives guided tours of the mill. (www.bobsredmill.com)

Pie Ranch, Pescadero, California
Organic 'Sonora' wheat berries and flour. Sold at the farm stand in Pescadero, March through October; Pie Ranch's flour (as well as its produce) also goes to make pies and other baked goods at local sustainable food businesses such as Mission Pie in San Francisco and Companion Bakers in Santa Cruz. $3 per 1-pound bag (www.pieranch.org).

Full Belly Farm, Guinda, California
Organic 'Sonora' wheat flour and wheat berries sold at various Bay Area farmers' markets and some grocery stores. $3 per 1 1/2-pound bag (www.fullbelly farm.com).

Eatwell Farm, near Dixon, California Organic 'Expresso' hard red wheat flour, as well as flour milled from several other varieties. Sold at San Francisco's Ferry Plaza Farmers Market on Saturdays. $1 per 1-pound bag wheat berries, $5 per 3-pound bag flour (www.eatwell.com).

Community Grains, Oakland, California Oliveto restaurant co-owner Bob Klein has just launched a new business that sells freshly milled, locally grown wheat flours, as well as super-flavorful polentas, at specialty stores in the Bay Area. "This is not health nut stuff," says Klein. "This is stepping into full flavor." The Web site, www.communitygrains.com, offers terrific in-depth information about wheat.

Wheat seeds

Whole Grain Connection, Mountain View, California Monica Spiller's Web site includes a history of wheat growing in America, recipes for bread made with barm (sourdough starter), and a report on field trials of various old wheat strains, plus a plan for how to bring them back into production. $1.25 per pound for seeds, plus

'Sonora' wheat

packaging and shipping (www.sustain ablegrains.org or 650/938-2865).

Wheat berries from Pie Ranch, Full Belly, and Eatwell Farm (see above, under whole-wheat flour) can be planted as seed. Wheat berries from the grocery store may not be viable, but theoretically could sprout, too.

Books

Homegrown Whole Grains, by Sara Pitzer (Storey Publishing, 2009). A charming, restfully designed, yet information-packed guide to growing your own, with helpful illustrations.

Professional Baking, by Wayne Gisslen (John Wiley & Sons, fifth edition, 2008). Although intended primarily for culinary-school students, this is an invaluable book for home bakers, too, and answers questions you didn't know you had.

Small-Scale Grain Raising, by Gene Logsdon (Chelsea Green Publishing Company, 2009). First printed in 1977, this book explains how to grow, thresh, winnow, grind, and store all kinds of grains at home, including wheat.

WINTER

Bright, chilly weather with an occasional frost, followed by a few months of rain—this is winter in the Bay Area. Even though it's nothing like the long, hunker-down, snow-blanketed hiatus of the Midwest or the Northeast, it's still a slow time that made us take stock of where we were and what we had.

Our wines sat quietly aging in their carboys. The olive oil, stored in small dark bottles, was a little over a year old and starting to lose some of its oomph. But we had cases and cases of it, enough to last several more months if we kept it cool and dark. The vinegar thrived, despite our forgetting to feed it several times. Our hens were doing fine, laying eggs regularly, and they liked the heat lamp we'd turn on for them whenever the temperature hit freezing. They'd hang out in the henhouse all morning until the sun could warm up the yard. Their favorite new treat was maggoty olives. They hailed down from our trees daily, tiny weights on the collective conscience of Team Olive—which hadn't yet found a practical and affordable solution for dealing with the infestation of olive fruit flies. But at least the chickens were happy. They scarfed up those black, wormy nuggets like party crashers at a caviar bar.

We were especially reluctant to treat our trees because we didn't know whether the spray would harm our bees. And the poor bees! As it was, they were battling a seemingly unending stream of pests and diseases. The latest two were the small hive beetle, which eats brood, bees, and honey; and nosema, which is sort of like bee flu. We dealt with the first by using traps and pouring a concrete slab under the hives so the beetles couldn't pupate in the ground beneath, and the second miraculously seemed to go away on its own.

Mites were a more persistent problem. We had already tried dusting the bees with powdered sugar (when they clean themselves, they knock off the mites) and using Apiguard, a mite-killing gel that the bees track all through the hive. Now it was time for pads soaked with formic acid, which gives off awful, powerful fumes that make your throat burn and your eyes water. It was a good thing that the women of Team Bee were utterly smitten with the hives—with their uncanny collective intelligence, their hardworking drive, and their sheer power, which Margaret would sometimes describe as "a tiger in a box." They would do whatever they could to help those hives survive.

❊

When we had finished surveying all of our projects, we felt pretty happy about them—and the sheer fact that we'd managed to keep them going, given how busy our lives were. They provided great holiday presents for our friends and families: jars of honey, fragrant hand salve (from our own beeswax, which Team Bee had carefully melted in a homemade solar wax melter), and bottles of olive oil and vinegar and beer. Cheeses weren't added to the list of gifts, because they took so long and we had made so few. We labeled all our jars and bottles (see How to Make Your Own Labels, page 165) and it felt good to be giving gifts that represented more than what they were— but were fine just *as* they were, too.

Our winter menu garden had been planned and mostly planted in the fall. This time around, we were going for a cozy supper of big food: A giant, bright winter salad of frilly escarole and crisp endive, with poached eggs and croutons from homemade bread (we had a bit of

Pouring beeswax hand salve

wheat carefully set aside for flour). Then we'd have a huge stew or a creamy hot chowder of winter greens and other vegetables, and a loaf of bread on the side with homemade butter. For dessert, Stephanie would make one of her specialties, a tender olive oil and orange cake. We told ourselves (blithely, as it turned out) that we would adapt

Our partly fermented mead, with airlock inserted

Tasting escargots

the cake to use the ingredients on hand. We wouldn't make beer this time around, since at long last we would have our Syrah as well as Chardonnay—and, in a surprise development, mead.

Sooner or later, every beekeeper considers making mead, or honey wine. Team Bee had visited a local meadery in the fall and been completely inspired by what they had sipped. This was no cloying, supersweet Renaissance faire beverage. It was crisp and simple, with "the luscious flavor of the honey shining through," Brianne said. Mead, as explained to them by the meadery's owner, seemed easy to make, too: Mix water, honey, and yeast. So that's exactly what the newly formed Team Mead did—using some of the same equipment we had used for beer—and now the result was fermenting in a glass carboy.

❖

The winter garden was shaping up to be a beauty. It was laid out in a U shape facing the path, compact and tidy—unlike our fall garden, which had no particular design other than to give the plants optimum sun exposure. The two arms of the U were meant to mirror one another, each planted with the same pleasing symmetry of greens, with brassicas like cauliflower, cabbage, and

weird, beautiful broccoli romanesco also worked into the pattern. The garden department threw in some red butterhead lettuce, too (in our mild winter, it would do fine). Our hardy thyme and oregano beds neatly capped each end of the U.

Among the garden's many admirers were snails. As in just about every California garden, we had tons of them, thanks to some well-meaning immigrant in the 1800s who brought these edible gastropods (known as *petit gris* in France) to the West thinking they could form a great new food supply—and instead introduced a major agricultural pest. Whenever Johanna found them snacking on our pretty garden, she would mercilessly crunch them with her boot or feed them to the chickens, who loved them.

Then one day, it occurred to her that they could fulfill their original nineteenth-century purpose, right here on our one-block table. She walked into the test kitchen and persuaded Amy, who is a lot less squeamish than your average cook (her father was a hunter), to form Team Escargot.

Within a week, they had purged, fattened, and even *named* about a dozen snails. Amy, not having had time to research snail cooking—do you pound them like abalone and flash-cook? or braise like octopus?—relied on French-style panache and threw Shelli, Chelle, Shelby, and the rest of the clan into a sauté pan with our wine, butter, and herbs. We tasted bravely and regretted it. Turns out it takes more than a quick sauté to remove mucus from a snail.

But Amy always rises to a challenge. Boiling, she read, would help deslime the snails. This produced lots of bilious green goo and some screaming from Amy, who refused to ever cook snails again: "The French can have them!" Several weeks later she got her mojo back, added a salting step to the process to reduce the slime, and made some incredibly tasty escargots. We did not add them to the menu, though—making snails for the entire staff was too much to ask of any cook.

⁜

Sixteen months after we had picked our Syrah grapes, crushed and destemmed them, fretted over them as they cold-soaked, went through two separate fermentations, pressed them, and then figured out how to siphon off the lees, our wine was at last ready to be bottled. We had to make sure with a final taste test, and used a turkey baster to sip from our first carboy. The wine was more than just okay—it was a flood of dark, delicious fruit. Cheers broke out all around. "We did it!" said Sara, and danced a little jig. She swirled, swished, and sipped, and got to analyze her own wine: brambles (good in Syrah) and blackberries, plus leafy tobacco, mocha, and black pepper.

We tasted each of our seven carboys and were amazed by how different they were—proof, as Sara said, that wine

Sampling the Syrah

is alive, and how tiny molecular shifts along the way can affect the "yum factor." The star carboys were definitely 1 and 5. Carboy 2 was good but with sweeter-seeming fruit, said Sara, and molasses character. Number 3 would need some age to smooth out its rough spots.

Then we got down to work. The entire team pitched in, including Dan Brenzel, our wisecracking advisor and perpetual provider of home wine-making equipment. Using the same techniques from a couple of months earlier, when we bottled the Chardonnay, we siphoned the inky wine into the 135 bottles we had saved up and sanitized, and then used Dan's nifty floor corker to drive each cork home. We ended the day with purple hands, purple teeth, and high spirits.

⁜

We hadn't exactly been hibernating in winter, what with most of our projects needing tending of one kind or another. Then we really started to bustle: We launched Team Cow.

For months, I'd been dreaming of finding our own cow. We'd been "importing" excellent store-bought organic milk and cream from Straus Family Creamery, north of San Francisco, but getting milk from our own cow—preferably a Jersey, which produces the richest milk in cowdom—would take our dairy products to a whole new level. Imagine the butter, ice cream, and cheese we could make from her superfresh, unadulterated, unhomogenized milk! Plus, we'd get to know an actual cow, an animal once common in backyards and farms across the country. Now they're familiar to most of us only as a picture on a milk carton.

We already knew we couldn't keep a cow at Sunset (even though our city regulations allow it, amazingly enough). The twice-daily milkings weren't the main issue. In order to lactate, cows must get pregnant and give birth, and the impregnation part—and then the delivery-of-calf part, and the dealing with calf (possibly many calves) afterward—seemed a little intense for people with desk jobs. Sharing a cow with a knowledgeable owner seemed like the best solution.

We looked and looked for a cow. Once there were small dairies all over the San Francisco Peninsula, but those are gone now. Finally we found her in Pescadero, on the coast to the south, at Pie Ranch Farm. She was an adorable Jersey named Adelaide, with a thick, glossy coat and sparkling brown eyes. Her owners, Jered and Nancy Lawson, had already set up a share arrangement, and we would be one of several owners.

We ground flour with a sausage grinder

Unfortunately, Adelaide got a staph infection in her udder right before our first visit. The Lawsons decided she had to dry up, which would help her heal, and then go through a whole new pregnancy (about nine months, just like humans) before her milk would be available. So Team Cow, with much regret, had to press the pause button.

At least our bees were on the mend. Both hives had lots of baby bees, enough to ensure that they would survive their mite infestation. Also, because mites prefer to lay their eggs in the larger drone cells rather than worker bee cells, we got in the habit of removing the drone frames every few weeks and freezing them. This killed the drone larvae along with the mites, but drones are relatively expendable, and, as Margaret remarked, "beekeeping is not all sweetness and honey."

❖

The garden had lived up to its promise and was a gorgeous, dense display of textures and colors—reds, burgundies, jade, lime green. The snowy heads of cauliflower were like pom-poms. Broccoli rabe towered at the back, with sprays of spicy yellow blossoms. The broccoli romanesco could mesmerize you for minutes with its perfectly symmetrical, spiraling turrets, like something out of an Escher engraving. And with their curvy, frilly leaves, the chard and kale and lettuce looked like the feathers on Vegas showgirls.

It was almost heartbreaking to have to harvest it for our feast. We managed to stop thinking about how barren and forlorn it looked once we had carried our huge, luscious basketfuls into the kitchen and started cooking. What a pleasure it is to cook with vegetables that still have life-force in them! Everything was crisp, tight, and juicy.

We were missing the escarole (a seed shortage prevented us from ever planting it) and the endive (it never germinated), so we changed our salad to use what we did have: red butterhead lettuce and arugula. We hard-cooked the eggs instead of poaching them, because liquidy poached yolks, great on crisp endive and escarole, would have turned the tender lettuces into a sticky clump.

For bread to go with our chowder, we ground some of our wheat berries, first coarsely (and laboriously) in a sausage grinder, and then finely in tiny batches in an electric coffee grinder. (We probably should have gotten a home grain mill, but we had so little to grind.) We turned the flour into a couple of rough, rustic loaves of ciabatta; we could just imagine butter pooling and melting in its nooks and crannies. So Elaine made butter, using nothing but cream and a food processor.

I had hoped we'd be able to preserve some onions and a few garlic bulbs from the summer—they are crucial kitchen workhorses, and we really needed them for this winter menu. But they had barely lasted through fall; we hadn't grown good storage varieties. We caved and added both to our winter "imports" list, telling ourselves we would grow storage types next year. Surprisingly, though, we did have a few remaining Yukon Gold potatoes, which we had experimentally stored in an old fridge (see page 82 for details). We had just enough for our winter chowder.

❖

Given the chilly weather, we ate our winter feast indoors, at a couple of long tables in the kitchen. We poured our deep, dark Syrah along with our Chardonnay, and I think it's the first time I've ever made a toast *to* wine as well as with it.

I had worried that this dinner would somehow be lumpy and bland. But it was as vigorous and pretty as the garden it came from. The salad had bits of juicy tangerine and yellow egg scattered among its red and green leaves. We sprinkled the chowder with yellow broccoli rabe and blue rosemary flowers, and it looked and tasted great with hunks of the dark, shaggy ciabatta. Dessert actually *had* started out lumpy and bland—it's why I'd been worried. Several days earlier, when Stephanie tried to make her olive oil cake with whole-wheat flour and honey instead of the usual refined white flour, baking powder, and sugar, it cooked up into a dark, heavy mass. She ditched it and instead made a lovely big flan for the

dinner, glistening with caramelized honey and bits of tangerine peel. It looked like a golden moon.

I'd also wondered whether our winter menu would be substantial enough. When it's cold, you need some rib-sticking food. Thanks, though, to the cream in the chowder, the butter, the whole-grain bread, and all those hearty winter vegetables—plus eggs, milk, and honey in the flan—it had sturdiness as well as freshness.

We ended dinner with another toast, this time to (and with) our mead, poured into tiny frosted shot glasses. It was a baby, really not meant to be tasted until it had aged for at least a year, better two. Even so, it was surprisingly drinkable—not "like cough syrup," Brianne's biggest fear. Like so much else in our one-block project, it was living and evolving, and every taste in the months to come would teach us more.

HOW TO MAKE YOUR OWN LABELS

We labeled nearly all of the foods we made, because it was fun and because we gave away lots of food as gifts, especially around the holidays. It's not difficult to produce your own labels. Here's how:

Create the design Use a design/graphics program like Adobe Illustrator, or work with your local home wine-making/home-brew store to create a label on their software.

Print the labels We laser-printed each design onto white Avery 5265 full-sheet labels (available at office-supply stores and www.officemax.com).

Cut the labels On a self-healing mat (available at craft stores and www.dickblick.com), line up a metal ruler along the label's edge and use a craft knife (available at craft stores and www.dickblick.com) to cut out each label. (We also tried trimming labels with a paper cutter, but sticky bits gummed up the blade.)

Stick them on Make sure the surface of the container to be labeled is clean and dry. Peel back one corner of the label and use that sticky spot to help you position the label on the surface. Then reach under the label and gently remove the backing with one hand; with the other, smooth down the label as you peel off the backing. Use a paper towel to do the smoothing, to keep the label clean. With wine, wait at least 48 hours after you bottle to start labeling; you want to give your wine some time to adapt to the bottle.

THE WINTER GARDEN

The leafy greens and succulent cruciferous vegetables we raised for our winter menu grow best when air temperatures are cool. Yet they thrive in sunny locations (at least 6 hours of sun per day). Arugula is easy to grow from seeds, while other crops, including lettuce, yield plentifully from nursery plants. (For seed-starting and planting tips, see pages 9 to 13.) If you can, avoid planting in any "frost pockets"—low areas that can get frost earlier than other parts of your garden.

Arugula

Broccoli Rabe

Broccoli rabe, also called broccoli raab or rapini, is a choice cool-season crop to grow alongside cabbage and carrots. It resembles broccoli, but instead of producing one giant head, it grows many longer, smaller budding stalks that you can selectively harvest all winter and spring. The plant grows 12 to 15 inches tall, and usually resprouts from the stalks until hot weather settles in.

BEST SITE Full sun, though it can tolerate some shade, and well-drained soil. Prefers cool weather.

DAYS TO HARVEST 60 days from seeds.

PLANTING AND CARE Plant in well-composted soil in early fall, sowing seeds 2 inches apart in rows 6 to 8 inches apart. When seedlings are 3 to 4 inches tall, thin them to 6 inches apart. Keep the soil evenly moist.

HOW TO HARVEST Clip stalks when buds appear, or allow a few of their yellow flowers to bloom for splashes of garden color (the blooms are edible, too). Plants will keep shooting out new buds for an extended yield.

SEED SOURCES (search under "broccoli raab") Johnny's Selected Seeds, www.johnnyseeds.com, and John Scheepers Kitchen Garden Seeds, www.kitchen gardenseeds.com.

Arugula

Arugula or rocket (*roquette* in French) has tender, deep green leaves that add a peppery bite to salads. Crops come fast: You can pick baby leaves in as little as 3 weeks. To prolong the harvest, sow in succession every 3 weeks.

BEST SITE An open, sunny spot and well-drained soil.

DAYS TO HARVEST 35 days from seed.

PLANTING AND CARE Sow seeds during cool weather in ground that has been raked or hoed clean of weeds and clods. You can either broadcast (scatter) the seeds or sow thinly in rows, and cover lightly with $1/4$ inch of soil. Water the plot lightly and often to bring up the seedlings, then regularly (once a week or so) as they grow. To speed them up, apply a high-nitrogen fertilizer after the first unformed leaves appear. Thin seedlings to about 6 inches apart (the thinnings are great in salads). Arugula also thrives in pots at least 6 inches deep and 14 inches wide.

HOW TO HARVEST Pick the leaves as needed once plants are larger.

SEED SOURCE Burpee, www.burpee.com.

Broccoli Romanesco 'Veronica'

This variety's round heads, made up of chartreuse florets that spiral into little peaks, make it look like cauliflower from another planet. It has a texture and flavor similar to mild, sweet cauliflower, too. The florets turn a slightly deeper, more olive green when cooked, and can also be eaten raw as whole florets (good with dips) or sliced in salads.

BEST SITE Grow it in loamy soil that's been well amended with compost, and make sure it gets full sun (though it can tolerate some shade). Broccoli Romanesco prefers cool weather.

DAYS TO HARVEST 77 days from seed.

PLANTING AND CARE In mild climates, plant in late summer or early fall for a winter harvest. (Plants develop the best heads when they mature in cool weather; in heat, the flower buds open prematurely.) Start seeds in flats or small pots indoors 6 weeks before transplanting into the garden. Before planting in the garden, work some well-aged compost and a granular complete fertilizer into the soil. Space the plants 18 to 24 inches apart, keep the soil evenly

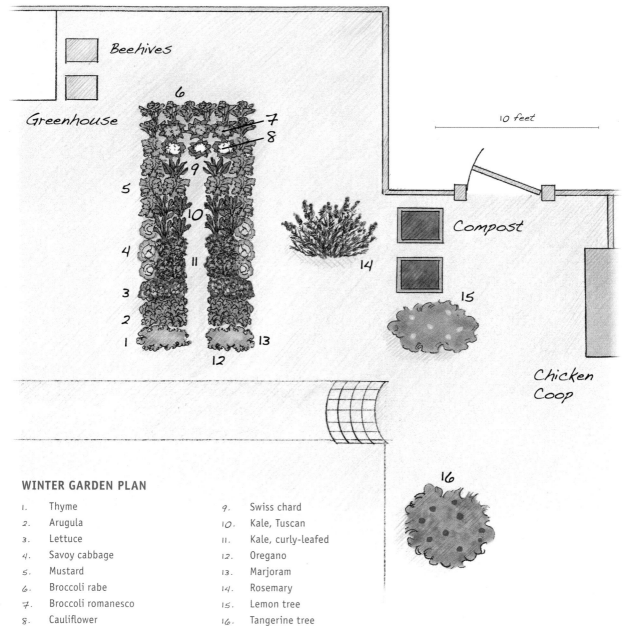

Beehives

Greenhouse

6

7

8

9

5

10

4

11

3

2

1

13

12

14

10 feet

Compost

15

Chicken
Coop

16

WINTER GARDEN PLAN

1.	Thyme	9.	Swiss chard
2.	Arugula	10.	Kale, Tuscan
3.	Lettuce	11.	Kale, curly-leafed
4.	Savoy cabbage	12.	Oregano
5.	Mustard	13.	Marjoram
6.	Broccoli rabe	14.	Rosemary
7.	Broccoli romanesco	15.	Lemon tree
8.	Cauliflower	16.	Tangerine tree

Broccoli Romanesco 'Veronica'

summer months. We started our plants from seeds, sowing them in flats in our greenhouse 4 weeks before planting the seedlings outdoors in garden beds in September. Space the seedlings 24 to 30 inches apart. Water the plants often enough to ensure they never wilt, and give them frequent light feedings of dilute liquid fish emulsion (follow package directions).

HOW TO HARVEST When the heads feel firm and look well formed, cut them off at the base with pruners or loppers. The plants can take light frost, which sweetens their flavor, but heavy freezes can knock them down.

SEED SOURCE Johnny's Selected Seeds, www.johnny seeds.com.

Cauliflower 'Cassius'

We grew this variety because it produces round, creamy white heads 7 to 8 inches across—the perfect size for a compact kitchen garden. Some varieties need to have their leaves tied together over the heads to keep the sun from discoloring them, but 'Cassius' is a self-blanching variety, so it didn't need all that fussing. Its flavor is mellow and sweet.

BEST SITE Full sun and well-drained soil.

DAYS TO HARVEST 65 to 75 days from seed.

PLANTING AND CARE Start seeds in flats or small pots indoors 4 to 6 weeks before transplanting into a garden bed that has been well amended with compost. Space seedlings 18 to 24 inches apart. Keep soil moist until seedlings get growing, then water deeply and regularly, especially in dry weather. Feed once or twice with complete fertilizer before heads start to form.

HOW TO HARVEST Use a sharp knife to slice the entire head from the mature stem. It's a bit of a dance to know when cauliflower is ready to harvest. The head should be firm and fully formed; harvest it before the curd (the white part) separates into flowers (check it regularly). Make the cut beneath the top set of leaves.

SEED SOURCE Territorial Seed Company, www.territorialseed.com.

Kale, Curly-Leafed and Tuscan

Rich and nutrient-packed (high in vitamins A and C), kale is indispensable for winter soups and stews. We grew two varieties: 'Winterbor', whose curly-edged, blue-green leaves

moist, and cover the seedlings with floating row covers (available at nurseries) until they're big and leafy enough to withstand cabbage worms.

HOW TO HARVEST For the best quality, harvest the heads when they are firm and tight. As they get older, they open up and lose their crunch.

SEED SOURCE John Scheepers Kitchen Garden Seeds, www.kitchengardenseeds.com.

Cabbage, Savoy 'Alcosa'

This curly-leaved Savoy cabbage forms tight heads that are ideal for closely spaced planting. Also, its leaves are dense, crinkled, and colorful—blue-green outside, lighter green to creamy white inside—and pretty in garden beds with other greens. We love this cabbage in stir-fries, because it retains its crunch, and in salads. It has an exceptionally mild, sweet flavor.

BEST SITE Full sun in mild coastal areas, part shade in hot-summer interiors, and loose, fast-draining soil enriched with compost.

DAYS TO HARVEST 72 days from seed.

PLANTING AND CARE Time your planting so heads will mature in cooler weather before or after hot

'Alcosa' Savoy cabbage   'Cassius' cauliflower   Red Butterhead lettuce

form low rosettes that stretch out to 2 feet, and 'Nero di Toscana', a Tuscan heirloom kale whose strappy, dark green leaves form statuesque, upright plants that reach 3 feet. (Tuscan kale is also often labeled lacinato or dinosaur kale.) Both kale types are ornamental and cold-hardy and add texture and color to the winter garden. Light frost sweetens their flavors.

BEST SITE Full sun or light shade in mild climates, part shade in hotter inland areas.

DAYS TO HARVEST 55 to 65 days for 'Winterbor' and 60 days for 'Nero di Toscana' from seed.

PLANTING AND CARE Plant in September for a winter crop. Till the soil and mix in compost or aged manure before planting. Sow seeds in place and thin seedlings to 24 to 36 inches apart. Or, set out nursery seedlings at the same spacing. Keep the soil moist during the growing season.

HOW TO HARVEST Remove leaves from the outside of the clusters as needed, or harvest the entire plant by pulling it up and cutting off the base.

SEED SOURCE John Scheepers Kitchen Garden Seeds, www.kitchengardenseeds.com.

Lemon 'Eureka'

See the Summer Garden, page 31.

Lettuce, Red Butterhead

Lettuce is one of the most satisfying vegetables you can grow: It's fast and easy from seed as long as you plant it at the right time of year (fall or spring in mild climates).

We chose 'Marvel of Four Seasons' ('Merveille des Quatre Saisons'), a French heirloom variety whose loosely cupped green leaves are tinged with shades of ruby, rose-pink, and bronze.

BEST SITE A sunny spot in cool areas, part shade where it is hot, and loose, well-drained soil.

DAYS TO HARVEST 50 to 60 days from seed.

PLANTING AND CARE Sow seeds about 4 inches apart in well-prepared soil, then barely cover the seeds with about 1/4 inch of soil. Thin seedlings to 12 inches apart. Spray the seedbed with water regularly until the seeds germinate, then water regularly to keep the soil moist. Feed once or twice during the growing season with dilute liquid fish emulsion.

HOW TO HARVEST Pick leaves any time from the seedling (thinning) size on. Harvest after loose heads form.

SEED SOURCES The Cook's Garden, www.cooksgarden.com, and John Scheepers Kitchen Garden Seeds, www.kitchengardenseeds.com.

Marjoram, Sweet

See the Summer Garden, page 31.

Mushrooms

See How to Grow Mushrooms, page 126.

'Green Wave' mustard

Mustard 'Green Wave'

Mustard comes in different colors and textures, but we like 'Green Wave' for its lime-green hue, ruffled edges, and pungent, peppery flavor. The plant looked so good in the garden that we neglected to harvest it and ended up with very big (and very spicy) leaves. Luckily, they were perfect when braised with other winter greens (see recipe, page 190).

BEST SITE Full sun and well-drained soil.
DAYS TO HARVEST 50 days from seed.
PLANTING AND CARE We planted mustard in October for our winter dinner. You can also plant in early spring or late summer; the key is to avoid exposing the plants to too much heat, which causes premature bolting (setting of seed). Start seeds indoors or plant them directly in well-fertilized soil $1/2$ inch deep, eventually thinning the seedlings to 6 to 12 inches apart. Water regularly, and feed with a complete fertilizer every 2 to 3 weeks.
HOW TO HARVEST Pick outer leaves as needed, or let the plant reach about 6 inches tall, then snip it down to an inch above the soil (new leaves can shoot up again from the base).
SEED SOURCE Territorial Seed Company, www.territorialseed.com.

Oregano, Italian

See the Summer Garden, page 30.

Rosemary 'Tuscan Blue'

See the Summer Garden, page 35.

Swiss chard

See the Fall Garden, page 102.

Tangerine 'Dancy'

'Dancy' is the standard variety that appears in markets before Christmas: smallish and seedy, but with excellent, complex flavor. We picked from a tree that has been at Sunset for decades. Like all tangerines, it's a member of the mandarin family.

BEST SITE Full sun and deep, fast-draining soil.
DAYS TO HARVEST Plants start bearing fruits in early winter.
PLANTING AND CARE Plant after spring frost but before summer heat. Dig in a 4- to 6-inch layer of compost before planting, then dig a hole twice as wide as the root-ball and mix a granular, controlled-release general-purpose fertilizer into the backfill. Or, plant in large containers (at least 18 inches in diameter) in fast-draining potting mix. Mulch with compost. Water established trees every other week, soaking the soil thoroughly. Feed several times during the growing season with a fertilizer formulated for citrus (follow package directions).
HOW TO HARVEST Citrus fruits ripen only on the tree. Pluck one and taste for ripeness.
PLANT SOURCES Shop nurseries, or online at Four Winds Growers, www.fourwindsgrowers.com.

Thyme, French

See the Summer Garden, page 36.

—Kathleen N. Brenzel and Johanna Silver

THE "IMPORTS"

We went outside our garden for these local foods:
Milk, whole and unhomogenized (for butter, page 154, and cheese, pages 46 and 117); seawater (for salt, page 172); active dry yeast (for bread, page 182); sweet mead liquid yeast (for mead, page 177); whole-wheat flour and wheat berries ('Sonora' and 'Expresso', page 156); garlic (ours ran out); 'Spanish White' onions (ditto); walnuts

THE WINTER PROJECTS

HOW TO MAKE
SALT

Of all the projects we attempted as part of our One-Block feasts, this may have been the most far-fetched. We had read of other people's efforts, most memorably Michael Pollan's in *The Omnivore's Dilemma*, in which he scavenges water from trash-strewn wetlands and evaporates it on his stove top into brown salt that, he writes, "tasted so metallic and so much like chemicals that it actually made me gag."

But we persisted because we knew we had to have seasoning for our dinner, and figured—what with the San Francisco Bay to one side of us (the same bay that Pollan harvested, actually) and the Pacific Ocean on the other, we had some water to choose from. Also, the other raw materials that we had "imported" for our feast—grapes for the wine, olives for the oil, and milk for the cheese—at least were transformed from their natural state by our own hands. It would be copping out to just go buy salt.

The process proved surprisingly easy, and the yield was much higher than we had expected. And our salt looked pretty (pure white), smelled fresh, tasted exactly like the ocean, and made a fine seasoning for our feast. As to whether it was safe to consume or would behave like normal salt in cooking, we weren't sure. We were just happy that we had, in fact, made our own salt from local seawater.

PACIFIC SEA SALT

We hauled drums filled with Pacific seawater to our Menlo Park offices and reduced several gallons to salt.

WHAT TO USE

Food-grade plastic drums We had a few clean 5-gallon food-grade plastic drums left over from making olive oil (see page 131), so we used them to transport the brine. Any thoroughly washed bucket will do. Drums cost about $15 each, plus $20 handling fee if your order is less than $100, at The Olive Oil Source, www.oliveoilsource.com or 805/688-1014.

Coffee filters or a triple layer of cheesecloth For filtering the water. About $4.50 for 2 square yards at a hardware store or cookware store.

Pyrex liquid-measuring cups To measure the hot brine.

Stockpot For boiling the brine. From $60 online or at a cookware shop.

Two Pyrex 9 by 13 inch baking dishes For baking and evaporating the brine. About $7 each at a cookware shop.

Rigid metal spatula Once the salt crystals have formed, you have to scrape them off the pan.

HOW TO DO IT

1. Collect seawater After thinking about the nearest cleanest portion of the ocean, we settled on Bean Hollow State Beach near Pescadero, since no streams (which can carry toxins and other runoff) flow into the ocean there. We collected 40 gallons of the chilly Pacific in our plastic drums. Another time, we collected seawater near Fort Bragg, a small coastal town north of San Francisco. Both batches were processed the same way.

2. Filter Back at the office, we poured a test batch of water through a coffee filter (or layered cheesecloth) into the stockpot.

Our Pacific sea salt

3. Boil We brought the filtered water to a rolling boil and held it there for 20 minutes to kill any noxious bacteria. We were aware that this would have no effect on other toxins or heavy metals. In fact, if they were present, the cooking might concentrate them.

4. Filter again To remove any remaining particles, we filtered the water again, this time into heatproof measuring cups.

5. Bake The first time we made salt, we used aluminum baking sheets, which gave us a large yield—but the salt was grayish and tasted like aluminum. We then switched to Pyrex baking dishes and got salt as white as snow with no funny taste. Here's how: We poured the filtered water in 3-cup batches into the pans, then baked it in a 350°F oven for about 2 1/2 hours, checking often toward the end to make sure we didn't burn the crystals as they formed.

Sun evaporation as an alternative. Feeling sheepish about the fossil fuel consumed by baking, we also tried putting the brine-filled baking sheets outside to evaporate in the sun. This didn't work very well, owing to spotty weather and to lots of leaves and other debris blowing into the exposed salt. We tried again, covering

the pans with cheesecloth, and after several days, we had salt. The yield was much lower than what we got with the baking method, however.

Or stovetop boiling. Another early attempt involved boiling filtered seawater until the liquid completely evaporated and salt lined the inside and bottom of the pan. This ended with a steamy kitchen and burning hot crystals of salt flying out of the pot like popcorn and hitting us on the arms. Plus, boiling down all that water and then running the fan to cool off the kitchen wasn't energy efficient, so baking became the best choice.

6. Scrape At the end of baking, the crystals rimmed the pan, and we scraped them off with the metal spatula. The yield varied depending on the source of the brine: We got about 2 tablespoons good-tasting, snowy white salt from 3 cups brine collected at Pescadero. The same amount of brine from Fort Bragg yielded between 1/3 and 1/2 cup.

7. Taste We sent a sample of our Fort Bragg salt to salt expert Mark Bitterman, owner of the specialty shop The Meadow in Portland, Oregon. Here's what he said: "[It] has a lovely opaque, crème fraîche color that comes from an abundance of the sea's trace minerals. The crystals are marvelously diverse in form, ranging from finely fringed micro-grains to layers of laminated flakes. And the flavor: a roiling oceanic assault on the senses—only nice, like being caught in a wave of sun-warmed water, briny and bitter and butter-sweet." He further pointed out that, unlike commercial salt manufacturers, we had reduced all the available salts in our brine, each of which has a different salinity and flavor. The big guys tend to go for sodium chloride only, which provides most of the salt and precipitates first, because it is more efficient. "What you guys have done is grab it all, including the calcium and magnesium salts. You've got a big dynamo of saltiness. It has everything in it." This, it seems, is the hallmark of artisanal salts. We are artisans!

8. Test We spent some fruitless time contacting various clean-water agencies to ask about getting our water samples tested. One officer, with a branch of the Environmental Protection Agency, said to us, "Why would anyone want to drink salt water?" He had a point. So we moved on to the salt itself.

We then considered sending a salt sample to a food lab, but a heavy-metals screening would have cost $275 for each possible contaminant (and there are many), and a test for pesticides at least $100. Kind of pricey for seasoning, we thought. As Bitterman pointed out, salt is extremely dilute in the ocean—and is not a bioaccumulator of toxins—so the chances of it containing large amounts of bad stuff are probably not all that high.

At this point, we are happy to have produced salt that tastes good and, we hope, might be harmless.

HELPFUL INFORMATION

Salt is a fascinating subject. It has roughly fourteen thousand applications, from de-icing roads to food preservation, and was so valued in Roman times that soldiers were paid wages in it.

BOOKS

- *Neptune's Gift: A History of Common Salt*, by Robert P. Multhauf (Johns Hopkins University Press, 1978).
- *Salt: A World History*, by Mark Kurlansky (Penguin Books, 2002).
- *Salted: A Manifesto on the World's Most Essential Mineral, with Recipes*, by Mark Bitterman (Ten Speed Press, 2010).

OTHER RESOURCES

- "How to Make Salt from Sea-Water," by John Leconte (Governor and Council of South Carolina, 1862). An oddly engrossing pamphlet written at the request of the state's governor by a chemistry and physics professor at South Carolina College. At a time when the oceans were cleaner than they are today, Leconte spells out how to boil down seawater in 20-foot sheet-iron pans over wood fires. You'll find yourself engrossed in the details of sludging and soccage (crystallization). For the free download, visit www.docsouth.unc.edu/imls/lecontej/leconte.html.
- The Salt Institute, an association of salt producers, puts forth all sorts of information about salt on its Web site—everything from stats on world production (China leads) to solution mining to nutrition (www.saltinstitute.org).

—Amy Machnak

Our first stab at making salt

HOW TO MAKE
ESCARGOTS
(FROM YOUR OWN GARDEN SNAILS)

Growing edibles inevitably means growing snails, especially because our garden is organic and hospitable to wildlife. We have a big snail population snacking on our carefully tended leafy vegetables. One day Johanna, our test-garden coordinator, suggested that we eat them. Eat them? As in—*escargots?*

That was definitely the French approach to dealing with snails in the garden. In fact, the French don't consider them a nuisance at all, but a reason to spend time with the family, walking with buckets through their yards—even grassy fields—in pursuit of their prize. They refer to it as "hunting."

But were ours the type of snails that could be eaten? Maybe they produced toxins. And, most important, how would we make them taste like the French gourmet item served in overpriced restaurants?

First, we experimented with sautéing them, and discovered that preparing snails wasn't as simple as tossing them around in butter in a frying pan. They were, er, slimy. So we did some research and consulted many authorities on the cooking of France, including M. F. K. Fisher and Georgeanne Brennan, and reread our own article on escargots, published in 1988. All advised pretty

Helix aspersa in the one-block garden

much the same technique for cooking snails, with slight variations: Purge the snails (put them on a cornmeal diet in a closed dish for several days to clear their innards of any noxious stuff they may have been nibbling), boil them, extract them from their shells, and then use them in whatever recipe you have in mind.

Having now nabbed and cooked several batches of snails, let's just say that making escargots, though not difficult, is not for the squeamish. In fact, it reminds us of a sixth-grade science project. But the final outcome is delicious.

ESCARGOTS

We plucked our little shelled nuisances from the garden.

WHAT TO USE

About 12 live snails Choose the biggest snails possible. Unfortunately, we didn't seem to have any big snails. Ours were all small to medium.

Bowl For collecting snails.

Kitchen towel To drape over the snail-collecting bowl, to keep your catch from crawling out.

Roasting pan A large, rimmed pan, such as a 10-by-14-inch roasting pan. About $10 at most cookware stores or online.

About 2 cups yellow cornmeal For the purge. About $3 for 1 pound at most grocery stores.

Several thyme sprigs For the purge.

2 tablespoons fine sea salt For salting to remove slime, plus more for seasoning when sautéing.

Small bowl For salting the snails.

Large saucepan

1/2 cup white wine

Fresh herbs

1/2 small onion

1 carrot

2 celery stalks

Garlic

Flat-leaf parsley

Lemon juice

White wine

Butter

1. Choose wisely Determine the species of snail you have; not all are edible. The most popular snail in France is the big, fat Burgundy snail, *Helix pomatia*. Ours are common brown garden snails, *Helix aspersa*, also considered fine to eat. They were brought to this country, probably by the French, in the 1850s and are now a major pest in gardens everywhere. Make sure you hunt for snails in a garden free of pesticides. This isn't a problem for us, as Sunset has had a no-spray policy for decades.

2. Collect We found the majority of our snails on the inside rims of potted plants, mostly edibles but occasionally flowers, too. They tend to like plants that give shade in the afternoon heat, such as agapanthus, but they also like to hang out in whichever plant they are eating, especially radicchio, lettuce, kale, cabbage, and strawberries. Just pull them off and put them in a basket or bowl, covered with a towel, for transporting to the kitchen.

3. Wash Since snails crawl around in dirt, you need to make sure they are really clean. Rinse them in a colander under cold running water while rubbing them together.

4. Purge This controlled feeding of the snails ensures that their digestive tracts are clean of impurities, toxins, and dirt. Put the snails into the roasting pan with a small dish of fresh water, about ¼ cup yellow cornmeal poured into the corner of the pan, and a few sprigs of thyme from the garden. Cover the pan with a double layer of cheesecloth secured around the edge of the pan with rubber bands or tied string. Every other day, take the snails out of the pan, wash the pan, return the snails to the pan, and replace the cornmeal, the bowl of water, and the thyme. Do this for about 2 weeks. You'll know the purge is working when you see little yellow and green dried poop trails in the pan.

5. Salt Put the snails in a small bowl and sprinkle them with the 2 tablespoons salt. This kills them and also helps to pull the slime from them. Cover the bowl with aluminum foil and poke a few holes in the foil. Let sit for about 12 hours.

Fill the bowl with water and then drain. Repeat as needed, rinsing off the salt and mucus each time, until the water runs clear.

6. Boil In a large saucepan, bring 4 cups water and the ½ cup white wine to a boil. Add a few herb sprigs, such as thyme and flat-leaf parsley. Then chop the onion, carrot, and celery and add them to the pan. Simmer for 30 minutes to create a flavorful broth. Drop the snails into the broth and simmer them, skimming off any green, slimy foam that appears on the surface (this is the science-project part), until the meat releases easily from the shell when prodded with a toothpick, about 15 minutes (longer if you have larger snails). Lift the snails out with a slotted spoon, letting any slime and mucus drip off the spoon, and transfer to a plate. Then use the toothpick to pluck the snails from their shells. The standard instruction is to cut the tough "foot" off the snail. Our snails were so small that the cut was more like a scrape, but we did it anyway.

You can save the shells, dry them completely, and serve the cooked snails in them for a lovely presentation. Our shells were too small and not worth the trouble.

7. Cook: Garlic Butter Escargots At this point, the snails can be used in any recipe you like (we've seen recipes for everything from baked escargots to spaghetti with escargots). We went the traditional French route and tossed them in a little garlic, parsley, lemon, white wine, and, of course, butter—lots of melted butter. We ate them in a little dish with a side of warm crusty bread and were instantly transported to a sidewalk cafe on the Champs-Élysées.

HELPFUL INFORMATION

BOOKS

- *The Food and Flavors of Haute Provence*, by Georgeanne Brennan (Chronicle Books, 1997).
- "Fifty Million Snails," from *Serve It Forth*, by M. F. K. Fisher (Harper & Brothers, 1937; reprinted by North Point Press, 1989).

OTHER RESOURCES

- "Snails as Food: Escargot" by Robert Hawthorne (8-page pamphlet from the University of California, Davis; publication #2222; revised 1975; order through http://anrcatalog.ucdavis.edu/snails)
- "The Snail Eaters," a reminiscence by Joyce Hanson on Leite's Culinaria, http://leitesculinaria.com/47375/writings-snail-eaters.html.
- For general information about snails and about cooking them, visit www.en.wikipedia.org/wiki/Heliciculture#Turning_snails_into_escargots.

—Amy Machnak

HOW TO MAKE
MEAD (HONEY WINE)

Most people think of mead as an overly spiced and unbearably sweet beverage found only at Renaissance faires, but there is a whole world of delicious, easy-to-drink mead, both sweet and dry. Along with beer and wine, it is one of our most ancient drinks, thought to have been made as early as 7000 BCE. We tend to associate mead with the Vikings and the Celts of northern Europe, but it's been quaffed in many other places around the globe, including China, India, Greece, and Africa (it is still popular in Ethiopia, where it's called *tej*). In places where grapes could not be grown, mead offered a different way to make wine. Dozens of different styles of mead exist, from morat (made with mulberries) to cyser (honey and apple juice fermented together) to metheglin (a traditional Welsh brew involving herbs and spices).

We were inspired to have a crack at it ourselves after accompanying our local beekeepers' guild to Rabbit's Foot Meadery, in Sunnyvale, California. We chatted with the owner and acclaimed mead maker, Michael Faul, and realized that basic mead was not hard to make: Honey, water, and yeast are all it takes.

After doing some research, we came up with a streamlined recipe that is easy to re-create. We left out all spices and refrained from boiling the honey to preserve more of its character. This gentle treatment also retains more of the nutritional benefits of the raw honey.

Our mead still needs a few years of aging to mellow fully, but even after eight months, it already tastes better to us than many of the professionally made meads we have tried. The flavor of the honey shines through, undisguised by fruit flavors or excessive spices. Follow Team Mead's blog (oneblockdiet.sunset.com/team-mead) to watch our progress as we embark on future batches of dry mead and of melomel, mead flavored with fruit.

··

TRUE MEAD

Sweet, crisp, unspiced honey wine, showcasing the floral and faint eucalyptus flavors of our one-block honey.

MAKES 5 gallons TIME at least 6 months

WHAT TO USE

Unless otherwise noted, all of our materials came from More Beer in Los Altos, California (www.morebeer.com or 800/600-0033).

Saniclean For sanitizing all equipment, including containers, tubing, and bottles. Safe for septic systems and doesn't stain. Use 2 ounces for 5 gallons of water. About $13 for a 1-quart bottle from Williams Brewing Company, www.williamsbrewing.com.

5-gallon plastic bucket For mixing up batches of Saniclean solution. About $7 at a hardware store.

Water Room-temperature tap water is fine. If your water contains heavy chlorine or minerals, use bottled water (not distilled).

6-gallon, food-grade plastic bucket with spigot Used for mixing the must and for fermenting and bottling. About $13. We actually used a 5-gallon glass carboy (see photo, page 178) since we happened to have a few on hand, but this is much cheaper.

About 12 pounds honey From our own hives.

Hydrometer A probe-like tool that measures the specific gravity (density) of the must relative to water. Dissolved sugars make up the density of the must, and sugars are what ferment into alcohol, so the beginning hydrometer measurement is a good indicator of your mead's potential alcohol level. (The higher the specific gravity, the higher the potential alcohol level.) The MT300 hydrometer has a potential alcohol scale included. About $6 from morebeer.com.

Hydrometer jar A plastic tube with a flat base, sized to fit the hydrometer; for holding the must and mead samples. Some hydrometers come with their own jars. An 11^1/$_2$-inch jar is about $5.

Yeast We used 1 vial of White Labs Sweet Mead liquid yeast. About $6.25.

Stirring paddle or spoon Any sort of long-handled spoon or spatula will work.

5-gallon glass carboy The main fermentation container. From $20 to $30 at a home wine-making or home-brewing shop.

Rubber stopper You want a no. 7 stopper with a small hole (to accommodate the airlock) for sealing the opening at the top of the carboy. $1.50.

Airlock You fill this small plastic cylinder with water and insert it into the rubber stopper on top of the carboy. This keeps bacteria and other airborne impurities from entering the mead, which is highly susceptible to contamination in its early stages. It also allows carbon dioxide to escape, rather than build up inside the carboy. About $1.25.

Blanket or a large, dark cloth For wrapping the mead as it ferments. It blocks sunlight, which can stimulate the growth of bacteria.

Racking cane This cane-shaped stiff plastic tube (^{3}/$_8$ inch in diameter by 21 inches long) attaches to the vinyl tubing (below) used to rack the must. $2.50.

4-foot length of food-grade vinyl tubing Made of clear vinyl, and with a ^{3}/$_8$-inch interior diameter, the tubing is used to both rack the mead (siphon it off its sediment to another container) and bottle it. Cut it into a 3-foot section and a 1-foot section. About 30¢ per foot online or at a home wine-making or plumbing-supply store.

Bottles You'll need 48 pry-top bottles (screw-top bottles are harder to seal) in a dark green or brown glass (sunlight shining through clear glass can stimulate growth of bacteria). We got ours from friends, family, and colleagues. Free.

Jet bottle washer This fits on any outdoor hose thread faucet, like those on an outdoor or garage sink. About $12.

Bottle tree Invert your newly washed and sterilized bottles on this multipronged "tree" for easy drying of lots of bottles at once. We like the 81-bottle model from Williams Brewing Company (www.williams

brewing.com or 800/759-6025; it's the same one we used for our beer). About $30.

Beer caps A pack of 50 pry-type caps costs about $1.50.

Capper The only way to cap your bottles. We like the double-armed, easy-to-use Emily capper from Williams Brewing Company (above). About $14.

HOW TO DO IT

1. Sterilize your equipment Sterilize everything with a Saniclean solution in the 5-gallon plastic bucket. Rinse the equipment well and set on clean dish towels to dry.

2. Make the must (honey water) Add 4^1/$_2$ gallons tap water to the 6-gallon bucket. Add enough honey to give the must your target specific gravity, which predicts potential alcohol content. For example, for a potential alcohol content of 10.74 percent, the beginning specific gravity needs to be 1.08. To get a specific gravity reading, insert the hydrometer in its jar, drizzle in enough must from the bucket's spigot to make the hydrometer float, and read off the original specific gravity (OG). Make a note of the OG. If your hydrometer does not include a potential alcohol scale, you can use a handy online potential alcohol

Racking the mead

calculator (see Helpful Information, below) to figure out the corresponding specific gravity.

The thickness of the honey you use, not the amount, will determine the specific gravity of the must. We recommend first adding about 2 cups honey to the water, then stirring in more, $1/2$ cup at a time, measuring the specific gravity with your hydrometer after each addition. Be sure there is enough liquid in the bucket to fill a 5-gallon carboy. If it is looking short, add more water and honey, paying close attention to the specific gravity.

3. Pitch the yeast Add the entire vial of liquid yeast to the must and stir for 5 minutes.

4. Primary fermentation Transfer the liquid from the bucket (through the spigot attached to the 1-foot tubing) into the clean glass carboy, leaving 2 inches of headspace at the top. Seal the carboy with the rubber stopper and insert the airlock into it. Store the carboy in a warm room (70° to 80°F) and cover it with a blanket or dark cloth to keep out the light. Within a week, fermentation will begin.

When the mead stops bubbling and the dead yeast particles have sunk to the bottom, it will be time to rack the mead. This typically takes between 1 and 3 months. (It took our mead 2$1/2$ months.)

5. Secondary fermentation and racking To rack your mead, put the carboy on a counter and the plastic bucket with the spigot on the floor below. Remove the airlock and stopper from the carboy. Attach the 3-foot length of vinyl tubing to the racking cane and insert the tip of the cane into the carboy. Start gently sucking on the end of the tubing to get the mead flowing; when the mead begins to move down the tube, pinch the end, set it in the bucket, and let the mead flow down. Stop when you see that you're getting close to the sediment. Remove the siphoning tubing and racking cane. Clean and sterilize your carboy and siphon the mead back into the carboy (switch positions with the bucket). Replace the rubber stopper and airlock and store in a cool, dark place (60° to 70°F) for 3 months. Re-rack the mead every 2 to 4 months until it is clear (this may take up to a year).

When your mead is clear, it is ready to bottle. Take one more specific gravity reading. As the sugars in the must convert to alcohol, the mixture becomes less dense, and the reading goes down. The reading won't tell you what the alcohol content is. The point, rather, is to let you know whether fermentation has worked. Our specific gravity sank from 1.08 to .998, so we knew we had been successful.

6. Bottle the mead Mix up a plastic bucketful of Sani-clean, put a batch of bottles into the solution, and let them sit there for a few minutes. Make sure the solution fills the bottles completely. Then empty the solution out of the bottles back into the bucket and rinse out the bottles with hot water using your jet bottle washer. Be sure to rinse the lip and neck of the bottles, too, to wash off any excess sanitizer. Invert the bottles on the bottle tree to drain.

To bottle the mead, siphon the mead from the carboy into the 6-gallon bucket with the spigot. Set the bucket on a counter and attach the 1-foot length of vinyl tubing to the spigot. Put the other end of the tubing in the neck of your first empty bottle. Open the spigot and fill the bottle about halfway up the neck. Cap each bottle as soon as it's filled.

7. Cap the bottles Put a cap on the bottle, place the capper over it, and push down on the capper's arms to seal.

8. Let the mead age Your mead will be fine for drinking once you have bottled it, but we recommend you let it age in a cool, dark place (60° to 70°F) for a minimum of 2 to 3 years. From everything we've heard, it only gets better.

HELPFUL INFORMATION

- For recipes, supplies, discussion boards, and information about the art of mead making, visit www.gotmead.com.
- For a potential alcohol calculator, visit www.gotmead.com/index.php?option=com_content&task=view&id=745&Itemid=16.
- The Web site of the National Honey Board, www.honey.com, offers a handy backgrounder on mead, including recipes and a great resources guide, at www.honey.com/images/downloads/makingmead.pdf#search='mead'.

—Brianne McElhiney

THE WINTER RECIPES

❋ ARUGULA AND RED BUTTERHEAD LETTUCE SALAD WITH TANGERINES AND HARD-COOKED EGGS

We wanted a hearty salad for our winter menu, with lots of different textures and flavors. The core idea was eggs on toast—which we translated into wedges of hard-cooked egg and crunchy, garlicky croutons. The lettuces lighten everything up and the tangerines are nuggets of juicy sweetness.

If you use eggs from your own chickens, or are buying eggs from the farmers' market, let them sit in the fridge for at least a week before you cook them (if eggs are too fresh, they're hard to peel).

MAKES 6 to 8 servings TIME about 1 hour

6 to 8 large eggs (not super-fresh)
2 teaspoons freshly squeezed tangerine juice
1/2 teaspoon finely grated tangerine zest
3/4 teaspoon fine sea salt
1/2 cup extra virgin olive oil
2 cloves garlic
3 thin slices Wheat Berry Ciabatta (page 182),
    cut into 1/2-inch cubes (about 11/2 cups)
5 cups loosely packed arugula leaves
6 cups loosely packed red butterhead lettuce leaves
    (about 1/2 small head)
2 large or 4 small tangerines

1. Preheat the oven to 400°F. Put the eggs in a small pot and cover with water by about 1 inch. Bring to a boil, immediately reduce the heat to a simmer, and cook, uncovered, for 10 minutes. Remove from the heat, immerse the eggs in ice water to cover, and let cool for 1 minute. On the countertop, crack each egg all over and return to the ice water for 5 minutes. Peel under cold water. Quarter eggs lengthwise and set aside.

2. Meanwhile, in a small bowl, whisk together the tanger-ine juice, zest, and 1/4 teaspoon salt. Whisk in 1/4 cup of the oil to make a dressing and set aside. Mince the garlic,

sprinkle it with the remaining 1/4 teaspoon salt, and mash to a paste with the flat side of a chef's knife.

3. In a heatproof measuring cup, combine the remaining 1/4 cup olive oil and the garlic paste and microwave it for 10 seconds. Put the bread cubes on a rimmed baking sheet, drizzle with the garlic oil, and toss to coat evenly. Spread in a single layer and bake, stirring once or twice, until crisp, about 15 minutes. Set aside.

4. Rinse the greens and dry twice in a salad spinner. Peel the tangerines and remove the thready white pith. Cut the tangerines crosswise, and separate into chunks, discarding any seeds.

5. In a large bowl, toss the greens gently but thoroughly with just enough of the dressing to coat. Add the tangerines and the croutons and toss gently. Divide the salad among individual plates. Add a quartered egg to each and drizzle the eggs with a little more dressing.

PER 2-CUP SERVING 288 cal., 64% (184 cal.) from fat; 9.7 g protein; 21 g fat (3.9 g sat.); 17 g carbo (2.9 g fiber); 359 mg sodium; 212 mg chol.

❋ WHEAT BERRY CIABATTA

We ate this shaggy-crumbed, chewy, steamy loaf slathered with homemade butter and sprinkled with sea salt. Although you will need to start it the day before, it requires very little effort that first day. We used sweet buttermilk left over from making Homemade Butter (page 154), and 'Expresso' (hard red) wheat berries and whole-wheat flour (for more on local flours, see the Allure of Local Wheat, page 156). Hard red wheat berries are the most common type sold in stores, and any brand will work; any regular whole-wheat flour will work, too.

MAKES two 1½-pound loaves (about 22 slices per loaf)
TIME 7 to 8 hours (mainly unattended time), plus overnight to chill starter

1 cup wheat berries
4½ cups whole-wheat flour, plus more for dusting
    and sprinkling
¾ teaspoon active dry yeast
¼ cup honey
¼ cup Homemade Buttermilk (page 154) or
    whole milk
About ⅓ cup extra virgin olive oil
2 teaspoons fine sea salt
3 cups ice cubes or ice-cold water

1. In a saucepan, combine the wheat berries and 4½ cups water and bring to a boil over high heat. Reduce the heat to a simmer, cover, and cook until the berries are very tender and at least half of them have burst, 1 to 1½ hours. Remove from the heat and let cool in the pan to room temperature. Drain the berries; you should have about 3 cups. (They can be cooked up to 3 days in advance and stored, tightly covered, in the refrigerator.)

2. In a bowl, stir together 1 cup of the flour, ¼ teaspoon of the yeast, and 1 cup cold water to make the starter. Cover and refrigerate overnight.

3. The next day, let the starter sit at room temperature for 1 hour; then scrape it into the bowl of a stand mixer fitted with a dough hook. Add the remaining 3½ cups flour, 1 cup cold water, the honey, the buttermilk, and ¼ cup of the oil. Knead the mixture on low speed until just combined but still shaggy, about 2 minutes. Turn off the mixer and let the dough sit for 45 minutes to allow the flour to absorb the moisture.

4. Sprinkle the remaining ½ teaspoon yeast over the dough and knead on low speed until a smooth dough forms, about 4 minutes. Add the salt and knead for 1 minute more. Add the reserved wheat berries and continue to mix on low speed just until most of the berries are incorporated.

5. Use about 1 tablespoon of the oil to grease a large deep baking dish. Transfer the dough to the dish along with any loose wheat berries and cover the pan with oiled plastic wrap. Let the dough sit in the dish in a warm spot until almost doubled in size, about 1½ hours.

6. Line 2 baking sheets with parchment paper and set aside. Turn the dough out onto a floured work surface and divide it in half. Flour your hands; then, using your palms, press each portion flat to release any air. Fold both long sides of each piece of dough into the center, forming 2 rectangular loaves each 10 to 12 inches long. Place each loaf seam side down on a baking sheet.

7. Loosely cover the loaves with oiled plastic wrap and let them sit in a warm spot until doubled in size and very puffy, 1 to 1½ hours.

8. Set 2 oven racks in the oven with 4 inches between them. Put a large rimmed baking pan on the oven floor. Preheat the oven to 500°F.

9. Peel the plastic wrap from the loaves, being careful not to tear their surfaces. Lightly sprinkle the loaves with whole-wheat flour and put them, still on the baking sheets, on the center racks in the oven. Before closing the oven door, pour about 3 cups ice cubes into the baking pan on the oven floor, then quickly close the oven door to trap steam. Reduce the oven temperature to 450°F.

10. Bake the loaves, switching the positions of the baking sheets once, until an instant-read thermometer inserted into the center of a loaf registers 190°F, 20 to 25 minutes.

11. Transfer the loaves to racks and let cool to room temperature. You can eat the bread right away, but if you rip into a loaf while it's still hot, it will be gluey when it cools. We usually eat one hot and let the other one cool.

PER 1/2-INCH SLICE 160 cal., 22% (35 cal.) from fat; 5.2 g protein; 4.1 g fat (0.61 g sat.); 28 g carbo (4 g fiber); 213 mg sodium; 1 mg chol.

• •

EGG CLOUD (*NUVOLONE*)

A dish from the Italian Alps, *nuvolone*—the word means "big cloud"—is like a deconstructed soufflé, with the whites piled in a fluffy peak above the liquid yolk. This recipe is based on one in Manuela Darling-Gansser's *Winter in the Alps: Food by the Fireside*. It's great for a weekend breakfast.

If you want to make multiple egg clouds, beat all the egg whites together, but put each yolk in a separate little bowl (or in its eggshell) until using, which makes it easier to keep them intact. Prep all of your ingredients before you whip the egg whites—and reduce the cooking time to 9 minutes.

MAKES 1 serving TIME about 20 minutes

1 teaspoon unsalted butter, homemade (page 154) or store-bought, plus more for greasing
1 large egg, separated (keep the yolk intact)
Pinch of fine sea salt
1 1/2 tablespoons coarsely shredded aged Gouda, homemade (page 122) or store-bought
2 teaspoons heavy cream
1/4 teaspoon dried or 1/2 teaspoon fresh minced marjoram

1. Preheat the oven to 375°F. Generously butter a ramekin 3 inches in diameter and 1 1/2 inches deep.

2. In a small bowl, beat the egg white until soft peaks form. Add the salt and beat into stiff peaks. Quickly and gently fold in 1 tablespoon of the Gouda. Spoon the beaten white into the ramekin, pushing it up the sides of the dish and leaving a well in the center.

3. Ease the egg yolk into the well. Top the yolk with the cream, marjoram, butter, and the remaining 1/2 tablespoon Gouda. Smooth the white over the yolk and build it up into a frothy pile. Put the ramekin on a rimmed baking sheet.

4. Bake until the top is pale gold and the white is set around the rim of the ramekin, 9 to 10 minutes. Inside, the yolk will be liquidy and the white will be cooked. Serve immediately.

PER SERVING 164 cal., 75% (123 cal.) from fat; 9.3 g protein; 14 g fat (7.1 g sat.); 1.1 g carbo (0.06 g fiber); 324 mg sodium; 241 mg chol.

FEATHERLIGHT PANCAKES

These are based on a recipe *Sunset* published years ago for German "egg cakes" (*Eierkuchen*) from the Elk Cove Inn, in the Northern California coastal town of Elk. They are good with whipped cream and berries, too.

MAKES 8 pancakes, or 4 servings TIME about 30 minutes

Unsalted butter for cooking and serving
1 cup whole-wheat pastry flour*
1/2 cup whole milk
1/4 teaspoon fine sea salt
1 tablespoon honey
6 large egg yolks
4 large egg whites
1 teaspoon freshly squeezed lemon juice
Warmed honey for serving

1. Preheat an electric griddle to 300°F or a nonstick frying pan over medium-low heat. Preheat the oven to 200°F. Butter a rimmed baking sheet.

2. In a medium bowl, whisk together the flour, milk, salt, honey, and egg yolks until well blended. In a large bowl, beat the egg whites with the lemon juice until moist, soft peaks form. Gently fold the whites into the yolk mixture.

3. When the griddle is ready, butter it and spoon on 1/2-cup portions of the batter. Cook until golden on the bottom and slightly puffed, about 3 minutes. Flip and cook until golden on the other side and cooked through (break into one to check), 1 to 2 minutes more. As they are cooked, put the pancakes on the buttered baking sheet, cover with aluminum foil, and keep warm in the oven.

4. Serve hot, with butter and honey.

* *We used finely milled local 'Sonora' soft white whole-wheat flour, which behaves like commercial whole-wheat pastry flour in recipes. See the Allure of Local Wheat, page 156, for more on local flours.*

PER 2-PANCAKE SERVING 267 cal., 37% (100 cal.) from fat; 12 g protein; 11 g fat (4.8 g sat.); 30 g carbo (4 g fiber); 241 mg sodium; 325 mg chol.

EGG AND GOUDA CREPES

Simple yet elegant, these egg-topped crepes make an excellent brunch or a light dinner. The nuttiness of the whole-wheat crepes pairs well with the butterscotch notes in the Gouda.

MAKES 4 servings TIME about 35 minutes

4 large Whole-Wheat Crepes, made in a 12-inch pan (recipe follows)
1 tablespoon extra virgin olive oil
1/2 cup finely chopped white onion
1 cup finely shredded Gouda, homemade (page 122) or store-bought
1 teaspoon unsalted butter, homemade (page 154) or store-bought
4 large eggs
Fine sea salt
About 1/2 cup small arugula leaves

1. Preheat the oven to 250°F and warm the crepes in the oven while it is heating. In a large nonstick frying pan, heat the oil over medium heat. Add the onion and cook, stirring often, until translucent, 4 to 5 minutes.

2. Working with 1 crepe at a time, evenly spread about 1 heaping tablespoon of the onion in the center of the crepe. Sprinkle 1/4 cup of the cheese over the onion. Fold the sides of the crepe over the filling, overlapping to form a square, and press to seal. Put the crepe on a rimmed baking sheet, folded side down. Cover with aluminum foil and keep warm in the oven. Repeat with the remaining crepes, onion, and cheese.

3. In the same pan, melt the butter over medium heat and swirl to coat the bottom. Crack the eggs into the pan, trying to keep them from touching. Cook, turning once, until the whites are set but the yolks are still runny.

4. Place each crepe on a plate and top with an egg. Sprinkle each egg with a pinch of salt and then scatter a few arugula leaves on top.

PER CREPE 367 cal., 61% (224 cal.) from fat; 19 g protein; 25 g fat (12 g sat.); 17 g carbo (2.4 g fiber); 770 mg sodium; 342 mg chol.

WHOLE-WHEAT CREPES

These crepes have a delicately nutty flavor and supremely tender texture.

MAKES 8 large (12-inch), 10 thickish medium (8-inch), or 16 small (6-inch) crepes TIME about 30 minutes

1 1/2 cups whole milk
About 3 tablespoons unsalted butter, homemade
   (page 154) or store-bought, melted
3 large eggs
1 cup whole-wheat pastry flour*
1/2 teaspoon fine sea salt

1. In a saucepan, combine the milk and 2 tablespoons of the butter and heat over low heat until warm.

2. Put the eggs in a blender and pulse just to mix. Add the flour, salt, and 1/4 cup of the warm milk mixture and whirl to combine. With the blender running, slowly pour the remaining milk mixture into the blender through the lid opening. Strain the batter into a bowl.

3. Heat a 12-inch, 8-inch, or 6-inch nonstick frying pan over medium heat. Brush the pan with a little of the remaining 1 tablespoon butter, then pour about 1/3 cup batter into the largest pan, 1/4 cup batter into the medium-size pan, or 2 tablespoons into the smallest pan and swirl to coat the bottom of the pan evenly. Cook, turning once, until set and starting to brown, about 2 minutes total.

Transfer the crepe to a plate or a baking sheet. Repeat with the remaining batter, brushing the pan with more butter as needed and stacking the crepes as you go.

MAKE AHEAD Crepes can be made up to 4 days ahead, wrapped in plastic wrap, and chilled, they can also be frozen, stored between layers of wax paper, for 1 month.

* We used finely milled local 'Sonora' soft white whole-wheat flour, which behaves like commercial whole-wheat pastry flour in recipes. See the Allure of Local Wheat, page 156, for more on local flours.

PER LARGE CREPE 148 cal., 48% (71 cal.) from fat; 5.3 g protein; 7.9 g fat (4.2 g sat.); 14 g carbo (2 g fiber); 187 mg sodium; 95 mg chol.
PER MEDIUM CREPE 118 cal., 48% (57 cal.) from fat; 4.3 g protein; 6.3 g fat (3.3 g sat.); 11 g carbo (1.6 g fiber); 149 mg sodium; 76 mg chol.
PER SMALL CREPE 74 cal., 47% (35 cal.) from fat; 2.7 g protein; 4 g fat (2.1 g sat.); 6.9 g carbo (1 g fiber); 93 mg sodium; 48 mg chol.

KALE COLCANNON

Colcannon is one of the genius ways that the Irish have with potatoes—mashing them up with milk, good butter, and cooked kale or cabbage. It is simple but delicious.

MAKES 4 to 6 servings TIME about 40 minutes

1 1/2 pounds Yukon Gold potatoes, unpeeled, cut into
   large, evenly sized chunks
1/2 pound Tuscan kale, tough ribs removed and leaves
   coarsely chopped
1/3 cup whole milk, or as needed, warmed
2 tablespoons unsalted butter, homemade (page 154)
   or store-bought, plus more for serving (optional)
3/4 teaspoon fine sea salt

1. In a saucepan, combine the potatoes with cold water to cover by 1 inch and bring to a boil over high heat. Reduce the heat and simmer, covered, until the potatoes are tender, about 20 minutes.

2. Meanwhile, pour water to a depth of 1/2 inch in another saucepan, insert a steamer basket, cover, and bring to a boil over high heat. Add the kale to the basket and cook, covered, turning the kale occasionally with tongs, until tender, about 20 minutes.

3. Drain the potatoes, return them to the pan, and add the milk, butter, and salt. Mash with a potato masher, keeping the potatoes slightly chunky. Add the kale and

stir to combine. Stir in a little more milk if the mixture seems too thick.

4. Serve the colcannon with a pat of butter if you like.

PER 3/4-CUP SERVING 145 cal., 27% (39 cal.) from fat; 3.8 g protein; 4.4 g fat (2.7 g sat.); 23 g carbo (1.7 g fiber); 309 mg sodium; 12 mg chol.

....

VEGETABLE SHEPHERD'S PIE

Creating a hearty shepherd's pie without meat was challenging, but meaty mushrooms and hearty greens and beans did the trick.

MAKES 4 to 6 servings TIME about 1³/4 hours

1¹/2 pounds Yukon Gold potatoes, peeled and quartered
1 tablespoon plus 2 teaspoons extra virgin olive oil
1/2 white onion, cut into slivers
1¹/4 teaspoons fine sea salt
1 clove garlic, finely chopped
2 tablespoons plus 2 teaspoons whole-wheat flour*
1/4 cup Chardonnay
2 cups Herb Vegetable Broth (page 140)

1/4 pound Tuscan kale, tough ribs removed and leaves chopped
1/2 pound Swiss chard, ribs removed and leaves chopped
6 ounces oyster mushrooms, halved if large
1 cup drained cooked flageolet beans (see method, page 142)
2 tablespoons unsalted butter, homemade (page 154) or store-bought
3 tablespoons whole milk
1 large egg plus 1 large egg yolk

1. In a saucepan, combine the potatoes with cold water to cover by 1 inch and bring to a boil over high heat. Reduce the heat, cover, and simmer until the potatoes are tender, about 20 minutes. Drain the potatoes, return them to the pan, and cook over low heat, stirring occasionally, until dry and floury, about 5 minutes.

2. While the potatoes are cooking, in a large pot, heat the oil over medium heat. Add the onion and 3/4 teaspoon of the salt and cook, stirring often, until the onion is softened and lightly golden, about 7 minutes. Add the garlic and cook until fragrant, about 1 minute.

3. Whisk the flour into the onion mixture and cook, whisking, for 1 to 2 minutes. Gradually whisk in the wine and continue whisking to break up any lumps. Then gradually whisk in the broth and bring the mixture to a simmer. Preheat the oven to 425°F.

4. Add the kale and chard to the broth mixture, cover, and cook over medium heat until the greens are tender, about 10 minutes. Stir in the mushrooms and cook, covered, until the mushrooms are almost tender, about 6 minutes.

5. Add the flageolets, return the mixture to a simmer, and cook until the consistency of thick but pourable gravy, about 5 minutes.

6. Meanwhile, press the potatoes through a ricer into a bowl (or mash with a potato masher). Mash the butter and milk into the potatoes, then stir in the egg, egg yolk, and the remaining 1/2 teaspoon salt.

7. Transfer the vegetable mixture to an 8-inch square baking pan, patting it into an even layer. Carefully spread the potato mixture on top, covering the vegetable mixture evenly. If you like, using a spoon, sculpt the top into freeform peaks or waves.

8. Bake until the potatoes are lightly golden and slightly puffed, about 25 minutes. Let stand for 5 to 10 minutes to thicken and cool slightly before serving.

* We used 'Expresso' whole-wheat flour, a hard red winter wheat. See the Allure of Local Wheat, page 156, for more about local flours. Any regular whole-wheat flour will work in this recipe.

PER SERVING 248 cal., 40% (98 cal.) from fat; 10 g protein; 11 g fat (3.9 g sat.); 36 g carbo (6.8 g fiber); 924 mg sodium; 81 mg chol.

RICOTTA MANICOTTI

Maria Helm Sinskey, author of *The Vineyard Kitchen: Menus Inspired by the Seasons*, makes her manicotti with crepes instead of dried pasta—just like her great-grandmother did. Ethereal and rustic at the same time, they were the inspiration for this recipe.

If you prefer crisp-edged manicotti, put the filled crepes on an oiled rimmed baking sheet in pairs (no tomato sauce beneath), leaving about an inch of space between the pairs. Top with two-thirds of the tomato sauce (leave the ends of manicotti bare) and bake in a 450°F oven until the edges are nicely browned, about 10 minutes, rotating the pan back to front halfway through so the manicotti brown evenly.

MAKES 10 manicotti or 4 to 6 servings
TIME about 40 minutes

3 cups 'Sweet Million' Tomato Sauce (page 79) or other tomato-based pasta sauce
1/4 cup Chardonnay
3 1/2 cups ricotta, homemade (page 117) or store-bought
1/2 cup chopped fresh basil
2 tablespoons freshly squeezed lemon juice
1 teaspoon crushed dried red serrano or árbol chile
1 teaspoon fine sea salt
10 medium Whole-Wheat Crepes (page 185), made in an 8-inch pan (they will be quite thick)
1/2 cup finely shredded Gouda, homemade (page 122) or store-bought

1. Preheat the oven to 450°F. In a small bowl, mix together the tomato sauce and wine. Spread some of the sauce in the bottom of a 9-by-13-inch baking dish.

2. In a bowl, mix together the ricotta, basil, lemon juice, chile, and salt. Spoon about 1/3 cup of the filling over each crepe, leaving a 1/2-inch border around the edges. Roll up the crepes and place them seam sides down in the baking dish. Spread the remaining tomato sauce evenly over the filled crepes.

3. Bake the crepes until hot and bubbling, about 15 minutes. Sprinkle the Gouda evenly over the top and continue to bake until the cheese melts, about 2 minutes more.

PER MANICOTTO 343 cal., 57% (197 cal.) from fat; 17 g protein; 22 g fat (12 g sat.); 20 g carbo (3 g fiber); 691 mg sodium; 127 mg chol.

❄ WINTER VEGETABLE CHOWDER

Cold rain hits the San Francisco Bay Area in January and February. A big bowl of this creamy chowder gives lasting, delicious warmth. To make it pretty, we sprinkled it with broccoli rabe and rosemary flowers.

MAKES 12 cups, or 6 main-course servings
TIME about 1¹/₂ hours

2 pounds 'Yukon Gold' potatoes, unpeeled, cut into
    ³/₄-inch chunks (about 6 cups)
1 head cauliflower, about 2¹/₂ pounds, cut into florets
1 head broccoli romanesco, about 1¹/₄ pounds, cut into
    florets
4 cups (about 1 bunch) chopped broccoli rabe plus
    any flowers
3 tablespoons extra virgin olive oil, plus more
    for serving
1 tablespoon fine sea salt
3 tablespoons chopped garlic
1 cup chopped white onion
¹/₂ cup heavy cream (optional)
Chopped fresh rosemary, plus any flowers, for garnish

1. Preheat the oven to 350°F. Put half the potatoes on a rimmed baking sheet. Pick out 3 cups bite-size cauliflower florets and combine them with the broccoli romanesco and broccoli rabe on another rimmed baking sheet (set aside any broccoli rabe flowers). Chop the remaining cauliflower and set aside. Drizzle 1 tablespoon of the oil and sprinkle 1 teaspoon of the salt over each baking sheet.

2. Roast the vegetables, stirring often, until golden brown and tender when pierced with a fork, about 20 minutes for the mixed vegetables and 25 minutes for the potatoes.

3. Meanwhile, heat the remaining 1 tablespoon oil in a large pot over medium heat. Add the garlic and onion and cook, stirring often, until translucent, about 5 minutes. Add the remaining potatoes, the chopped cauliflower, and 6 cups water and bring to a simmer. Cover and cook until the vegetables are tender, about 15 minutes. Remove from the heat and let cool slightly.

4. Working in batches, ladle about 2 cups of the liquid and vegetables into a blender and process until smooth. Pour through a fine-mesh strainer set over a large bowl, using the back of the ladle to push the soup through.

5. Pour the puree back into the pot and bring to a simmer over low heat. Stir in the cream and the remaining 1 teaspoon salt, then add the roasted vegetables and heat through.

6. Serve the chowder into deep soup bowls, drizzled with oil and sprinkled with chopped rosemary and broccoli rabe and rosemary flowers.

PER 2-CUP SERVING 273 cal., 23% (64 cal.) from fat; 11 g protein; 7.5 g fat (1.1 g sat.); 43 g carbo (5.3 g fiber); 1,205 mg sodium; 0 mg chol.

WHEAT BERRY "RISOTTO" WITH ROASTED TOMATOES AND BROCCOLI RABE

Many grains other than rice can be cooked like risotto, and wheat berries from soft winter wheat are one of them. As you stir them, they drink in hot liquid and their starchy outer hulls dissolve into delectable creaminess. We used local 'Sonora' soft white wheat berries from Pie Ranch in Pescadero, California. Despite the name, they are actually pale yellow, and have a lovely, fresh, slightly corny flavor. Hard red wheat berries are what you are likely to find in the grocery store, and while they won't become as creamy, their earthier, deeper flavor is good in this recipe, too.

We ate this as a main course, with a chunk of homemade feta (page 120) and some hot bread on the side.

MAKES 8 cups or 4 to 6 servings TIME about 3 hours

2 cups wheat berries, preferably soft white wheat such
    as 'Sonora'
5 tablespoons extra virgin olive oil
1 bunch broccoli rabe, about 1 pound, tough ribs
    removed and leaves chopped into 1-inch pieces
1 teaspoon fine sea salt
4 large cloves garlic, finely chopped
1 white onion, chopped (about 1¹/₂ cups)
³/₄ cup Slow-Roasted Tomatoes for the Freezer (page
    84), thawed; or sun-dried tomatoes packed in oil
1 cup chopped walnuts
2 tablespoons unsalted butter, homemade (page 154)
    or store-bought

1. In a large pot, combine the wheat berries and 2¹/₂ quarts water, cover, and bring to a boil over high heat. Remove from the heat and let sit, covered, for 1 hour. Bring back to a boil, then reduce the heat to a

5. Add 1/2 cup of the simmering water and cook, stirring, until completely absorbed by the wheat berries. Continue adding water, 1/2 cup at a time, stirring until each addition is absorbed before adding the next, until the berries look creamy, 15 to 30 minutes. You will have water left over. Keep the pot at a steady simmer throughout, reducing the heat to medium-low if the mixture starts to boil.

6. Chop the tomatoes and add them and the cooked broccoli rabe to the wheat berries. Heat, stirring, until heated through, 2 to 4 minutes.

7. Remove the pot from the heat and stir in the walnuts and butter. For a looser risotto, stir in 1/2 to 1 cup of the remaining simmering water. Serve immediately.

PER SERVING 535 cal., 52% (277 cal.) from fat; 15 g protein; 32 g fat (5.6 g sat.); 56 g carbo (11 g fiber); 490 mg sodium; 10 mg chol.

BRAISED WINTER GREENS WITH PRESERVED LEMON AND RED CHILE

If you have a jar of preserved lemons and some dried chiles on hand, you can make these supremely satisfying greens quickly. We especially like the combination of sweet Savoy cabbage with mildly pungent mustard greens, but you can use any greens in your garden.

MAKES 4 to 6 servings TIME about 25 minutes

3 tablespoons extra virgin olive oil
2/3 cup finely chopped white onion
2 tablespoons chopped preserved lemon peel (page 195)
1/4 to 1/2 teaspoon crushed dried red serrano chiles or árbol chiles
3 1/2 quarts loosely packed whole leaves of mixed greens such as Savoy cabbage, mustard, Swiss chard, and/or kale that have had the tough stems and ribs removed
Fine sea salt (optional)

1. In a 5- to 6-quart saucepan, heat 1 1/2 tablespoons of the oil over medium heat. Add the onion and cook, stirring often, until translucent, 4 to 5 minutes. Stir in the preserved lemon and chile and cook, stirring, for about 1 minute.

2. Add half the greens and 3/4 cup water and raise the heat to medium-high. Cover the pan and cook until the greens

simmer. If using soft white wheat berries, simmer until about half of the berries have just burst, about 30 minutes. If using hard red wheat berries, simmer until about half of the berries have burst wide open, 2 to 2 1/2 hours. Drain the wheat berries and set aside.

2. In a large nonstick frying pan, heat 3 tablespoons of the oil over medium heat. Add the broccoli rabe and cook, stirring occasionally, until wilted, about 4 minutes. Sprinkle 1/2 teaspoon of the salt over the greens, cover, reduce the heat to low, and cook until just tender, about 15 minutes more. Add the garlic, raise the heat to medium, and cook, stirring occasionally, for 3 minutes. Remove from the heat, cover, and set aside.

3. In a saucepan, bring 6 cups water to a simmer. Cover and keep at a simmer over low heat.

4. In a heavy-bottomed 8-quart pot, heat the remaining 2 tablespoons oil over medium heat. Add the onion and cook, stirring occasionally, until translucent, about 10 minutes. Add the wheat berries and the remaining 1/2 teaspoon salt and cook, stirring often, until hot, about 3 minutes.

have wilted, 2 to 3 minutes. Add the remaining greens and cook, covered, until all are wilted, about 5 minutes more. Stir, reduce the heat to low, and cook, covered, until the greens are tender, about 5 minutes more.

3. If there is too much liquid in the pan, uncover and boil over high heat for a few minutes to evaporate most of it. Stir in the remaining 1¹/₂ tablespoons oil and season to taste with salt.

PER ²/₃-CUP SERVING 118 cal., 53% (63 cal.) from fat; 4.6 g protein; 7.3 g fat (1 g sat.); 13 g carbo (6.5 g fiber); 401 mg sodium; 0 mg chol.

••••••••••••••••••••••••••••••••••••

CARAMELIZED TANGERINE AND RICOTTA TART

Bellwether Farms, in Sonoma, California, produces some of America's finest ricotta, and head cheese maker Liam Callahan taught us how to make ricotta at home (see page 117). It is terrific in this tart, which was inspired by one that Liam and his mother, Cindy, serve to guests at Bellwether. Their version is based on a tart by chef Emeril Lagasse, who invented it using Bellwether cheeses.

If you make the rectangular tart, you'll have enough pastry dough, filling, and topping left over for a 4- to 5-inch mini tart. Instead of the caramelized tangerines, you can top the tart with any ripe, in-season fruit and glaze it with some warmed jam.

MAKES 1 round 9- or 10-inch tart, or 1 rectangular 4¹/₂- by-14-inch tart plus 1 round 4- to 5-inch mini tart
TIME about 4 hours, plus at least 2 hours to chill

TOPPING
1¹/₃ pounds small, firm tangerines (avoid the loose "zipper-skin" type)
7 tablespoons honey
1 cup freshly squeezed tangerine juice, plus more if needed

CRUST
1¹/₂ cups 'Sonora' whole wheat flour* or whole-wheat pastry flour, plus more for dusting
¹/₄ teaspoon fine sea salt
¹/₂ cup cold unsalted butter, homemade (page 154) or store-bought, cut into cubes
1 tablespoon honey
3 to 4 tablespoons ice water

FILLING
1 cup ricotta, homemade (page 117) or store-bought
³/₄ cup fromage blanc, homemade (page 118) or store-bought**
¹/₂ cup crème fraîche, homemade (page 70) or store-bought
2 tablespoons honey
2 tablespoons Sticky Chewy Tangerine Marmalade (page 194) or store-bought tangerine or orange marmalade

1. To make the topping, preheat the oven to 275°F. Wash the tangerines well, but don't peel them. Slice them very thinly crosswise. Arrange half the slices in an 8-inch square baking dish, keeping them more or less in a single layer. Drizzle the slices with 1¹/₂ tablespoons of the honey. Top with the remaining tangerine slices and drizzle with another 1¹/₂ tablespoons honey. Pour the tangerine juice over the layered slices. It should almost cover the fruit; if it doesn't, add more as needed. Cover the dish with aluminum foil and cook until the peels are very soft, 2 to 2¹/₂ hours.

2. Meanwhile, make the dough for the crust. Sift the flour and salt into a food processor and whirl briefly to blend.

Scatter the butter cubes over the top and pulse until the mixture looks like shaggy fresh bread crumbs. Drizzle the honey over the mixture. With the motor running, drizzle in the ice water, adding just enough for the dough to come together. Turn the dough out onto a work surface and press together into a rectangle or disk, depending on the shape of the tart you are making. Wrap the dough in plastic wrap and refrigerate for at least 1 hour or up to 2 days.

3. While the dough is chilling, make the filling. In a bowl, beat the ricotta, fromage blanc, crème fraîche, and honey until smooth with a wooden spoon. Then beat in the marmalade. Cover and refrigerate until needed.

4. When the tangerine slices are ready, drizzle with another 2 tablespoons honey and raise the oven temperature to 350°F. Roast the slices, uncovered, until they start to brown, about 50 minutes. Remove from the oven and drizzle with the remaining 2 tablespoons honey.

5. While the tangerines are roasting, bake the crust. Lightly dust a work surface with flour. Unwrap the dough, set it on the floured surface, and let it warm up for 10 minutes. With a lightly floured rolling pin, roll out the dough about 1/8 inch thick to fit a 9- or 10-inch round tart pan with a removable bottom or a 4-by-14-inch rectangular tart pan with a removable bottom. Using a pastry scraper or a thin metal spatula, scoot the dough off the surface and gently ease it into the tart pan. Trim the dough even with the pan edge. If you are making a rectangular tart, gather up the scraps and reroll to a line a 4- or 5-inch tartlet pan.

6. Prick the bottom of the crust all over with a fork. Line the crust with parchment paper and fill with pie weights or dried beans. Slide the crust into the oven alongside the tangerines and bake until golden, 30 to 40 minutes. Remove from the oven, remove the pie weights and parchment, and bake the crust until deep golden, 10 to 15 minutes more. Let cool on a rack.

7. Spread the filling in the cooled crust to within 1/2 inch of the rim. Arrange the warm or cooled tangerines over the filling and drizzle with any accumulated juices. Chill for at least 2 hours before serving.

* We used local 'Sonora' soft white wheat flour because it behaves like commercial whole-wheat pastry flour. See the Allure of Local Wheat, page 156, for more about local flours.

** Store-bought fromage blanc is often much drier than homemade fromage blanc. If you use it, stir in enough heavy cream (at least 3 tablespoons) to give it the consistency of softened cream cheese.

MAKE AHEAD The tart can be made up to 1 day ahead and refrigerated. You can also make the crust, filling, and topping up to 1 day ahead (keep the crust at room temperature; refrigerate the filling and topping), then assemble and chill for 2 hours before serving.

PER SLICE OF ROUND TART 342 cal., 44% (152 cal.) from fat; 6.5 g protein; 17 g fat (10 g sat.); 42 g carbo (3.8 g fiber); 236 mg sodium; 49 mg chol.

❄ TANGERINE HONEY FLAN

Without baking soda or baking powder, we couldn't make cakes. But we could make this fantastic flan—smooth, rich, cool, and creamy.

MAKES 1 (9-inch) flan TIME about 2 hours, plus 2 hours to chill

1/3 cup plus 1/2 cup honey
2 1/2 cups whole milk
1 tablespoon finely shredded tangerine zest
4 large eggs plus 2 large egg yolks
Thinly sliced tangerine peel for garnish (optional)

1. Preheat the broiler and position the rack 5 inches from the heating element.

2. Spread 1/3 cup honey in an ovenproof 9-inch quiche dish or pie pan.

3. Broil the honey until bubbly and medium amber, 5 to 10 minutes. Watch closely to make sure it doesn't burn. Remove from the oven and swirl gently if unevenly colored, then let the honey cool (it will solidify and become fairly hard). Reduce the oven temperature to 325°F and reposition the rack in the center of the oven.

4. In a small saucepan, combine the milk and tangerine zest and heat over medium-low heat until steaming. Meanwhile, whisk together the remaining 1/2 cup honey, the whole eggs, and the egg yolks in a bowl.

5. Slowly drizzle the warm milk mixture into the egg mixture while whisking constantly. Strain the custard through a cheesecloth-lined strainer into a clean bowl.

Put the quiche dish of honey in a roasting pan and pour the custard into the dish.

6. Pull out the center oven rack halfway and put the roasting pan on the rack. Pour hot water into the pan to come halfway up the sides of the quiche dish. Carefully slide the rack into place. Bake until the custard jiggles only slightly when the dish is gently shaken, about 1 hour.

7. Carefully remove the roasting pan from the oven. Let stand for 10 minutes, then transfer the custard dish to a rack to cool to room temperature.

8. Cover the custard and chill for at least 2 hours or up to overnight. To serve, carefully run a knife along the inside edge of the dish to release the custard. Invert a large rimmed plate over the custard, carefully invert the dish and plate together, and then lift off the dish. Top with the tangerine peel.

PER SERVING (1/12th OF FLAN) 135 cal., 27% (37 cal.) from fat; 4.2 g protein; 4.1 g fat (1.7 g sat.); 22 g carbo (0.1 g fiber); 48 mg sodium; 111 mg chol.

· ·

STICKY CHEWY TANGERINE MARMALADE

This Scottish-style marmalade is based on a recipe from my family's friend Mary Latker, whose relatives owned the R. & W. Scott jam factory in Carluke, near Glasgow. It's thick and delectably chewy, with a pleasantly bitter edge.

The recipe has three stages: an overnight soak, a first boil, and a second boil in small batches, with sugar added (we used honey instead). Preserves made this "small-batch" way have a better consistency and a fresher, brighter taste. You can double the recipe if you like, but you must still do the second boil in small batches.

We don't process the marmalade jars in boiling water, and have had no trouble (the jars seal properly and the marmalade keeps for several months at room temperature). That said, water-bath processing has the advantage of driving out every last bit of air from the jars, and marmalade or preserves that are processed this way keep their color longer. If you'd like to try it, follow the instructions that come with canning jars, or download directions from the National Center for Home Food Preservation at www.homefoodpreservation.com; look under Make Jam & Jelly, then go to Processing Jams and Jellies.

MAKES 3 half-pint jars, plus a little extra
TIME about 3 hours, plus overnight to soak

2 pounds firm tangerines (9 to 15, depending on size)
1/2 lemon
2 1/4 cups honey

1. Wash 2 or 3 tangerines, then score their peels into quarters and remove them. Slice the peels into thin slivers (you should have about 1/2 cup) and put the slivers in a large, wide heavy-bottomed pot.

2. Peel the remaining tangerines and remove most of the thready white pith from all the tangerines, including those from step 1. Separate the tangerines into segments, cut the segments in half crosswise, and remove any seeds. Put the segments in the pot.

3. Wash the lemon half, then cut it, peel and all, into 1/4-inch dice and remove any seeds. Add to the pot. Measure the contents of the pot. You should have about 5 cups (add a little extra peel or fruit if you are short.) Return the fruit to the pot and add 1 1/2 cups water for every 1 cup fruit. Cover and refrigerate overnight.

4. The hard boil: Cover the pot and bring to a boil over high heat. Boil rapidly until the peels are very soft and

cooked through, 25 to 30 minutes. The tangerine peels can toughen after seeming soft, so cook them well.

5. Meanwhile, put 3 half-pint canning jars on a rack (or on several cookie cutters) in a stockpot and fill with hot water. Bring to a boil, then boil for 10 minutes to sterilize. Wash canning lids and rings for the jars with hot, soapy water.

6. The small-batch boil: Measure the fruit pulp, including the liquid; you should have about 6 cups. Working in batches, put 2 cups pulp in a heavy-bottomed medium saucepan (plain steel, no dark coating inside; this helps you see the true color of the marmalade as it darkens). Stir in 3/4 cup of the honey. You can do more than one batch at a time if you have enough equipment.

7. Put a small plate in the freezer to chill. Bring the fruit mixture to a boil over medium-high heat and cook, uncovered, at a hard, foaming boil, stirring occasionally with a wooden spoon, until the mixture starts to thicken, about 20 minutes. To test, spoon a dollop onto the chilled plate. If the dollop has rounded "shoulders" instead of flattening out, and nearly holds its shape when you run a finger through it, the marmalade is ready. (It will thicken as it cools.) If it seems too thin, continue to boil, watching carefully (honey burns easily) and testing periodically the same way. If the marmalade begins to burn, reduce the heat and simmer until it is thick enough to set.

8. Empty the jars of hot water and set them on a counter. Ladle in the marmalade to within 1/4 inch of the rims and skim any foam from the surface. Wipe the rim edges clean with a damp kitchen towel. Set the inner lids on the jars, then screw on the bands. Transfer the jars to a cooling rack until they self-seal (they give off an audible "snick" as the lid is sucked in toward the surface of the jam). Test a seal by pushing on the center of the lid. If it doesn't spring back, it is sealed.

9. If you have not been making batches simultaneously, repeat steps 6, 7, and 8 with the remaining fruit pulp. The marmalade will keep in a cool, dark place for several months. If a jar did not seal properly, store it in the refrigerator and use within a month. If you have leftover marmalade, or if the final batch failed to make a full jar, store that in the refrigerator too.

PER TABLESPOON 56 cal., 1% (0.42 cal.) from fat; 0.18 g protein; 0.05 g fat (0.01 g sat.); 15 g carbo (0.41 g fiber); 0.95 mg sodium; 0 mg chol.

PRESERVED LEMONS

Most preserved lemons take a good month to cure. Freezing them overnight speeds up the softening of the lemons' cells, and they are ready in about a week. Slice or chop the peel and put in salads, cooked greens, or quinoa, or puree with cooked vegetables for soup—carrot is especially good. We used 'Eureka' lemons, because it's what we grew; but if you have Meyer lemons, by all means use them.

MAKES 2 cups TIME about 10 minutes, plus at least 1 week to stand

5 to 7 lemons
5 tablespoons fine sea salt

1. Rinse the lemons well. Quarter 5 lemons lengthwise, put in a bowl, and sprinkle with the salt. Mix with your hands to coat the lemons evenly with the salt, then crush them with your hands or a potato masher until the juices seep out. Pack the lemons into a 1-pint widemouthed jar with a clamp lid. The lemon quarters should be immersed in the juice. If not, squeeze the juice from the remaining 2 lemons and add as needed to cover the lemon pieces.

2. Cover the jar with plastic wrap, roll a rubber band down around the rim to hold the wrap in place, and freeze for at least 8 hours or up to overnight.

3. Let the lemons thaw at room temperature. Remove the plastic wrap and close the jar lid. Let stand at room temperature until the peels have softened, 7 to 8 days. Invert the jar twice a day to make sure the lemon pieces are evenly moistened.

4. The lemons are now ready to use. They can be stored in the refrigerator for up to 1 year (they will turn a deeper yellow). To use them, scrape the pulp from the peel and discard the pulp. If you want a less salty flavor, rinse the peel under cold running water. Cut the peel as directed in individual recipes.

PER 1/4 LEMON 3.8 cal., 0% from fat; 0 g protein; 0 g fat (0 g sat.); 1.3 g carbo (0.5 g fiber); 1,680 mg sodium; 0 mg chol.

SPRING

Spring starts early in the San Francisco Bay Area. In February, stone-fruit trees puff out in popcornlike balls of pink and white. With every passing week, new flowers open on trees and from bushes and beds: mock orange and rose and lilac vine, sending out a sweet blended perfume.

Around the beginning of the month, our bees began pouring from the hives. We saw them everywhere, dancing over the flowers and herbs, their golden bodies glinting in the sun. Despite the pleasure of watching them and anticipating the honey to come, Team Bee braced itself. Spring is swarm season.

Swarming typically happens because the hive is overcrowded. The crammed-in bees will raise a new queen (or several), and then she and up to half of the colony will fly away. It can seriously deplete the hive, and beekeepers try to prevent this by stacking on another box to give their bees more room.

We had added boxes to both hives a few weeks earlier, but it wasn't enough to keep Betty from swarming. One morning, we spotted a big, buzzing clump of bees up in a nearby tree—and more bees cascading thickly down the front of Betty. Luckily, bees are gentle when swarming; their goal is to protect the queen (hidden in the buzzing ball) and find a new home, not attack, so even though we had rushed out without suits or veils, we had little to worry about. But we were helpless to intervene.

Two days later, Betty (now ex-Betty, most likely) swarmed again. An "afterswarm" is rare, but does happen when the bees raise more than one queen. The air was thick with darting, roaring bees, and Kimberley and Margaret stood in the middle of it, engulfed by the tornado. "It felt like being encompassed by the Other," said Margaret later. "You could feel their weird, humming, crackling energy." Even for those of us standing at the edge, it was an awesome sight. We watched for half an hour, and the bees kept flying crazily back and forth. By

the end of day, they still hadn't managed to locate a new place to live and were pooled forlornly under the hive.

The next morning, Brianne found the swarm clustered on some empty clay pots nearby. She had just been to a lecture on swarm catching, and without hesitation gently slid an empty box under the bees while brushing them in with a bee brush (kind of like a duster). We gave the swarm to the head of our local beekeeper's guild. And we left the twice-swarmed hive alone for a while to settle down with, we hoped, a new resident queen.

The One-Block Spring Feast

Radishes, Fresh Homemade Butter, and Salt (page 223)
Favas and Ricotta on Buttermilk Crackers (page 223)

❧

Mesclun Salad with Spring Beets and Dill (page 226)
Grilled Carrot Salad (page 228)
Fava Leaf and Parsley Quiche (page 232)

❧

Strawberries with Fromage Blanc and Lemon Honey (page 235)

❧

Chardonnay (page 110), Belgian Abbey Ale (page 52),
Strawberry Lemonade (page 236)

❧

We had been excited about all of our menus. But spring seemed especially wonderful, because the contrast between the dense, minerally, sulfurous vegetables of winter—kales, cabbages, cauliflowers—and the light, fresh crops of spring—strawberries, peas, carrots—was so dramatic. With the sun came sunny, sweet-tasting food.

After our now-customary Food and Garden meeting to figure out what we would like to grow versus what we actually could grow, Johanna began the planting. She started the more tender herbs—like dill (even though it's more of a summer herb, it would still grow in our spring), tarragon, and feathery chervil—in the greenhouse, since the ground wasn't quite warm enough yet. She planted carrots, strawberries, and soft mixed lettuces that we would be able to snip when barely formed and toss into salads. Green onions went in, and radishes, and three kinds of beets. We craved peas, preferably English peas or sugar snaps, but if planted now, in March, they wouldn't be ready for a feast in May.

This was terribly disappointing. What is a spring menu without peas? Then we spotted some distinctly legume-like plants climbing up the side of the greenhouse. Johanna reluctantly revealed that they were fava beans, which she had planted specifically as a cover crop

back in October to deliver nitrogen to a spot that needed it. Ah! Fava beans could be just as good, if not better, in our spring menu. Maybe the test garden could spare a few? "Please let us eat some. They're so delicious," I wheedled. "And we have no peas." Johanna graciously gave in. Team Kitchen lucked out, and next year, we will plan ahead for peas.

❧

Chickens are tamer than bees, but they care less about the good of the collective. Honey—the henpecked chicken for whom we had built her own separate protective enclosure the year before—was again being tormented by the rest of the flock: more bleeding comb, more hiding in the nest box, serious wasting away of plump chicken body. We fretted. This could not go on.

Finally, we realized that Honey was just being broody. This is common among chickens, and we felt a bit silly that it had taken so long for us to recognize it. Poor Honey was trying to hatch eggs; that was why she refused to leave the box, not because she was avoiding the sorority from hell down in the yard. However, non-brooding hens, we learned, do typically attack a brooder whenever she's off the nest. It's as though they're telling her to get back on the job.

Our tactic was to haul Honey out of the nest box, plop her down next to the food, and stand guard long enough so she could eat and drink. She would puff up her feathers until she looked like a big yellow dandelion, and she'd make wet, squelchy clucks that sounded as though she were babbling. This completely enraged the other chickens. We'd fend them off with menacing foot thrusts while Honey chowed down. Within several days, she was back to her usual sleek self, and Team Chicken was able to relax.

❖

At last, Team Beer attempted its most ambitious brew, using our own hops and our own agonizingly threshed and winnowed wheat and barley. Now we had to malt the grains—that is, make them sprout, which naturally converts their starches to sugars. Malted grain, once ground up and soaked in warm water, produces wort, the sweet liquid that yeast feed on and convert to beer.

Team Beer's leader, Rick LaFrentz, is also Sunset's head gardener and has a knack for making seeds sprout. He soaked our wheat and barley for hours and then enclosed the seeds in plastic bags to keep them moist. Within days, fine little root hairs and shoots appeared. A bit of drying and rubbing off of roots and shoots, and the malted grain was ready.

For help on brewing day, we enlisted a friend with lots of experience in home brewing from grain: Chuck Schwalbach, husband of Diane, who works in manufacturing at Sunset. Chuck brought in some very useful tools, including a plate chiller, which cools the hot wort almost instantly. As the ripe smell of wort filled the kitchen, we hoped that the grains had fully converted their starches to sugars. Without sugars, our beer would bomb. So it was a big relief when, at the end of the day, Chuck measured the new brew's density and found that it had plenty of sugar: enough, he predicted, to give our beer 7 percent alcohol. We toasted our success with mugs of the grainy, sweet wort, tinged with bitterness from the hops.

Beer wasn't the only thing we planned to brew for the spring feast. Months earlier, Chris Ryan, our executive editor and a dedicated tea drinker, had observed that our project lacked caffeine. We had assumed that growing coffee and tea would be impossible, that the plants needed to be shrouded in tropical mists. But no! Tea could survive our climate, apparently, if coddled. Back in the fall, Chris had tracked down some plants at a South Carolina nursery that were mature enough to yield leaves in spring, and sent away for three of them.

Picking tea

They survived the winter, and as soon as the weather warmed up, they began to unfurl small, shiny green leaves. It only took about a week and a half to wither, roll, ferment, and dry our minuscule harvest. To celebrate, it seemed fitting to have a tea party. We summoned up our inner Britons and made dainty tea sandwiches—and, not having the ingredients for scones, little tarts filled with clotted cream and preserves.

Team Cow was celebrating, too. We'd finally found a new cow. It had taken months of calling all over the area and beyond—to 4-H clubs, farms and ranches, even backyard cow owners. Our cow lived about one hundred miles to the south, at Claravale Farm, a raw-milk dairy near Pinnacles National Monument. It was a beautiful place set in a remote, grassy valley framed by mountains, with chickens clucking in the bushes, a pistachio orchard, several century-old buildings from the town that once stood there, and a milking herd of fifty-five Jersey cows.

Ron Garthwaite and his partner, Collette Cassidy, let us pick out a young, good-looking, chocolate brown Jersey, No. 64. We named her Holly, after Hollister, the nearest big town, and arranged to buy her (she would continue to live at Claravale, though.). We got to milk her by hand, which is much harder than you might think:

milk shoots sideways, down your sleeve, or refuses to come out at all. It is, however, extremely relaxing to put your shoulder against a big warm animal and (once you get the hang of it) rhythmically squirt milk from soft, stretchy teats into a bucket. Mainly, though, we used an individual milking machine, with tubes that attach to each teat and pipe the milk straight into an enclosed container. This is more efficient (the cow is milked in ten minutes, versus up to forty-five), more comfortable for the cow, and more sanitary, since the milk is never exposed to the air, flies, or whatever might happen to fall into an open bucket.

And Holly's milk was a revelation. It tasted sweet and pure, with an indescribable lightness of texture and the slightest hint of grass. "It hasn't been homogenized, pasteurized, standardized, or fortified," said Ron. He'd just described the milk we'd all taken for granted as the real thing—until now.

After each visit, we took Holly's milk home in one-gallon canning jars that we buried in a giant cooler full of ice. At Sunset, we drank it as it was, from the jars. If we felt we hadn't kept the milk cold enough, or if anyone at Sunset requested it, we gently pasteurized some (the method is on page 214). So far, we've used the milk to make rich, delicious, sweet-tasting ricotta with a much higher yield than from store-bought milk—doubtless because Jersey milk has more butterfat and proteins than the milk of any other breed. We'll be trying out all kinds of other cheeses, too, in the months ahead—and yogurt, butter, and ice cream.

❖

By March, our spring garden had sprouted in a neat rectangle of green leaves of various hues and textures. Johanna had broadcast the herb seeds—meaning she scattered them the way nature would—and sowed the other crops in rows, so we had a combination of soft masses and orderly lines. The carrots had been heavily seeded in case some refused to germinate, but most of them had sprouted, forming a dense patch. Johanna carefully pulled out more than half to make some growing space for the rest. The thinnings were delicious in salad.

While out in the garden one day, we noticed that Alana, layer of pretty green eggs, was not her perky self. Her tail was drooping and she had a sad, lethargic look in her eyes, as though something very bad were going on internally.

Elizabeth read up on droopiness and lethargy. She concluded that it was most likely egg binding, which is when an egg gets stuck in the oviduct; it can be fatal if not fixed.

Ron Garthwaite and Collette Cassidy with their Jerseys

The home remedy involves helping the chicken relax. So, following the standard advice, we massaged Alana's vent with mineral oil (not as bad as it sounds) and gave her a warm bath. We also massaged her stomach in the direction of the vent to coax the egg out, but felt nothing.

Alana got worse and worse. After about five days, she was nearly unable to stand, and kept her eyes closed most of the time. By this point in our chicken keeping, we had decided we would limit veterinary care. We didn't want to be cruel to our chickens, but they were, after all, farm animals, and if they were in pain we would give them a quick, merciful end. Also, their diseases were often not treatable. That said, we did want to know whether Alana had something that could harm the rest of the flock.

So Elizabeth took Alana to an avian vet in nearby Mountain View. He was stumped, too, but he came up with many untreatable possibilities, from Marek's disease (a deadly contagious virus) to botulism to heavy-metal poisoning. "Her prognosis doesn't look good," he told her. The choice was pretty clear. We decided to put her out of her misery and send her body to the state lab, to understand what had happened to her.

This was the first death in our one-block project. Okay, it was the first warm-blooded death—we'd had hundreds, if not thousands, of dead bees. After investing a lot of time and concern in one chicken, Elizabeth found the death difficult, not only because she was present for it but also because she had made a real effort not to get attached to any of the hens. Plus, she had always tried to keep in mind that she (like the rest of us on Team Chicken) enjoyed a good chicken curry and that our own chickens were perfectly edible. So her sadness took her by surprise.

We each ended up feeling differently about Alana's end. Jim, an animal lover to his core, sensed even more acutely the innocence and vulnerability of animals that come under the care of humans. "It lays superiority and responsibility at your feet, even when you don't want them," he said. Elizabeth said it gave her some insight into empathy and how it should be directed. "The chickens are not pets. They're animals that have a job to do. I had to ask myself, how sad do I feel about this? And I had to control my empathy, which was an eye-opening experience. I might not give them human names next time." Other people on staff (not on Team Chicken, however) had no qualms about killing one of our flock, whether to end suffering or to put meat on the table. As for me and where I stood on the detachment scale, well, probably near Elizabeth. Mostly, I felt gratitude for that chicken and her beautiful, delicious eggs, which she had so generously produced day after day.

❊

Several weeks after Alana's body went off to the lab, we got the results back. She didn't die of anything infectious, but of kidney failure, and she had some inflammation around the heart. Also, a lot of internal fat. We were probably overfeeding the chickens. No more enchiladas, girls! We cut back on kitchen scraps and started giving them only greens, with a few other fruit and vegetable bits. And Johanna put together a movable garden enclosure for them out of chicken wire and rebar, so they could run around a little more and scarf up slugs at the same time. Unfortunately, we couldn't give them free rein of the garden because they would also eat our vegetables, which we were coaxing toward maturity for our spring feast.

We had had phenomenal luck getting our winter garden to ripen all at once. That was not going to happen with this one. The favas were ready now, in April (right on schedule for favas), and so were the radishes, but everything else needed a few more weeks of grow time. We weren't worried: Favas keep well layered between damp paper towels or newspaper, and we quickly replanted the radishes (they grow fast). We harvested twenty-five pounds of big, meaty pods from those fava vines in about half an hour and packed them away, along with their entirely edible greens, in the fridge.

Beverage-wise, we were moving right on schedule. Our beer had taken a couple of days for fermentation to kick in, but when it did, it blew the airlock clean off the carboy. Now, after six weeks of racking it and letting it percolate, Team Beer filled and capped a grand total of fifty-one bottles. We tasted it expectantly. Even though it wasn't yet carbonated, it seemed balanced, with a nice graininess and fragrant hops. After all that work, we had probably made some decent beer.

Three weeks later, when carbonation was complete, we popped a few caps for a group taste. Maybe we hadn't cleaned our bottles quite well enough, or maybe something had crept into the brew while we were bottling, but the beer was undeniably funky. At first we tried to deny it, saying things like, "It has a zingy, citrusy edge," and "Boy, is that blond." The more honest among us noticed flavors of plastic jug and bathroom cleanser, and then we all did. Team Beer drew on its inner Buddhist and tried to think about the journey, not the end.

❊

Nothing we seemed to do could keep the mites from swarming all over our bees. At best, we kept them at bay. Our newest tactic was to bring in an alternative hive called a top-bar. So far, we'd been using traditional Langstroth hives, which have stacked boxes and frames with preexisting foundation on which the bees build honeycomb and brood cells. The top-bar is a long single-story box you build yourself, with strips of wood (the bars) running across the top. The bees build their own comb, as they do in the wild, and anchor it to the bars. The top-bar was reputed to reduce disease and pests, and we were willing to try anything.

For this hive, we installed bees for the first time. We had purchased our first two hives as nucs (new colonies complete with queens). We built this one from scratch. The bees had arrived by mail, in a very buzzy shoebox-size box, with the queen in a small, separate capsule inside. During the trip, she had been emitting the powerful pheromones that were gradually bonding the other bees to her, but without her own traveling compartment, they might have killed her first. We named her Califia, after the queen of the mythical island of California. She was a beautiful bee, the color of a ripe apricot.

We removed the cork from the bottom of the queen's capsule and stuffed in a marshmallow instead, which the other bees would chew through in a few days, giving the queen time to fully cast her scent-spell over her subjects before they released her. We hung the little cage inside the hive. Kimberley shook the box of bees over the open hive, and they fell in with the sound of rice pouring from a box. After a couple of hours, they were already out on scouting flights. Three weeks later, fourteen of the fifteen bars had comb descending from them in snowy white lobes. Our new bees were busy and capable. Now we hoped they would stay healthy, too.

❄

A couple of days before our spring dinner, we checked out the favas. The pods were fine, and enough of the greens had lasted to give us a filling for two big quiches, which together formed the centerpiece of our menu. Then we went into the garden with Johanna and harvested our crops, pulling up golden and red beets and dusty pink ones—the amazing 'Chioggias' that, when sliced crosswise, looked like swirly peppermint lollipops. The carrots were just a matter of pulling, too, and all the herbs were easy—we just snipped. Pull on a green onion, though, and it snaps off. You have to dig around each one and then tug to get the whole thing.

In the kitchen, we tasted our vegetables so we would know how best to cook them. With a bowl of water for swishing and a knife for root trimming, we chomped straight from the basket. Everything was sweet and juicy, especially the radishes, which were as crisp and mild as apples, and the green onions, which had only a hint of heat sneaking in toward the end of the chew. The frilly little chervil had a clean, good flavor. French tarragon numbed our tongues with a hit of potent licorice, like it was supposed to. The strawberries were best of all—dead ripe and supersweet. We were glad our plan for them was simple: We wouldn't get in their way.

A breeze kicked up on the day of our feast, so we ate inside, next to sliding doors open to the garden. The beer was there for the curious, and we still had plenty of Chardonnay to sip as we stood around eating freshly baked buttermilk crackers with sweet ricotta, mint, and fava beans. We had a platter of radishes, too, with fresh butter and salt—it was all they needed.

We covered the table with pink roses that Johanna had picked, and bottles of wine and pitchers of strawberry lemonade. Everything was served on platters: mesclun salad with paper-thin circles of red, golden, and

Harvesting fava beans

lollipop-swirled beets; tall, custardy quiches laced with sautéed fava leaves; and a warm salad of grilled carrots with tarragon. Elaine was in charge of dessert, and she had been experimenting with our strawberries for several days. In the end, she turned away from strawberry fromage blanc cheesecake (because we already had a crusty dish, the quiche) and strawberries simmered in wine syrup (it tasted wintry). Instead, she spooned homemade fromage blanc into bowls, added the strawberries, and drizzled warm lemon-infused honey on top. It was so simple, and it was just right.

The dinner looked like a garden in full bloom, and it tasted wonderful, too. And yet the real triumph—as with each of the feasts that preceded it—happened on the way to the table.

We had coaxed food from pure nature, and that had required forming a relationship with it. We'd been moved to tears and totally frustrated; we'd been overjoyed and awestruck. We'd seen into the microscopic heart of cheese, beer, and wine; worked with bees, chickens, and a cow; and made gardens that grew like green symphonies, each little plant playing its part, contributing its flavor and beauty to the whole. Our project had taken place, more or less, on one block, but what we learned from it went far beyond.

Spring

THE SPRING GARDEN

Tender greens, crisp green onions, and plump radishes are cool-season crops, meaning they grow best in cooler temperatures. Long periods of hot weather can cause them to turn bitter and to bolt (set seed) before they produce edible parts. In mild-winter climates, plant them in very early spring so they will mature before summer heat settles in, or in late summer for a fall or winter crop. Because growing conditions vary by region (and even within neighborhoods), check the planting times for your area on pages 250 to 257. Many of the crops we planted thrive in full sun in cooler areas, which means the planting location needs at least 6 hours of sun per day. In hot climates, give them part shade. Some crops, such as mesclun and radishes, are easy to grow from seeds. Others on our spring menu, including strawberries, are easier if you start with bare-root plants or nursery seedlings. For seed-starting and planting tips, see page 9.

Arugula

See the Winter Garden, page 167.

Beets

Best known for their edible roots, beets also send up leaves that are tasty in soups and salads if picked when they are young and tender. The plump, heart-shaped bulbs come in various colors, from red and deep plum to golden. We chose three heirlooms: 'Bull's Blood', with blood red foliage that adds color to salads; golden, which forms sweet, mild-tasting globes; and supersweet 'Chioggia', whose roots reveal alternating rings of white and pink when sliced.

BEST SITE Full sun and fertile, well-drained soil enriched with compost.

DAYS TO HARVEST 40 to 52 days for 'Bull's Blood', 55 days for golden, and 54 days for 'Chioggia' from seed.

PLANTING AND CARE In mild climates, sow seeds in early spring or late summer so plants will mature in mild weather. Space them 1 inch apart, then cover with 1/4 inch of compost. (To prolong the harvest, sow at monthly intervals.) When the plants are small, thin them to 3 inches apart. Keep the soil evenly moist, and apply a dilute fish emulsion after the tops are up.

HOW TO HARVEST Pull up the roots when they are about 3 inches wide (the bigger they grow, the woodier they get).

SEED SOURCES Burpee, www.burpee.com, and Ed Hume Seeds, www.humeseeds.com.

Carrot 'Nantes'

Pulled straight from the earth and showered at the sink, homegrown carrots taste sweeter than any you can buy at the grocery store. But flavor, even among homegrown types, differs by variety. We grew 'Nantes', which forms blunt-tipped orange carrots about 7 inches long—great for munching raw. They are also delicious roasted with other root vegetables or grilled with thyme (see recipe, page 228).

BEST SITE Full sun with light, deep, well-drained soil free of clods and stones. Raised beds filled with planting mix are nearly perfect.

DAYS TO HARVEST 70 days from seed.

PLANTING AND CARE In mild-winter climates, sow seeds in early spring when the soil is warm (carrots are at their sweetest when the last few weeks of growth occurs in cool weather). Or, sow in early fall. Soak the bed, then scatter the seeds thinly on top, in rows 15 inches apart. Cover with 1/4 inch of compost to keep the soil surface from crusting. When the tops are 1 to 2 inches tall and have two or three leaves, thin the seedlings to 2 inches apart (eat the thinnings in salads or steam them in butter). Keep the soil evenly moist throughout the growing season. After the first thinning, work a narrow band of complete fertilizer into the soil about 2 inches beyond the row.

HOW TO HARVEST Begin to harvest when the carrots are fully grown (about 7 inches long; pull one up to check) and the tops are green and full.

SEED SOURCE Burpee, www.burpee.com.

Chervil

This lacy annual herb—one of French cooking's four classic fines herbes, along with tarragon, parsley, and chives—resembles parsley, but is paler green and more delicate. It tastes like parsley, too, but with overtones of anise. We like to add the fragile whole leaves to salads, fold them into omelets, or float them on soups. As the plant matures, 1- to 2-foot-tall flower stems topped with white blossoms will rise above the low mound of ferny foliage. Cut those off—ideally before they open—to keep the tasty leaves coming (flowering causes the foliage to lose its flavor and aroma). Spring crops bolt (flower and set seed) quicker than fall crops, because they mature in warmer weather.

BEST SITE Part shade and well-drained soil.

DAYS TO HARVEST 6 to 8 weeks from seed.

PLANTING AND CARE Plant seeds in early spring or in fall (where winters are mild), sowing them about 1/4 inch deep and 2 inches apart. When the seedlings are up (they germinate in 10 to 14 days), thin them to about 4 inches apart. Keep the soil evenly moist, and don't let the plants dry out completely between waterings or they will set seed. Feed every 3 weeks or so with liquid fish emulsion.

HOW TO HARVEST Snip off tender young leaves as needed and use them immediately. The delicate flavor of chervil is volatile and can dissipate soon after harvest (add it to cooked dishes at the last minute).

SEED SOURCES Renee's Garden, www.reneesgarden.com, and John Scheepers Kitchen Garden Seeds, www.kitchengardenseeds.com.

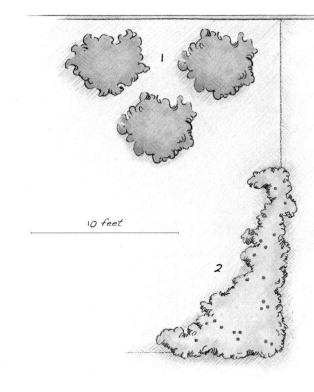

10 feet

Dill

Big, umbrella-like clusters of yellow flowers and soft, feathery foliage make dill as pretty as a spring wildflower. The blooms that poke above the stately 3- to 5-foot-tall plant provide nectar for butterflies and beneficial insects. But the most compelling reason to grow dill is the pungent aroma of its seeds and leaves, which can flavor so many dishes. You can use the seeds in pickling and in vinegar and the leaves to flavor sauces and soups.

BEST SITE Full sun and well-drained soil; protect from the wind.

DAYS TO HARVEST 40 to 50 days to harvest leaves, 85 to 105 days to harvest seed.

PLANTING AND CARE In early spring, sow seeds directly in the ground, 1/2 inch deep and 1 to 2 inches apart in rows 6 inches apart. (Once the plants' deep tap roots get growing, transplanting will be difficult.) Thin the seedlings to 12 inches apart when they are 2 to 3 inches tall. Water regularly—about once a week during dry periods. If you don't want plants to resow (which they will, vigorously), shear off

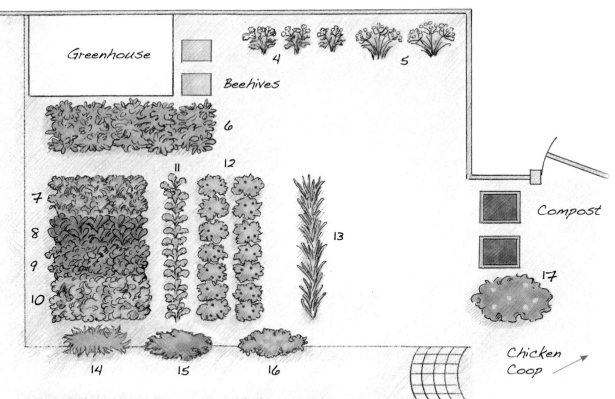

Greenhouse

Beehives

4

5

6

12

11

7

8

9

10

13

Compost

17

14

15

16

Chicken Coop

18

3

SPRING GARDEN PLAN

1. Tea
2. Nasturtiums
3. Peppermint
4. Chervil
5. Dill
6. Fava beans
7. Carrots
8. Beets
9. Arugula
10. Mesclun
11. Radishes
12. Strawberries
13. Green onions
14. Tarragon
15. Thyme
16. Parsley
17. Lemon tree
18. Tangerine tree

the heads before they set seed, or watch the seeds carefully and harvest them promptly (see below).

HOW TO HARVEST Snip off leaves as you need them. To collect the seeds, tie small paper bags or tightly woven cheesecloth (double or triple layers if necessary) over the seedheads when the seeds begin to turn brown, and leave the bags in place for a week or so. Then snip the stems below the bags, bring the heads into the kitchen, and shake the seeds out onto a tray. Store them in airtight containers.

SEED SOURCE Renee's Garden, www.reneesgarden.com.

Fava Bean

Not a true bean, the fava is actually a giant vetch (an ancient type of legume). Unlike true beans, it is cold hardy, which means gardeners in mild climates can plant it in the fall for harvest in late winter or early spring (as we did). As long as the weather stays cool, the plants can last into midspring. You can cook and eat the immature pods like edible-pod peas, or let the pods hang on the plant to ripen into dry shelling beans. One caveat: Some people of Mediterranean, Asian, and African ancestry have an enzyme deficiency that can cause severe reactions to these beans and their pollen.

BEST SITE A mild, sunny location with loose, fast-draining soil.

DAYS TO HARVEST 65 days from seed.

PLANTING AND CARE Sow seeds as soon as the soil is warm. Heavy leaves must push through the soil, so be sure the soil is loose and open. For a bush type of fava, which is what we grew, plant seeds 1 inch deep and 1 to 3 inches apart, allowing 24 to 36 inches between rows. Moisten the soil thoroughly before planting, then do not water again until seedlings have emerged. Keep the soil evenly moist throughout the growing season. Fertilize the soil after the plants are in active growth and again when the pods start to form, working a complete fertilizer into the soil along the row.

HOW TO HARVEST To eat the pods, pick them when they are small (about 3 inches long), plump, and deep green. To eat the fresh beans inside (but not the pod), wait until the pod and beans are larger but are still bright green. For dry yellow shelling beans, wait until the pods have blackened and drooped.

Fava beans

'White Lisbon' green onions

SEED SOURCE John Scheepers Kitchen Garden Seeds, www.kitchengardenseeds.com.

Green Onion 'White Lisbon'

Sometimes called scallions, green onions are either bulbing onions that you harvest young (before the bulbs grow), or bulbless bunching onions. We grew 'White Lisbon', a green bunching type with delicate stems and sweet, juicy tops.

BEST SITE Full sun and loose, fertile, well-drained soil.

DAYS TO HARVEST 60 to 65 days from seed.

PLANTING AND CARE Plant green onions from seed or nursery seedlings. Sow seeds $1/4$ inch deep and $1/2$ inch apart in rows 12 to 15 inches apart. Plant seedlings 4 to 5 inches apart. Keep the soil evenly moist and feed plants regularly with a dilute liquid fish emulsion.

HOW TO HARVEST Pull up green onions when the tops are 12 to 18 inches tall.

SEED SOURCE Botanical Interests, www.botanical interests.com.

Lemon 'Eureka'

See the Summer Garden, page 31.

Mesclun

The word *mesclun*, from a southern French word for "mixture," refers to an assortment of greens picked when young and tender. Sweet red and green lettuces, piquant green arugula, spicy mustard, peppery red Komatsuna, tender Swiss chard leaves—some or all might turn up in one of these colorful mixes. Succulent "weeds" such as purslane and tender mâche might be included, too. You can choose a mix that contains the greens you like.

BEST SITE Full sun in fall, winter, and spring in mild climates, and well-drained soil enriched with plenty of compost.

DAYS TO HARVEST 35 days from seed.

PLANTING AND CARE Scatter seeds over the prepared seedbed in spring. To prolong the harvest, sow seeds every 2 or 3 weeks. Thin seedlings to about 3 inches apart. Keep the soil evenly moist, and apply half-strength liquid fish emulsion after the first fully formed leaves appear.

HOW TO HARVEST Snip off the young plants above ground level. Most will produce new leaves for your next harvest.

SEED SOURCE Burpee, www.burpee.com.

Nasturtium

Round, bright green leaves of this pretty annual (*Tropaeolum majus*) have a refreshing herbal fragrance. When young and tender, they also have an appealing, dewy sweetness and a peppery flavor (as do the buds and flowers) that adds zip to salads. You can grow vining nasturtiums to trail over the ground or climb (to 6 feet), or you can plant bushy dwarf types that top out at 18 inches. Either way, they will reseed themselves: We still have offspring of 'Copper Sunset' popping up here and there, even though we haven't planted it for years.

BEST SITE Full sun or part shade and well-drained or sandy soil.

DAYS TO HARVEST 45 to 60 days from seed.

PLANTING AND CARE For an early summer harvest, sow seeds in March or April, or for a spring harvest, sow in October in mild-winter or hot-summer areas. Plant the large seeds 10 to 12 inches part and 1 inch deep. Keep the soil well watered throughout the growing season. Dig a little compost into the soil before planting and your nasturtiums won't need fertilizer.

HOW TO HARVEST Pick leaves and flowers as you need them. For the best flavor, harvest them early in the morning when temperatures are cool.

SEED SOURCE Renee's Garden, www.reneesgarden.com.

Parsley 'Gigante Italian'

See the Summer Garden, page 33.

Peppermint

See the Summer Garden, page 34.

Radish 'Easter Egg II'

Among the easiest vegetables to grow, radishes are also fast to mature. We especially like 'Easter Egg II', a feast for the eyes that blends pink, rose, purple, and white radishes in one colorful mix. All have crisp, juicy white flesh. The best part: You can harvest from 2 to 5 pounds per 10-foot row!

BEST SITE Full sun in mild climates and part shade where it is hot; fast-draining soil that's been well amended with compost.

DAYS TO HARVEST 25 days from seed.

PLANTING AND CARE Sow seeds as soon as the soil is workable in spring, then at weekly intervals until warm weather approaches (plants go to seed when temperatures rise). In mild climates, you can also sow seeds at regular intervals in fall and winter. Plant the seeds ¹/₂ inch deep and 1 inch apart in rows 1 to 1¹/₂ inches apart. Keep the soil evenly moist from seed to harvest. Ten days after planting, feed with a dry or liquid fertilizer (any kind), applying it alongside the rows.

HOW TO HARVEST Pick as soon as radishes reach full size (about 3 weeks after sowing, as noted above, but longer for slower varieties). If you leave them in the ground too long, they will turn woody and too pungent to eat.

SEED SOURCE Burpee, www.burpee.com.

Strawberry 'Sequoia'

Nothing tastes sweeter than a plump, sun-warmed strawberry picked at the peak of ripeness. It is nature's best dessert—divinely succulent and juicy, low in calories (about 50 per cup), and high in vitamin C. If you only have room for growing one crop, we suggest this one, since many commercial harvests are treated with chemicals.

We chose 'Sequoia', a locally adapted variety that bears its entire crop once a year. (It is called a "June bearer," but we had berries in May.) The plants reach 6 to 8 inches tall and spread by runners about 12 inches across. The berries are large and luscious.

BEST SITE Full sun and loose, well drained, well-amended soil.

DAYS TO HARVEST 90 to 104 days from January-started bare-root plants.

PLANTING AND CARE Set out bare-root plants in January or February (trim their roots back to about 6 inches and soak them in water for about 30 minutes before planting). You can also set out plants in late summer or fall for a spring harvest. Plant seedlings from small pots in late February or March. Plant with the crown (the point where the leaves come together at the stem base) slightly above the soil level (a buried crown will rot); the topmost roots should be about ¹/₄ inch below the soil. Mulch to deter weeds (we used straw, which did a good job of keeping ripening fruit clean). Keep birds from stealing your berries by covering the bed with netting or floating row covers. Water regularly (at least once a week) during the bearing season. Feed June-bearers twice a year—lightly when new growth starts, and more heavily after fruiting. Give ever-bearing types regular light feedings throughout the growing season, and alpine strawberries once in early spring and

'Sequoia' strawberry

once after fruiting begins. For all strawberries, use a complete fertilizer.

HOW TO HARVEST After a fruit has colored up, pinch through the stem with your thumbnail to detach it.

PLANT/SEEDLING SOURCES Bare-root plants and seedlings are sold at nurseries.

Tangerine 'Dancy'

See the Winter Garden, page 171.

Tarragon, French

This sprawling, largely flowerless woody perennial (*Artemisia dracunculus sativa*) has dark green, aromatic leaves with an anise flavor and grows to less than 2 feet tall. The leaves are a classic seasoning for chicken dishes, sauces, and vegetables. Be careful not to plant plain old Russian tarragon—*A. dracunculus*—by mistake; it has tougher, narrower leaves and a pungent, bitter flavor.

BEST SITE Full sun and rich, well-drained soil.

DAYS TO HARVEST Leaves can be harvested any time.

PLANTING AND CARE In early spring, as soon as the soil starts to warm up, set plants about 24 inches apart in garden beds or put a single plant in an

French tarragon

8-inch-deep container. Water regularly and let the plants dry out between irrigations. Apply a complete fertilizer during spring growth and again after major harvests. To keep a fresh supply coming, cut plants almost at the ground during the growing season. Divide the plants every other year during early fall.

HOW TO HARVEST Pinch off leaves.

SEEDLING SOURCE Mountain Valley Growers, www.mountainvalleygrowers.com.

Tea

Camellia sinensis is the tropical shrub grown commercially in Asia for making green, black, and oolong teas. It is rare in the United States, and we couldn't find mature plants at nurseries or growers on the West Coast, so we ordered them from a source in North Carolina (Camellia Forest Nursery, www.camforest.com or 919/968-0504). But if you are patient, you can order seedlings from the two sources listed at right.

Our three pretty, round tea shrubs have leathery, dark green leaves and fragrant white fall blooms. Initially we planted them in big pots so we could move them under the eaves in winter (the plants are frost tender), but they weren't happy, so now they are in the ground (we will cover them when frost hits). The plants will eventually grow to 15 feet tall.

BEST SITE Full sun, or light shade inland, and well-drained soil enriched with plenty of compost, or use potting soil. Protect from wind and from winter frost.

DAYS TO HARVEST Plants must be at least 3 years old.

PLANTING AND CARE Set the plant in the soil so its base is above soil level, then keep the roots cool by applying a 1/2-inch-thick layer of mulch (keep it away from the stem's base). Young plants are best in light shade under tall trees. Water your tea plant regularly, at least weekly during the April to October growing season for the first few years; older plants can get by with less water. Feed occasionally with an acid plant food formulated especially for camellias.

WHEN TO HARVEST In spring, pick the two uppermost new leaves and the new buds. To prepare them for making tea, see How to Make Tea (page 219).

SEEDLING SOURCES Greer Gardens, www.greergardens.com, and Nichols Garden Nursery, www.nichols gardennursery.com.

Thyme, French

See the Summer Garden, page 36.

—Kathleen N. Brenzel

THE "IMPORTS"

We went outside our garden for these local foods: Milk, whole and unhomogenized, from our own cow (page 213); active dry yeast; whole-wheat flour ('Sonora' and 'Expresso', page 156); garlic (ours ran out); 'Spanish White' onions (ditto)

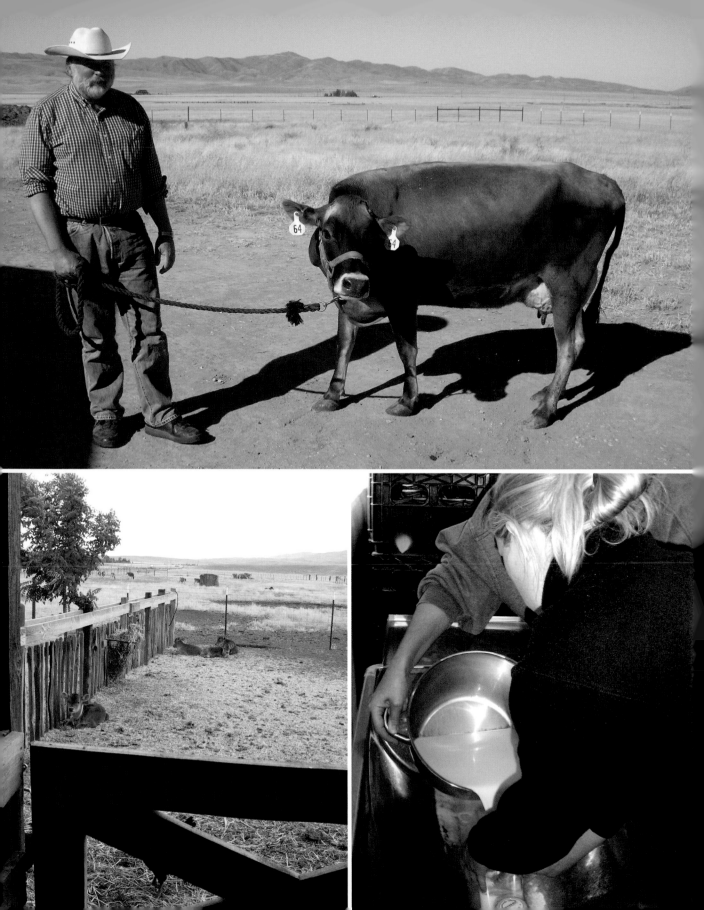

THE SPRING PROJECTS

A DAIRY COW

Getting a cow might seem like a large leap for us office-working suburbanites. (Like jumping over the moon, you say?) We had good reasons. Milk had been an integral part of our one-block feasts from the start, giving our vegetarian menus protein and making cooking more interesting; like eggs, milk is one of those building-block ingredients that open up all sorts of possibilities for recipes. We had been "importing" unhomogenized, pasteurized bottled milk from Straus Family Creamery (by buying it at the store). But if we could have a cow—especially a Jersey, a breed that gives particularly rich, delicious milk—we could make a key ingredient our own.

With a cow of our own, we'd see firsthand the fluctuations in milk from season to season. We'd be able to try fresh, unprocessed milk, a food that most of us, in our age of mass-produced dairy products, had never tasted—even though humans have been consuming it since at least 5000 BCE. And we'd understand more about how this taken-for-granted substance is made.

Also, several of us happened to really like cows, the way some people like horses. We wanted to get to know one of these patient, generous animals whose relationship with humans has profoundly shaped our culture.

To our amazement, our city, Menlo Park, allows backyard cows. We imagined what it might be like to have a brown Jersey hanging around the office, contentedly grazing on Sunset's lawn. For many reasons, including our complete and utter lack of experience, we quickly decided our cow would be better off living on a farm and being taken care of by people who knew what they were doing—and could teach us.

The rewards so far include learning to milk by hand (well, sort of); the pleasure of wandering around a beautiful and well-managed farm with healthy cows; the incomparable flavor of sweet, fresh Jersey milk; and the richness and nuance of the cheeses we've made. Because this is our newest project, what is written here reflects only our first steps. We'll be describing our continuing experiences on our blog, http://oneblockdiet.sunset.com/team-cow.

ONE DAIRY COW

Holly is an 800-pound, 2½-year-old Jersey. She gives between 5 and 6 gallons of milk a day.

HOW TO DO IT

You can own a cow three ways:

1. Buy the cow and keep her at home This is a serious commitment, involving twice-daily milkings and learning how to keep lactation going (by having your cow impregnated every 12 to 18 months; a cow has to have a calf in order to produce milk). It also involves figuring out what to do with the calves (sell or use them for beef? Occasionally keep a female calf to raise as another milk cow?). You also need to have enough space for a cow and her calf and be sure you can properly feed them (a lactating cow eats a lot) and keep them healthy (see "Raising Dairy Cows," page 218, for helpful resources that will tell you more). And a cow is expensive: A good adult dairy cow costs as much as $2,500, a calf around $500. That said, she will give you wonderful milk, enough to share, if you like; meat, if you choose (her calves); and manure for the garden and pasture. Keeping a single cow at home is also the safest way to have raw milk, because one cow is easier to keep clean than a herd, and you have more control over the milk.

Check with your city to see whether local rules let you keep a cow, and then start learning everything you can about cows, including differences between breeds. Jerseys are often suggested as ideal backyard cows because they are gentle and friendly, smaller than other breeds and thus easier to handle, and also produce richer milk but less of it—a volume that is easier to deal with than the 14-gallon-a-day flow of, say, a Holstein. You might also consider sharing your cow with neighbors to offset the expenses and to divide up the milk.

Ron Garthwaite and Holly, our cow, at Claravale Farm (top);
Pouring Holly's milk into bottles at Claravale Farm (bottom right)   213

Most sources say that beginners should look for a cow pregnant for the second or third time. She'll be "trained" in milking, and you won't have to deal with the impregnation aspect of owning a cow for at least a year.

2. Co-own or share a cow who lives on a farm Cow-sharing is most common in states where the sale of raw milk is banned, because it gives the owners legal access to their cow's fresh milk. The ownership fee, paid to the farmer, covers the cost of the cow's care and board. A cow-share contract can also be set up as a share in an entire herd. For more on how to find or set up a cow-share (or goat-share), see Helpful Information, page 218.

Perhaps you are wondering whether cow-shares exist at regular (non-raw-milk) dairies. To the best of our knowledge, they don't, and for two reasons: Most commercial dairies aren't set up to capture the milk of a single cow. They are very large operations that pump milk straight from the entire herd into refrigerated trucks, which then drive the milk to a separate facility—the creamery—for pasteurizing and processing. Also, their contract with the creamery is usually exclusive, which means they can't do business with outside parties. In any case, it might not be a good idea to share a cow from one of these dairies. Since the milk is destined for pasteurization, the allowable pathogen count is higher than at a raw-milk dairy. In other words, it would be risky to drink the milk unless it was pasteurized.

3. Own a cow who lives on a farm Like cow-sharing, this arrangement isn't common in California, because the sale of raw milk is legal in our state. However, Ron Garthwaite of Claravale Farm, a raw-milk dairy near Paicines, California, was willing to make a one-time arrangement with us to own one of his cows and board her at his farm. He has also agreed to manage her care and give us lessons in the art of cow keeping.

Although we did not set out to find a cow at a raw-milk dairy, we've since learned that the legal requirements for cleanliness at such an operation are much more stringent than for a pasteurized-milk dairy, since the milk will be leaving the premises raw. We also see how healthy Ron's cows are and notice the care with which he handles them. His farm is inspected regularly and has never been cited. He doesn't pool the milk with that of any other herd, he supervises every step of its (minimal) production, and he distributes it only in California. All this reassures us that the milk we're getting is of the highest quality.

WHAT TO USE

Claravale Farm supplied most of the equipment we needed, as part of our boarding contract. We've included prices anyway, should you be interested in keeping a cow at home. The source, unless otherwise mentioned, is Nasco dairy supply, 800/558-9595 or www.enasco.com/farmandranch/Dairy+Supplies.

HOW TO BATCH-PASTEURIZE MILK

1. For equipment details, see opposite. Fill the stockpot with water and bring to a boil. Add the thermometer (submerging only the stem) and the ladle; boil for 10 minutes. Transfer the ladle and the thermometer to a sanitized work surface and pour the hot water into the boiling-water canner. Add enough water to fill to within 1 inch below the top ring, insert the canning rack upside down (handles down and folded under), cover, and bring water to a boil over high heat. Meanwhile, fill a sink with cold water (your emergency cool-down spot).

2. Pour the milk into the stockpot. Attach the dairy thermometer to the side of the pot, and ease the pot into the hot-water bath until it rests on the canning rack. The water should come 2 1/2 inches up the sides of the pot; add more boiling water if you need to. Keep the burner on high.

3. Stir the milk with the ladle 20 times, using a slow surface-to-bottom circular motion to distribute the heat evenly. Watch the thermometer; when it hits 140°F, turn off the burner and let the milk rise to 145°F. Hold it at 145°F or just above, covered, for 30 minutes, boosting with a

blast of heat from the burner if necessary, or removing the pot from the canner if the temperature gets above 150°F (you can also put the pot in the sink to cool down rapidly).

4. Add plenty of ice to the sink of water and immerse the milk pot in the ice water. Let the milk cool, stirring with a slow surface-to-bottom circular motion every now and then. If you're making cheese, let it cool to the temperature specified in the recipe, then use immediately. Otherwise, cool the milk to room temperature, then pour it into the cleaned canning jars and refrigerate.

Teat Dip An iodine-based sanitizing solution for the teats. About $23 for a 1-gallon jug.

Plastic teat dipper A cup, filled with teat dip, that makes dipping each teat easier. About $3.

Individual cow milker Commercial dairies use a system of tubes to carry the milk of several (or more) cows at once into a large chilling tank. For one cow, you need a self-contained setup; this one includes a vacuum pump, an electronic pulsator, the "claw" (suction cups that attach to the teats), the tubing, and the milking pail. $1,749 from Hoegger Supply Co., 800/221-4628 or www.hoeggergoatsupply.com

Stainless-steel milk strainer Right after we collect the milk, we pour it through this to separate out any dirt. Includes a steel mesh strainer disk. $199.

6^1/$_2$-inch round milk filter disks (non-gauze) Thin, paperlike disks that fit into the strainer, on top of the steel mesh strainer disk. $6.25 per box of 100.

Aluminum milk pail or jug To hold the strained milk. $40.

1-quart widemouthed canning jars We like this size for transporting milk, because the jars are small enough for the milk to cool quickly when immersed in ice water. Also, they are easy to clean, and the wide top allows us to skim the cream without effort. From about $18 for a case of 12 jars (enough for Holly's afternoon-milk yield of 2^1/$_2$ to 3 gallons) at a well-stocked grocery store, hardware store, or cookware store.

A big cooler (about 2^1/$_2$ feet long), full of ice For rapid cooling and transporting of the milk in the trunk of our car. From about $75 for a 75-quart cooler at a hardware store.

Dairy thermometer For keeping tabs on the temperature of the milk during transport, and to measure the temperature of the milk if you pasteurize. Get the kind that you can clip onto the side of the pot, and make sure it's accurate (see page 46 for calibrating instructions). About $25 from the Beverage People, www.thebeveragepeople.com or 800/544-1867.

21-quart boiling-water canner with canning rack If you want to pasteurize (see opposite). When filled with hot water, the canner makes a great water bath for your milk pot. From $16 on www.amazon.com.

8-gallon heavy stockpot If you opt to pasteurize, you'll need this, too.

Stainless-steel perforated cheese ladle or large slotted spoon For pasteurizing. We like the large, flat surface of the cheese ladle because it's more efficient for stirring the milk. From $7 for the ladle at www.thebeveragepeople.com.

HOW TO DO IT

1. Find the cow For our best general advice, see page 213.

Cows are few and far between on the San Francisco Peninsula. Educational farms near us had cows, but they were already being milked to their limits. 4-H clubs focus on raising younger animals, not adult dairy cows. The backyard cow owners we tracked down had all decided to let their animals "dry off" for a while, meaning they weren't producing milk.

We finally found Claravale Farm, and Holly, through another farm (the owners had bought their cow from Claravale), and through a state brand inspector, who handles documentation when cows are sold and who pointed us in Claravale's direction. With the free assistance of the Farm-to-Consumer Legal Defense Fund (see Helpful Information: Cow-Shares, page 218), we drew up an initial bill of sale and a cow-boarding agreement.

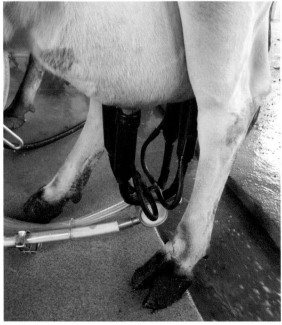

The "claw"

Filtering milk into a sanitized jug

Holly's price was $2,500, but we sold most of her milk in advance back to Claravale, since we knew we wouldn't be able to use it and the Claravale owners definitely could. The cost per year worked out to be $270.

2. Milk the cow She ambles into the milking barn, ideally 12 hours after the last milking, lowers her head to the trough, and starts chewing grain—the treat that puts her in a good mood and encourages the "letting down" of her milk. Meanwhile, a stanchion holds her head in place just in case she tries to back out.

Before milking starts, we dip each of her four teats in a bright red iodine sanitizing solution. The first few squirts go onto the ground, to clear the ducts of any dirt and also the iodine once it has done its job. Then we wipe off the iodine with a clean damp paper towel.

We tried hand milking, and it's quite a bit harder than you might think. Each teat fills up with milk when the cow "lets down." To keep it from shooting back up into the udder instead of into the pail, you have to close off the teat right where it meets the udder, using your thumb and forefinger; then you squeeze the milk in the teat down and out with your remaining fingers. Ron demonstrated on Holly and a thick stream of milk shot into the pail. When we tried, we got little dribbles. Well, room for improvement! The truth is that cows are usually milked with a milking machine, which gets the job done

in a fraction of the time and keeps the milk cleaner than a set of hands squirting into an open pail. It hooks up to the cow by means of a "claw," a configuration of four cylindrical suction cups, each of which attaches to a teat and rhythmically draws the milk off through pipes to a central chilling tank. So we could keep Holly's milk separate, Ron showed us how to attach a small, individual milking unit whose pipes end up in a portable canister. The claw goes on with a little *swooosh* of pressurized air and, when the milk flow slows, pops off easily. After milking, we again dip each teat in sanitizer, and Holly saunters back out to pasture.

3. Filter the milk We immediately lug the milk canister to the cool milk-tank room, where we pour it into the strainer, set atop a sanitized steel jug. The milk is quite warm—it's 102°F—and sweet-smelling steam rises from it as we pour.

4. Bottle the milk We've lined up our jars in a long stainless-steel sink. Now two of us lift the jug and pour the milk as accurately as possible into the jars, trying not to spill. Another Team Cow member screws the lids on the jars as soon as they are filled and plunges the jars into the ice-filled cooler. There's always one jar that ends up only partly filled. We insert the dairy thermometer into this jar and fit it into the cooler too, covering it with foil as best we can to prevent sloshing; it is our temperature gauge. Fresh milk should be cooled right away to at least 40°F. At Claravale, the pipes take the milk directly to the chiller tank, which drops its temperature to 36°F within minutes after it has been in the cow. We're not as fast, but we're not far behind.

5. Transport the milk (and taste) We drive back to Sunset and put the milk in the refrigerator. Usually we have a glassful first, because it is absolutely delicious.

6. Store the milk Chilled at 40°F or below, it stays fresh and sweet for a week or so. Whenever we haven't been certain that we've kept the milk cool enough on its long ride back to Menlo Park, we've pasteurized it using the low-heat, long-time "batch" method (see page 214), which destroys any harmful organisms but interferes least with the milk's light, fresh flavor. Most commercial dairies use what is known as the high- temperature, short-time (HTST) method, which means that the milk is heated to 162°F (sometimes up to 171°F) for 15 seconds, or the ultrahigh temperature (UHT) method, which blasts the milk at or above 265°F for 2 seconds.

7. Cook with the milk Jersey milk has more butterfat by weight than Holstein milk, the grocery-store standard, does (over 5 percent versus 3.6 percent), and more protein, too. This, and the fact that it's not homogenized or high-temperature pasteurized—both of which alter the structure of the milk—means it coagulates more readily and the cheese yield is higher. We made terrific, fluffy ricotta with Holly's milk, because the whey forms many more and fatter curds than whey from Holstein milk. When we made Gouda, though, it set so quickly and firmly that it turned into a sort of cheese superball. Our friends at Cowgirl Creamery, in Point Reyes, California (see How to Make Cheese, page 119), advised us to reduce the rennet by 40 percent when using Jersey milk. We'll try that next time.

HELPFUL INFORMATION

BUYING DAIRY COWS

- Your county's agricultural extension office; see www.csrees.usda.gov/Extension/index.html for a nationwide listing.
- Small dairy farms, which periodically have cows for sale. Claravale Farm, in Paicines, California, where we bought our cow, Holly (and where we

MILK: THE FRESH AND THE COOKED

In the world of food and drink, few controversies generate as much passionate outrage as the debate over raw milk. If you want to own a cow and drink her milk, you will have to decide where you stand. This is a simplified overview; to learn more, see Helpful Information, page 218.

The argument for fresh (raw)

Supporters say raw milk is a pure, healthful food that is not only nutritious, but also capable of curing such chronic conditions as eczema, asthma, and even hepatitis. They also claim that pasteurization destroys vitamins and beneficial bacteria.

The argument for cooked (pasteurized)

Detractors, which include the U.S. Department of Agriculture and the U.S. Food and Drug Administration, insist that raw milk should be universally avoided, and rules in many states ban the sale of it. They contend that pasteurization—heating the milk to kill harmful microbes—leaves the nutritional value of the milk intact.

Our opinion so far

Raw milk is not inherently harmful. It has to be invaded by bad bacteria to be unsafe, and if that doesn't happen, it's perfectly fine to drink. (Interestingly, if left to sour naturally, raw milk is inhospitable to those bad bacteria—but we'd rather drink the milk when it's sweet.) That said, bacteria love raw milk, and can quickly contaminate it if the cow is diseased or dirty or the milk is mishandled. Many outbreaks of foodborne illness have been connected to raw milk. (As they have to a range of other foods, from hamburger to spinach.)

Unfortunately, it seems pretty clear that our current system of mass production and distribution can't keep bacteria at bay. Raw milk needs to come from healthy cows, be checked vigilantly for pathogens, and be kept cold and very clean in order to be safe. It has to be handled as the fragile, fresh substance that it is, and requires a different and more careful (and more localized) way of selling.

We know our cow and how she is cared for, and how her milk is treated. We love how her milk tastes. So, when we know we've chilled it right and kept it cold, we drink it raw. And when we're in doubt, we pasteurize—gently.

keep her), sells cows occasionally. Contact owner Ron Garthwaite through www.claravaledairy.com or 831/628-3219.

- Large-animal veterinarians often have clients who will sell a dairy cow.
- Livestock brand inspectors in your state, who handle the paperwork whenever a cow is sold or moved, often know of cows for sale.

RAISING DAIRY COWS

- Your county's agricultural extension office may know of workshops near you. See www.csrees .usda.gov/Extension/index.html for a listing of offices nationwide.
- *The Backyard Cow*, by Ann Williams (Prism Press, 1979). A sweet, little British book that covers the basics of cow rearing.
- *Chore Time*, by Tim Wightman (Farm-to-Consumer Legal Defense Fund, 2008). Two DVDs take you through the ABCs of small-scale milk production.
- *The Encyclopedia of Country Living* (10th edition), by Carla Emery (Sasquatch Books, 2008). An invaluable resource for anyone interested in learning to live off the land, this personable, comprehensive guide (more than 900 pages long) covers everything from calculating harvest yields to stocking a fish pond to making your own furniture polish. The chapter on raising dairy cattle is an encouraging and friendly introduction, and it supplies a guide to breeds and where to find them, plus a handy list of questions to ask when buying a family milk cow.
- *The Family Cow*, by Dirk van Loon (Garden Way Publishing, 1976). A very good introduction to the dairy cow, complete with taking care of the land that feeds her and building fences to keep her in.
- www.motherearthnews.com offers a mother lode of articles, many dating back to the 1970s but others current, on keeping cows. Search under "Keep a Family Cow" for the most comprehensive listing.
- *Raw Milk Production Handbook*, by Tim Wightman (Farm-to-Consumer Legal Defense Fund in association with the Weston A. Price Foundation, 2008). A beginner's guide to buying, raising, and milking a healthy, happy cow; it's the most current resource we've found.
- *The Self-Sufficient Life and How to Live It: The Complete Back-to-Basics Guide*, by John Seymour (DK Publishing, 2009). Written in 1976 by Britain's "Father of Self-Sufficiency," this is an expanded edition. Like many DK books, it is beautifully illustrated, and the chapter on cows is inspirational.

COW-SHARES

- Farm-to-Consumer Legal Defense Fund, (703) 208-3276 or www.farmtoconsumer.org/cow-shares.html
- The Weston A. Price Foundation, a nonprofit devoted to promoting whole, unprocessed foods, has a list of state-by-state chapters that can help locate a share in your area, www.westonaprice.org/ chapters and also www.realmilk.com/cowfarm share.html.

RAW MILK

- www.realmilk.com (a branch of the Weston A. Price Foundation)
- www.fda.gov/Food/ResourcesForYou/Consumers/ ucm079516.htm
- "The Udder Truth," by Hannah Wallace; www.salon.com, January 19, 2007.
- *Safe Handling: Consumers' Guide*, by Peggy Beals (MI Fresh Milk Council, 2009). A guide to raw-milk handling from an advocate's perspective.
- "Should This Milk Be Legal?" by Joe Drape; www.nytimes.com, August 8, 2007.
- *The Untold Story of Milk—The History, Politics and Science of Nature's Perfect Food: Raw Milk from Pasture-Fed Cows*, by Ron Schmid, ND (NewTrends Publishing, 2009).

MILK HISTORY AND SCIENCE

- *Milk: The Surprising Story of Milk Through the Ages, with 120 Adventurous Recipes That Explore the Riches of Our First Food*, by Anne Mendelson (Alfred A. Knopf, 2008). One of America's finest food historians offers a well-researched, beautifully written exploration of milk as used by cultures over the globe, from ancient times to the present day. The book includes an extensive, worldly, and fascinating collection of recipes.
- *Nature's Perfect Food: How Milk Became America's Drink*, by E. Melanie DuPuis (New York University Press, 2002). A history of milk in the United States that does a good job of puncturing myths.
- *On Food and Cooking: The Science and Lore of the Kitchen*, by Harold McGee (Scribner, 2004). Chapter 1, "Milk and Dairy Products," is a compelling read that makes the science of milk a page-turner.

HOW TO MAKE
TEA

With all due respect to Teams Salt and Escargot, Team Tea submits that attempting to grow, here in Menlo Park, *Camellia sinensis*—a crop that's happiest in, say, the rain forests of Yunnan or the hill stations of Darjeeling—is *the* most far-fetched One-Block project.

As far as we can tell, only two tea plantations are currently operating in the western United States, and neither of them is in California. What's more, these two farms (one is in Hawaii, the other is in Washington) produce only Japanese-style green teas, not black tea. (Although green and black teas all come from the same kind of plant, they are processed in different ways.) Since some of us on the team are hopelessly addicted to the black stuff, that's what we had our hearts set on.

The first hurdle was finding mature tea bushes and figuring out where they would grow best on the Sunset grounds. After that, the actual processing of the tea turned out to be pretty simple.

We are still in the early days of tea growing. So far, we've had one very small harvest from our three bushes, which resulted in a single pot of pale yellow, very delicate, distinctly tea-flavored brew. But we're looking forward to learning, and drinking, more.

BLACK TEA

Our first harvest: 1 heaping tablespoonful of dried tea leaves, rolled into needles like Asia's finest.

WHAT TO USE

Tea bushes When we first started looking for tea bushes, we thought we'd be able to buy them from Forest Farm Nursery up in Williams, Oregon (www.forestfarm .com). But the nursery only had seedlings at the time, and a bush generally needs to be 3 years old before you can start plucking its leaves. Further research led us to Google Answers and a reference to the Camellia Forest Nursery, in North Carolina, which sells both seedlings and mature tea plants. There are hundreds of subvarieties and cultivars of *C. sinensis*, but we figured we could at least see which of the three main types—large leaf (Assam bush), medium leaf (Java bush), and small leaf (China bush)—does best in our

climate, so we ordered one of each, in late fall. Kind of a splurge, as they were $50 each. Camellia Forest Nursery, www.camforest.com or 919/968-0504.

Rimmed baking sheet Perfect for all stages of the leaf processing. About $7 at a cookware store.

Wine cellar or other cool, damp place We invaded the Sunset wine cellar, commandeering a side table where we left our tea leaves to oxidize. A regular cellar would work just as well, or even a garage. (But maybe park the car outside while your tea is oxidizing, to avoid adding the fine aroma of car exhaust.)

Reliable oven thermometer

Metal tin with an airtight lid Tea lasts much longer if kept in one of these. You can buy a fancy tea caddy, or you can reuse an old Peet's tin, which is what we do.

HOW TO DO IT

1. Have the tea bushes inspected One wrinkle we failed to foresee was that because our plants were coming from outside California, they needed to be inspected by our county's Office of Weights and Measures (California's title for its county agriculture departments) before we could put them outside. (They were also examined, en route, by California state inspectors, which added a few days to the estimated shipping time.) After a brief scare involving a mystery beetle (which turned out to be benign), the county guy lifted the quarantine. To find out whether your plants need to be inspected, contact your county's agriculture department.

2. Acclimate the plants After being shipped cross-country, the bushes were looking bedraggled. Our garden-department friends helped move them out into the test garden and then repotted them in three lovely green ceramic pots, staking them, too. The people at Camellia Forest told us that in our region, we wouldn't start seeing new growth (or picking leaves) until April. With winter coming on, we decided to leave them in the sun for the time being.

3. Transplant the plants By early spring, it was becoming clear that the bushes weren't loving the full sun, or being in pots: The leaves were spotty and blemished and the plants weren't thriving. We found a spot in dappled shade and dug three relatively shallow holes, maybe 16 inches deep. Like citrus trees, tea bushes don't like their crowns (where the stem meets the roots) covered with earth, so we were careful not to plant them too deep. According to what we had read, tea plants do best at higher elevations, where the summers are warm and wet and the winters dry and moderately cold—the opposite of our weather. But we also had read that they can "prosper surprisingly well in a range of adverse climatic conditions, tolerating dry summers and wet winters." And we had seen plenty of healthy, happy ornamental camellias growing in Northern California. So we crossed our fingers and waited. (For more on how to grow *C. sinensis*, see the tea entry under the Spring Garden, page 211).

4. Harvest the leaves (April) According to the people at Camellia Forest, we were supposed to pick 1 or 2 of the newly growing leaves *and* the leaf bud on each stem. At this early stage of the bush's life, the idea is to leave a couple new leaves on the stem unpicked, so some growing gets done. Then, after a week or two, you can go back and pick from that stem again. We played it safe: On our first sweep, we ended up with only about 25 leaves or buds. (We had to combine the leaves from all three plants to get that total; someday, we're hoping to have enough leaves from each bush so that we can try making single-variety teas.) We picked them in the morning, having read that

Newly transplanted *Camellia sinensis*

tea leaves picked in the afternoon can have unpleasantly higher levels of tannin.

5. Wither the leaves Basically, the first step in making black tea from our leaves was simple: Just spread the leaves out on the baking sheet for the rest of the day to let them wilt. Keep checking them—if the room is too dry or you leave them too long, some of the smaller leaves might dry to a crisp. You want them sad and wilty looking, like salad that's been left out too long. For us, that took from about ten in the morning until six that night.

6. Roll the leaves Roll the wilted leaves firmly, one at a time, between your fingers and thumbs. You're supposed to be bruising the leaves to release their enzymes, and you'll know you're doing it hard enough if you can feel the juices in the leaves being released. Then spread out the needle-shaped rolled leaves on the baking sheet.

7. Ferment the leaves This just means letting the leaves sit for a few hours or days to oxidize until all the green color is gone and they're completely brown. We let our first batch sit for 3 full days in the wine cellar, and by the end of that time, there were still patches of green amid the

Picking tender new leaves   Transplanting the young tea bushes

brown. At that point, since it was a Friday, we moved on to the next step. With our second batch of leaves (which we picked a couple weeks later), we gave them 5 days. Even so, we still saw a few hints of green.

8. Dry the leaves Although the tea looked plenty dry to us, we decided to follow Camellia Forest's instructions to dry the tea, still on its baking sheet, in a 250°F oven for 20 to 25 minutes. We let it cool thoroughly (for a few hours) and transferred the leaves carefully into our metal tin.

9. Brew the tea The finished product, once we poured briskly boiling water into a teapot with our precious tablespoonful of tea leaves and let it steep for 5 minutes, was more delicate than we had hoped, though it definitely had a tealike scent and a tannic afterbite. At this point, milk would probably have overwhelmed it. For our next harvest, we'll try picking the leaves in the afternoon—maybe that extra tannin will help add some body—and we'll let them oxidize for however long it takes for the leaves to turn entirely brown. And Team Cow will provide the milk.

HELPFUL INFORMATION

BOOKS

- In *For All the Tea in China: How England Stole the World's Favorite Drink and Changed History* (Viking, 2010), journalist Sarah Rose tells the tale of how Robert Fortune (he was kind of a nineteenth-century botanical equivalent to Indiana Jones) smuggled tea plants from China to India on behalf of the British East India Company.
- Sadly out of print but worth looking for used, *A Time for Tea* (Knopf, 1991), by British writer Jason Goodwin, is a beautifully and quirkily written history of tea through the ages.
- *The Tea Enthusiast's Handbook*, Mary Lou Heiss and Robert J. Heiss (Ten Speed Press, 2010), gives a good overall introduction to the topic of tea, with in-depth descriptions of the most famous types.

OTHER RESOURCES

- This link to the University of Florida IFAS Extension page leads to growing information aimed, of course, at gardeners living in Florida, but has helpful advice even for those living elsewhere: www.edis.ifas.ufl .edu/hs308.
- Here is the link to the Google Answers page that led us to Camellia Forest Nursery and provided lots of useful (albeit undocumented) information: www.answers.google.com/answers/threadview/ id/566527.html.
- On Google Books, we found a scanned copy of a classic prewar work on tea production that we're looking forward to reading, called *Indian Tea: Its Culture and Manufacture of Tea*, written by Claud Bald and published in Calcutta in 1903.

—Christine Ryan

THE SPRING RECIPES

❋ RADISHES, FRESH HOMEMADE BUTTER, AND SALT

This classic country French hors d'oeuvre could not be easier. And when both the radishes and butter are very fresh, it is delicious.

MAKES 6 servings TIME about 5 minutes

24 juicy, just-picked radishes
Unsalted butter, homemade (page 154) or store-bought
Fine sea salt

Cut the bigger radishes in half and leave smaller ones whole. Serve with butter, salt, and a butter knife or two.

PER SERVING (4 RADISHES AND 3/4 TEASPOON BUTTER) 28 cal., 93% (26 cal.) from fat; 0.15 g protein; 2.9 g fat (1.8 g sat.); 0.61 g carbo (0.28 g fiber); 7.4 mg sodium; 7.6 mg chol.

❋ FAVAS AND RICOTTA ON BUTTERMILK CRACKERS

Plump fava beans and milky-sweet ricotta are as springy as spring gets. A little bit of mint adds an extra spark. We used true peppermint, which is more mentholated than regular grocery-store spearmint, but spearmint works, too (use a little more of it).

Unless they are very small, when you can eat them pod and all, favas need to be shelled, and then each bean popped out of its tough skin. This takes a little time, but it is easy to do and strangely relaxing, like knitting. Do it while you're watching TV.

MAKES 8 servings (16 crackers) TIME about 45 minutes

Fine sea salt
3 pounds fava beans in the pod
16 Buttermilk Crackers (recipe follows)
  or store-bought crackers
1 cup ricotta cheese, homemade (page 117)
  or store-bought
About 1/2 cup finely sliced fresh peppermint leaves
About 1/4 cup extra virgin olive oil

1. Bring a small pot of salted water to a boil. Meanwhile, shell the fava beans (you will have about 2 cups beans). Boil the beans for 2 minutes. Drain into a colander and rinse with cold running water until cool.

2. To peel the tough skin from each bean, tear it open at the bean's round end with your fingernail or a paring knife and then pop out the bean.

3. Spread the crackers with a thin layer of ricotta and top with the mint and then the favas. Arrange on a platter, sprinkle with salt and drizzle with the oil.

MAKE AHEAD You can prepare the favas up to 1 day ahead and store them in an airtight container in the refrigerator.

PER SERVING 496 cal., 45% (226 cal.) from fat; 22 g protein; 26 g fat (8.7 g sat.); 57 g carbo (4.4 g fiber); 1,213 mg sodium; 32 mg chol.

BUTTERMILK CRACKERS

Homemade crackers are surprisingly easy to make and taste much fresher than the average store-bought cracker. If you have made your own butter (page 154), use the leftover buttermilk to make these crackers.

MAKES 16 crackers, each 2 by 4 inches TIME about 40 minutes

2 cups whole-wheat flour* or whole-wheat pastry flour, plus more for dusting
2 teaspoons fine sea salt, plus more for sprinkling (optional)
1½ teaspoons crushed dried red serrano or árbol chiles (about 2 chiles)
4 tablespoons cold unsalted butter, homemade (page 154) or store-bought, cut into small cubes
²⁄₃ cup Homemade Buttermilk (154) or whole milk
1 tablespoon honey
About ¼ cup extra-virgin olive oil

1. Preheat oven to 375°F. In a food processor, whirl together the flour, salt, and chile. Add the butter and pulse until the mixture looks like fine cornmeal. Pour in the buttermilk and honey and pulse just until incorporated.

2. Turn the dough out onto a lightly floured work surface, form into a ball, and then divide the ball in half. Set half of the dough aside and cover it with a damp kitchen towel to keep it from drying out.

3. Pat the remaining dough half into a rough rectangle, dust with flour, and roll out into a paper-thin rectangle. Trim off any ragged edges. (You can save the scraps and reroll them, though the resulting crackers will be a little tough.) Gently roll the dough around the rolling pin, and then unroll it onto a rimmed baking sheet. Using the tip of a sharp knife, score it into eight 2-by-4-inch rectangles. Brush with half of the oil and sprinkle very lightly with salt. Repeat with the remaining dough half. Poke both dough sheets all over with a fork.

4. Bake for 8 minutes, then switch the pan positions and rotate the pans back to front. Continue to bake until the dough is a pale brown with some slightly darker edges, about 3 minutes longer. Let cool on the pans on racks, then break into individual crackers along the scored lines.

* *We used 'Sonora' soft white wheat flour because it's local and because we like its delicate flavor and slightly nubbly texture in these crackers. But regular whole-wheat flour*

or whole-wheat pastry flour will work too. See the Allure of Local Wheat, page 156, for more on local flours.

MAKE AHEAD The crackers will keep for up to 1 week in an airtight container at room temperature.

PER CRACKER 118 cal., 50% (59 cal.) from fat; 2.6 g protein; 6.8 g fat (2.4 g sat.); 13.3 g carbo (2 g fiber); 292 mg sodium; 8 mg chol.

GOUDA GOUGÈRES

Choux pastry, made with just eggs, salt, butter, and flour, is the basis for all kinds of rich treats—éclairs, profiteroles, cream puffs, and these tasty, cheesy morsels.

MAKES 25 to 30 small puffs TIME about 40 minutes

4 tablespoons unsalted butter, homemade (page 154) or store-bought, cut into cubes
¼ teaspoon fine sea salt
½ cup whole-wheat pastry flour* mixed with ¼ cup whole-wheat flour
2 large eggs
2 ounces aged Gouda, homemade (page 122) or store-bought, coarsely shredded (about ½ cup)
½ teaspoon minced fresh rosemary

1. Preheat the oven to 425°F. Line 2 rimmed baking sheets with parchment paper.

2. In a heavy-bottomed medium saucepan, combine the butter, salt, and ½ cup water and bring to a rolling boil over high heat. Remove from the heat, add the flour all at once, and vigorously stir with a wooden spoon until smooth and shiny. Stir in the eggs, one at a time, mixing in the first egg completely before adding the second one. Stir in the cheese and then the rosemary.

3. Spoon the dough into a pastry bag fitted with a ½-inch plain tip. Pipe the dough onto the prepared baking sheets in 1 tablespoon mounds, spacing them about 1 inch apart. Or, snip a ½-inch hole in one corner of a resealable plastic bag, fill the bag with the dough, and use it to pipe the dough.

4. Bake for 10 minutes, then switch pan positions and rotate the pans back to front. Reduce the heat to 300°F and continue to bake until the puffs are golden brown, 10 to 12 minutes more. Serve warm.

*   We used freshly milled 'Sonora' soft white wheat flour because it is the closest local substitute for commercial whole-wheat pastry flour. See the Allure of Local Wheat, page 156, for more about local flours.

MAKE AHEAD You can freeze the puffs for up to 2 weeks. Let cool, then put in a resealable plastic bag and freeze. To serve, reheat in a 350°F oven for 8 minutes.

PER GOUGÈRE 36 cal., 61% (22 cal.) from fat; 1.2 g protein; 2.4 g fat (1.4 g sat.); 2.4 g carbo (0.4 g fiber); 39 mg sodium; 20 mg chol.

CARROT AND BEET CHIPS

Why not go beyond the potato and make seasonal chips? We love how colorful and flavorful these are. We used extra virgin olive oil to stay within our One-Block pantry, but it would be a waste otherwise, since the oil is expensive and high heat destroys its nuances. Several other cheaper, more neutral-flavored oils, such as safflower or canola, have a higher smoke point and would be ideal.

MAKES about 2 ounces carrot chips (2 cups) and about 1 ounce (1 1/2 cups) for each kind of beet chip
TIME about 1 hour

3 very large carrots, at least 1 1/2 inches in diameter, peeled and cut into 4-inch lengths
3 beets of any variety, about 5 ounces each, trimmed and peeled
Extra virgin olive oil for deep-frying
1 1/2 to 2 teaspoons fine sea salt

1. Using a mandoline or other handheld slicer, slice the carrots paper-thin lengthwise. Thinly slice the beets, slicing any red beets last so they don't stain the others.

(continued)

2. Pour the oil to a depth of 1/2 inch into a large frying pan and heat over medium-high heat to 375°F on a deep-frying thermometer. (Some olive oils have lower smoke points; if your oil starts smoking, reduce the heat until the thermometer registers 360°F).

3. Working in small batches, fry the carrot chips first, then the beet chips, stirring occasionally with a slotted spoon, until they are crisp, 1 to 2 minutes. Transfer to a double thickness of paper towels laid over a paper bag to drain. Return the oil to 375°F before frying each batch.

4. Sprinkle the chips with salt while they're hot.

MAKE AHEAD You can fry the chips up to 2 days ahead and store them in an airtight container at room temperature. If they get soggy, spread them in a single layer on a rimmed baking sheet and reheat in a 250°F oven for 10 minutes. Let them cool for at least 10 minutes in a single layer before serving.

PER 1/4 CUP CARROTS 51 cal., 61% (31 cal.) from fat; 0.47 g protein; 3.6 g fat (0.52 g sat.); 4.8 g carbo (1.4 g fiber); 401 mg sodium; 0 mg chol.
PER 1/4 CUP BEETS 50 cal., 62% (31 cal.) from fat; 0.76 g protein; 3.6 g fat (0.51 g sat.); 4.5 g carbo (1.3 g fiber); 403 mg sodium; 0 mg chol.

GARDEN BORSCHT

This is a gentle, fabulous soup that owes its subtle grace to fennel seeds that we harvested from our plants at the end of their cycle, when they stood nearly six feet tall.

MAKES 6 servings TIME about 1 1/2 hours

About 2 pounds large beets, with tops intact
1 tablespoon extra virgin olive oil
1 white onion, chopped
1 carrot, peeled and chopped
1 clove garlic, minced
1 tablespoon crushed fennel seeds (see page 98 for details on how to harvest)
4 cups Herb Vegetable Broth (page 140)
1/4 cup plus 4 teaspoons coarsely chopped fresh dill
2 teaspoons fine sea salt
Créme fraîche, homemade (page 70) or store-bought, for serving

1. Trim the leafy tops from the beets and chop them, including the stems. Peel the beets, quarter them through the stem end, and then thinly slice each quarter crosswise. Set the tops and beets aside.

2. In a large pot, heat the oil over medium heat. Add the onion, carrot, garlic, and fennel seeds and cook, stirring often, until the vegetables have softened, about 4 minutes. Add the beet tops, then pour in the broth, 3 1/2 cups water, and the 1/4 cup dill. Cover, bring to a simmer, and cook, stirring occasionally, until the beets have softened and the flavors have blended, about 1 hour.

3. Season the soup with the salt, then serve dolloped with crème fraîche and some of the remaining dill.

PER SERVING 112 cal., 39% (44 cal.) from fat; 2.6 g protein; 5.1 g fat (0.73 g sat.); 16 g carbo (4.4 g fiber); 1,396 mg sodium; 0 mg chol.

❋ MESCLUN SALAD WITH SPRING BEETS AND DILL

Lettuces are one of the most rewarding crops in the backyard garden. They are easy to grow, and you can harvest the young, tender leaves right before dinner to make a salad that is as fresh as it gets.

MAKES 4 to 6 generous servings TIME about 20 minutes

$^1/_2$ teaspoon finely shredded lemon zest

2 tablespoons freshly squeezed lemon juice

$^1/_2$ teaspoon sea salt

$^1/_4$ cup extra virgin olive oil

3 small to medium red and golden beets
('Chioggia', 'Bull's Blood', or other red beet, and
golden), trimmed and peeled

8 cups loosely packed mesclun (baby lettuces)

$^1/_2$ cup small sprigs dill

1. In a small bowl, whisk together the lemon zest, lemon juice, and salt, then whisk in the oil.

2. Slice the beets into paper-thin rounds, preferably with a mandoline or other handheld slicer. Slice red beets last so they don't stain the others. Put the red beet slices in a medium bowl and toss with 1 tablespoon of the dressing to coat evenly.

3. In a large shallow bowl, toss together the mesclun, dill, and any light-colored beet slices. Drizzle on the remaining dressing and toss to coat evenly. Tuck in the red beet slices.

PER SERVING 110 cal., 74% (81 cal.) from fat; 1.8 g protein; 9.4 g fat (1.3 g sat.); 7.8 g carbo (2.3 g fiber); 230 mg sodium; 0 mg chol.

NASTURTIUM SALAD WITH OMELET RIBBONS

Nasturtiums have been self-seeding at random in the Sunset garden for several years. They are at their peak in spring and early summer, blooming in billowy clusters of orange and yellow—and were hard to ignore when we were snipping lettuces for this salad.

MAKES 4 to 6 servings TIME about 20 minutes

1 tablespoon freshly squeezed lemon juice

1$^1/_2$ teaspoons honey

$^1/_8$ teaspoon plus $^1/_4$ teaspoon fine sea salt

2 tablespoons plus 1 teaspoon extra virgin olive oil

3 large eggs

3 cups loosely packed nasturtium leaves, stems
removed

3 cups loosely packed mesclun (baby lettuces)

1 to 2 cups nasturtium blossoms, stems removed

1. In a small bowl, whisk together the lemon juice, honey, and $^1/_8$ teaspoon salt. Whisk in 2 tablespoons of the oil.

2. In a 10-inch nonstick frying pan, heat the remaining 1 teaspoon oil over medium heat. Meanwhile, in another small bowl, whisk together the eggs and the remaining $^1/_4$ teaspoon salt until well blended.

3. When the oil is hot, pour the eggs into the pan. As the eggs begin to set, lift the edge with a spatula and tilt the pan to let the uncooked mixture on top flow underneath. Work your way around the omelet, lifting one section of the edge at a time and tilting the pan, until the omelet is set underneath. Continue to cook until the top is only slightly moist, 1 to 2 minutes.

4. Slide the omelet onto a heatproof plate. Invert the pan over the plate and, holding the pan and plate together with pot holders, flip them over together so the omelet falls back into the pan. Return the omelet to the heat until the underneath is just set, 1 to 2 minutes more. Slide the omelet onto a cutting board and cut into ribbons $^1/_4$ inch wide.

(continued)

5. In a serving bowl, combine the nasturtium leaves, mesclun, and omelet ribbons and toss gently to mix. Drizzle on the dressing and toss again. Sprinkle with the nasturtium blossoms and serve.

PER SERVING 92 cal., 75% (69 cal.) from fat; 3.6 g protein; 8 g fat (1.6 g sat.); 2.4 g carbo (0.25 g fiber); 184 mg sodium; 106 mg chol.

WHOLE-LEAF RADISH AND HERB SALAD

Instead of lettuces, this salad has lots of just-picked herbs plus radish leaves, which have a lovely, fresh, "green" taste.

MAKES 4 to 6 servings TIME about 20 minutes, plus 30 minutes to chill

3 cups loosely packed small, tender radish leaves (or use larger, tender leaves torn into pieces)
2 cups quartered radishes
2 cups loosely packed small fresh flat-leaf parsley leaves
3/4 cup loosely packed small sprigs dill
3/4 cup loosely packed sprigs chervil
3/4 cup loosely packed fresh tarragon leaves
1 teaspoon Syrah Vinegar (page 113) or 1 1/2 teaspoons other red-wine vinegar
1/2 teaspoon fine sea salt
3 tablespoons extra-virgin olive oil

1. In a large serving bowl, combine the radish leaves, radishes, parsley, dill, chervil, and tarragon. Cover and chill for about 30 minutes to crisp the leaves.

2. In a small bowl, whisk together the vinegar and salt, then whisk in the oil to make a dressing. Drizzle the dressing over the salad and toss gently to coat evenly. Season with salt to taste.

PER SERVING 99 cal., 67% (66 cal.) from fat; 3 g protein; 7.7 g fat (1.1 g sat.); 6 g carbo (1.8 g fiber); 234 mg sodium; 0 mg chol.

❦ GRILLED CARROT SALAD

We grew 'Nantes' carrots, an exceptionally sweet and juicy French variety with rounded tips. You can often find them at farmers' markets, too.

MAKES 6 servings TIME about 30 minutes, plus 1 hour to marinate

1/3 cup extra virgin olive oil
3 tablespoons Syrah Vinegar (page 113) or 4 tablespoons other red-wine vinegar
1/2 teaspoon fine sea salt
3 tablespoons fresh thyme leaves
1 1/2 pounds carrots
3 green onions, ends trimmed and halved crosswise

1. In a large bowl, whisk together the oil, vinegar, salt, and 2 tablespoons of the thyme leaves. Add the carrots and green onions, turn to coat evenly, and marinate at room temperature for about 1 hour.

2. Prepare a grill for medium heat (350° to 450°F; you should be able to hold your hand above the cooking grate for only 5 to 7 seconds).

3. Lift the carrots out of the marinade onto the grill and cook, turning often with tongs, until charred on all sides and tender when poked with a paring knife, about 10 minutes for smaller carrots and 15 minutes for larger ones. About 5 minutes before the carrots have finished cooking, lift the green onions out of the marinade, reserving the marinade, and cook them, turning once, until charred and softened on both sides, about 5 minutes total. As the carrots and green onions are done, return them to the marinade.

4. Transfer the carrots to a cutting board and cut each carrot on the diagonal into 3 equal pieces. Return the carrot pieces to the marinade and toss with the onions.

5. Arrange the carrots and green onions on a large serving platter (discard the marinade) and sprinkle with the remaining 2 tablespoons thyme leaves.

PER SERVING 157 cal., 69% (108 cal.) from fat; 1.3 g protein; 13 g fat (1.8 g sat.); 12 g carbo (3.5 g fiber); 267 mg sodium; 0 mg chol.

Opposite page: Grilled Carrot Salad (bottom); Mesclun Salad with Spring Beets and Dill (page 226)

ROASTED BEETS AND TOPS WITH TARRAGON

We especially like the deep, earthy sweetness of red beets in this recipe, but you can use any kind of beet.

MAKES 4 to 6 servings TIME about 1¼ hours

About 3 pounds large beets, with tops intact
4 tablespoons extra virgin olive oil
¼ cup fresh tarragon leaves
¼ teaspoon fine sea salt

1. Preheat the oven to 350°F. Trim the leafy tops, including stems, from the beets, rinse thoroughly, and set aside. Arrange the beets in a roasting pan just large enough to hold them in a single layer. Drizzle the beets with 1 tablespoon of the olive oil and cover the pan with aluminum foil.

2. Bake the beets until tender when pierced with a knife, about 50 minutes. Set aside until cool enough to handle.

3. While the beets are cooking, roughly chop the reserved beet tops, including the stems. Heat 1 tablespoon of the olive oil in a large pot over medium-low heat. Add the chopped beet tops and stems and pour in ¾ cup water. Cover and cook, stirring often, until they are wilted and tender, about 30 minutes.

4. Peel the beets, cut into large chunks, and add them to the beet tops in the pot. Stir in the tarragon and salt.

5. Turn the mixture into a serving dish and drizzle with the remaining 2 tablespoons oil.

PER SERVING 164 cal., 51% (84 cal.) from fat; 4.2 g protein; 9.7 g fat (1.4 g sat.); 18 g carbo (7 g fiber); 382 mg sodium; 0 mg chol.

FRESH PICKLED BEETS

This super-easy small-batch pickle is stored in the refrigerator (no canning required). We used our homemade Syrah Vinegar, which gives the pickles a tart, fruity depth.

If you want to can your own pickles using homemade vinegar, you'll need a recipe designed for canning, because proportions of ingredients are important for safety; for details, see the "USDA Complete Guide to Home Canning," (www.uga.edu/nchfp/index.html), and also follow their directions for water bath processing. Also, homemade

vinegars can vary in acidity, so you'll need to measure the percent of acidity (acetic acid) in your vinegar to be sure it's the same as what's listed on the bottle of commercial vinegar called for in the canning recipe. You can do a quick check with a Country Acid Test Kit ($8.95) from the Beverage People (www.thebeveragepeople.com or 800/544-1867); ask to have the instructions for titrating vinegar included.

MAKES about 1¾ cups beets, plus pickling liquid
TIME about 1 hour, plus at least 3 hours to chill

1 pound red beets
3 tablespoons honey
1½ teaspoons fine sea salt
⅓ cup Syrah Vinegar (page 113) or ½ cup other red-wine vinegar

1. Trim the leafy tops off the beets, leaving about 1 inch of the stem intact. (Reserve the tops for another use.) Put the beets in a saucepan with just enough water to cover, cover the pan, and bring to a boil over high heat. Reduce the heat to a simmer and cook until the beets are just tender when pierced with the tip of a sharp knife, about 20 minutes.

2. Drain the beets and let them cool until they can be handled. Peel, slice into ½-inch-thick rounds or wedges, and put the pieces into a heatproof bowl.

3. Meanwhile, in another saucepan, bring the honey, salt, and 2 cups water to a boil over high heat. Reduce the heat to a simmer and cook until the honey dissolves. Add the vinegar and stir well; pour over the beets.

4. Let cool, then cover and chill for at least 3 hours to let the flavors develop.

MAKE AHEAD The pickled beets will keep in the refrigerator for up to 2 weeks.

PER 1/2-CUP SERVING 58 cal., 0% (1 cal.) from fat; 1.1 g protein; 0.11 g fat (0.02 g sat.); 14 g carbo (1.3 g fiber); 530 mg sodium; 0 mg chol.

PICKLED EGGS

You can also put a few peeled hard-cooked eggs in with your beets, if you like. Add the whole eggs to the bowl of beets before you pour in the hot vinegar mixture. After 2 to 3 days of pickling, the whites will have acquired a brilliant outer ring of fuchsia, the yolks will have remained a vivid yellow, and the eggs will taste pleasantly pickled. They are best eaten right away. After 4 days or more, they will start to get rubbery.

PER EGG 78 cal., 62% (48 cal.) from fat; 6.3 g protein; 5.3 g fat (1.6 g sat.); 0.56 g carbo (0 g fiber); 62 mg sodium; 212 mg chol.

. . . .

FIVE WAYS WITH FRESH EGGS

When your backyard hens are just starting to lay eggs, it's nice to get to know them in the simplest possible recipes—you'll immediately see (and taste) how different they are from industrial eggs. For the following methods, we are assuming that your eggs are standard large (2 ounces in the shell). If they are small or jumbo, adjust the timings by a minute in either direction.

1 FRIED, OVER EASY

Use your most slick-surfaced, well-seasoned frying pan. It should be large enough to allow a bit of space around each egg so you can turn them easily. Heat the pan over medium-low heat until hot, then add a bit of unsalted butter, homemade (page 154) or store-bought. When the butter has foamed up and settled back and is just beginning to brown, crack an egg on your countertop, hold it close to the pan's surface, and open it into the pan. Repeat with another egg, being careful not to crowd them. Sprinkle with fine sea salt and let cook until the white is almost set (touch it to test). Gently turn each egg over (we like to use a spatula in each hand) and

remove the pan from the heat. Let the eggs sit in the pan for 30 seconds, then serve.

2 SCRAMBLED

Use the same well-seasoned frying pan you would use for frying eggs, above, and heat it over medium heat until hot. Meanwhile, crack the eggs into a bowl and sprinkle them with fine sea salt (and fresh minced herbs, if you like), but don't mix them. Add some unsalted butter, homemade (page 154) or store-bought, to the hot pan, let it foam up and settle back, and then pour in the eggs. When the whites are just starting to set, stir the eggs with a wooden spoon to mix the whites with the yolks. Keep stirring until they are almost but not quite as set as you like (they will continue to cook off the heat). Serve right away.

3 POACHED

Fill a saucepan with enough water to cover the eggs you are cooking and bring to a gentle simmer. At the same time, pour water to a depth of about $1^1/_2$ inches into a large frying pan and bring to a gentle simmer. Gently lower the eggs, still in their shells, no more than two at a time, into the saucepan of water. Simmer for 15 seconds to set the outermost layer of egg white, then lift out.

(continued)

Whisking eggs for an omelet

Crack 1 egg into a spouted measuring cup, then touch the spout to the surface of the simmering water in the frying pan and slip the egg into the water. Repeat with the remaining eggs. Cook the eggs until they look softly set, 2 to 3 minutes. Lift them out with a slotted spoon, slide them onto warmed plates, and serve right away.

MAKE AHEAD You can poach the eggs as directed, then arrange them in a single layer in a glass or ceramic baking dish, cover the dish, and refrigerate for up to 2 days (yes, really). To reheat, pour water to a depth of $1^1/_2$ inches into a large frying pan and heat until steaming hot (but not quite boiling). Gently lower the eggs into the water and let stand until they feel hot to the touch, about 5 minutes. Lift out the eggs with a slotted spoon and serve right away.

4 SOFT COOKED

This method produces tender but completely cooked whites and yolks that are still liquid in the center. They are not boiled, so we don't use this word to describe them. (To hard-cook eggs for use in salads or sandwiches, see page 241.) If the eggs are chilled, first bring them to room temperature, which helps keep them from cracking. Put the eggs into a saucepan just big enough to hold them, add warm water to cover by 1 inch, and let sit for about 5 minutes. Remove them from the water and bring the water to a boil. Gently lower the room-temperature eggs into the water, turning down the heat until it is at a barely bubbling simmer (a few bubbles rise from the bottom of the pan but don't break the surface). Simmer the eggs, uncovered, for 6 minutes. Remove from the water and let sit for 3 to 4 minutes before eating.

5 OMELET

Heat a 10-inch nonstick frying pan over medium heat. Whisk together 6 eggs, $1/_2$ teaspoon fine sea salt, and about 2 tablespoons minced fresh herbs (fines herbes—a mix of chervil, parsley, chives, and tarragon—is especially good). Add 2 teaspoons unsalted butter, homemade (page 154) or store-bought, to the pan. Once the butter is foaming but before it starts to brown, pour in the eggs and reduce the heat to low. As the eggs begin to set, lift one edge with a spatula and tilt the pan to let the uncooked mixture on top flow underneath. Work your way around the omelet, lifting one section of the edge at a time and tilting the pan, until the omelet is set underneath. Cover and cook until the top is set but still quite moist, 1 to 2 minutes. If you like, spoon some ricotta, homemade (page 117) or store-bought, over one-half of the omelet,

and gently fold the other half on top. Slide onto a warmed plate and serve right away. SERVES 3 TO 4.

....

❈ FAVA LEAF AND PARSLEY QUICHE

We like growing fava plants not only for their tasty beans, but also for their broad, abundant, easy-to-pick leaves, which have an earthy-sweet, faintly grassy flavor and can be cooked and eaten as you would spinach.

We borrowed our method for the quiche from a wonderful recipe in Thomas Keller's *Bouchon*.

MAKES one 10-inch quiche, or 8 servings TIME about 1 hour, plus $1^1/_2$ hours to chill and about 1 hour to cool

CRUST
$1^1/_2$ cups whole-wheat flour,* plus more for dusting
$1/_2$ teaspoon fine sea salt
$3/_4$ cup cold unsalted butter, homemade (page 154) or store-bought, cut into small cubes
$1/_4$ cup ice water

FILLING
2 teaspoons extra virgin olive oil
$1^1/_2$ teaspoons minced garlic
6 ounces baby fava or spinach leaves
$1/_3$ cup chopped green onions
1 cup fresh flat-leaf parsley leaves
$1/_2$ teaspoon fine sea salt

CUSTARD
$1^3/_4$ cups whole milk
$1^3/_4$ cups heavy cream
5 large eggs
1 teaspoon fine sea salt

1. To make the dough for the crust, put the flour and salt in a food processor and whirl briefly to blend. Add the butter and pulse until the mixture looks like cornmeal. Add the ice water and pulse again until the dough comes together, about 30 seconds. Turn the dough out onto a work surface and press into a disk. Wrap in plastic wrap and chill for at least 1 hour and up to 1 day.

2. Lightly dust a work surface with flour. Unwrap the dough, place it on the floured surface, and let it warm up for 15 minutes. With a floured rolling pin, roll out the dough into a 12-inch round. Roll the round gently around the rolling pin, then unroll over a 10-inch deep-dish pie pan. Press the dough evenly onto the bottom and up the

sides of the pan, fold the overhang under itself to create a high edge on the pan rim, and crimp or flute the edge. Chill for at least 30 minutes. Meanwhile, position an oven rack on the lowest rung in the oven and preheat the oven to 325°F.

3. Line the chilled crust with parchment paper and fill with pie weights or dried beans. Bake the crust on the bottom oven rack for 25 minutes. Remove the pie weights and parchment and continue to bake until the crust is slightly browned and looks dry, about 10 minutes more. Remove the crust from the oven and set it on a rimmed baking sheet. Raise the oven temperature to 375°F.

4. While the oven is heating, make the filling. In a large frying pan, heat the oil over medium heat. Add the garlic, fava leaves, green onions, parsley, and salt and cook, stirring often, until the leaves are wilted, about 4 minutes. Transfer the mixture to a cutting board and chop the leaves coarsely, then arrange evenly over the bottom of the warm crust.

5. To make the custard, heat the milk and cream in a large heavy-bottomed saucepan over high heat, just until the mixture begins to simmer. Remove from the heat. Put the eggs in a blender, add half of the hot milk mixture, and whirl for a few seconds to combine. Add the salt and the remaining hot milk mixture and whirl again just to combine. Pour the mixture into the crust, being careful to keep the greens evenly distributed.

6. Bake the quiche on the lowest rack until slightly browned around the edges and beginning to puff in the center, about 25 minutes. Let cool to warm or room temperature before serving.

*   We used finely milled 'Sonora' soft white wheat flour because it makes a particularly tender crust. Any whole-wheat flour will work in this recipe, however. Higher-protein flours (made with hard red or spring wheat) will produce a firmer, denser crust. See the Allure of Local Wheat, page 156, for more information on local flours.

PER SERVING 512 cal., 75% (386 cal.) from fat; 11 g protein; 43 g fat (25 g sat.); 24 g carbo (4 g fiber); 688 mg sodium; 255 mg chol.

ARE BACKYARD EGGS BETTER FOR YOU?

In 2007, *Mother Earth News* magazine, using an accredited, independent lab, tested eggs from fourteen different pasture-raised flocks around the United States for their nutritional content. Here is how the figures compare to data on commercial eggs, supplied by the U.S. Department of Agriculture.

Pastured eggs versus commercial eggs

- one-third less cholesterol
- one-third less saturated fat
- two-thirds more vitamin A
- two times more omega-3 fatty acids
- three times more vitamin E
- three times more beta-carotene
- at least three times more vitamin D

The *Mother Earth* hens roamed around all day, pecking up green plants, seeds, insects, worms, and some grain supplement. Our Sunset flock doesn't have free range of the garden (they tend to eat our tender seedlings to the nub), so they can't qualify as "pasture raised." We feed them organic layer pellets and greens from our kitchen, with occasional fruit and a few snails, and they do have the occasional (supervised) outing.

We were curious to see how eggs like ours—from average, not-very-cooped-up but not-pastured-either hens—would stack up nutritionally, since many backyard chicken owners have a similar setup. We sent off a dozen eggs to Columbia Food Laboratories in Corbett, Oregon, for testing, focusing on four nutrients: cholesterol

and saturated fat (the "bad" stuff), and omega-3s and vitamin D (two of the "good" elements). Current research suggests that vitamin D in particular may have all kinds of health benefits, including helping build bones, boost muscle strength, and reduce inflammation.

The results? Unimpressive when it comes to cholesterol and omega-3s (we were quite sad about this, but science doesn't lie). We are happy to report, however, that our eggs have *half* the saturated fat of commercial eggs—even less than pastured!—and *three times* the amount of vitamin D. If you are interested in getting your eggs tested, contact Columbia Food Laboratories, www.columbiafoodlab .com. or 503/695-2287.

3. In a glass measuring cup, combine the honey and lemon zest and microwave until beginning to bubble, about 30 seconds. Let cool about 5 minutes.

4. Drizzle the warm honey over the berries and fromage blanc. Top each bowl with 1 or 2 of the reserved berries.

* *Store-bought fromage blanc is often much drier than homemade fromage blanc. If you use it, stir in enough heavy cream (at least 3 tablespoons) to give it the consistency of softened cream cheese.*

PER SERVING 263 cal., 39% (103 cal.) from fat; 5.3 g protein; 11 g fat (6.8 g sat.); 36 g carbo (1.6 g fiber); 351 mg sodium; 44 mg chol.

STRAWBERRY CREPES

Although supremely easy, these breakfast crepes are elegant, too.

MAKES 6 servings TIME about 25 minutes

¹/₂ cup unsalted butter, homemade (page 154)
or store-bought
¹/₂ cup honey
4 cups hulled and quartered strawberries
12 small Whole-Wheat Crepes, made in a 6-inch pan
(page 185)

1. In a large frying pan, melt the butter over medium heat. Add the honey and strawberries and cook until the strawberries have begun to release their juices, about 2 minutes. Remove from the heat.

2. Fold each crepe in half and then in half again to form a triangle. On each of 6 plates, arrange 2 triangles, overlapping them. Spoon the strawberries and their sauce over the crepes.

PER SERVING 475 cal., 51% (244 cal.) from fat; 8.9 g protein; 28 g fat (16 g sat.); 52 g carbo (5.1 g fiber); 284 mg sodium; 184 mg chol.

❊ STRAWBERRIES WITH FROMAGE BLANC AND LEMON HONEY

Although technically a fresh cheese, fromage blanc tastes like a thicker, silkier version of sour cream, and is terrific with strawberries.

MAKES 6 servings TIME about 30 minutes

1¹/₄ cups (about 9 ounces) fromage blanc, homemade
(page 118) or store-bought*
¹/₄ cup heavy cream
2 pints strawberries, preferably small
¹/₂ cup honey
Finely shredded zest of 1¹/₂ lemons

1. In a bowl, whisk together the fromage blanc and cream until very smooth. Divide the mixture among 6 shallow bowls.

2. Set aside 6 to 12 small, perfect berries. Hull the remaining berries and halve or quarter lengthwise if large. Scatter the berries over the bowls of fromage blanc.

3. Fill a large bowl with ice cubes and water. Pour the puree through a fine-mesh strainer into a medium bowl, pressing the mixture with a spoon to extract as much liquid as possible. Discard the contents of the strainer. Set the bowl in the ice bath and let cool completely, stirring occasionally.

4. Add the crème fraîche to the cold strawberry liquid and whisk until smooth. Freeze in an ice cream maker according to the manufacturer's directions. Eat right away, or transfer to an airtight container and freeze until completely firm, about 6 hours, before serving.

MAKE AHEAD The sherbet can be stored in the freezer for up to 1 week.

PER 1/2-CUP SERVING 144 cal., 36% (52 cal.) from fat; 1.1 g protein; 5.8 g fat (3.6 g sat.); 24 g carbo (1.6 g fiber); 38 mg sodium; 13 mg chol.

❋ STRAWBERRY LEMONADE

This refreshing lemonade is just as much about the strawberries as it is about the lemons.

MAKES 71/2 cups, or 6 servings TIME about 20 minutes

2 pints strawberries, hulled
3/4 cup honey
1 cup freshly squeezed lemon juice
**   (from 5 to 6 lemons)**
Ice cubes for serving

1. In a blender, puree the strawberries and honey. Pour through a fine-mesh strainer set over a bowl, pressing the mixture with a spoon to extract as much liquid as possible. Discard the contents of the strainer.

2. Pour the strawberry juice into a pitcher and stir in the lemon juice and 4 cups water. Serve over ice.

MAKE AHEAD The lemonade can be made up to 4 days ahead and refrigerated.

PER SERVING 83 cal., 3% (2.5 cal.) from fat; 0.84 g protein; 0.29 g fat (0.01 g sat.); 22 g carbo (2.1 g fiber); 1.9 mg sodium; 0 mg chol.

STRAWBERRY CRÈME FRAÎCHE SHERBET

Rich, tangy crème fraîche takes the place of milk in this smooth, refreshing dessert.

MAKES 4 cups TIME about 1 hour, plus time to freeze

4 cups hulled and quartered strawberries
1/2 cup honey
1 teaspoon freshly squeezed lemon juice
1/8 teaspoon fine sea salt
Ice cubes
1/2 cup crème fraîche, homemade (page 70)
**   or store-bought**

1. In a large saucepan, combine the strawberries, honey, lemon juice, salt, and 1/4 cup water and cook over medium heat, stirring often, until the strawberries have softened and the mixture is simmering, about 20 minutes.

2. Remove the strawberry mixture from the heat and puree it in batches in a blender.

A SPRING TEA PARTY
(because we could)

As soon as we learned that we could grow tea in Menlo Park, actual *Camellia sinensis*—the civilizing sip of queens and commoners alike—the idea of trying to make a tea party seized hold. Proper British afternoon tea is all about nuance and delicacy, however, and we had relatively few ingredients to pull it off.

But we were determined. In the end, the tea party food we created had a hearty note (there's no getting around that with sandwiches made with whole-wheat bread), but it mostly qualified as dainty. We added a bowl of freshly picked strawberries and some thick whipped cream sweetened with honey, and thoroughly enjoyed ourselves one spring afternoon, with our afternoon tea out in the garden.

SCONE TARTS

What is afternoon tea without scones, clotted cream, and jam? With no baking powder or baking soda, we didn't even try to make scones, knowing they would be disastrous. In their place, we made mini tarts and filled them with scone toppings. They were buttery and delicious, crumbling as soon as we put them in our mouths.

You can use any shape of tart pan you like for this recipe, as long as it is small (1 to 2 inches in diameter). Even a mini-muffin pan will work. Also, this recipe can easily be doubled.

MAKES about sixteen 2-inch tarts
TIME about 1½ hours, plus 1 hour to chill

TART CRUSTS
3/4 cup whole-wheat pastry flour*
1/8 teaspoon fine sea salt
4 tablespoons cold unsalted butter, homemade (page 154) or store-bought, cut into small cubes
2 teaspoons honey
1 to 2 tablespoons ice water

FILLINGS
About 1/4 cup clotted cream, homemade (page 239) or store-bought
About 2 tablespoons Sticky Chewy Tangerine Marmalade (page 194) or store-bought citrus marmalade
About 2 tablespoons strawberry jam, homemade** (page 240) or store-bought
About 2 tablespoons lemon curd, homemade (page 239) or store-bought
A few tangerine segments, cut in half
1 strawberry, hulled and sliced lengthwise paper-thin
Several thin lemon zest strips

1. To make the tart crusts, sift the flour and salt into a food processor (discarding any bran) and whirl briefly to blend. Add the butter and pulse until the mixture looks like shaggy fresh bread crumbs. Drizzle the honey over the mixture. Then, with the motor running, drizzle in the ice water, adding just enough for the dough to come together. Turn the dough out onto a work surface and press into a disk. Wrap in plastic wrap and refrigerate for at least 1 hour.

2. Preheat the oven to 350°F. Lightly dust a work surface with flour. Remove the dough from the refrigerator, unwrap

it, place it on the floured surface, and let it warm up for 10 minutes. For each 2-inch tart shell, pull off a ball of dough about 1½ inches in diameter and put it in the bottom of a 2-inch tart pan. With floured thumbs, gently press the dough into the pan, rotating the pan as you press, until the dough is an even ⅛ inch thick on the bottom and sides. (You can use a smaller pan, but reduce the amount of dough; it should form a layer no more than ⅛ inch thick.) Trim the dough even with the pan rim by brushing outward across the rim with your fingers.

3. Prick the bottom of each tart crust all over with a fork. If you have extra empty tart pans in the same size, fit the empty pans on top of the pastry-lined pans, to create slightly neater shells (they won't shrink as much when baked). Put the pans on a rimmed baking pan and bake until thoroughly golden, 10 to 15 minutes. Let cool completely in their pans, at least 15 minutes but no more than 1 hour (or they will start to stick).

4. Invert each tart pan and squeeze gently to release the crust. Arrange the crusts on a large platter. Fill each crust partway with clotted cream, then fill to the top with the marmalade (warmed if too thick), strawberry jam, or lemon curd. Top each tart with a piece of tangerine, a strawberry slice, or a lemon zest strip.

* We used finely milled 'Sonora' whole-wheat flour, which behaves like commercial whole-wheat pastry flour. See the Allure of Local Wheat, page 156, for more information on local flours.

** If using our Strawberry Oven Jam recipe, sweeten to taste with honey before using.

MAKE AHEAD Tart dough can be made up to 2 days ahead and refrigerated. Tart crusts can be baked up to 1 day in advance and stored in an airtight container at room temperature. The tarts can be assembled up to 1 hour before serving and kept at room temperature. (Do not refrigerate them or the crusts will become soggy.)

PER 2-INCH TART 69 cal., 57% (39 cal.) from fat; 0.63 g protein; 4.4 g fat (2.8 g sat.); 7.1 g carbo (0.75 g fiber); 32 mg sodium; 19 mg chol.

CLOTTED CREAM

A star of the English tea tray, clotted cream is produced by slowly heating pure cream until it forms a devastatingly rich, thick layer on top, which is then scooped off for slathering onto warm scones.

MAKES about 1¼ cups TIME 2 days

5 cups heavy cream (not ultrapasteurized)

1. Preheat the oven to 175°F. Pour the cream into a wide, heavy-bottomed pot, cover, and heat for at least 8 hours and up to 12 hours.

2. Remove the pot from the oven, cover, and refrigerate the cream overnight (at least 8 hours).

3. Using a wide, flat spoon, skim the thick layer of clotted cream from the chilled cream and place in a bowl or jar (reserve the remaining thin cream for another use). Cover and refrigerate until firm enough to spread, about 4 hours.

MAKE AHEAD The cream will keep, refrigerated, for up to 1 week. It will get thicker the longer it sits.

PER TABLESPOON 70 cal., 97% (68 cal.) from fat; 0 g protein; 7.5 g fat (5 g sat.); 5 g carbo (0 g fiber); 2.5 mg sodium; 23 mg chol.

LEMON CURD

You can use any citrus you like to make this rich, tangy spread. We spooned it into little tart crusts (page 237) for our one-block tea party. It is also delicious blended with vanilla ice cream or used as a cake filling.

MAKES about 1½ cups TIME about 15 minutes

½ cup unsalted butter, homemade (page 154) or store-bought
½ cup freshly squeezed lemon juice (from about 3 lemons)
⅔ cup honey
8 large egg yolks

1. In a heavy-bottomed medium saucepan, melt the butter with the lemon juice over medium-high heat. In a bowl, whisk together the honey and egg yolks until blended.

(continued)

Strawberry Oven Jam, Lemon Curd, and Clotted Cream

2. Slowly whisk the hot lemon-butter mixture into the honey-egg mixture, $1/2$ cup at a time. Pour the mixture back into the saucepan and cook over medium-high heat, whisking constantly, until the mixture is thick and just starts to boil, about 4 minutes.

3. Remove from the heat, pour into a bowl or other container, and press plastic wrap directly onto the surface to prevent a skin from forming. Let cool, then refrigerate.

MAKE AHEAD The curd will keep in the refrigerator for up 1 week.

PER TABLESPOON 82 cal., 57% (47 cal.) from fat; .99 g protein; 5.3 g fat (3 g sat.); 8.4 g carbo (0.04 g fiber); 3.7 mg sodium; 80 mg chol.

STRAWBERRY OVEN JAM

Making strawberry jam without sugar or commercial pectin is challenging. Honey tends to burn over high heat, resulting in a bitter jam. A slow-cooker yields a jam that is too liquidy. We kept at it and finally arrived

at this easy method, which produces a not-too-sweet, fresh-tasting jam with a nice, spreadable consistency.

MAKES about 1 cup TIME about 3 hours

2 pints strawberries, hulled
2 tablespoons honey, plus more to taste (optional)
1 tablespoon freshly squeezed lemon juice

1. Preheat the oven to 200°F. Combine the strawberries, honey, and lemon juice in a food processor and pulse 20 to 30 times to chop the berries, stopping to scrape down the sides of the work bowl as needed. Be careful you don't puree the berries.

2. Spread the strawberry mixture in a thin, even layer on a rimmed baking sheet. Bake, scraping up and stirring with a flat, wide metal spatula every hour and then respreading into an even layer, until the jam is as thick as you like, 2 to 3 hours. It will continue to thicken slightly as it cools.

3. Let cool, then transfer to an airtight container. Stir in more honey before serving if you want a sweeter jam.

MAKE AHEAD The jam will keep in an airtight container in the refrigerator for up to 1 week or in the freezer for up to 3 months.

PER TABLESPOON 20 cal., 5% (1 cal.) from fat; 0.25 g protein; 0.11 g fat (0.01 g sat.); 5 g carbo (0.73 g fiber); 0.67 mg sodium; 0 mg chol.

. . . .

TEA SANDWICH TRIO

There is something particularly pleasing about sitting in your garden and eating dainty tea sandwiches filled with the garden itself. We made three kinds of sandwiches: hard-cooked egg and peppery nasturtium; Gouda with arugula; and, in a tribute to James Beard's famous onion sandwiches, green onion and parsley.

MAKES 36 miniature sandwiches, or 6 servings
TIME about 20 minutes, plus 30 minutes to chill

18 very thin slices Whole-Wheat Honey Sandwich
    Bread (page 243)
Egg-Nasturtium Filling (recipe follows)
Gouda-Arugula Filling (recipe follows)
Green Onion–Parsley Filling (recipe follows)

1. Fill the sandwiches as directed in each filling recipe, using 6 slices of bread to make 3 large sandwiches with each filling. Chill the sandwiches until cold, at least 30 minutes.

2. Trim the crusts from each sandwich and cut into 4 small squares, rectangles, or triangles. Arrange on a platter or individual plates to serve.

MAKE AHEAD The sandwiches can be assembled up to 2 hours ahead, covered with a barely damp kitchen towel and plastic wrap, and chilled.

PER EGG-NASTURTIUM SANDWICH 60 cal., 65% (39 cal.) from fat; 1.7 g protein; 4.6 g fat (0.87 g sat.); 3.6 g carbo (0.52 g fiber); 109 mg sodium; 40 mg chol
PER GOUDA-ARUGULA SANDWICH 46 cal., 57% (26 cal.) from fat; 1.8 g protein; 3 g fat (1.8 g sat.); 3.5 g carbo (0.53 g fiber); 74 mg sodium; 9.5 mg chol
PER GREEN ONION–PARSLEY SANDWICH 35 cal., 34% (12 cal.) from fat; 1.3 g protein; 1.3 g fat (0.75 g sat.); 4.6 g carbo (0.62 g fiber); 111 mg sodium; 4.7 mg chol

EGG-NASTURTIUM FILLING

MAKES enough for 12 miniature sandwiches TIME about 20 minutes

2 large eggs, at least 1 week old (superfresh eggs
    are difficult to peel)
3 tablespoons Green Chile Mayonnaise (page 73),
    made without garlic or chile, or regular mayonnaise
    flavored with a little freshly squeezed lemon juice
3 tablespoons coarsely chopped nasturtium leaves,
    plus 6 whole leaves
Fine sea salt (optional)
12 nasturtium blossoms

1. Put the eggs in a small pot and cover with water by about 1 inch. Bring to a boil, immediately reduce the heat to a simmer, and cook, uncovered, for 10 minutes. Remove from the heat, immerse the eggs in ice water to cover, and let cool for 1 minute. Crack each egg all over on the counter and return to the ice water for 5 minutes.

2. Peel the eggs under cold water and put them in a bowl. Chop them with a pastry blender or mash them with a fork. Stir in the mayonnaise and chopped nasturtium leaves and season with salt.

3. To fill the sandwiches, spread half of the bread slices with the egg mixture, then top each one with 2 whole leaves and 4 blossoms. Top with the remaining bread slices.

GOUDA-ARUGULA FILLING

MAKES enough for 12 miniature sandwiches
TIME about 5 minutes

About 1^1/$_2$ tablespoons salted butter, homemade
    (page 154) or store-bought, softened
About 2 ounces young or aged Gouda, homemade
    (page 122) or store-bought, thinly sliced
^{1}/$_3$ cup loosely packed small arugula leaves

1. To fill the sandwiches, lightly spread each bread slice on one side with butter. Layer the cheese and then the arugula on the buttered side of 3 bread slices.

2. Top with the remaining bread slices, with the buttered side down.

GREEN ONION–PARSLEY FILLING

MAKES enough for 12 miniature sandwiches
TIME about 10 minutes

**¹/₃ cup fromage blanc, homemade (page 118)
    or store-bought mixed with 3 tablespoons
    heavy cream
3 tablespoons finely chopped green onions
¹/₄ cup finely chopped fresh flat-leaf parsley
¹/₈ teaspoon fine sea salt**

1. In a small bowl, stir together the fromage blanc, green onions, parsley, and salt.

2. Spread the mixture on 3 of the bread slices, dividing it evenly. Top with the remaining bread slices.

· ·

WHOLE-WHEAT HONEY SANDWICH BREAD

This mild-tasting loaf tastes equally good with something savory, like cheese, or something sweet, like jam. It makes great toast, too.

MAKES 2 loaves; each loaf yields about twenty
¹/₂-inch-thick slices TIME about 2¹/₂ hours

**2 packages (2¹/₂ teaspoons each) active dry yeast
¹/₄ cup honey
6¹/₂ cups whole-wheat flour,* plus more for dusting
2 tablespoons unsalted butter, homemade (page 154)
    or store-bought, melted
1 tablespoon fine sea salt
About 1 teaspoon extra virgin olive oil**

1. Put the yeast, honey, 1 cup of the flour, and 3 cups warm water (100° to 110°F) in the bowl of a stand mixer fitted with a dough hook. Let stand until the yeast dissolves and bubbles appear, about 5 minutes. Add the remaining 5¹/₂ cups flour and mix with the dough hook on low speed just until the flour is no longer dry, about 1 minute. Add 1 tablespoon of the butter and the salt and mix on medium-low speed until the dough is smooth, begins to pull away from the sides of the bowl, and feels a bit tacky, 5 to 7 minutes.

2. Use some of the oil to grease a large bowl. Transfer the dough to the bowl and turn the dough to coat it evenly on all sides with oil. Cover the bowl with plastic wrap and let sit in a warm spot until the dough is doubled in size, about 1 hour.

3. Use the remaining 1 tablespoon butter to grease two 8¹/₂-by-4¹/₂-inch loaf pans. Dust each pan lightly with flour, tapping out the excess, and set the pans aside.

4. Turn the dough out onto a lightly floured work surface and divide in half. Using the palm of your hand, flatten 1 piece into a rectangle, popping any air bubbles. Position the rectangle with a long side facing you. Fold the farthest edge toward you ¹/₂ inch at a time, alternating with folds of the shorter sides toward the center, until you reach the long side nearest you. With the heel of your hand, press all along the length of the seam to seal it. Place the loaf, seam side down, in a prepared pan. Repeat with remaining dough half and place in the second pan. Loosely cover each pan with lightly oiled plastic wrap and let them sit in a warm spot until the dough is doubled in size, 30 to 45 minutes. Meanwhile, preheat the oven to 350°F.

5. Peel the plastic wrap from the pans, being careful not to tear the surface of the loaves. Bake until the loaves are browned and sound hollow when tapped on the bottom or sides (use pot holders to tip the loaf out of the pan, then tap), 45 to 50 minutes. Turn the loaves out onto racks and let cool completely before slicing.

* *We used 'Expresso' whole-wheat flour, but any regular whole-wheat flour will work. See the Allure of Local Wheat, page 156, for more information on local flours.*

PER SLICE 80 cal., 12% (9.6 cal.) from fat; 2.8 g protein; 1.1 g fat (0.45 g sat.); 16 g carbo (2.5 g fiber); 169 mg sodium; 1.5 mg chol.

WHOLE-WHEAT ROLLS
Follow the recipe through step 2. Butter and flour two 12-cup standard muffin pans. Divide the dough into 24 equal pieces. Roll each piece into a ball and place a ball in each prepared cup. Cover the pans loosely with lightly oiled plastic wrap and let sit in a warm spot until the dough doubles in size, about 50 minutes. Bake the rolls in a 350°F oven until they are browned and sound hollow when tapped on the bottom (lift a roll out of the pan with a knife tip, then tap), about 15 minutes. Turn out onto racks to cool completely.

PER ROLL 134 cal., 10% (14 cal.) from fat; 4.8 g protein; 1.6 g fat (0.72 g sat.); 27 g carbo (4.2 g fiber); 282 mg sodium; 2.5 mg chol.

Epilogue

We haven't exactly had a smooth ride with this one-block project of ours. And yet, to a person we think it's been worth it.

We've had to do without so many ingredients we regularly use unthinkingly all the time, like baking soda and baking powder, cinnamon, black pepper, vanilla, chocolate, and coffee—and sugar, which is much more versatile than honey because it doesn't burn as easily or ooze. Crops we were counting on failed or were destroyed by pests (most perniciously, our lovely olive trees). Our first prospective cow got mastitis, and one of our chickens died. And, most recently, Team Bee member Brianne had to be rushed to the emergency room with a suddenly developed allergy to bee stings. (She recovered well, and is undergoing desensitization therapy so she can work with the hives again.)

And yet. All that we've done, successfully or not, has changed our whole outlook on food—and on ourselves.

Now that we've made beer, for instance, and understand more about all the ways in which it can go wrong, we're in awe of the artisans who create great beers like Chimay, time after time.

We have a deeper way of seeing and relating to the natural world. Margaret can tell the age of a bee by the condition of its wings. Brianne seems to spot mushrooms wherever she goes—she just has an eye for them now. Jim is so gentle with the hens that even skittish Charlotte lets him pick her up. Erika says that one of the best rewards of making wine was "getting to feel alive in a new way. We got to be part of nature—and be low-tech, without our computers glaring at us." In the kitchen, we cooks look at plants differently now. We consider a vegetable's potential from top to bottom, beyond the parts normally considered edible. Fava leaves and radish greens are delicious, we've found, and so are crisp, juicy pineapple guava blossoms, and pod-on shelling beans if you eat them when they are very small.

THE ONE-BLOCK TEAM. *Back row, left to right:* Erika Ehmsen (with wine), Julie Chai, Sara Schneider, Sarah Epstein, Sara Jamison, Rachel Levin, Alan Phinney, Elaine Johnson, Sheila Schmitz. *Middle row, left to right:* Lauren Bonar Swezey, Christine Ryan, Sophie Egan, Katie Tamony, Vanessa Speckman, Kimberley Burch, Margaret Sloan, Stephanie Dean, Kathy Brenzel, Rick LaFrentz, and Erin Shitama. *Front row, left to right:* Jim McCann, Brianne McElhiney, Margo True, Amy Machnak, Elizabeth Jardina, and Johanna Silver. *Not pictured:* Ryan Casey, Christine Ciarmello, Dale Conour, Trina Enriquez, Barb Newton.

And finally, we cooks (okay, mainly me) have come to understand the gardener's point of view. At the beginning of this project, I thought that a garden could be planted to follow a menu. Now I know that a menu follows a garden. Nature always leads, and a smart cook learns how to dance.

That said, I'm not sure we would have had as much fun without a menu as our roadmap. It was the idea of a well-thought-out, well-cooked meal that drove us to figure out a cooking fat (olive oil) and sweetener (honey), seasoning (salt), and protein (eggs and cheese)—and really everything else, too.

And it was our projects that led to us getting to know one another. Our office is sort of like a neighborhood, in that most of the people here see each other nearly every day and say hello and maybe chat in the hall. But that's often where the conversation ends. Through collaborating on cheese and wine, bees and olive oil, and so on, we learned who likes to camp, whose kids play baseball, about musical tastes and books being read, and who tells a good joke—all the small things that give texture to life. I'm not sure whether this has helped us in our professional work together, but I'd like to think so.

Of course, we are all proud that we have managed to produce some excellent food, using skills more common a few generations ago. Beyond having had four thoroughly enjoyable dinners and plenty of good food in between, we have learned a lot, even though we are far from being experts in anything. We fling around terms like hydrometer and titration, rennet and rumen, sodium metabisulfite and GF-120 as though they were spare change. We're more capable now.

There's something else going on here, too. Part of what is compelling about these projects is that they're somewhat mysterious and unpredictable. They involve cooperating with other living beings, some human, some not, and most of them microscopic. There is no single way to succeed, so the projects have truly become our own, with results that reflect us and everything around us: the weather, the earth, our tastes and choices, our skill levels. And what we've produced—the weird torpedo-shaped eggs and the carrots with crooks in them, the superfloral honey and the supersharp vinegar—seems unique, too, and wonderful in a world that persists in prizing Red Delicious apples, all the same size, shape, and color.

What we like most about our One-Block project is that it has connected us to nature itself, free of standardized packaging and predigested ways of seeing. It has given us the quirks and surprises we didn't even know we craved until we had them, and didn't know we'd lost until we'd found them.

The One-Block Team

Kathy Brenzel • Garden Editor • Team Vinegar
Every year, Kathy's husband makes wine, most recently using grapes from their neighbors' merlot, cabernet, and zinfandel vines. With so much wine aging in carboys and oak barrels in their garage, Kathy decided it was time to learn how to turn some into equally delicious vinegar for dressing salads.

Kimberley Burch • Imaging Specialist • Teams Bee, Mead, Olive, and Salt
With the exception of a college year abroad in Wales, Kimberley has lived her entire life in the West, where *Sunset* magazine was always around. A love of nature led her to become a photographer, and now she is in heaven as Sunset's imaging specialist, photographer for the one-block website, and "Queen Bee"—leader of Team Bee.

Ryan Casey • Organic Farmer and Former Test Garden Coordinator • Team Garden
A true nature nerd and lover of good food, Ryan found the One-Block garden a perfect place to get his hands dirty, watch birds, and discover the vast amount of edible possibilities to grow. He now produces fresh vegetables, fruits, and flowers at Blue House Farm (www.bluehouseorganic farm.com) in Pescadero, California.

Julie Chai • Associate Garden Editor • Teams Vinegar and Cheese
As a member of Team Vinegar, she's dug deep into crocks of fermenting wine to pull out the aging "mother" with her bare hands, and has stirred pots of milk for hours as a member of Team Cheese. In coming years, she's hoping to find a way to create Team Chocolate.

Christine Ciarmello • Features Editor • Team Cheese
Ever since she learned to churn butter as a Girl Scout, Christine has been fascinated with the chemistry of food. Team Cheese gave her a peek into the wonderful world of curds. The San Francisco–based editor says her desert island food is definitely ricotta.

Dale Conour • Partner and Head of Strategy at Dial House brand strategy agency and Former Executive Editor • Teams Bee and Beer
As fascinating as the bees were, Dale simply enjoyed the opportunity to wear a pith helmet. His beer-making experience deepened his respect for beer craftsmen everywhere, and he now always performs a silent salute to the brewmaster before imbibing. A native of the West, he lives in San Francisco.

**Stephanie Dean • Test Kitchen Coordinator •
Teams Beer, Kitchen, and Cow**

Before Sunset, Stephanie worked for chocolate and olive oil producers and in a food product development lab, and has a master's degree in nutrition. What she loved most about the One-Block project was how cooking with what's available forced us to be creative.

Sophie Egan • Researcher • Teams Tea and Cow

Getting close to one's food sources is thrilling to Sophie, a recent Stanford graduate and Seattle native. After learning that green and black tea all come from the same plant, she was excited to tackle the tea-making process. And she couldn't pass up Team Cow's offer to milk her first cow.

Erika Ehmsen • Copy Chief • Team Wine

This comma jockey relished the chance to pursue perfection in a glass, eagerly blending *I Love Lucy*–inspired grape stomping with a high school affinity for chemistry. After tucking her young kids into bed, Erika sneaks off to her laptop to mince words for her next Team Wine post on the One-Block blog.

Trina Enriquez • Copy Editor • Team Olive

Even though Trina's dad grows a jungle of backyard fruit—nectarines, persimmons, kiwis, avocados, pluots—Trina herself took it all for granted as a kid. Living in the Bay Area and working at Sunset finally opened her eyes, though. Her dad still cures olives from one of his trees, a process that piqued her interest in Team Olive.

Sarah Epstein • Recipe Retester • Team Wine

Sarah's background in agriculture and plant science fueled her curiosity about how wine happens, from planting and picking to sipping and pairing. She spends her days testing recipes in the Sunset kitchen, where she has used (and tasted) products from all the One-Block teams.

**Elizabeth Jardina • Freelance Writer and Former Researcher •
Team Chicken**

Elizabeth is a friend to chickens and a former vegetarian. A native Texan, she now lives in San Mateo in Merv Griffin's childhood home.

Sara Jamison • Former Photo Style Coordinator • Team Wine

Before Sunset, Sara taught arts and crafts to elementary-school children. At Sunset, she transferred her artistic vision to the photo department, styling and propping sets and managing day-to-day details. She has always loved a good glass of wine, so when Team Wine started up, she was ripe for the picking.

**Elaine Johnson • Associate Food Editor •
Teams Mushroom, Kitchen, Cheese, Cow, and Bee**

Ever since she pruned her first lemon tree (badly) at age 10, Elaine has been fascinated with growing her own food. She took up canning and vegetable-gardening in college in Corvallis, Oregon, and still grows and preserves food year-round out of her home garden in Palo Alto, California.

Rick LaFrentz • Head Gardener • Team Beer

Rick has worked in the gardens at Sunset for over 31 years. What he did before that he can't remember. He'd had some experience making beer (from extract), but it's been quite an education trying to make a beer completely from scratch.

Rachel Levin • Senior Editor • Team Olive

As a travel editor-writer who loves to cover all things food, too, Rachel jumped at the chance to join a One-Block team. Team Chicken seemed like too much responsibility. Olives sounded easier (until she met the olive fly).

**Amy Machnak • Recipe Editor •
Teams Salt, Olive Oil, Vinegar, Kitchen, and Escargot**

Amy grew up in the suburbs of Detroit, in a family of avid hunters and gardeners who instilled the foraging and farm-to-table philosophy in her long before it was trendy. A former pastry chef turned writer and devout Western enthusiast, she was giddy at the idea of making recipes from only what grew at Sunset, and often tells people at cocktail parties that she made salt.

James McCann • Art Director • Team Chicken

Jim hooked up with Team Chicken because as a city boy, he's always had a hidden desire to be a farmer and know what it's truly like to live off the land. Plus, he claims he's never had enough straw in his hair, feathers in his mouth, or poop on his shoes.

**Brianne McElhiney • Editorial Assistant •
Teams Bee, Cheese, Mead, Mushroom, Chicken, and Cow**

A native of the Bay Area, Brianne is no stranger to the innovative and forward-thinking lifestyle of the West. A graduate of Pepperdine University with a degree in business administration and a passion for food, she is balancing her enthusiasm for business with the adventurous and sustainable spirit of Western living—a life made, not bought.

Barb Newton • President • Team Cow

Barb is a proud member of Team Cow. She came to Sunset from Wisconsin—need she say more?

Alan Phinney • Managing Editor • Teams Wine and Beer

In his 19-year stint at Sunset, Alan has had his hand in covering many aspects of growing and gardening, and food and wine. Yet literally handling grapes and grain as they went from field to bottle has meant a whole new world of learning and appreciation.

Christine Ryan • Executive Editor • Team Tea

Wondering whether true black tea could thrive in Northern California, Christine (a five-cup-a-day drinker) volunteered to head up Team Tea. Apart from her tea-fermenting duties, she serves as executive editor of the magazine; before coming to Sunset, she was abusing caffeine at *7x7*, *Travel Holiday*, *Gourmet*, and *European Travel & Life* magazines.

Sheila Schmitz • Sunset.com editor

Sheila coached the One-Block team in the art of blogging, and she loves to grow tomatoes, peppers, cucumbers, lettuces, herbs, and fruit in her San Jose, California backyard. She keeps the garden imperfect to leave room for daydreaming and surprises.

Sara Schneider • Wine Editor • Team Wine

Writing about wine makes it irresistible to produce it if you get the chance—to get inside this chemically alive, fascinating beverage. Heading up Team Wine was a true career highlight for this former English teacher, culinary school grad, and food editor.

**Erin Shitama • Assistant to the President •
Teams Bee and Mushroom**

Erin grew up foraging for wild berries and onions around her home on the eastern shore of Maryland, and was drawn to the locavore lifestyle long before she knew locavore was a word. She's happiest when she's on the road with only her passport and a backpack, sampling local food, language, and culture along the way.

**Johanna Silver • Test Garden Coordinator •
Teams Garden, Escargot, Chicken**

Johanna came to Sunset with a background in organic farm apprenticeships and garden education. She's since added ornamental gardening to her list of loves while at the magazine, but participating in the One-Block project keeps her in touch with her edible roots—er, beginnings.

Margaret Sloan • Production Coordinator • Team Bee

Margaret wears many hats at Sunset; she researches stories, illustrates maps, squares up page designs, and makes sure the magazine will print properly. She's been fascinated by bees ever since a swarm settled on a tree near her house years ago, but never dreamed she'd have a job that required her to wear a beekeeper's helmet, or that she'd learn to like bugs.

**Vanessa Speckman • Photo & Imaging Assistant •
Teams Bee and Mead**

Vanessa grew up in an Italian and Irish family with a hands-on kitchen, learning how to do everything from crush grapes and construct wine barrels with her *nonno* to making good chicken broth. Harvesting honey at Sunset and understanding how vital bees are to the environment inspired Vanessa and her brother to make their own mead at home.

**Lauren Bonar Swezey • Former Garden Special Projects Editor •
Teams Garden, Wine, Chicken**

As manager of the Sunset test garden and long-time garden writer and editor, Lauren helped identify which vegetable varieties were best for Menlo Park's mild climate, and oversaw planting, care, and harvest. Her favorite part of the project? The excitement of witnessing the garden's daily transformation from bare plot into veritable vegetable factory, and then sampling the tasty harvest.

Katie Tamony • Editor-in-Chief • Team Mushroom

She was so intrigued by the idea of "making" her own mushrooms—a favorite food! Katie's usual job at Sunset is to direct the editorial work of our incredibly creative group in magazines, books, our web site, and television. And to greenlight projects like this!

**Margo True • Food Editor •
All teams, but especially Kitchen, Chicken, and Cow**

What a journey it's been. What's next? How about Team Fish?

Acknowledgments

For almost every one of our projects, we relied on the advice of people wiser and more knowledgeable than us. These generous people helped steer us in the right direction:

Bees Randy Oliver, of Scientific Beekeeping, for shifting our paradigm; master beekeepers Tom Vercoutere and Tina and Thomas Keller, for their help, support, and soothing influence in the face of panic; and the Beekeepers' Guild of San Mateo County, for patiently answering our questions and lending us a honey extractor.

Beer Chuck Schwalbach, for sharing his extensive beer knowledge and vast array of brewing equipment, and for being so calm and organized.

Cheese Sue Conley, Peg Smith, Jonathan White, and Maureen Cunnie at Cowgirl Creamery; and Liam Callahan and his mom, Cindy Callahan, at Bellwether Farms, for their inspiring cheesemaking lessons and followup advice.

Chickens Jody Main, for a demystifying day with her hens.

Cow Ron Garthwaite and Collette Cassidy, of Claravale Farms, who made Team Cow possible.

Garden Renee Shepard, of Renee's Garden Seeds, for always encouraging us to start from seed; also Darryl Wong, of Free Wheelin' Farm, for being our on-call crop advisor.

Olives Chris Banthien at Valencia Farms, where we picked olives, and Alessio Carli, olive oil and winemaker at Pietra Santa Winery, where we crushed them, as well as the winery's director of marketing, Jayme Nunn; Dan Flynn, for backyard tree harvesting advice; and Alexandra Devarenne, Bill Krueger, Frank Zalom, Paul Vossen, and Ernie Simpson, for their excellent tips on olive fruit fly control.

Salt Mark Bitterman, "selmelier" at The Meadow, in Portland, Oregon, for his infectious enthusiasm and for helping us make better salt.

Vinegar The incomparable Paula Wolfert, cookbook author, who taught us the ways of vinegar-growing and gave us pieces of her vinegar mother.

Wine Thomas Fogarty Winery's Dr. Thomas Fogarty, Anne Krolczyk, and especially winemaker Michael Martella, who visited Sunset to check up on the wine; also Dan Brenzel, home winemaker and retired chemist, who kindly loaned us just about every scrap of equipment we needed—and whose wisecracks still make us laugh.

To all of them, we owe a giant debt of gratitude. Many others contributed along the way, including my sweetheart, Peter Lang, who trapped Nugget the rooster and spent many hours tending chickens on weekends; Andrew Hash, who collected gallons of Pacific Ocean; and Hank Shaw, our friend at http://honest-food.net, who gave us pointers on cooking snails; and the readers of our blog, http://oneblockdiet.sunset.com, who have offered countless good suggestions and stories of their own food-from-scratch adventures.

In the kitchen, we salute our amazing team of retesters—home cooks who come to Sunset and test our recipes with diligence and dedication to make sure they'll work for anyone. We are grateful for all their work on this book. Thanks also to Molly Watson, former Sunset recipe editor, for creating some of the recipes for our first one-block menu back in the summer of 2007.

Every now and then, we've needed to construct things like a hen yard or a concrete pad to shield our beehives from ants. Tony Soria and Dan Strack, whose talent and hard work keeps Sunset's office and grounds operating smoothly, have been our heroes and helped us out whenever we asked. Speaking of construction, we have possibly the prettiest henhouse in Menlo Park, built by James Stamp of Wine Country Coops; thank you, James.

The photos of our feasts were art directed by Sunset's creative director, Mia Daminato, whose graceful aesthetics set the tone for this book. Our luscious recipe shots are the work of staff photographer Tom Story and photo editor Sue Smith—thank you so much—and the garden shots were coordinated by photo editor Linda Peters with good-natured aplomb. A big thank you to photo director Yvonne Stender, for overseeing the photography and making sure it came in on time and on budget. Warm thanks to Sunset's imaging specialist, Kimberley Burch, for efficiently cataloguing hundreds of possible images for this book and adding to them with her own photography. You went above and beyond! Thanks too to Spencer Toy, for our fine group portrait and for the many other shots he contributed to these pages.

At Ten Speed Press, Melissa Moore was our champion editor and warm guiding hand, assisted with aplomb by Emily Timberlake. Nancy Austin and Katy Brown created the beautiful design. We much appreciated Sharon Silva and Linda Bouchard for their scrupulous attention to every word. And we are very thankful to Aaron Wehner, who instantly understood what we were doing and signed us on. Working with all of them has been a wonderful experience.

And lastly, heartfelt thanks to Katie Tamony, our editor in chief at Sunset, for saying Yes to this quirky project and committing the time, resources, and enthusiastic support to help it blossom and grow—and to Barb Newton, our president, who was always ready for the next adventure.

Appendix

Regional Planting Calendars for Your Own One-Block Feasts

The planting and growing information in this book is for Northern California, where Sunset is located. Over the decades, we've defined a series of 32 climate zones for the entire West—based on winter low temperatures as well as elevation, latitude, rainfall, and proximity to climate-altering mountains, oceans and lakes—with the aim of helping our readers figure out what to plant in their areas and how best to care for those plants. This information is presented in detail in the *Sunset Western Garden Book* (Sunset Publishing, Eighth Edition, 2007). We've applied that knowledge to the planting timelines that follow to help you grow our one-block crops no matter where in the West you live.

Whereas our timelines on pages 4 to 7 reflect how we planted crops in Northern California, the calendars here show you all the seasonal plantings and harvests possible in your area, to give you maximum choice for planning menus. The calendars begin in March simply for the sake of consistency.

Edamame sprout

One-Block Feasts across the Country

In certain regions of the country, planting times roughly resemble those in parts of the West. If you live in one of the following areas, consult the timeline suggested for your region, but make allowances for your different climate conditions.

- **New England** (Connecticut, Massachusetts, Rhode Island). Check out our Mountain and Intermountain West timeline.
- **Midwest** (Illinois, Iowa, Michigan, Wisconsin). Your spring planting dates are much the same as in the Pacific Northwest, but your summers are hotter and winters colder.
- **Mid-Atlantic States** (Maryland, Delaware, Virginia). Your spring planting dates are much the same as in the Pacific Northwest, but your summer summers are hotter and winters colder.
- **The Mid-South** (parts of Georgia, Alabama) Your region shares some planting dates with parts of California, but heat, humidity, and rainfall significantly shift the harvest and summer planting dates.
- **A National Climate Map** For more precisely tailored information for your climate, see our map of 45 national climate zones at www.sunset.com/usclimatezones. The accompanying descriptions will tell you when to plant warm-season crops and when to start cold-season crops in your area, so you can apply that information to growing the plants in this book; refer to the seasonal garden guides for specific information on planting and harvesting each crop. For a print copy of the national zones and much more on countrywide gardening, pick up a copy of the *Sunset National Garden Book* (Sunset Publishing, 1997; available on www.amazon.com).

Because growing conditions can vary so much by region and even microregion, the best source for local planting information is your county's agricultural cooperative extension office; find yours at www.csrees.usda.gov/Extension/index.html. Local independent nurseries are excellent sources of advice, too.

MARCH

Plant

Arugula (through Apr)
Beets (through May)
Broccoli rabe
Carrots (except interior valleys)
Chervil
Dill
Florence fennel
Green onions (through Apr)
Lettuce (through Apr)
Mesclun (through Apr)
Mustard
Parsley (through Apr)
Potatoes
Quinoa
Radishes (through Apr)
Swiss chard (through May)
Tea

Harvest (Jan or Feb planting)

Arugula
Beets
Broccoli rabe
Broccoli romanesco
Cabbage
Carrots
Green onions
Kale
Lemons
Lettuce
Mesclun
Mustard
Parsley
Radishes

WARM SEASON
....

APRIL

Plant

Basil (through Jun)
Beans (through Jul)
Chiles
Corn (through Jul)
Cucumbers (through May)
Edamame (through Jul)
Herbs (perennial)—chives,
    marjoram, oregano,
    peppermint, rosemary, sage,
    French tarragon, thyme
Lemon tree
Lemongrass
Melons, all kinds (through Jun)
Nasturtiums
Peppers
Pineapple guava
Purslane
Squash, butternut
Squash, summer (pattypan and
    zucchini)
Tangerine tree
Tomato

Harvest

Beets
Broccoli rabe
Broccoli romanesco
Cabbage
Carrots
Cauliflower
Fava beans
Green onions
Herbs (perennial)
Lemons
Lettuce
Mesclun
Mustard
Parsley
Radicchio
Radishes
Strawberries
Swiss chard
Tea

MAY

Harvest

Barley
Basil
Beets
Broccoli rabe
Broccoli romanesco
Cabbage
Carrots
Cauliflower
Chervil
Dill
Fava beans
Florence fennel
Green onions
Herbs (perennial)
Lemons
Lettuce
Mesclun
Onions, 'Spanish White' and
    cippolini
Parsley
Strawberries
Swiss chard
Wheat

JUNE

Harvest

Barley
Basil
Beets
Cabbage
Carrots
Chervil
Dill
Edamame
Florence fennel
Garlic
Herbs (perennial)
Lemons
Lemongrass

Lettuce
Nasturtiums
Onions, 'Spanish White' and
    cippolini
Parsley
Potatoes
Purslane
Quinoa
Squash, summer (pattypan and
    zucchini)
Swiss chard
Wheat

JULY

Plant

Corn

Harvest

Basil
Beans
Cucumbers
Chiles
Dill
Edamame
Florence fennel
Garlic
Herbs (perennial)
Lemons
Lemongrass
Melons
Nasturtiums
Peppers
Potatoes
Purslane
Quinoa
Squash, summer (pattypan and
    zucchini)
Tomatoes

COOL SEASON
....

AUGUST

Plant

Broccoli romanesco (through
    Oct)
Cabbage (through Oct)
Cauliflower
Lettuce (through Feb)
Potatoes (through Sept)

Harvest

Basil
Beans
Chiles
Corn
Cucumbers
Edamame
Herbs (perennial)
Hops
Lemons
Lemongrass
Melons
Nasturtiums

Peppers
Purslane
Squash, butternut
Squash, summer (pattypan and
    zucchini)
Tomatoes

SEPTEMBER

Plant

Arugula (through Feb)
Beets (through Feb)
Broccoli rabe (through Feb)
Carrots
Chervil
Green onions
Kale (through Oct)
Mesclun (through Feb)
Mustard (through Oct)
Parsley
Radicchio (through Feb)
Radishes (through Feb)
Swiss chard

Harvest

Beans
Chiles
Corn
Cucumbers
Edamame
Herbs (perennial)
Hops
Lemons
Melons
Mesclun
Peppers
Radishes
Squash, butternut
Squash, summer (pattypan and
    zucchini)
Tomatoes

OCTOBER

Plant

Barley
Carrots (except interior valleys)
Fava beans (through Nov)
Green onions
Onions, 'Spanish White' and
    cippolini (through Nov)
Parsley (through Feb)

Harvest

Arugula
Beans
Broccoli rabe
Chiles
Corn
Edamame
Herbs (perennial)
Kale
Lemons
Lettuce
Mesclun

Mustard
Peppers
Pineapple guava
Radishes
Tomatoes
Squash, butternut

NOVEMBER

Plant

Cabbage (except interior valleys through Jan)
Carrots (except interior valleys through Dec)
Garlic (through Dec)
Kale (except interior valleys through Jan)
Mustard (along coast through Dec)
Potatoes
Wheat

Harvest

Arugula
Beets
Broccoli rabe
Broccoli romanesco
Cabbage
Carrots
Cauliflower
Green onions
Herbs (perennial)
Kale
Lemons

Lettuce
Mesclun
Mustard
Parsley
Pineapple guava
Potatoes
Radicchio
Radishes
Swiss chard

DECEMBER

Harvest

Arugula
Beets
Broccoli rabe
Broccoli romanesco
Cabbage
Carrots
Cauliflower
Chervil
Green onions
Herbs (perennial)
Kale
Lemons
Lettuce
Mesclun
Mustard
Parsley
Potatoes
Radicchio
Radishes
Swiss chard

Tangerines

JANUARY

Plant

Broccoli romanesco (except interior valleys through Feb)
Cauliflower (except interior valleys through Feb)
Hops (through Feb)
Mustard
Onions, 'Spanish White' and cippolini (except along the coast)
Strawberries (through Feb)

Harvest

Arugula
Beets
Cabbage
Carrots (except interior valleys)
Chervil
Green onions
Herbs (perennial)
Kale
Lemons
Lettuce
Mesclun
Mustard, along coast
Parsley
Radicchio
Radishes
Tangerines

FEBRUARY

Plant

Cabbage
Carrots
Chervil
Dill
Florence fennel
Green onions
Mustard
Onions, 'Spanish White' and cippolini (through Nov)
Potatoes
Swiss chard

Harvest

Arugula
Beets
Broccoli rabe
Cabbage
Carrots (except interior valleys)
Green onions
Herbs (perennial)
Kale
Lemons
Lettuce
Mesclun
Mustard (along coast)
Parsley
Radishes
Tangerines

SOUTHWEST DESERTS (in New Mexico, Arizona, Utah, Nevada, and California)

This calendar has no warm or cool seasons. That's because growing seasons here are especially diverse. Instead, follow planting times for one of the four regional climate zones: zone 10, high desert; zone 11, intermediate deserts of California and southern Nevada; zone 12, Arizona-Sonoran desert; zone 13, low deserts of California and Arizona. If no zone is noted, the information pertains to all Southwest gardens.

MARCH

Plant

Basil (zone 12)
Beans (zone 12)
Beets
Broccoli rabe (zones 10, 11)
Broccoli romanesco (zones 10, 11)
Cabbage (zones 10, 11)
Carrots (zone 10, 11)
Cauliflower (zones 10, 11)
Chervil (zones 10, 11, 12)
Corn (zones 12, 13)
Cucumbers (zone 13)
Dill (zone 11)
Edamame (zone 13)
Fava Beans (zone 11)
Florence fennel (zone 11)
Hops (zone 10)

Kale (zones 10, 11)
Lettuce (zones 10, 12)
Melons (zones 12, 13)
Mesclun
Mustard (zones 10, 11)
Onions, 'Spanish White' and cippolini (zone 10)
Parsley (zones 10, 11)
Potatoes (zone 11)
Purslane (zone 13)
Radicchio (zone 11)
Radishes (zones 10, 12)
Strawberries
Squash, summer (pattypan and zucchini) (zones 12, 13)
Swiss chard (zones 10, 12)
Tomato (zone 12, 13)
Squash, butternut (zone 13)

Harvest

Arugula (zone 12)
Beets
Carrots (zones 12, 13)
Fava Beans (zones 12, 13)
Florence fennel (zones 12, 13)
Green onions
Lettuce (zones 12, 13)
Mesclun
Parsley (zones 12, 13)
Quinoa (zone 13)
Radicchio (zone 12)
Radishes (zones 12, 13)
Swiss chard (zone 12)

APRIL

Plant

Basil (zones 10, 11, 12; from mid-month)

Carrots (zone 10, 11)
Chervil (zones 10, 11, 12)
Chiles
Corn (zones 10, 11)
Cucumbers (zone 11; from mid-month, 13)
Dill (zones 10, 11)
Edamame (zones 12, 13)
Fava Beans (zone 10)
Florence fennel (zones 10, 11)
Herbs (perennial)—chives, marjoram, oregano, peppermint, rosemary, sage, French tarragon (zone 10 only), thyme
Lemon tree (zones 12, 13; outside potted for wintering indoors elsewhere)
Lemongrass
Lettuce (zone 10),

Mesclun
Nasturtiums (zones 10, 11, 12)
Onions, 'Spanish White' and
  cippolini (zone 10)
Parsley (zones 10, 11)
Peppers
Pineapple guava (zones 12, 13)
Potatoes, (zone 10)
Purslane (zones 10, 11, 12)
Quinoa (zones 10, 11, 12)
Radicchio (zone 10)
Radishes (zones 10, 11, 12)
Squash, butternut (zone 10)
Squash, summer (pattypan and
  zucchini) (zones 12, 13)
Tangerine tree (zones 12, 13;
  outside potted for wintering
  indoors elsewhere)
Tea (zone 12)
Tomato (zones 10, 11)

Harvest
Barley (zones 12, 13)
Basil
Beans
Beets
Broccoli rabe (zones 10, 11)
Carrots (zones 12, 13
Cucumbers (zone 13)
Dill (zones 12, 13)
Florence fennel (zones 12, 13)
Green onions
Lettuce (zones 10, 11)
Mesclun
Onions, 'Spanish White' and
  cippolini
Parsley (zones 12, 13)
Quinoa (zone 13)
Swiss chard (zones 10, 12)

MAY

Plant
Arugula (zone 12)
Basil (zones 10, 11, 12)
Carrots (zone 11)
Chiles
Corn (zone 10)
Cucumbers (zone 10, 11),
Edamame (zones 11, 12)
Mesclun (zones 10, 12)
Melon (zones 10, 11)
Peppers (zones 10, 12)
Squash, butternut (zones 10, 11)
Squash, summer (pattypan and
  zucchini) (zones 10, 11)
Tomato (zones 10, 11)

Harvest
Barley (zones 12, 13; late in
  month)
Basil
Beans
Beets
Broccoli rabe

Broccoli romanesco
Carrots
Chervil (zones 10, 11, 12)
Corn (zone 13)
Cucumbers (zone 13)
Dill (zones 10, 11)
Florence fennel (zones 10, 11)
Garlic
Green onions
Lettuce (zones 10, 11, 12)
Mesclun
Nasturtiums (zone 13)
Potatoes (zone 13)
Onions, 'Spanish White' and
  cippolini
Parsley (zones 10, 11)
Purslane (zone 13)
Radicchio (zones 10, 11)
Radishes, zones 10, 11, 12
Strawberries
Swiss chard (zones 10, 12)
Tea
Wheat

JUNE

Plant
Cabbage (zone 10)
Carrots (zone 11)
Corn (zone 10)
Edamame (zone 10)
Squash, summer (pattypan and
  zucchini) (zones 10, 11)

Harvest
Arugula (zone 12)
Barley
Basil
Beans
Beets (zones 10, 11)
Carrots (zones 10, 11)
Chervil (zones 10, 11, 12)
Corn (zones 12, 13)
Cucumbers
Dill (zones 10, 11)
Edamame (zone 13)
Florence fennel (zones 10, 11)
Green onions
Herbs (perennial)
Lemongrass
Lettuce (zone 10)
Melons (zones 12, 13)
Mesclun (zone 10, 12)
Nasturtiums (zones 10, 11, 12)
Onions, 'Spanish White' and
  cippolini
Parsley (zones 10, 11)
Potatoes (zones 12, 13)
Purslane
Radicchio (zone 10)
Strawberries
Swiss chard (zone 10)
Tomatoes (zones 12, 13)

JULY

Plant
Beans (zone 12; last half of
  month)
Beets (zone 10)
Cabbage (zone 10)
Carrots (zone 11)
Corn (zones 10, 11, 12)
Mesclun (zone 10)
Radicchio (zone 10)
Squash, butternut (zones 12, 13)

Harvest
Basil
Carrots (zone 11)
Chiles
Corn (zones 10, 11)
Cucumbers (zones 10, 11)
Edamame (zones 12, 13)
Fava beans
Garlic
Herbs (perennial)
Lemongrass
Mesclun (zones 10, 12)
Nasturtiums (zones 10, 11, 12)
Peppers
Potatoes (zone 11)
Purslane
Quinoa (zones 10, 11, 12)
Squash, butternut (zone 13)
Squash, summer (pattypan and
  zucchini) (zones 10, 11)
Tomatoes

AUGUST

Plant
Beans (zones 12, 13)
Beets (zones 10, 11)
Carrots (zone 10)
Corn (zones 12, 13)
Cucumbers (zones 12, 13)
Lettuce (zone 10)
Mesclun (zone 10)
Radicchio (zone 11)
Radishes (zones 10, 11, 12)
Swiss chard (zone 10)

Harvest
Carrots (zone 11)
Chiles
Corn (zone 10)
Edamame (zones 11, 12)
Fava beans
Herbs (perennial)
Hops
Lemons
Lemongrass
Melons (zones 10, 11)
Mesclun (zone 10)
Peppers
Potatoes (zone 10)
Purslane
Quinoa (zones 10, 11, 12)

Squash, butternut (zone 10)
Squash, summer (pattypan and
  zucchini) (zones 10, 11)
Tomatoes (zones 10, 11, 12)

SEPTEMBER

Plant
Arugula (zones 10, 11, 12)
Beets
Broccoli romanesco
Cabbage
Carrots (zones 12, 13)
Cauliflower
Chervil (zones 12, 13)
Chiles
Dill (zone 12)
Florence fennel (zone 12)
Kale
Lettuce (zones 10, 11, 12)
Mesclun
Mustard
Nasturtiums (zone 13)
Parsley (zone 12)
Peppers
Radicchio (zones 12, 13),
Radishes (zones 11, 12, 13)
Swiss chard (zones 12, 13)

Harvest
Beets
Carrots (zone 11)
Corn (zone 10)
Edamame (zone 10, 11, 12)
Herbs (perennial)
Lemons
Lemongrass
Mesclun
Radishes (zones 10, 11, 12)
Squash, butternut (zones 10, 11)
Swiss chard (zone 10)
Tomatoes (zones 10, 11, 12)

OCTOBER

Plant
Arugula (zones 12, 13)
Beets (zones 12, 13)
Broccoli rabe (zones 12, 13)
Broccoli romanesco (zones 12,
  13)
Cabbage (zones 12, 13)
Carrots (zones 10, 12, 13)
Cauliflower (zones 12, 13)
Dill (zones 12, 13)
Fava Beans (zones 12, 13)
Florence fennel (zones 12, 13)
Garlic
Herbs (perennial)—rosemary,
  sage, thyme
Kale (zones 12, 13)
Lettuce (zones 12, 13)
Mesclun (zones 12, 13)
Mustard (zones 12, 13)
Parsley (zones 12, 13)

Radicchio (zones 12, 13)
Radishes (zones 11, 12, 13)
Swiss chard (zones 12, 13)

Harvest
Arugula (zones 10, 11, 12)
Beans
Beets
Cabbage
Chervil (zones 12, 13)
Corn (zones 10, 11, 12)
Cucumbers (zones 12, 13)
Edamame (zone 10)
Herbs (perennial)
Lemons
Lettuce (zone 10)
Mesclun
Nasturtiums (zone 13)
Radishes (zones 11, 12, 13)
Squash, butternut (zones 12, 13)
Swiss chard (zone 10)

NOVEMBER

Plant
Arugula (zones 12, 13)
Barley (zones 12, 13)
Beans
Beets (zones 12, 13)
Broccoli rabe (zones 12, 13)
Broccoli romanesco (zones 12, 13)
Cabbage (zones 12, 13)
Carrots (zones 12, 13)
Cauliflower (zones 12, 13)
Dill (zones 12, 13)
Fava Beans (zones 12, 13)
Florence fennel (zones 12, 13)
Garlic
Kale (zones 12, 13)
Lettuce (zones 12, 13)
Mesclun (zones 12, 13)
Mustard, transplant (zones 12, 13)
Onions, 'Spanish White' and cippolini
Parsley, seedling (zones 12, 13)
Quinoa (zone 13)
Radicchio (zone 12)

Radishes (zones 12, 13)
Swiss chard (zones 12, 13)
Wheat

Harvest
Arugula
Beets
Corn (zones 12, 13)
Cucumbers (zones 12, 13)
Herbs (perennial)
Lemons
Lettuce
Mesclun (zones 12, 13)
Nasturtiums (zone 13)
Pineapple guava
Radicchio (zones 12, 13)
Radishes (zones 11, 12, 13)
Squash, butternut (zones 12, 13)
Swiss chard (zones 12, 13)
Tangerines

DECEMBER

Plant
Arugula (zones 12, 13)
Barley (zones 12, 13)
Beets (zones 12, 13)
Carrots (zones 12, 13)
Dill (zone 13)
Florence fennel (zone 13)
Lettuce (zones 12, 13)
Mesclun (zones 12, 13)
Onions, 'Spanish White' and cippolini
Parsley (zones 12, 13)
Potatoes (zone 13)
Radicchio (zone 12)
Radishes (zones 12, 13)
Swiss chard (zones 12, 13)

Harvest
Arugula
Beets
Carrots (zones 12, 13)
Dill (zones 12, 13)
Florence fennel (zones 12, 13)
Lemons
Lettuce (zones 12, 13)
Mesclun (zones 12, 13)

Parsley (zones 12, 13)
Radicchio (zones 12, 13)
Radishes (zones 12, 13)
Swiss chard (zones 12, 13)
Tangerines

JANUARY

Plant
Arugula (zones 12, 13)
Basil (zone 13)
Beets (zones 12, 13)
Carrots (zones 12, 13)
Dill (zone 13)
Florence fennel (zone 13)
Hops (zone 10)
Lettuce (zone 12)
Mesclun (zones 12, 13)
Parsley (zones 12, 13)
Potatoes (zone 13)
Radicchio (zone 12)
Radishes (zones 12, 13)
Strawberries (through Mar)
Swiss chard (zone 12)

Harvest
Arugula (zones 12, 13 through Feb)
Beets
Broccoli romanesco (zones 12, 13)
Cabbage (zones 12, 13)
Carrots (zones 12, 13)
Cauliflower (zone 13)
Dill (zones 12, 13)
Florence fennel (zones 12, 13)
Green onions
Kale (zones 12, 13)
Lemons
Lettuce (zones 12, 13)
Mesclun (zones 12, 13)
Parsley (zones 12, 13)
Radicchio (zones 12, 13)
Swiss chard (zones 12, 13)
Tangerines

FEBRUARY

Plant
Basil
Beans (zone 13)
Beets
Carrots (zones 12, 13)
Corn (zone 13)
Cucumbers (zone 13)
Dill (zone 13)
Florence fennel (zone 13)
Hop (zone 10)
Lettuce (zones 11, 12)
Mesclun (zones 11, 12)
Nasturtiums (zone 13)
Potatoes (zones 12, 13)
Radishes (zones 12, 13)
Swiss chard (zones 10, 12)

Harvest
Arugula (zones 12, 13)
Beets
Cabbage (zones 12, 13)
Carrots (zones 12, 13)
Cauliflowe (zones 12, 13)
Dill (zones 12, 13)
Fava Beans (zones 12, 13)
Florence fennel (zones 12, 13)
Green onions
Kale (zones 12, 13)
Lemons
Lettuce (zones 12, 13)
Mesclun (zones 11, 12, 13)
Parsley (zones 12, 13)
Radicchio (zones 12, 13)
Radishes (zones 12, 13)
Swiss chard (zones 12, 13)

MARCH

Plant

Arugula (through May)
Beets (through May)
Broccoli rabe (through Apr, warmest zones)
Broccoli romanesco (through Apr, warmest zones)
Cabbage (through Jul)
Carrots (through Jul)
Cauliflower (through May)
Chervil
Hops
Lettuce (through May)
Mesclun (through Jul)
Mustard (through Apr)
Onion (through Jun) (Green onions only)
Parsley (through May)
Potatoes (through May)
Radicchio (through Jul)
Radishes (through Apr)
Strawberries
Swiss chard (through May)

Harvest

Herbs (perennial)
Lemons

WARM SEASON
....

APRIL

Plant

Dill (through Jun)
Florence fennel (through Jul)
Herbs (perennial)—chives, oregano, peppermint, rosemary, sage, French tarragon, thyme (thorough May)
Hops (through May)
Lemongrass
Marjoram (through May)
Pineapple guava (warmest location)
Tomato (last half of month and through May)

Harvest

Arugula
Cauliflower
Chives
Lemons
Mesclun
Mustard

MAY

Plant

Basil (through Jul)
Beans (through Jun)
Broccoli rabe (cooler zones through Jun)
Broccoli romanesco (cooler zones through Jun)

Chiles
Corn
Cucumbers
Edamame
Honeydew melon
Lemon tree (through Jun; outside in summer, sunroom in winter)
Melons
Nasturtiums (through Jun)
Peppers
Pineapple guava
Purslane (through Jun)
Quinoa
Radishes (except in hottest zones)
Squash, butternut (through Jun)
Squash, summer (pattypan and zucchini, through Jun)
Tangerine tree (through Jun; outside in summer, sunroom in winter)
Watermelon

Harvest

Arugula
Beets
Broccoli rabe
Carrots
Cauliflower
Chervil
Fava Beans
Green onions
Herbs (perennial)
Lemons
Lettuce
Mesclun mix
Mustard
Radicchio
Radishes
Wheat

JUNE

Plant

Beets (cooler zones only)
Cabbage (cooler zones only through Jul)
Cauliflower (cooler zones, through Jul)
Fava Beans
Lettuce (cooler zones, through Jul)
Radishes (cooler zones)

Harvest

Arugula
Basil
Beets
Broccoli rabe
Broccoli romanesco
Cabbage
Carrots
Cauliflower
Dill leaves

Garlic
Green onions
Herbs (perennial)
Lemongrass
Lemons
Lettuce
Marjoram
Mesclun
Mustard
Parsley
Potatoes
Radicchio
Radishes
Strawberries
Swiss chard

JULY

Plant

Arugula (late in the month)
Beets (warmer zones)
Radishes (except in hottest zones)

Harvest

Barley
Basil
Beans
Beets
Broccoli rabe
Broccoli romanesco
Cabbage
Carrots
Cauliflower
Cucumbers
Dill
Edamame
Fennel
Green onions
Herbs (perennial)
Lemongrass
Lemons
Lettuce
Marjoram
Mesclun
Nasturtiums
Onions, 'Spanish White' and cippolini
Parsley
Potatoes
Purslane
Radicchio
Radishes
Strawberries
Squash, summer (pattypan and zucchini)
Swiss chard
Tomato

COOL SEASON
....

AUGUST

Plant

Arugula (through Oct)

Basil
Beets
Broccoli rabe
Broccoli romanesco
Cabbage
Carrots (through Sept)
Cauliflower
Chervil (last half of month)
Kale
Lettuce (except in warmest zones)
Mesclun (through Sept)
Mustard (through Sept)
Onions, 'Spanish White' and cippolini (through Sept)
Parsley
Radicchio (through Nov)
Radishes (except in warmest zones)
Swiss chard

Harvest

Basil
Beans
Beets
Cabbage
Carrots
Chiles
Corn
Cucumbers
Dill leaves, seeds
Edamame
Fennel bulbs
Green onions
Herbs (perennial)
Hop flowers
Lemongrass
Lemons
Lettuce
Honeydew melon
Marjoram
Melons
Mesclun
Nasturtiums
Onions, 'Spanish White' and cippolini
Parsley
Peppers
Potatoes
Purslane
Radicchio
Radishes
Strawberries
Squash, summer (pattypan and zucchini)
Swiss chard
Tomato
Watermelon

SEPTEMBER

Plant

Broccoli rabe
Broccoli romanesco

Cabbage
Cauliflower
Chervil
Fava beans (through Oct)
Herbs (perennial)—rosemary,
  sage, thyme (through Oct)
Kale
Lettuce
Purslane
Radishes

Harvest
Arugula
Basil
Beans
Beets
Broccoli rabe (late)
Broccoli romanesco
Cabbage
Cauliflower
Chiles
Corn
Cucumbers
Dill
Edamame
Fennel
Green onions
Herbs (perennial)
Honeydew melon
Kale
Lemongrass

Lemons
Lettuce
Marjoram
Melons
Mesclun
Mustard
Parsley
Peppers
Quinoa
Radicchio
Radishes
Strawberries
Squash, butternut
Squash, summer (pattypan and
  zucchini)
Tomato
Watermelon

OCTOBER

Plant
Barley (through Nov)
Garlic (through Nov)
Wheat (through Dec)

Harvest
Arugula
Broccoli rabe
Broccoli romanesco
Cabbage
Carrots

Cauliflower
Chervil
Dill
Fennel
Herbs (perennial)
Kale
Lemons
Lettuce
Marjoram
Mesclun
Mustard
Parsley
Pineapple guavas
Radicchio
Radishes
Squash, butternut
Swiss chard
Tomato

NOVEMBER

Plant
Fava Beans (first half of the
  month)

Harvest
Arugula
Broccoli romanesco
Carrots
Chervil
Lemons

Mustard
Parsley

DECEMBER

Harvest
Arugula
Lemons

JANUARY

Plant
Hops (through Mar)
Strawberries (through Feb)

Harvest
Herbs (perennial)
Lemons

FEBRUARY

Harvest
Herbs (perennial)
Lemons

MOUNTAIN AND INTERMOUNTAIN WEST (Mountainous areas of all Western states, including the Northwest)

MARCH

Plant
Beets (through Apr in mildest
  areas)
Fava Beans (mildest areas)
Hops
Lettuce (in mildest areas,
  through Apr)
Mesclun (through Jun)
Mustard (mildest areas)
Onions, 'Spanish White' and
  cippolini
Potatoes (mildest areas)
Radicchio
Radishes (mildest areas, through
  Apr)
Strawberries (through Apr)
Swiss chard (milder areas
  through Jun)

Harvest
Lemons
Tangerines

APRIL

Plant
Arugula
Broccoli rabe (through Jun)
Broccoli romanesco
Cabbage
Carrots (through Jun)
Cauliflower (through May)
Chervil
Fava Beans
Hops
Onions, 'Spanish White' and
  cippolini
Quinoa (through May)

Harvest
Lemons
Mesclun
Radishes
Swiss chard
Tangerines

WARM SEASON

MAY

Plant
Basil (through Jun)
Beans (through Jun)
Beets
Broccoli romanesco (through
  Jun)
Cabbage (through Jun)
Chiles
Corn
Cucumbers
Dill (through Jun)
Edamame (through Jun)
Florence fennel
Herbs (perennial)-chives,
  oregano, peppermint, sage,
  French tarragon, thyme
Lemon tree, (outdoors in frost-
  free season, sunroom in cold
  months)
Lemongrass
Lettuce (everywhere through
  Jun)

Marjoram
Melons
Mustard (coldest-winter areas)
Nasturtiums
Peppers
Potatoes (everywhere)
Purslane
Radishes (colder areas)
Rosemary (though Jun)
Squash, butternut
Squash, summer (pattypan and
  zucchini)
Tangerine tree (outdoors in
  frost-free season, sunroom in
  cold months)
Tomato (cold-winter areas)
Watermelon

Harvest
Arugula
Beets
Broccoli rabe
Green onions
Lemons
Lettuce
Mesclun

Radicchio
Radishes
Swiss chard
Tangerines

JUNE

Plant

Cucumbers
Potatoes (cold-winter areas)
Swiss chard (cold-winter areas)

Harvest

Beans
Beets
Broccoli rabe
Broccoli romanesco
Cabbage
Carrots
Cauliflower
Fava Beans
Garlic
Green onions
Lemons
Lettuce
Mesclun
Radishes
Swiss chard
Tangerines

JULY

Plant

Beets (mild-summer areas)
Lettuce (except in hot-summer areas)
Mesclun (except in hot-summer areas)

Harvest

Basil
Beans
Beets
Broccoli rabe
Broccoli romanesco
Cabbage
Carrots
Cauliflower
Chervil
Chiles
Corn
Cucumbers
Edamame
Fava Beans
Garlic
Green onions
Herbs (perennial)
Hops

Lemons
Lemongrass
Lettuce
Marjoram
Mesclun
Nasturtiumss
Peppers
Potatoes
Purslane
Rosemary
Strawberries
Squash, summer (pattypan and zucchini)
Swiss chard
Tangerines
Tomato
Wheat

COOL SEASON

AUGUST

Plant

Arugula (except in hot-summer areas)
Lettuce (except in hot-summer areas)
Mesclun (except in hot-summer areas)
Radicchio

Harvest

Barley
Basil
Beans
Beets
Broccoli romanesco
Cabbage
Carrots
Cauliflower
Chervil
Chiles
Corn
Cucumbers
Dill
Edamame
Fava Beans
Florence fennel
Herbs (perennial)
Honeydew melons
Hops
Lemons
Lemongrass
Lettuce
Marjoram
Melons

Mesclun
Nasturtiums
Onions, cippolini
Pepper
Potatoes
Purslane
Quinoa
Rosemary
Squash, summer (pattypan and zucchini)
Swiss chard
Tangerines
Tomato
Watermelons

SEPTEMBER

Plant

Barley
Mesclun
Mustard (mildest areas)
Radishes
Wheat (through Oct)

Harvest

Arugula
Basil
Beans
Beets
Corn
Cucumbers
Chiles
Dill
Edamame
Herbs (perennial)
Lemons
Lemongrass
Lettuce
Marjoram
Melons
Mesclun
Nasturtiums
Onions, 'Spanish White'
Peppers
Potatoes
Purslane
Rosemary
Squash, butternut
Squash, summer (pattypan and zucchini)
Tangerines
Tomato

OCTOBER

Plant

Barley

Garlic (last half of month through Nov)
Radishes (mild-winter areas)

Harvest

Arugula
Herbs (perennial)
Lemons
Lettuce
Marjoram
Mesclun
Potatoes
Radishes
Rosemary
Squash, butternut
Tangerines

NOVEMBER

Harvest

Lemons
Radicchio
Radishes
Tangerines

DECEMBER

Harvest

Lemons
Tangerines

JANUARY

Harvest

Lemons
Tangerines

FEBRUARY

Plant

Swiss chard (in mildest areas)

Harvest

Lemons
Tangerines

Index